The Fading of the Scars

Orrin Michael Carpenter

TABLE OF CONTENTS

TRIBUTE

This novel I dedicate to the people of Chicago, and police officers everywhere, to whom I feel such a deep kinship.

PREFACE

In times of great sorrow we look for the silver lining. God's love is that lining. A tragic story leaves no room for celebration, for to celebrate one's rescue from the evil that was perpetrated upon others does not afford the respect due them, the victims. Appreciate my deliverance if you desire to do so, but never celebrate it.

ACKNOWLEDGMENTS

Many thanks to Mary Jo for encouraging me in the writing of this novel with her enthusiastic optimism. Please be aware that this does not necessarily mean she endorses every principle set forth in this book. It instead signifies that in the spirit of friendship she was supportive of my literary efforts along the challenging and difficult road to completion. My undying appreciation is hers to be had.

* * *

My heartfelt and ongoing gratitude to a certain policeman and his wife for urging me to come to terms with my past. They will surely forever hold a special place in my heart.

* * *

To the man who symbolizes eventual victory over all that's terrible that's happened; I so value the privilege to have known you.

SPECIAL REQUEST

It is the author's fervent request that this novel, or the reasons why it was written, not be spoken of to him in the public domain. The private setting is the appropriate place for discussion of it, preferably the living room, his favorite room in the house, for The Living Room is symbolic of living. The Living Room is symbolic of his rescue.

CHAPTER 1

SCHOOL BLUES

Dwight Enhart had not always been withdrawn. As a small child he was quite outgoing. He played actively with other children and really knew happiness; but then, when he grew older, something happened, for in a relatively short period of time he was cast into a burdened, constrained existence which left only pity, or indifference, or in some cases even indignation in the hearts of those who knew him.

People had their theories as to why he had changed so drastically. Some said that his mother was too overprotective of him as a young boy, and that later on in his emotional development she ceased to give him the security of her love because of the anger she channeled against him for his father's leaving her to raise two small children alone, while others felt that in the more recent years of his life he had become far too detached from his general associations with people in the community. Indeed, to one degree or another, these factors contributed to his present state of mind, yet one thing was most evident beyond any shadow of a doubt, it being that something was in great need of taking place to alleviate his life of discontent.

Sitting worriedly on the front steps of his home at the age of fourteen, he felt the full impact of his anxieties penetrate the very core of his emotions, for he knew that in a matter of minutes a bus would be coming along to carry him off to his first day of school at Fulton High. Yes, the moment he had been dreading and losing sleep over for weeks was almost upon him, and it tormented him to think that he would be forced into meeting new people and confronting unfamiliar surroundings after becoming accustomed to a three room country grade school in the small town of Chism, Mississippi. For the life of him he could not contemplate in dealing with all the nagging fear within him; and so suddenly he yearned to rush to the bosom of his mother for the comfort and reassurance he had known as a little boy, yet he realized this was no longer for the choosing, because she despised the sight of him.

In the ensuing moments, as he sadly beheld the white picket fence which surrounded the yard so perfectly, he heard the distressingly distant sound of the bus travelling down Kirkland Road just to the south, which, in turn, contributed to the escalation of his fears. Oh, how he wished things were not this way. He did not want to be so anxious and insecure. He did not want to run away and hide from the inevitabilities of life. Still, at times, the urge to do just that seemed to lurk within him in nearly uncontrollable proportions.

Slowly rising to a standing position, he gazed longingly at the nearby safety of the woods, strongly sensing the temporary relief which could be afforded him. It was all so closely within touch, and yet so far, for even if he managed to avoid addressing the dreaded demands of his life for today, he knew that there would always be tomorrow. *I guess I better get my lunch*, he therefore told himself before reluctantly turning to enter the kitchen, genuinely not realizing in doing so how commendable it was that his inner reserves of strength had persuaded him to do the right thing.

"Clair, the bus is coming," he murmured in a distinct southern accent as he made his way to the small counter next to the refrigerator.

"It's about time," his sister of seventeen commented while primping before the mirror that hung on the wall above the sink. "I can't wait to see people again. There should be so much to talk about." She stated this in the hopes that her mother happened to be listening, for whether or not Dwight heard her concerned her very little. "I've been anxious to get filled in on all the latest news."

"I'm sure you won't miss a thing," her mother told her as she entered the kitchen from the nearby living room. "That is if you're anything like I used to be. But now, why the heck should I care?"

The manner in which she shrugged her shoulders made her disdain ever so evident.

As Clair turned to face her one could see in her eyes the proof that their relationship had become strained.

"That's my problem, mama," she told her in the emergence of an outlook that was unusually forthright. "I'm probably too much like you." And through force of habit of days of innocence gone by, she rushed to her mother's side and gave her a gentle kiss on the cheek in an open desire for understanding. Yet when her mother uncomfortably drew away from her, she backed off as she felt her emotions take on a pronounced hardening by way of the hurt and disappointment that this outward display of rejection represented. Abruptly grabbing her lunch from the table, she headed for the door. "See ya later," she concluded with feigned indifference, an indifference which so symbolized a further digression from the satisfied mind.

"Bye," her mother responded with little regard for what happened. As she focused on Dwight, who had delayed his departure, an apathetic expression came over her features.

"So this is your first day of high school," she said while coolly eying him. "Ya don't look any too happy about it."

"I'm not. I've never been to high school before," he spoke in labored words as she casually reached for a pack of cigarettes from the table. "I'm kinda scared."

In what seemed to be an instant his mother's mood became one of intolerance.

"You get going now!" she as a result snapped. "I've got enough on my mind without listening to this nonsense! .... Get going!" she boldly pressed on when he showed no sign of moving. "That bus isn't gonna wait for you!" In her frustration she turned to escape the sight of him, for he was a responsibility she didn't want to acknowledge.

Without saying another word Dwight walked out of the house and down the steps with a look of defeat on his face. It seemed like no one understood him or cared enough to listen, not even mama. But then his mother seemed to blame all of the male gender for the way in which she chose to feel about one man, and she wanted Clair to think as she did, unwisely believing that it was the right thing to do to prepare her for the real world. It was all so short-sighted and self-defeating, which made it oh so heartrending.

* * *

When the creaky old bus pulled to a stop before the Enharts' mailbox, Dwight was so distressed he felt as though he would not be able to mount its stairs. Then, in looking upward, he was filled with an awakening though troubling sensation, for there before his eyes seated in the front right seat was Sara Treson, a girl whom he unpleasantly recalled had made a habit out of making him the butt of her jokes. But at least he was considered attractive by earthly standards, which was quite convenient, for even though a person's outward appearance shouldn't matter, and even though one's outward appearance could never assure one's happiness, a person such as him gladly welcomes not having to deal with the added burden of being criticized about their looks in a world of the flesh.

As he boarded the bus behind his sister in the hopes that Sara wouldn't notice him, Dwight found, much to his dismay, that his effort proved to be in vain.

"How many friends have you made lately, Dwight?" she jested in restrained laughter when he was standing beside her. "I hear you've got 'em all lined up."

There was immediate mirth when Dwight softly responded, "I hardly think so." Why, even his sister had broken out in laughter as she stopped in the aisle to delay his advancement.

"Good, then I can have you all to myself," Sara giddily stated while turning toward her best friend, Julie Kent, who was seated behind her.

In a combination of humiliation and embarrassment Dwight stood with his head lowered, just waiting for Clair to allow him to get by. Then, much to his relief, the bus driver came to his defense by ordering Clair to seat herself so that he could resume to drive onward.

When Clair was no longer in his way, Dwight darted to the rear of the vehicle to avoid any further tongue lashings.

Seated alone, he stared out the window and envisioned a crystal clear waterfall. It was a place of refuge where he would meditate or write poems to deal with the pain in his life. Oh, how he wished he were there now, for he wanted so much to be set apart from people who treated him badly. .... And he could hardly be blamed.

* * *

By the time the bus arrived at Fulton High it was filled with students.

In envy Dwight had noticed for the greater part of the ride how everyone seemed to have somebody to talk to, a friend. He once had a friend named Timothy to whom he felt very close, but he moved away to Chicago when they were both ten years old. He took it quite hard and especially missed him now. *But perhaps he, too, would feel differently towards me*, he suddenly assumed, for most people seemed to these days.

Stepping off the bus moments later, Dwight felt as though he were in some strange city, for so many of the faces were unfamiliar to him. It was a scary sensation, because he didn't know who these people were or what they felt. But most of all he didn't know how they would end up treating him. Still he managed to forge onward, though, amongst the bustle of students; yet by the time he reached the main entrance of the school, his legs began to quiver in fearful anticipation of what the future held in store for him.

It wasn't until he entered the building that it suddenly dawned on him that he did not know where to find the gymnasium for his first class of the day. Too shy to ask anyone which floor it was on, he decided to follow someone he suspected would be in that class. Gazing about, he happened to see a fellow classmate from Chism, Scott Weston, who was a very athletic person.

Drawing towards Scott in the hopes he'd be led where he was required to go, Dwight was surprised to discover that Scott was none the wiser than he as to which direction they should proceed in, for he had now stopped a very attractive girl to ask her for guidance.

"Do you know where the gymnasium is?" Dwight overheard him ask her.

"Oh, yes, it's on the ground floor," the girl informed him with a smile, "but you won't be reporting there just yet. Everyone's to meet in the auditorium on the first day of school to be welcomed by the principal and advised on school rules and regulations. Would you like to walk there with me? It's on the second floor."

"Sure," Scott eagerly accepted the offer as he took in her beauty. "I suppose I had better introduce myself," he added then. "My name is Scott Weston. I live in Chism."

"Pleased to meet you," the girl replied while extending a hand. "My name is Jana Rossi. I live here in Fulton." As Scott returned the gesture, she commented, "You must be a freshman to not know your way around here."

"Yes, I am," Scott informed her. "Are you surprised by that?"

"As a matter of fact I am," Jana let it be known. "At first I thought you were new to the area. You don't look like a freshman. You look... older."

"Oh," he laughed freely. "I'll take that as a compliment."

"Good," she said a bit relieved. "I really didn't mean anything by it."

Gazing at one another with soft smiles, Scott eventually asked, "What grade are you in?"

"Oh, I'm a freshman also, but I'm familiar with this school because I live down the road only a short distance from here. Maybe we'll be in some of each other's classes."

"That would be nice," Scott stated with clear interest. "In fact I hope I'll be seeing you around here a lot."

Jana lowered her gaze in flattered emotions. Then, in noticing the thinning ranks of the students, she said, "We better get going. It looks like most everyone is already upstairs."

Scanning the area, Scott was just about to walk away with the girl when she suddenly stopped in her tracks at the sight of Dwight. Curiously she found herself unable to stop looking at him, for he seemed so in need of a friend. Yet even then there was more to it than that. Yes, there was something about him which brought a strange feeling to her heart, so much so that she felt obligated to speak of him, for never before in her life did she recall being so captivated by another human being.

"Do you know who he is?" she asked Scott while yet regarding

Dwight, who had now turned sideways so as not to be confronted by her stare.

Looking in the direction she had indicated, Scott became quite puzzled when he discovered whom she was concerned with. *Why on earth would she ask about him?* he thought. ... *But of course, she doesn't understand,* he remembered in a flash.

"Ah... his name is Dwight," he reluctantly informed her. Then, in an effort to steer her attention away from him, he said with emphasis, "We had better get going, like you said!"

With a look of lingering intrigue Jana regarded Scott.

"Oh... yes... of course," she stammered, barely realizing the mental state she had entered into. Yet as they proceeded to walk away, she could not seem to get Dwight off her mind, though she wasn't sure why.

When Dwight noticed their departure from the corner of his eye, he began to follow them, wishing as he did so that he, too, had an outgoing personality, the type which was conducive to better human relations. What he did not comprehend was that with the aid of caring people he would eventually acquire that which he yearned for, yet not without the tempering effect of trial and tribulation.

* * *

The auditorium was nearly filled to capacity by the time Dwight made his way through one of its three doors. Never had he seen so many people together at once, and the anxiety he consequently felt as he advanced toward the many rows of seats actually caused his body to shake. Earnestly he sought to recapture some sense of composure in an effort to sway the attention of they whom he imagined to be noticing his awkwardness, but try as he may, the symptoms of his self-consciousness continued to overpower his desires. In fact it was not until he had seated himself in one of the few remaining seats that he felt somewhat at ease.

Shortly thereafter, the principal, Mr. Tailor, walked onto the stage to welcome the students to Fulton High. He was a robust man with a deep, strong voice that was clearly audible.

At first Dwight found it nearly impossible to concentrate on what Mr. Tailor was saying because of the closed in, cramped feeling he was witnessing. But then, finally, the conditioning qualities of time's passing allowed him to calm down considerably, which enabled him to listen to what the principal had to say with some degree of focus.

When Mr. Tailor had finished his oration, the students were instructed to go to their first class of the day.

Rising from his seat to head for gym class, Dwight again felt anxiety protrude his emotions, for he had in recent years developed a terrible phobia over failing in sports, a feeling that to perform less than perfect would result in harsh criticism. The irony of it all was that he was actually a very capable person, a quick learner who had a certain gracefulness about him. Unfortunately, though, his poor opinion of himself suppressed his hidden attributes.

Mr. Milter, the gym instructor, turned out to be a strident man, whose stern appearance made it all the more evident. He demanded quickness when responding to the roll call and made it seem as though the boys were being recruited into the army.

Calisthenics were first on the agenda, and by the time twenty-five sit-ups, fifty jumping jacks, and twenty-five push-ups had been performed, most of the boys were quite exhausted. Yet Dwight held up quite well to this workout, for he did a lot of walking and running, and occasionally chopped wood also, so he was in good physical condition. Sadly, however, his mental condition was not sound, and so he did not feel in the least as though he had performed satisfactorily, so critical was he of his every effort.

When gym class at last came to an end, the boys eagerly hit the locker room.

While Dwight showered, he found himself wondering how many teachers would require oral reports of their students, which was something he sought to avoid if at all possible. In fact he was so wrapped up in his anxious thoughts that he barely stirred when he heard a voice sound out beside him. Looking to his left, he realized he was being spoken to when he noticed a blonde haired boy staring at him.

"What did you say?" he forced himself to inquire.

"I asked you how ya liked gym today?" the boy repeated himself.

"It was okay," Dwight managed to say without looking at him.

Though sensing something amiss, the boy yet tried to carry on a conversation with him.

"I noticed that you did pretty well at those exercises. Do you do that sort of thing often?"

Initially Dwight eyed the boy in pleasant surprise over his comment; but then, all too soon, it changed into distrust.

"No," he would only say as a result, most certain that the young man had said exactly the opposite of what he meant in an aim to insult him.

A puzzled expression now came over the boy's features, because he could not understand why Dwight was treating him in such a standoffish manner.

"My name is Sam Harris," he nevertheless pressed on. "What's yours?"

"Dwight Enhart," he responded in words which were barely audible before turning off his shower and quickly walking away with a towel wrapped around his waist.

In eventual anger over Dwight's odd behavior the boy stated to a nearby listener, "He's not much of a talker, is he? I was only trying to be friendly!"

"I know," the other young man agreed. "He didn't seem to want anything to do with you."

"Well, I tried!" Sam commented with conviction. "What a snob!"

"Don't let him bother you," the other boy advised him. "A person like that isn't worth it. Believe me, I know the type."

"Maybe so, but it still makes me mad to be brushed off for no good reason," Sam disgustedly stated, not understanding Dwight's mentality. "I think he'll have to change if he wants to get along around here."

"I don't think he'll cause any trouble," the other boy said. "All ya have to do is ignore him."

Shutting off his shower and grabbing hold of a towel, Sam observed Dwight from afar and stated, "That's fine with me."

* * *

Beginning with Dwight's second class of the day things began to improve. In some respects school wasn't as bad as he had anticipated. True, his personality was not conducive to promoting friendship, but at least he was coping with today, which was something worthwhile. *Yet maybe I feel alright because I'm not being called on to answer any questions*, he surmised later that afternoon from where he sat in math class. *Today is the first day of school, though, and assignments haven't been given yet*, he further realized. *Oh, I hope oral reports aren't required.* Through his manner of thinking nervousness began to pervade his body once again, which induced him to shuffle his feet while gazing restlessly about. He had developed the distinctly bad habit of making himself feel uneasy when all seemed to be going well. It was as though he would not allow himself any lasting peace. Did he think about the things which scared him too much? Perhaps so, but as of now that was the stark reality of his existence.

When the bell rang to signify the end of class, Dwight experienced a sense of relief, for he was anxious to get up and walk, this always seeming to help him whenever he felt troubled, provided he wasn't being stared at by anyone.

Rising from his desk, he noticed Jana and Scott leaving the room together and wished he, too, were doing so with someone. Then, scoping a wider area and laying eyes on Sara and Julie along with a few other students from Chism, he realized that here before him were people he had known since childhood, kids he had laughed and played with, yet now seemed to have so little in common with. They went about their business and he went about his, they not seeming to want anything to do with him, and he too emotionally handicapped to implement a change. And yet it does take an individual of rare character to effectively deal with a shy person, for many people are uneasy when they're met with the challenge of contributing to the greater part of a conversation between themselves and someone else, which in essence is initially the case when reaching out to the constrained. Thus they do nothing at all. *I can't help them*, some may say in an attempt to justify their complacency, when in actuality they're uncomfortable with the notion of trying.

Once Dwight was out of the room walking down the hall toward his locker, he noticed a freshman from Fulton named Carl Barnet kidding around with his fellow classmate and frequent companion, Ben Kustover. Carl, being a bully ever since he had started going to school, was quick to seek out and take advantage of anybody he could easily dominate. His ways were unmerciful, and once he got it in his head to pick on someone they were in for a terrible ordeal until they made up their mind to stand up to him once and for all. Then, and only then, would he target someone else to abuse.

In total ignorance of the type of person before him, Dwight advanced onward. Then, just as he neared the two boys, Carl purposely pushed Ben into him to test his reactions.

It was with wide-eyed unease that Dwight regarded Ben.

"Excuse me," he shifted the blame to himself in an attempt to gain the boy's approval. Much to his dismay, however, Carl immediately sensed his vulnerability and forcefully pushed him back against some lockers.

"No, you're not excused!" Carl dismissed his apology while firmly pinning his arms back. "I don't like troublemakers like you walking into people, especially my friends!"

"But I'm not a troublemaker. I just want to be left alone,... please," Dwight beseeched him with pleading eyes.

By this time a group of students, including Jana and Scott along with Sara and many others, had gathered to catch a glimpse of the tense-filled scene.

Seeing these spectators caused Dwight to undoubtedly feel very humiliated. Yet when he tried to break free, Carl pushed him back against the lockers.

"So you wanna be left alone," he spoke loudly. "Did you hear that everybody? He wants to be left alone. Well, first of all I wanna hear you say you're sorry," he belittled him in a high pitched, mocking voice.

By this time Dwight was so desperate for relief that he managed to break free. In a flash, however, Carl grabbed him by the arm and swung him about.

"I didn't say you could leave, kid!" he sneered.

Unable to resist the opportunity to impress everyone, and mainly motivated by the personal attention it would thus create,

Scott suddenly decided to step in on behalf of Dwight.

"Leave him be!" he spoke up with false concern. "I saw what happened here and I don't think Dwight started this."

Without surrendering his hold on Dwight, Carl turned his attention to Scott. The tension mounted to the point where there seemed to be a temporary stillness, as though time was no longer passing. ... But then, when Carl realized that Scott was not about to relent, he angrily released his hold on Dwight without saying a word.

Deeply relieved, Dwight sped to his locker, fearing as he did so that Carl might decide to attack him at any given moment. Nervously retrieving a book, he made a fast-gaited exit down the hall, yet not before catching sight of Jana. She seemed to be trying to comfort him by way of a look; and although this was something he was not able to express any appreciation over at this time, he very much wanted to. How she appeared to have empathy for him. ... *But no, it must have been pity*, he told himself moments later. Yet even though he thought this way, he could not forget her serene face and calming ways. It seemed to be the only positive aspect of the whole episode, the only thing which helped him cope with the shame he so keenly felt. And so, for obvious reasons, he suddenly felt like crying, but restrained from doing so, because he expected people would never understand his emotions.

* * *

When the last bell rang to dismiss school for the day, Dwight wondered whether Carl would bother him again. For that reason a sense of relief only came when he had retrieved a few books from his locker and was boarding the bus. Still he could not put the incident out of his thoughts. Yet the reason did not solely rest with him, for he strongly sensed that people were talking about what a coward he had been in that occasionally he would either hear high-pitched whispers, or catch somebody staring at him either pitifully or sardonically.

I wish that boy hadn't treated me so badly, he thought from where he sat on the bus. *I tried to mind my own business, but he wouldn't let me,* he racked his mind. Peering out the window in shattered spirits, he happened to take notice of Jana and Scott walking out of the school together and felt a bit better. It was no wonder, though, because even though he had taken Scott's intervention on his behalf to be founded on mainly pity, at least it had served a purpose.

"Thanks for showing me around today," Scott told Jana as they neared the bus. "It made things a lot easier for me."

"My pleasure," she assured him while flipping back a few tresses of her dark hair. "I'll see you tomorrow."

"I miss you already," Scott said in an anticipating tone of voice.

"Go on now," she laughed in response. "You'll miss your bus and end up walking otherwise."

Scott smiled widely.

"If I knew you'd be walking with me, I wouldn't mind."

"My father would probably ground me," Jana chuckled as she commenced to stroll the half mile or so down the road to her house.

Scott also laughed. Then he boarded the bus without saying another word, confident he was gaining her affections.

* * *

Jana was nearly halfway home when she heard the Chism bus approaching from behind. As it passed, she happened to catch a glimpse of the boy who had been picked on in school. *He's different than most*, she pondered. *So withdrawn ... I wonder why*? Slowly she ceased walking to stare at the bus as it disappeared from sight down the road, leaving behind only a cloud of dust. Moments later, her train of thought was broken as her best friend, Cybil Adams, yelled out to her while approaching at a fast gait.

"I was looking for you after school," she informed her a bit out of breath when she was standing beside her. "I thought you were gonna wait for me by your locker."

A look of embarrassment came over Jana, for she usually didn't forget such things.

"Oh, I'm sorry," she as a result told her. "I was with Scott Weston and it slipped my mind."

"For that reason I'll forgive you," Cybil stated with a smile. "I might have forgotten, too, if I had been with him."

"Ya, he's a nice guy I suppose," Jana casually commented.

"Just nice?" Cybil probed. "Is that all you have to say about him?"

"Well, I just met him, Cybil! I don't even know that much about him!" Jana defensively reacted.

Realizing she made good sense, Cybil grew to regret her shallow remark.

"Yes, I can see your point," she acknowledged. Searching her mind for another topic of conversation, she suddenly recalled the incident that had taken place in the hall at school. "Hey, did you hear about Carl Barnet bullying some kid today," she made mention of.

"I didn't have to hear about it! I saw it!" Jana informed her. A troubled expression shown on her features as she recalled what she had witnessed. "It was terrible. That poor guy seemed so scared. He didn't stand up to Carl at all."

"Well, Carl is threatening," Cybil maintained, "but that kid should've stood up to him. I mean how else does he expect to have self-respect if he doesn't? And not only that," she continued, "everyone knows it's the only way to rid themselves of Carl once and for all."

Jana nodded her head as they proceeded to walk onward.

"Yes, Carl will be after him again, I'm sure," she had to assume. "I only wish there was something I could do about that."

"He's got to make up his own mind to do that for himself, Jana," Cybil told her. "You really can't do much to help him. Nobody can."

"Scott helped him, though," Jana brought to her attention. "He told Carl to leave him alone and he did." Sighing lightly, she added, "I was so glad somebody did something."

"But Scott isn't going to be around every time," Cybil reminded her. "Next time who knows what might happen."

Stopping to gaze down the road once again, Jana softly uttered, "Sadly that's true I guess." Then, as she continued along her way, Cybil began talking up a storm about something else.

* * *

The bus came to a slow halt near the Enharts' white picket

fence. As Clair and Dwight got up from their seats to unboard, Sara was quick to take advantage of the situation.

"Bye, Dwight, don't beat up too many guys," she poked fun at him as he neared her. From an open window she laughed while he descended from the vehicle.

Without saying a word in response to her jibes, Dwight stood with a subdued bearing. As the bus began to depart he felt relieved to think he'd be left alone. ... But no, as it turned out he was forced to deal with yet another unpleasant episode, for much to his disappointment he became consciously aware of his sister's piercing stare.

"You'll never learn, will you?" she voiced her resentment. "I'm ashamed to even tell people you're my brother!"

In response to her words Dwight shifted his eyes to a large elm tree which stood so beautifully across the road.

"I can't seem to take control of my life," he spoke up then. "I want to be different, but I haven't discovered what it'll take." Looking intently at his sister, he repeated himself by saying, "I really do wanna be different."

"Well, you're failing miserably!" she strongly reminded him. "Can't you understand that that's why people don't like you?"

Regarding her with a wounded gaze, Dwight said quite candidly, "I've never been sure what they expect of me. I'm not sure they even know." With added emphasis he felt inclined to add, "I'm just looking for unconditional love."

At this point Clair looked at him as if to suggest he made no sense at all. Turning abruptly about, she headed for the house without saying another word.

Dwight knew that disdain could very easily creep into his thoughts. Surely a coping mechanism was in order; and so, turning aside and laying his books on the ground, he proceeded to run through the woods. He ran faster and faster until he came upon a small cliff where a waterfall splashed forth crystal clear water.

Sitting on a large rock, he held his head between his hands and trembled in his humility while tears dampened his cheeks. Finally he had a reprieve from his tormentors.

* * *

Two hours had passed before Dwight came plodding into the dimly-lit living room by way of the back door. Immediately laying eyes on his mother, he saw that she was sitting on the couch listening to the radio with a cigarette resting between her fingers.

"Where ya been?" she apathetically questioned him without shifting her gaze.

"Just out," he answered her.

"Well, don't expect me to warm you any supper," she muttered.

Only briefly Dwight eyed her before advancing toward the kitchen to discover what he could find to eat. When there, he opened the refrigerator and withdrew a few pieces of chicken and half a quart of milk.

Sitting down at the table with his meager meal before him, he was so hoping he'd be able to enjoy it in peace, but it was not to be realized. Clair came walking into the room shortly thereafter with her hair up in curlers.

"I was beginning to wonder if you'd ever come back," she spoke up while nearing the cupboard for a glass.

"I'm sure it didn't bother you any," Dwight gravely contended without looking at her.

Clair pretended to think about it as though she could not make up her mind.

"No, I can't say that it did," she stated then with seeming indifference.

Concluding that it was pointless to speak to her, Dwight resumed eating without paying her any more attention. *Why talk when it's only in wasted words*, he thought, fully aware that he had had enough of humanity for one day.

CHAPTER 2

THE ATTACK

As dark rain clouds commenced to roll in early the following morning, thunder began to rumble in the distant air.

Having spent a restless night tossing and turning in broken sleep over the emotionally wrenching memory of what had happened the day before, Dwight easily awoke only minutes later to the pitter-pattering of rain upon his window. Lying there, he found himself staring with childlike interest at the tiny droplets of water flowing down the panes in gathering streams, which compelled him to realize that the world wasn't always unsettling, for if it were, such peaceful moments as this would never be felt.

It was not until he became consciously aware of his alarm clock ticking away the time of day that discontent began to enter his emotions, an abiding discontent which brought a terrible sensation to his stomach over the thought of attending school. Shifting his gaze to the clock and discovering that he only had five more minutes to remain in bed, he pulled the covers over his head in the empty hope that time would stand still. Such was the reality of his world, this boy who was not only troubled in the presence of others, but also at times when alone. He couldn't escape his inner self, and so a prison within himself was the bondage he bore, trapped in disturbed thoughts concerning an uncertain future.

In due time Dwight was able to motivate himself to get out of bed. After eating breakfast, he went out to the barn to tend the livestock. He was glad to be out of the house, for he didn't enjoy the company of his mother or Clair as he had in the past. They were different. He was different. It seemed as though they didn't want to acknowledge his existence any longer. True, they cooked for him and did his laundry, but it was more out of force of habit than anything else; or so he currently believed anyway.

Having entered the barn, he grabbed a wooden bucket to fetch water from a faucet that was situated against the wall to the right of the door. Commencing to fill it, he heard the impatient bellows of their milking cow, Hazel, a black and white holstein that he had been fond of for quite some time. Being a boy of seven when his father bought her as a calf from a neighbor, he made a big fuss over her right from the start. Why, on the very first night Hazel was brought home he tried to sneak her into the house so that she wouldn't have to spend the night alone in the barn, but her unceasing cries soon alerted the entire household of his deed. Forbidden to keep the animal indoors, he managed to persuade his mother and father to allow him to sleep in the barn with her until she was content with her new environment; and so there he slept for three nights in a row loving every minute of it.

"How's Hazel," he talked gently to avert her impatience. "You're a thirsty one, aren't you?" Seeming to sense his meaning, the animal quieted down and stared at him, just as she had done on so many other mornings.

When he had finished filling the pail, Dwight carried it over to her, smiled, and said, "Aren't you the good girl?" As she drank, he gently stroked her head and neck with his right hand while holding the bucket in his left. How he did love animals, for they so often responded with trust when someone treated them well. .... But oh yes, he knew full well that trust had to be earned, and that sometimes it was broken. Where mankind was concerned he had come by this knowledge the hard way.

* * *

The sky began to clear by the time school buses pulled up to the high school to unboard students.

Dwight did not want to leave the safety of the bus. Nervously he sat in his seat staring at the dull brown building in delayed reaction, wondering what the day would have to offer.

When the moment inevitably did come to step down from the vehicle, lastly by choice, he slowly began walking toward the main entrance, at which time he happened to notice Jana talking with Scott by the doorway. He was particularly glad to see her again, for from what he discerned the day before, he believed he would like her if the opportunity to get to know her ever presented itself. Yet even though he felt this way, he realized that he would not allow himself to say anything to her at this time. As he approached where she stood, however, much to his pleasant surprise she released a smile as he glanced her way.

"Hello," she said in a cheerful manner.

Dwight was compelled to cease his advancement. Then, while squarely eying her, he forced himself to return the greeting despite the fact that he was somewhat distrustful of her motive for being so friendly toward him. ... Yet all of a sudden he felt some of the anxiety he carried within him drift from his very being. Indeed there was such a soothing air about her that he could not help but continue to look at her in eased emotions, that is until it came to an abrupt halt when he was bumped into by a student entering the school.

Heading indoors to face another day of tension, Dwight continued to think of Jana. *Is she really willing to be my friend?* he wondered as he proceeded along his way. ... A disturbing notion now occurred to him. Perhaps if Jana did gain his trust she would betray that trust in the future, just as his mother and sister had done. In light of that suspicion, he lowered his head as a certain sadness engulfed him, a sadness which disappointed him in more ways than one.

By the time he arrived at his locker Dwight was so uncomfortable with his surroundings that he could not even breathe normally, proof enough that one's mental state affects one's physical state. Opening the locker door to place away his lunch and books, he was puzzled to discover a folded up note taped to the front portion of the bookshelf. Curiously removing it, he was swept with apprehension, for written on the paper were the threatening words, "The worst is yet to come!"

As the note began to tremble at Dwight's fingertips, a raging fear sent his heart pounding in what seemed to be wild, irregular beats. He wanted so desperately to run and hide, but he knew he had nowhere to go to escape reality, so instead he forced himself to scan the immediate area in search of an explanation. .... And he soon enough discovered it, for staring at him a few feet down the hall with a self-satisfied smirk on his face was Carl. Ben was standing beside him.

To Dwight's disappointment he had been correct in his reservations concerning what the future held in store for him. With injured feelings he slowly returned his gaze to the disturbing message, then closed his eyes tightly and thought, *The day has just begun and already I'm being threatened. I can't take much more of this... and yet I feel I must go on.* ... Crumbling the note, he threw it in his locker and headed for gym class in sober resignation of life as he knew it to be, not realizing in doing so that he was being brave by forcing himself to do that which filled him with such fear. No, he just didn't know at this stage in his life that it was bravery, a bravery which he was beginning to acquire in a desperate aim to rise above adversity.

When Dwight had disappeared from sight down the hall, Carl shifted his attention to Ben.

"Are you gonna get him today?" Ben inquired.

Carl's eyes narrowed as he folded his arms and crossed his legs while leaning against a locker.

"I'll scare him some," he said in a scheming voice, "but nothing too serious just yet. What I really want is to get him alone where no one can help him." Upon standing upright, he added, "I'll have to wait for that, though. It'll take time." Smugly regarding Ben, he proceeded to head for the same class as Dwight.

So it was that Carl took sadistic delight in seeing people squirm, pitifully not realizing the why behind his behavior, or the additional unrest he consequently brought upon himself in the midst of his unhealthy choices, even though his unrest was such a clear and obvious certainty in the eyes of God.

* * *

Mr. Milter divided the boys into two teams that were lined up at either end of the basketball court. At the center of the gym floor he placed a soccer ball that a total of four boys from the ends of each team's line were to pursue at the blow of his whistle. The object was to kick the ball past the opponent team's line and thereby score.

Carl and Dwight turned out to be on the same team, but Carl wasn't concerned about that. All he did was count off each player from the center of his team's line until he came to Dwight. Then he did the same thing in the opposite direction; and there he went, squeezing in between two other boys. Now all he had to do was wait until the time came when he would be out on the floor at the same time as Dwight.

As for Dwight, he was nervous enough about participating in this event, but now he had the added worry of encountering Carl. *Oh, I hope I can avoid him,* he thought in his uncomfortable state of mind, not yet having conditioned himself to look to God in his hour of need.

When the boys were well into the game with the score three to two in favor of the opposing team, the whistle once more blew.

Scott was up, and it was he and Cliff Roberts, a boy who was also from Chism, who rushed out for the ball along with two other boys.

Beating everyone there, Scott advanced toward Dwight's team while guiding the ball along the floor. Yet just as he was getting close enough for a chance to score, the ball was suddenly kicked away from him by one of the defenders.

With quick thrusts of his long legs Scott was able to bypass the boy. Then, turning and charging him head on, he managed to regain possession of the ball. Heading down the court once again, he gave the ball a strong kick sending it right past the defense. With the score his teammates cheered and hoorayed in jubilation as he proceeded to return to the center of his team's line with a wide grin of triumph on his face.

When the ball was placed in the center of the court once again, the next four players readied themselves for action.

Dwight was up and tried his best to appear eager to participate in the game even though his anxiety was quite pronounced.

While awaiting the dreaded sound of the whistle, he thought, *Why must I go through this*? even though he knew that all freshmen were required to take gym class. Eying his teammates, he further thought, *I wish I believed in myself. I just....* Suddenly he was overtaken with fear, for maliciously eying him from the other end of the line was Carl as he anticipated the coming moments.

Dwight was desperate to assume a different position in the lineup, but before he was able to make any attempt whatsoever to do so, the whistle blew to signal the resumption of play. He started off rather slowly, but then somehow gained confidence and speed as he approached an opposing team member who was readying himself for an offensive kick of the ball.

By the time a minute of play had passed, no one yet had scored, but still Dwight managed to handle himself quite well; he even got off a few good shots at the opponent team's defensive line. But then suddenly Carl made his move against him to spoil the self-confidence that was gradually beginning to wind its way into his sentiments. Running beside him, he deliberately placed his right foot between his legs, which propelled him so abruptly forward that he ended up landing flat on his face.

Now Dwight was a downcast spectacle for all to see. Nobody moved, because it was generally realized that Carl was out to get him, and they were anxious to find out what would happen next.

Dwight remained in a subordinate position, afraid to risk getting up and being knocked back to the floor. Through each passing moment the stares of his classmates seemed to be all the more intensified. Then, finally, he raised his head to regard Carl with a look that seemed to implore him to explain why he had behaved so badly. It was a distressing moment, but an ever angry Carl was not about to relinquish his abusive ways.

"You disgust me, you weakling!" he jeered in a clench-toothed whisper. Yet as he turned to walk away, he, being a bully, seemed to sense that it was a weakness to target and lash out at the very people who put forth the least resistance. What he did not realize, however, was that there was another way for a wronged person to respond to the persecutions directed against them. Indeed, in the passage of time, he would come to see and know this different type of resistance within Dwight. Yet for now, hardened in heart as he was, he thought with sole purpose while continuing to leave the scene of his recent offense, *I'll get him some other time... yes, some other time.*

The whistle blew and play continued when Dwight had at last returned to he center of his team's line. Naturally he felt relieved that this latest incident was behind him, yet he was far from satisfied by the manner in which he had handled it. He did not comprehend, however, that he was well on his way to being touched by God to overcome his difficulties in a manner not commonly put into practice by the general population.

Looking across the gym floor at the other team, Dwight saw some boys talking while staring at him. *What do they think of me?* he thought. .... *They think I'm a coward, I guess,* he finally concluded as Mr. Milter warned Carl against such acts in the future from where he spoke with him near the locker room doorway.

CHAPTER 3

THE ACQUAINTANCE

As the weeks passed, Dwight managed to avoid any further disturbing episodes such as those which had taken place in the hall and the gym. He was constantly alert when around people, though, growing less trustful of them through each passing day it seemed, and living, he thought, for only two things; the advent of weekends, and the occasional, friendly smiles he received from Jana. She did not dismiss him as other students were prone to do, even though he made no effort to talk to her because of his handicapped personality. This puzzled him so. Why would a girl that attractive and popular even notice him? She had her friends. It really didn't make any sense to him at this point in his life.

Jana did want to be his friend, though, possibly because he seemed to have no others. And yet it went deeper than that, for he had a certain attribute about him which drew her to him. She found herself wanting to make a difference in his life, and not out of pity, but out of a genuinely heartfelt desire to befriend someone whom she believed would be receptive to her efforts. .... Therefore one sunny Friday afternoon in late October, after school had been dismissed for the day, she decided to take the initiative to approach him.

Standing outside the school waiting for his bus to arrive on the scene, Dwight did not notice Jana walking towards him.

"Hello," she spoke up with an air of ease. "Are you going to the football game tomorrow afternoon?" She was glad that his bus was not yet present, for she knew he would already have been seated on it.

Even though Dwight was somewhat relieved to discover who had spoken to him, he still became self-conscious over the thought of talking to her. But he couldn't and wouldn't be rude by saying nothing at all, he convinced himself.

"Ah... I don't think I'll be able to make the game," he stammered with a forced smile before looking away as though the conversation were ended, and not because he wanted it that way, but because he wasn't composed enough to enable speech to flow freely.

Although Jana immediately sensed his reticence, she decided to press on anyway in an honest attempt to gain his trust.

"Well, if you change your mind, please come," she said despite knowing that he probably wouldn't risk encountering Carl at the event.

Dwight could feel her concern for him, and he was grateful for it.

"I'll remember that," he said as his bus pulled up beside them and opened its doors. "Thank you."

"You're welcome," she told him as more and more students began to exit the school. "Have a nice weekend."

Though Dwight said nothing, he did manage to nod his head before entering the bus and heading for a rear seat. How grateful he was to have finally spoken to her. *She's so friendly*, he thought. *Could it be she understands me? ... No, it's not possible*, he concluded shortly thereafter. *How could she? She'd have to live it.*

Let it cross the collective minds of all mankind that there is someone who does understand us all. Let us reap comfort from that fact in our present condition, whatever that condition may be.

* * *

Cheerleading practice had been a trying ordeal for Jana, for she was tired from studying late the night before for a history exam. Thus her main inclination was to go straight home, and she certainly would have done so had she not told Scott she'd accompany him to Sam's Place for a burger and fries after football practice.

While she changed in the girl's locker room, she was neared by

Sara Treson, who had also made the squad along with Cybil and three other girls.

"It looks like we've got everything down pat," Sara spoke up as she, too, began to undress. "I just hope that we win!"

"Yes, so do I," Jana uttered with much less zeal.

Sensing her fatigue, Sara said, "I could tell that you were a bit tired during practice. Were you out with Scott last night?"

"No, not on a Thursday night. That's a school night," Jana reminded her. "It's just that I was up late studying. And now Scott wants to take me out to eat."

"Well, I'm sure you'll live through it." Sara smiled suggestively. "You two seem to get along quite well. And Scott's the best catch there is in Chism. You're lucky."

Without understanding the complete reasoning, Jana immediately thought of Dwight. It was not that she wasn't currently interested in Scott, but she found Sara's comment to be so narrowly conceived, so subjective, that it prompted her to challenge the accuracy of it.

"Who may be a best catch to you may not be to the next person," she wisely pointed out. "For instance a person might find Dwight Enhart very appealing."

Sara laughed so loudly that Jana became somewhat startled. Then, when Sara had regained some semblance of composure in the midst of Jana's questioning stare, she said, "But he's so backward." Giggling without reservation, she added, "I just love to tease him. He's so easy to embarrass and he never fights back."

Jana was quickly annoyed, for it bothered her to hear of anybody taking advantage of another person's vulnerabilities. Nobody gained anything of value to enrich the quality of their lives in the process.

"Do you mean to tell me that you deliberately try to embarrass him because you find it funny?" she questioned her in near disbelief while squarely eying her.

"Why... yes," Sara acknowledged in stunned response. "Does that bother you?"

Jana felt as though she could become angry enough to shake some sense into her, but she could not bring herself to violence, so instead she tried as best she could to take the rational approach.

"It bothers me very much. He doesn't deserve such treatment. Nobody does," she told her in the hopes that she'd realize the error of her ways. But unfortunately it didn't serve its intended purpose, for Sara only grew resentful.

"You live your life and I'll live mine!" she rebounded indignantly, thereby putting an abrupt end to their conversation, which Jana was secretly thankful for.

* * *

It was nearly five thirty by the time Jana and Scott entered Sam's Place, a small restaurant with an informal atmosphere that had an adjoining game room. On occasion Jana would come here, for it was located less than a mile's walk from her home.

Behind a white counter, which provided seating for about ten people, they immediately laid eyes on Sam, who was busily flipping burgers on the grill.

"Hey, Scott and Jana," they now heard a voice call out from the second of five booths set against the wall. "Come sit with Ben and me." Turning aside, they discovered Carl beckoning them to join him with an upheld hand.

Jana grew noticeably tense as she approached the booth with Scott, for she did not like to be in Carl's presence. Under the circumstances, however, she felt as though she had little choice in the matter, given that Scott seemed quite willing to accept Carl's invitation, which puzzled her plenty considering how Scott had come to Dwight's defense in school.

"Hi," they exchanged greetings as Carl and Ben slid over in their seats to make room for them. "I sure hope we win the big game tomorrow, Scott!" Carl told him.

"We'll sure do our best," Scott asserted as he and a very hesitant Jana sat down. "Coach Milter says we're the best team he's ever had."

"What'll it be?" they were suddenly interrupted by Molly, a no nonsense waitress who appeared to be impatient with many of her more frequent customers without it actually being the case.

"Two burgers and cokes," Scott stated with a smile. "And two fries. ... Molly, you never change, do you?"

"No, and I guess I never will. It's not that I'm stubborn, you understand. It's just that I'm already molded," she noted with a suppressed grin before walking comically away amongst everyone's laughter, except Jana's, for she was not at all in a humorous mood, and Carl understood why this was so. You see earlier in the day he happened to see her speaking with Dwight, so he knew perfectly well she did not wish to be in his company. He was bent on defiance, however, therefore when the mirth had subsided, he made it a point to force her to address him by asking, "How do ya think ya did on today's history test? I thought it was pretty hard myself."

"I guess I did alright," she responded with rigid courtesy as Carl casually took a bite from his half-eaten burger. "But I studied for it." Indeed she assumed he probably had not.

"This guy seems to think he can get away without studying," Ben reinforced her unspoken presumption. "Then he wonders why tests seem so hard." And he shook his head unknowingly.

"I've got other things on my mind that keep me occupied!" Carl sharply rebounded. "So just keep your mouth shut!"

"Okay, I'm sorry," Ben cringed. "I didn't mean any harm."

I know what other things he's got on his mind, Jana thought in growing resentment as she reflected on what he had done to Dwight.

There was now a brief period of silence in which tension could be readily felt in their midst.

"Hey, let's go play pool, Carl," Ben sought to appease him then, much to Jana's delight over the thought of their leaving. "I wanna find out if I can beat you for a change."

"I guess so," Carl said while he finished his burger. "But you supply the money."

"Of course," Ben responded as Jana and Scott got up from their seats to let them out. "What's new?"

"We'll see ya both later," Carl stated when he and Ben were standing. "I guess I'll have to show this kid up again." Sardonically he smirked at Jana in his ongoing defiance.

"Ya, see ya both around," Scott told them as Jana looked to the floor. "May the best man win."

"Oh, gee, I think I just lost then," Ben predicted as they started to walk away.

Jana had to force herself to say good-bye to the boys. Then, when she and Scott were seated in the booth once again, Scott spoke up over the discomfort he sensed within her.

"What's wrong with you?" he asked in apparent bewilderment.

"It's not me! It's you!" she swiftly informed him. "Why did you agree to sit with them?"

"Because I was asked to," he nonchalantly stated while she anxiously clasped her hands together.

"But surely you must have realized by now that I don't like Carl's ways!" she implored him. "In fact I thought you didn't either." Her eyes revealed her yearning for an explanation.

"I never told you I disliked Carl," he informed her. "And besides, what was I suppose to do, ignore him?"

"No, I'm not saying you should have taken things that far, but you could have told him we wanted to be alone, anything!" she sought to reason with him. "I hope this doesn't happen again. I don't like to associate with mean-spirited people."

"Alright, you win!" Scott gave in with disgust. "I'll only associate with him when you're not around, okay!"

For a moment or two Jana could only stare at him in utter confusion, for she was discovering a side to him she didn't think existed.

"You saw how Carl treated Dwight Enhart and yet you still want to be around him!" she straightforwardly declared.

Meeting her gaze squarely, Scott blurted out in blind words of frustration, "Ya, maybe I like Carl because he confronts people!"

Shaking her head in a fit of exasperation over the logic he was employing, Jana stated, "If you think bullying people is a good way to confront people... well, I think you had better seek counseling!" Reflecting on what had taken place in school weeks earlier, she confoundedly inquired, "And if you approve of Carl's ways so much, then why on earth did you stand up for Dwight that day?"

"I guess I wanted to draw attention to myself," he had the nerve to admit. "And it worked."

In her dismay Jana took on silence, believing it was pointless to continue speaking to him in his current frame of mind. *He's a lot like Carl*, she thought in her disappointment. *And they're the weak ones, not Dwight*. Yes, she knew that whenever anyone was truly strong in character they did not feel the need to prove it, real strength in character not carrying with it the desire to impress and/or oppress others, but the desire to help others through the self-confidence which accompanies a healthy self-image. Yet instead she was looking at someone who was admitting to having exploited a situation for a selfish and most insecure of reasons.

Moments later, when Molly brought them their order, Jana ate in sullenness as Scott began to rattle on about the upcoming game, amazingly acting as though all was fine and well, and that he had not said or done anything wrong.

* * *

The Gulf was located only a few miles from Dwight's home. Often he would go there to walk on the white sand beach or run in the breaking waves to sort out his thoughts. For certain it could be said he drew comfort from this place to cope with the unsettling aspects of his life.

As he strolled along the deserted beach, he thought about how relieved he was to be away from home. It was sad, yet understand-able, because it seemed as though his mother was becoming more and more embittered through each passing day. Even Clair seemed to be at odds with her as of late. He didn't know how much longer he could tolerate such an unhealthy environment, and yet in spite of feeling this way he presumed he could survive it indefinitely if he found a truly inspiring reason to live.

When he noticed a seashell that had washed up on the beach, he bent over to pick it up. Inspecting it, he heard the lonely cry of a solitary gull, and wondered what the future held in store for him. Looking upward, he saw it flapping its wings speedily in the wind as though it were searching for something; and so could not help but think of himself. Eventually shifting his attention down the beach to a rather small sand dune, he got the urge to ascend it. Dropping the shell, he dashed forth in the energy of his youth.

Indeed, in moments such as this, when he channeled his thoughts away from his problems, he became an active participant in the world around him instead of the repressed individual people envisioned him to be. Perhaps it was the freedom he felt in the wide-open spaces which filled him with such inspiration: the sea, the earth, the endless sky.

Dwight took it upon himself to gaze at the ocean from atop the dune for quite some time before turning to walk down the knoll that blended into the dirt road that led home. He thought about staying longer to view the sunset to the west, but he was growing weary. He knew, however, that he had succeeded in boosting his spirit on this day, and he suddenly felt the pressing desire to thank God for the ability to bring that about.

* * *

Mr. Weston picked Jana and Scott up from Sam's Place at six thirty. He was a muscular man with well-defined facial features. Being an attorney, his attire was usually one of suit and tie.

"Hey, dad, what are your plans for tomorrow afternoon?" Scott asked when he and Jana were seated in the back seat of the car.

"I'm sure hoping to make it to your game, son," his father sought to assure him as he began to drive away. "But like I told you this morning, I might be busy. ... By the way, how was your evening together?"

"It was alright," Scott told him despite the heated conversation he had had with Jana. "And we both enjoyed the burgers at Sam's Place. They're the best."

"Yes, they are good," his father agreed. "I haven't had one in awhile, though. Lately I've been so busy with work I hardly find time for anything else."

"Dad's been involved with a big case in Jackson," Scott enlightened Jana.

Jana grew curious.

"May I ask what it's about?"

"I'm representing a girl who claims she was raped by a man from Jackson when she visited her cousin there last month," the man confided with a deeply concerned tone of voice. "Of course I believe she's telling the truth and the evidence falls into place, but still," he shook his head, "rape is a difficult thing to prove, and in this instance, since the accused is from a rich and influential family, it makes it all the harder. Suffice it to say he's got the support and financial backing to have the charges dropped."

"I've heard of that sort of thing happening before where money and power are concerned," Jana responded as she thought of how terrible it was for a woman to be so violated.

"And whenever that does happen, justice isn't served," Mr. Weston continued. "Sometimes people even scorn the rape victim, going as far as to blame her for the crime as though she caused it. That attitude doesn't encourage women to come forth."

Jana felt as though Mr. Weston was right in what he had said, yet before she could make any comment to that effect, Scott spoke up on the issue.

"I sure would like to get my hands on the guy who did that to that girl," he angrily stated. "I'd break every bone in his body."

Being a lawyer, Mr. Weston quickly informed his son that that wouldn't be a wise approach; yet Jana, though disagreeing with the violent method Scott advocated, felt moved by his desire to stand up for the protection of women. *He has concern for others after all,* she gladly thought. *Perhaps everything between us can be fine if we work at it.* She was relieved to think there was a glimmer of hope for better relations between them.

When Mr. Weston pulled to a stop before the Rossis' house in the midst of approaching twilight, one could see the beauty of the huge white home's exquisite features. Ironclad masonry and wide French windows along with a large gallery and huge white supporting columns made it a truly elegant maison of traditional old South elegance and charm.

"I'll see you soon," Scott told Jana as she got out of the car.

"Yes," she rather tentatively responded. "Mr. Weston, I do hope you make it to the game tomorrow." Bending over, she regarded him directly.

"I'll do my best. Good-bye."

Returning the farewell, Jana proceeded through a splendid iron gate, down a wide sidewalk, and up a flight of stairs to the front door. Turning momentarily, she waved in final parting before entering the foyer.

Hearing the murmur of voices down the hall in the library, Jana smiled softly. *Mother and father must be playing chess again*, she surmised. Walking down the dimly-lit corridor to the doorway of the room, she found herself to be correct in her assumption, for seated on a chair on one side of a game table was her mother, while seated across from her on a black sofa was her father.

"Hello," Jana alerted them of her presence as her father made a move on the chessboard.

"Oh, hello, dear," her mother stated with an accent which bespoke French ancestry. "How was your day?"

"Tiring." Her mother's question made her realize how exhausted she really was. "I'm glad to be home." Making her way to the sofa, she sat down beside her father. Placing her undivided attention upon him, she inquired, "And how was your day, father? I hope it wasn't too demanding."

Mr. Rossi was no longer a youthful man, being in his fifties at the time of Jana's birth, and now under the close supervision of the family doctor for dizzy spells he'd been experiencing as of late. Jana, her sister Cynthia, and their mother wished he'd take on a less demanding workload as bank president. So did his doctor; but no, he insisted on doing as much as ever. *Would he even be alive much longer?* Jana at times fretfully wondered, for she did love him a great deal, even though her relationship with him had never been satisfying, his personality being too austere to endorse displays of affection between family members. As far as he was concerned everything was to be conducted in a formal fashion. He did things out of necessity and a sense of obligation more than pleasure, and such was the case where the parenting of his daughters was concerned. Mrs. Rossi had come to accept this about him. So had Cynthia. But Jana, being the warmhearted girl that she was, was driven by the sincere hope that a much desired change in the type of relationship she had with her father would soon be forthcoming.

"My day was just fine," Mr. Rossi uttered in a deep voice. "You must not worry about me. ... I do hope the lawyer's son walked you up to the door?" He spoke without tearing his attention away from the chessboard.

"No, father... we said good-bye at the car," Jana was reluctant to inform him.

"Well, then I must have a talk with that young man about proper etiquette when I see him," he told her with firm resolution.

In the ensuing moments, as Mr. and Mrs. Rossi planned their next move on the chessboard, Jana felt the desire to ask them their opinion about something that had been nagging within her for quite some time now.

Resting her head against the back of the couch, she stared at the high-ceilinged room in search of the right words before finally saying, "What do you think of people who treat other people badly just because they think they can get away with it?"

Immediately a distinguishable look of worry could be detected on her mother's face, but her father remained unmoved.

"Has somebody been treating you badly, Jana?" the woman questioned her then.

"No, it's not me, mother," Jana sought to assure her. With solemn reflection and ever so grave undertones, she added, "It's this shy boy from school. Some kids don't like him very much, and they're making a point of it."

"I myself have never liked shy people either," Mr. Rossi frankly spoke up. "They don't make good speakers, and if you can't communicate well in life, you'll never go places."

Jana was not surprised in the least by her father's position on the matter, but she pressed on anyway in the hopes that her mother would feel differently.

"But he doesn't deserve to be scorned," she pointed out in earnest. "And I really think he'd be able to see past his fears once he took that first step. What do you think, mother?" Intently she fixed her gaze upon her.

Mrs. Rossi felt cornered, so much so that she was at a loss for words, for she did not feel comfortable giving advice which ran contrary to her husband's, her role as his wife having been that submissive ever since their marriage.

"I... don't think he should be treated badly of course," she was slow to say, "but I really wouldn't worry about him if I were you. ... Let him fend for himself. You can't do much to help him really."

Upon finishing what she felt so pressured to say, she obediently looked to her husband.

"Bravo," Mr. Rossi wholeheartedly supported her. "Now enough of this foolish talk." Finally removing his gaze from the chessboard, he beheld his daughter before adding, "Just listen to what we said and everything will be fine. Don't fret about matters that don't concern you. You've got to learn to mind your own business!"

Meeting her father's gaze, Jana knew that her mother had not spoken her true feelings because of the man's strong influence in her life. And yet even though this was so, she, on the other hand, was not about to follow suit. She was determined to pursue her interest in Dwight, and nobody, not her father or anyone else, was about to dissuade her, for she believed the day would dawn when Dwight would look upon her as his friend. And perhaps the day would also dawn when she would be saying to her father that mankind was her business after all.

CHAPTER 4

THE WILLARDS

A s the clock ticked away the remaining seconds of the game and the crowd rose to its feet in excitement, Coach Milter felt relieved. With the score twenty eight to twenty four in favor of Fulton, he thought for a minute or two that the team's unblemished record would include a loss. *Thank goodness for Scott Weston*, he quite elatedly told himself as the siren blew to signal the end of the well played event.

Mr. Weston felt proud seeing Scott become the star of the game, scoring three touchdowns in all. The man was even inclined to wonder if his son's athletic talent would fast make him the most admired boy at Fulton High.

Once inside the noisy locker room after being literally mobbed by teammates and fans alike, Scott approached Coach Milter.

"We did it, coach!" he ecstatically spoke up. "I can hardly wait until the next game!" His eyes confirmed his enthusiasm.

"I'm not sure my heart can take this!" the coach emphasized. "It was a close one. Keep this up and you'll go places. You've got possibilities kid."

"Thanks," Scott heartily stated as a fellow teammate, Joe Darreth, summoned him from afar. Joe was a husky junior with a reputation for being a good guard.

Scott excused himself from the coach's presence and walked over to where Joe was undressing a short ways off.

"What's up?" he inquired.

"First of all I wanna congratulate you on a great game," Joe told him. "We're really hot this year!" His grin was from ear to ear.

"We sure are!" Scott wholeheartedly agreed. "I'm sure glad my dad made it here to see it happen!" Yelping in jubilation, he added, "It sure is great to be a winner!"

"Ya, and last year we only won two games for the entire season," Joe reminded him. "I guess it speaks for itself."

"I guess it does at that," Scott stated without the least hint of modesty.

Focusing on the main reason he had called Scott over, Joe whispered while scanning the general area for eavesdroppers, "By the way, do you wanna go to Hickory Lake later? There's gonna be a party." Removing his grimy shirt, he continued, "We planned it this morning. Fred and Cliff managed to get hold of some beer."

"That sounds like fun," Scott welcomed the idea even though he knew Coach Milter and his father would not want him to be drinking. Thinking of Jana, he then asked, "Should we take dates with us?"

"Sure, the more the merrier," Joe told him. "Girls make a party all the more fun." Expressively he eyed Scott and laughed.

"I'll talk to Jana about it," Scott eagerly informed him. "But we'll need a ride there."

"Don't worry about that," Joe stated. "I have my dad's car for the day. Some of the other guys have cars, too. We'll be leaving in an hour."

"Where should we meet?" Scott inquired.

"Behind the school. Don't be late. I don't wanna miss out on any of the fun."

* * *

Jana and Cybil walked out of the school with Scott and Bill Willard, a boy from Fulton whom Cybil had only recently begun to see on a regular basis. Bill, like Scott, was on the football team, but rarely had Coach Milter ever put him in a game. Being optimistic, though, he took it all in stride, for he had a confident outlook which was linked to his upbringing. His parents were very loving people who believed in their children's potential, guiding them well in life with good advice, fair discipline, and ample affection. Bill cherished them immensely.

"Hey, do you wanna take a walk to Sam's Place?" Bill suggested. "I haven't been there in a while."

"I've got a better idea," Scott intervened and apprised them of the party at Hickory Lake. "We could have a great time!"

"But you know that the coach doesn't want us to drink, not to mention our parents," Bill levelheadedly pointed out. "We might get in trouble."

"He's right," Cybil maintained. "Don't get involved with that sort of thing, Scott. You've got a lot going for you."

Scott realized that Cybil and Bill made good sense, but he became angry with them anyway, and here is why. He was extremely defensive of the counsel of others when it called into question the wisdom behind his choices. Also, because of his popularity, he had assumed he could easily persuade them to do what he wanted, and it irked him to think he did not have authority over their behavior.

Jana, in seeing resentment building up within Scott, grew very ill at ease.

"And how do you feel about this?" Scott asked while sternly turning to face her. "I suppose you agree with them!" He made out that he knew her mind.

Jana was unsure whether she should speak at all. She felt as though Cybil and Bill were absolutely right in what they had said to him, and yet she did not want to run the risk of upsetting him any further. In spite of her mixed emotions, however, she finally did decide to discourage him from going through with his plans by saying with his best interest at heart, "You know they're right. Let's go to Sam's Place instead." She seemed on the verge of begging him to be cooperative.

"Don't tell me what to do!" he angrily replied, startling all present with his outburst. "I can see that none of you know how to have a good time! Well, I'm not missing out on this because of all of you!" Obstinately fixing his gaze upon Jana, he bluntly concluded, "You know where I'll be!" In a huff he began walking toward the back of the school.

At first Jana made a motion to call out to him in a vain last attempt at dissuasion. Judiciously deciding against it, she simply watched him leave.

Approaching her, Cybil gently laid a hand upon her shoulder in an effort to console her.

"I'm sorry, Jana," she said. "I never knew he got this way. If I had I wouldn't have agreed with what Bill said."

"Try not to feel badly about that," Jana defended her actions as tears began to cloud her vision. "You were right. False guilt will do none of us any good."

"Do you want to go home?" Bill asked of her. "We'll understand."

Shifting her focus upon him, Jana managed to reveal her appreciation.

"Yes, I think that'd be for the best," she replied. "Thank you."

"Do you want us to walk with you?" Cybil inquired.

"No, I'd rather walk alone. You understand."

"Of course," she assured her. "I'll call on you tomorrow."

Jana slowly proceeded homeward. Never in her wildest dreams did she think today would end up like this. Her world seemed so fragile. But in the course of time the future was yet to be molded. Surely, if nothing else, she could take comfort in the fact that she had acted wisely on this day.

"I can see now that Scott isn't good for Jana," Cybil pointed out to Bill once Jana was out of hearing range. "He just isn't considerate enough."

"It appears so," Bill had to admit. "And if there's one thing I've learned from my parents throughout the years, it's that consideration is what we should give everyone."

* * *

Supper turned out to be very repetitious for both Clair and Dwight, but their mother could not have cared less. She prepared whatever was easiest for her without attempting to implement a variety in the weekly menu.

So there they all sat picking away at grits and fried potatoes in the poor family relations they had come to know. As time went by meat was becoming less and less common in their diets, even though Clair did occasionally work at the bakery to help out financially. But more and more lately their mother was calling in sick at the local factory where she worked part-time simply because she didn't feel like being there. Her life and the way she had allowed it to become was affecting her in a much broader way than financially or emotionally. Through the jailing of her soul she was stifling the attainment of the glorious inner freedom which could have been.

They were almost finished eating when Clair suddenly broke the silence by crying out, "I can't take this any more! This rotten food!" She pushed her plate away in distaste. "Day after day, rotten food, boring people, I just can't take it any longer!"

Taken aback by her outburst, Dwight stared at her with widened eyes, but his mother seemed unmoved, unaffected, the epitome of apathy.

As Clair began to sob, Dwight felt compelled to encourage her to seek some semblance of hope in the midst of her terrible feelings.

"Things can still change for the better, Clair," he dared to suggest. "If we cared enough to make it happen that is."

"But we don't!" she bitterly exclaimed. "That's the point, isn't it! We don't care enough and I expect we never will!" Standing up, she raced from the kitchen and flew up the stairs while weeping all the harder.

Hearing Clair's bedroom door loudly slam shut, Dwight shifted his attention to his mother. Strangely she still seemed unmoved by Clair's outburst, for she was casually lighting a cigarette as though nothing of significance had happened. Had he been the one who complained, he would not have been surprised by her reaction, but in the not-too-distant past she had expressed some concern for Clair's feelings. Now even that seemed to have eroded. It was a blatant reminder of the deterioration that had taken place within her intellect. *How she must have depended on father*, he now thought, for ever since that day when the man left home never to return, her life had been torn further and further apart. She found it difficult to cope with all that happened because she had given her husband her complete devotion. A broken trust, real or imagined, wounds deeply and leaves a scar. Yet if only she saw her hardened heart as a condition of her own choosing, she would be so much better off. She was so unenlightened about many things, and for that reason had no intention of trying to restructure her life.

Mustering all the courage he could, Dwight ultimately stated, "I agree with Clair that some changes need to take place around here. This is a frustrated home."

With a blank expression his mother stated, "And how would you know what a frustrated home is? Are you an expert?" Standing up, she strode to the refrigerator, removed a beer from it, and made her way into the living room in total disregard over conditions as they stood.

Dwight somberly left the house and made his way to the barn. Upon entering the structure, he immediately approached Hazel.

Stroking her neck as he hugged her, he thought about his life and wept. What was there to really live for? He searched his mind for an answer. With longing eyes he could not help but think of the contented person he used to be. Wishing would not bring that kind of feeling back, though. He had to rise above adversity and change his life for the better. Hence, like never before, he focused on the realization that he held something positive within his grasp, it being the ability to determine how he responded to whatever was cast his way. It was tied in to a quote he had once read: "Faith is the substance of things hoped for, the evidence of things not seen."

Never give up faith, Dwight Enhart, for you can have redemption if you desire it enough. To a large extent your difficulties came about because you felt as though you had to constantly be on guard around people. You are filled with unrest and you cringe at life now, it is true, but change is always possible. The worst can return to laughter.

* * *

Arriving home around seven o'clock, Bill found his parents, his brother, and three sisters gathered in the living room listening to the radio. Their home was quite plain and unadorned with a fireplace set against one wall and a couch against another. Here and there about the room a few chairs had been placed, and there was a large oval rug in the center of a hardwood floor.

Seated on the couch, Mrs. Willard was in the process of telling her husband about a raffle the church was planning to have in order to raise funds to help the needy in the community, while in the meantime their seven-year-old son, Jerry, and nine-year-old daughter, Sandy, carried on a minor sibling squabble about who would get the last piece of carrot cake left over from supper. Indeed there was rarely a moment of silence in this house, for everyone communicated quite openly with one another. Any disagreements that did happen to arise were eventually worked out with order once again established in the mainstream of their lives. Truly there was great love in this house, but it was no coincidence. The strong bond between Mr. and Mrs. Willard brought this atmosphere about. The essence of their values didn't rest within these four walls, however, for Mrs. Willard often volunteered to help others through church projects, and whenever she put up jams or canned vegetables from the garden, she made sure to it that someone received something from her. And where Mr. Willard was concerned, he assisted people in need by repairing things around their homes, or delivering extra firewood he had cut. What a good example they set for their children to emulate. It was no wonder their small grocery store did such good business, because people saw what helpful, honest folks they were in the community. This family was wealthier than words could express for they knew how to attain fulfillment in life through the joy of giving.

"Hello, everybody," Bill heartily greeted them as he walked into the room.

Seeing his big brother, Jerry immediately stopped arguing with Sandy and ran to his side. He was a cute kid with light brown hair, dense freckles, endless energy, and a deep admiration toward his big brother Bill.

When everyone had returned Bill's greeting, Jerry quickly asked him if he'd play catch.

"I wanna try out my new ball!" he anxiously anticipated.

With a confused expression Bill inquired, "How did you get a new ball?"

"I saved up money from my newspaper route," Jerry proudly informed him.

"Oh, I see," Bill replied. "Well, it must be a beauty."

"I'll go get it," Jerry told him and darted for the stairs.

Jerry's parents could have afforded to buy him the new football, but they wanted to teach him and all their children the value of working for something they wanted. They knew that so often parents made the mistake of overindulging their children, thereby leaving them ill prepared to deal with the responsibilities of everyday living.

When Jerry had disappeared from sight, Bill's ten-year-old sister Eliza spoke up from where she sat beside her father on the couch.

"Hey, Bill, ma and dad said that if tomorrow is nice we're going on a family picnic to The Gulf! I sure hope we do! I love The Gulf!"

Immediate interest shown on Bill's face, for he, along with everyone else in the family, enjoyed these outings to a great extent.

"That sounds like fun! Would it be alright if I asked Cybil to come along?" He shifted his gaze from his mother to his father for approval.

"Of course," his mother assured him. "We'd love to have her along." Pleasantly she smiled.

"Yes, by all means ask her," Mr. Willard wholeheartedly supported the idea.

At first glance one might say that Mr. and Mrs. Willard were not attractive people, but all one had to do was get to know them personally and the precious beauty of their character beamed forth to project them as the most handsome people possible, the quality of their inner being taking charge.

Walking to a small table near the stairwell upon which the phone was situated, Bill said, "I'll call her up to make sure she can make it. What time would we be leaving?" Picking up the receiver, he began to dial Cybil's number.

"Around noon," his father told him as Jerry came rushing down the stairs clutching his prized possession.

While Jerry stood before Bill waiting for him to get off the phone, Bill widened his eyes in a display of approval over the fine ball he had purchased.

"Yes, Mrs. Adams," he then spoke up. "Is Cybil there please?"

As Bill discussed the next day's plans with Cybil, Eliza and his twelve-year-old sister, Mary Ann, went upstairs to their room to do their homework, while in the meantime Sandy brought a broken doll crib to her father.

"Can you fix this, daddy?" she asked while placing it in his hands. "I really like it."

"I don't imagine this will be too much of a problem," he said while inspecting it. "I'll have it looking good as new." Reassuringly he smiled at the child to ease her concerns.

Sandy hugged him in appreciation.

"Thank you, daddy," she said. ... Then, turning her attention to her mother, she asked if she could have the last piece of carrot cake.

"You can have half of it," she told her. "You want Jerry to have some, don't you?"

There was now a brief silence as Sandy deliberated.

"Well, I guess so," she finally decided. "But mom, next time make a bigger cake." Her astute remark compelled both of her parents to break out in laughter.

"I'll be sure to remember that next time," her mother obliged her with a lingering smile before the child hurriedly scampered off to the kitchen for her snack.

Immediately upon hanging up the phone from his conversation with Cybil, Bill picked up Jerry's ball to inspect it.

"Boy, Jer, this is really nice. I bet you really like it," he surmised.

"Ya, I do," he freely admitted. Yet then suddenly, in a somewhat subdued manner, he looked slightly downward.

"What's wrong?" Bill asked in response to the boy's unusual behavior.

Shrugging his shoulders a bit, Jerry stated, "It's just something that my friend Jimmy told me."

"And what was that?" Bill pressed the issue.

Rather hesitantly Jerry related, "He told me that you weren't good enough to play in the game today. He said that you'll never be put in a game."

Bill put a hand to his chin in deliberation.

"Well, Jer, the coach didn't put me in the game today because there's other players who play better than me," he honestly informed him. "It may not seem fair, but it's the way it is. I hope that doesn't mean you'll stop coming to the games." He spoke with gentle urging as he recalled his family's devotion in attending the events. "I may get to play one of these days. I work hard in practice."

It was only seconds later that Jerry looked up at him in appeasement.

"I'll be at the next game," he gladly told him. "To me you're the best player of all."

Giving him a rub on the head, Bill said in simulated sternness, "Get out of here." He motioned his eyes toward the door. "I'll be out in a minute to help you break in your new ball."

Jerry's face beamed with delight.

"Sure!" he exclaimed and rushed for the door.

"That was wonderful what you told Jerry," Mrs. Willard commented from across the room. "He looks up to you so much."

"Well, I think he's pretty special, too," Bill confided as he approached his parents. "And because I do, I didn't want to lie to him."

"You did the right thing, son," Mr. Willard told him. "It wouldn't have been good to tell him otherwise."

"I guess it's part of being a big brother," Bill chuckled. "He's something else."

Standing up at this time, Mrs. Willard proceeded to head for the kitchen to make some tea.

"Oh, by the way, is Cybil planning on coming with us tomorrow?" she asked of Bill while turning to face him.

"Oh, ya," Bill informed her. "She said she hasn't been to The Gulf in a long time. She's really looking forward to it."

"I do hope she likes fried chicken," she said as she neared the dining room doorway.

"Who wouldn't like your chicken, mama?" Bill complimented her with teasing overtones.

"Oh, go on," she said while throwing out a hand at him in modest response. Her mild laughter could be heard as she disappeared from sight.

Turning aside and heading for the door, Bill said to his father, "I better not keep Jer waiting too long."

"Have a good time."

"Jer will see to that," Bill laughed.

It was only a few minutes later that Mrs. Willard returned carrying a tray with a tea service and cookies on it. As she placed it upon the coffee table before the couch, she suddenly recalled a conversation she had had the day before with a poor, elderly widow she had visited.

"By the way, I was talking with Dolores Horton yesterday in her yard," she informed her husband while pouring the tea, "and I noticed that there's a broken board on her front steps. I was wondering if you could find the time to fix it."

Mr. Willard regarded her in an approving manner.

"I'll tell her in church tomorrow that I'll repair it as soon as we get back from our picnic. I wouldn't want her to get hurt."

Affectionately eying him, his wife stated, "I knew you'd do it but I didn't want to commit you." Sitting down, she placed a hand atop his and added, "You're a wonderful man, and I'm fortunate to have you in my life."

Putting his other hand upon hers and clutching it tightly, he said, "And I'm fortunate to have you. You encourage me to help people." Tenderly kissing, they sat back to enjoy their tea. Contentment flowed within them.

Their children were very fortunate to be blessed with them as parents. It's people like them who deserve to have children, for they make one realize that there is indeed great hope for a better world tomorrow.

* * *

Hickory Lake was located five miles out of Fulton at the end of a dusty dirt road which intersected the main highway. It was a small body of water surrounded by elm, chestnut, and dogwood trees, and here and there any number of camp sites could be seen. In the summer months this spot was popular indeed as a recreational area for community members and tourists alike.

With a bonfire blazing intensely from old broken limbs the boys had collected from the forest floor a few feet into the woods, the chilly evening air seemed less prevalent, this along with the fact that the ale being consumed was having a numbing effect on the senses.

Seated in a slumped position, Scott was barely aware of his surroundings.

"Get me another beer," he stated in slurred words to anyone who might be listening.

"Don't you think you've had enough?" Carl laughed at his impaired condition. He was glad that Cliff had asked Ben and him to the party, for he liked alcohol a lot and had been drinking it on and off ever since he was ten years old. It was sad to know, but had he been able to get his hands on it whenever possible, he would in all likelihood have been highly addicted to the brew by now.

"I said get me another beer!" Scott insisted as he unsteadily rose to his feet.

"Okay," Carl gave in while grabbing for a bottle. "It'll probably be your last one anyway. Our supply is getting low."

"He might not even be able to finish that one," Cliff commented with a slight grin. "He's about as surefooted as a two year old on stilts."

Awkwardly staring at him, Scott said, "What do you mean?" Yet then, as he tried to walk forward, he fell flat on his face.

Lying there amongst the renewed laughter, Scott raised one of his hands and extended his index finger in a dictating position.

"I'm a good football player," he stuttered while staring with glassy eyes at Cliff, who was on the other side of the fire. "I have to be surefooted to be such a good player." Turning over on his back and seeing Carl standing over him with his beer, he attempted to reach for it only to fall to the ground in an unconscious state.

"It looks like he won't be having that beer after all," a tall, dark haired junior named Fred said while extending his hand. "Here, I'll take it."

Granting Fred's request, Carl looked at Scott with mischievous eyes.

"Hey, I've got an idea on how we can sober Scott up a little," he said and pointed at the lake. "I think a cold swim would do him wonders, don't you?"

In immediate and enthusiastic support of the idea Joe and Cliff each took hold of one of Scott's legs while Carl and Fred each grabbed an arm. Carrying him to the lake amongst cheers of support, they readied themselves for the eventful toss.

"Alright, we'll swing him three times, then throw him in!" Cliff commanded; whereupon, in unison, the boys went through the motions before flinging a still unconscious Scott up into the air and under the lake's surface with a big splash.

No sooner had Scott entered the cold water than it brought him to a state of awareness as an unpleasant, tingling sensation permeated his body. Jumping to his feet while yelling out, one could see the shocked expression on his face.

"How's the water?" Joe hilariously shouted amongst the laughter.

"He's awake now!" Carl joked. "It works every time!"

Realizing by now what had happened, Scott gazed at his merry onlookers in anger from where he stood in the knee deep water.

"Why'd ya do this!" he interrogated them in disgust over their prank. Crossing his arms against his chest, he began to shiver. "Look, I'm freezing to death!"

"Well then you better get out of there," Cliff stated while yet laughing as he put out a hand. "Here, let me help you."

"Sure," Scott complied and pulled his arm hard, forcing him to fall face first beside him.

The hilarity now mounted to a new height as Cliff came coughing to the surface.

"Why are you picking on me?" he gasped when he was standing beside Scott. "I wasn't the only one involved!"

With a self-satisfied grin Scott told him, "No, but you were the only dummy who trusted me." Trudging from the lake with some measure of difficulty, he walked to the bonfire as everyone made way for him to pass.

"Don't tell me you're mad at us for just that!" Carl pestered while following a close distance behind him.

Kneeling before the fire to place his hands over the flames, Scott shouted, "You darn right I'm mad!" Looking at him, he saw fit to bring to his attention, "I see you're still dry!"

"Ya, but you sure got Cliff good!" Carl laughed. "He looks like a drowned rat!"

In annoyance over his inability to get through to him, Scott looked away as though Carl were no longer there. It was then that Joe's girlfriend, Ginger Waine, approached the fire in ill intentioned defense of Scott. She was a girl with an especially vain interest in him. For quite some time now she had had her eye on him, yet her motivation was based solely on the fact that he was popular in school. It had nothing to do with a worthy desire. She wanted to be around him for reasons of social standing only, and it concerned her little that she might slight someone in the process of achieving her goal.

"I can understand your being upset, Scott," she spoke up with false concern. Then, kneeling beside him, she looked up at Carl and added, "I didn't want them to do it, but what could I do?"

Miffed by her contention, Carl challenged her integrity by stating, "It didn't seem to me that you were upset at all. In fact I thought I saw you laughing."

In defense Ginger turned to Scott, glad that Joe was still on his way back from the lake with the others.

"Oh, no, he's mistaken," she persisted in her lie. "I was very upset over their childish behavior."

Believing her to be sincere, Scott released a smile in thanks.

"It's nice to know someone sees my side," he told her just as Cliff and the others arrived on the scene.

Noticing that Scott was shivering, Ginger stated, "We had better get you home or you might catch pneumonia." Before he could even consider responding, she rose to her feet to approach Joe. Being wrapped up in the excitement, he was not aware that she had even spoken to Scott.

"Joe, I think it's time we left," she urged him. "Scott is shivering something awful." It was her aim to encourage Scott to be impressed by her conduct so that she could successfully charm him at some future date.

"Alright, whatever you say," Joe cooperated. Facing Scott, he added, "Come on, let's get going before you can't move." He was yet in a jovial mood. "It's a sorry sight you are."

Scott awkwardly stood up in his less than comfortable state.

"I'm well aware of that, Joe," he said in eased emotions as Ginger cast him a flirtatious smile.

* * *

The ride home was nauseating for Scott in the back seat of the car. Every bump along the road seemed to turn his stomach into knots. Yet in spite of his condition, he began to imagine what it would be like to be involved with Ginger. No regrets crept into his mind over this fantasy, even though he knew Joe wouldn't have liked what he was thinking. Ever since his mother died three years earlier, however, he had been searching for someone he could open up to in trust, and he found himself wondering if Ginger might be that person. A significant reason for his search had to do with the emotional support he craved from his father, but hadn't been given, in the aftermath of his mother's death. How vividly he recalled the apprehension he felt over shedding tears, or talking about his inner-most feelings. This was not to say his father was an incompassionate man. He was actually known to be benevolent at heart, yet he simul-taneously believed that a man should not express his emotions. "Don't ever cry. Boys don't cry," he would always tell Scott, and Scott did his best to please him in that regard by acting out the part, neither one of them seeming to comprehend that it was tearing at the root of their relationship as father and son.

"I sure hope your dad won't be mad about what time you're getting home," Joe inadvertently put an end to Scott's train of thought as he stopped to pull onto the main road. "I lost track of the hour."

"Ah... no, he won't be mad," Scott predicted. "If tomorrow were a school day he'd be upset, but it's not."

"Good," Joe responded while continuing to drive along. In regarding Ginger, he noted, "You're kinda quiet tonight. Is anything wrong?"

"No, nothing," she maintained, though in actuality she had been thinking of Scott. "I'm just tired. That's all."

"So do you want me to take you home now, or after I drive Scott home?"

"I'd rather go home right now," she stated, for tonight she did not want to be alone with him.

"Alright," Joe freely accepted her wish. Moments later he said to Scott, "It's too bad Jana couldn't make it. I think she would have had a good time."

Recalling his previous conversation with her, Scott grew resentful. It seemed to him that Jana did not care for him all that much, for if she did, she would have done what he wanted, he thought in selfish disappointment. It did not occur to him that his attitude was unreasonable, his previous actions toward her unwarranted.

"I wish she could have made it, too, but like I said before, she wasn't feeling well," he once again lied in his reluctance to admit he didn't have control over her behavior, as though it were a personal shortcoming of some sorts. He seemed not to comprehend that life could be so much better if he stopped caving in to pretense.

CHAPTER 5

TECUMSEH

Despite what had recently occurred at the supper table, Dwight began to feel better emotionally. In a very significant way he sensed optimism making its way into his life; and so much he hoped it would become the rule more than the exception.

Later, after having entered the barn and milked Hazel, he made his way into the coop to see to the chickens' needs and collect any eggs that had been laid. In all there were twenty hens and six roosters of mixed colors and breeds, but he had especially taken an interest in a Rhode Island Red rooster he named Tecumseh. This bird was not as aggressive as the others, basically detaching itself from the rest of the flock. In a vicarious sort of way, its place in the pecking order reminded him of the life he had come to know; and so, if for no other reason than that, he felt drawn to it.

"Hello, Tecumseh," he spoke while retrieving a dried piece of bread from his pants pocket. "I've got a treat for you." Having gained the rooster's trust, it immediately approached him and began pecking at the morsel. "You're one chicken I'll never eat," he stated as he recalled butchering a few of the birds from time to time for his mother to prepare for supper.

"You're strange!" Clair blurted out from where she arrived in the doorway. "Who ever heard of talking to a chicken?"

For a few seconds Dwight coolly eyed her.

"There's nothing wrong with it," he mildly reproached her

before resuming to watch the bird.

"Well, I suppose you've got to talk to something," she poked fun at him.

Without commenting, Dwight continued to feed Tecumseh what remained of the bread, determined not to let Clair get to him.

Looking away, Clair proceeded toward the rows of boxes which served as nests for the hens. After withdrawing any eggs she could find, she turned and walked to the doorway, pausing only briefly to regard Dwight before departing.

Turning to make sure she was gone, Dwight thought about how unhappy she was. With such resentment built up within her it was impossible to be anything else.

"I feel sorry for her," he whispered. "She makes life worse for herself." Yes, he knew that she was her own worst enemy in that she had allowed herself to become shortsighted, which should never be used as an excuse for inappropriate behavior, because we have override. There is a thing called The Golden Rule, and it has served as a powerful influence in more than one instance throughout history. Steer clear of the ways of hate, and ye shall discover a viable mechanism for achieving a noble goal, possibly even finding a way to reach one's family.

* * *

By one o'clock that afternoon the Willards and Cybil were seated on the beach with a delicious meal set before them. And good it was to see this strong family unit together on this sunny day.

"Mother, you sure know how to prepare a picnic basket," Bill complimented her as everyone ate.

"I've had a lot of practice," she stated with an appreciative smile. "I'm just glad we didn't have to eat at home today. The fresh air is so invigorating." She breathed in to experience it fully.

"I can agree with that," her husband remarked. "I remember greeting the ocean air when I came here with my parents as a boy. We'd fish from the shoreline and then my mother would fry up our catch. A kid remembers those things."

"Can we fish today, dad?" Jerry spoke up. "We haven't done it in a long time."

"It just so happens I have a few fishing poles in the trunk," he informed him with a wink of his eye. "I'll get 'em as soon as we finish eating."

With a wide grin Bill addressed Cybil.

"I bet you never thought you'd get the chance to fish today, did you?"

Surprised that he would even suggest she attempt it, she exclaimed, "I've never fished in my life! I wouldn't even know what to do. As a matter of fact I'd probably end up snagging someone." At the very thought of it she began to giggle.

Laughing along with her, Mr. Willard stated, "Perhaps you'll change your mind after you see everyone else try. It's really not that difficult."

"Perhaps," Cybil reluctantly contemplated. Then, facing Mary Ann and Eliza, who were seated beside her on the sand, she stated, "Am I correct in assuming you girls have fished before?"

"Don't look so shocked," Mary Ann humorously responded. "Father and mother have taken us fishing many times to streams and rivers, but rarely The Gulf."

Touched by the closeness of this family, Cybil said, "Well, I think it's great that y'all do so much together, and I'm really glad to be here today."

"We're glad to have you," Mrs. Willard convinced her. "It's always nice to share a good day with friends."

"I'll remember that," Cybil told her as Jerry and Sandy began to disagree about who should get the last piece of chicken.

"I wanted it first," Sandy pouted. "It'll only be my third piece."

"But I only had two pieces, too," Jerry protested with the same determination. Swiftly snatching it up, Sandy made a move to grab his arm, at which time, in his hurried effort to avoid her, he lost his balance and fell over, dropping it into the sand.

Getting up, Mrs. Willard walked before them with intent purpose.

"Enough is enough!" she scolded them. "Now stand up, Jerry!"

Slowly rising to his feet, both he and Sandy faced her with their heads held down in submission.

Encouraging herself to gather her thoughts, their mother said, "There are some people who haven't had any chicken at all. Now you know how I feel about wasting food." Eying them squarely, she continued, "If the two of you would have shared, this wouldn't have happened."

In the onset of regret Sandy regarded her mother before shifting her gaze to Jerry.

"I'm sorry for not sharing," she stated. Attempting reconciliation, she suggested, "Do you wanna share a ham sandwich instead?"

Gladdened by her desire to make amends, Jerry smiled and nodded his head.

"I'd rather have a ham sandwich anyway," he contended as their mother smiled upon them.

"That's better," she welcomed their decision. "I'm pleased by that."

Chances were that the sound advice and fair discipline of the Willards would serve their children well, for they were likely to grow up respecting their parents' standards. How sobering it is to know that many children are not so enriched. ... So take heed, for it behooves a person to find out what God expects of them.

Later, while Cybil observed Mr. Willard, Eliza, and Mary Ann fishing from the shoreline, Jerry and Bill played catch with Jerry's new football a short distance away on the beach.

Adventurous as always, Sandy approached her mother, who was packing a few things for the return trip home, and asked if she could go down the beach to look for shells.

"Maybe I'll fish when I get back," she anticipated.

Looking upon her, the woman consented.

"But don't be too long," she made certain to add. "I'm not sure when we'll be leaving."

"I move pretty fast," Sandy humored her before darting off.

As she walked along scanning the shoreline, the girl soon came upon an oyster shell and quickly snatched it up. Thoroughly inspecting her discovery, she put it in her dress pocket and proceeded onward until she came to an expanse of small sand dunes that graduated into a knoll. With hopeful glances she then noticed a very attractive conch shell half buried in the sand about twenty five feet away by the water's edge.

Dashing forth as though she were afraid the shell would disappear in the next breaking wave, Sandy, in her hurried effort, twisted her ankle.

"Ow!" she instinctively cried out as she fell to her knees and cringed in pain. ... "Somebody help me! ... I can't walk!" she yelled, but she was too far away for her family to hear her pleas.

From atop one of the dunes Dwight had been lying on his back for quite some time listening to the waves crash to shore while staring skyward at the wandering gulls. Thoroughly caught up in the moment, he did not heed Sandy's wails at first. ... But then, when he finally did become aware of them, he raised his head with due concern.

"Somebody, help!" Sandy continued to plead above her sobs. "My ankle hurts!"

In noticing the girl, Dwight immediately stood up and proceeded toward her.

"Sit down. Don't try to walk," he advised her as he neared where she was struggling to stand. Grasping her by the arm, he guided her to a sitting position. "What happened?" he asked.

"I saw that conch shell." She motioned her eyes toward it. "But... I hurt my ankle trying to get it." It was clear that her pain was quite acute.

"Then I had better take your shoe and sock off to check it," he suggested while looking downward. Bending over, he began to remove the articles with great care.

As Dwight examined Sandy's ankle, she looked down the beach and stated while pointing, "My parents are over there. We came here on a picnic."

"That's nice," he responded as he continued to inspect her ankle. ... "There doesn't seem to be much swelling yet. ... I don't think it's broken."

"Oh, but it hurts something awful," she reminded him with tear filled eyes. "I wish my mom and dad were here!"

Respecting her desire to return to her family as soon as possible, Dwight helped her to her feet.

"Put your arms around my neck," he advised her.

Doing as she was told, Dwight lifted Sandy into his arms and commenced to walk onward, yet before he had even made it ten feet, she exclaimed, "Oh, please get me the conch! I really think it's nice, and I might never see one that nice again!" The look on her face was both persuasive and hopeful.

"Alright," Dwight consented, for he did not want to disappoint the girl.

Placing Sandy on the beach, Dwight started for the much desired shell. After retrieving it from the wet sand, he washed it off in an incoming wave while standing on a slightly raised area of the beach very close to the shoreline. With the water swirling about him it made it seem as though he were on a small island, yet moments later this vision disappeared as the water receded back to the beckoning sea to make way for a new flood of the foaming liquid.

"Here ya go," he told Sandy once he had returned to where she sat waiting for him.

"Thank you. ... It's even prettier than I thought," she proclaimed, her face beaming so brightly that Dwight concluded she had momentarily forgotten her pain.

"Yes, it is quite nice," he told her as a warm feeling entered his heart. ... "Are you ready to go now?"

"Yes," she said while smiling up at him. "I feel much better now, but I don't know if I can walk yet."

"I'll carry you," Dwight stated as he again lowered himself to pick her up. "You might make matters worse by trying to walk too soon."

When Dwight had resumed transporting the girl down the shoreline, he began to experience nervous anticipation over the thought of encountering her family, so much so that he became consciously aware of his quickening heartbeat.

"What's your name?" Sandy eventually asked him while they continued along their way.

"Dwight Enhart," he told her.

"Mine is Sandy Willard," she informed him. In growing curious as to why she had not seen him on the beach earlier, she asked him why this was so.

Increasingly uptight over her inquiry, Dwight stammered, "Ah... I took the road and cut across over there." He looked to their left. "That's always the route I take." He lied, because he did not think she would understand his fear of strangers, or, in some cases, even someone he knew for that matter. Perhaps if he had known of her upbringing he would have confided in her by telling her he purposely avoided her family, for she really was quite understanding for a child of her age. At this early stage in their relationship he had no idea of this quality within her, however, and so remained silent about his repressions.

Glancing in their direction, it was Eliza who noticed Dwight making his way down the beach with Sandy. At first her face conveyed a somewhat puzzled expression, but very soon after that it changed into one of grave concern.

"Look!" she exclaimed as she dropped her fishing pole to the sand and pointed towards them. "Something's wrong with Sandy!"

Mrs. Willard was still packing a few things away at the time, so she did not hear Eliza's outburst, but everyone else heeded it by stopping what they were doing to gaze in the direction she had indicated, in the event of which they simultaneously rushed forth.

"What's wrong?" they began to shout all at once as Mr. Willard relieved Dwight of his burden by taking his daughter into his own arms.

"Don't worry," Sandy urged everyone with an air of ease, for she was no longer in very much pain. "I just hurt my ankle, but Dwight helped me."

It was only seconds later that Mrs. Willard arrived on the scene breathing a bit heavily from her dash to her daughter's side.

"What's going on here?" she inquired with searching glances.

"I'm not sure how everything happened," Mr. Willard informed her, "but Sandy's alright, and that's the main thing."

"Well, what did happen, Sandy?" her mother pressed her for information.

Upon telling her and the others the whole story in detail, Sandy looked up at Dwight from where her father had in the meantime placed her on the sand.

"I think he's my friend now," she said while smiling freely, compelling Dwight to take on an ardent expression.

"He is your friend, and for what he did he's our friend, too," Mrs. Willard said so emphatically that Dwight truly believed she meant it. Turning aside, she looked directly at him and added, "Thank goodness you heard her pleas."

"I'm glad I could help," Dwight stated a bit nervously while looking slightly downward. "Ah... I think her ankle will be fine. It'll just be sore awhile." He swallowed as though a lump were in his throat.

Everyone sensed his discomfort, for it was blatantly evident. But to Sandy and Mr. and Mrs. Willard in particular he was so strikingly genuine that they gladly accepted him for what he was, even though it was their immediate concern to assist him in feeling at ease in their presence.

"We'll make sure to keep an eye on it," Mr. Willard assured him. "I, too, want to thank you," he then said.

Dwight merely nodded his head in response to the man's words. Slowly walking backwards, he put up his hand and barely waved.

"Bye," he said. "I had better go now."

In an attempt to delay his departure Mr. Willard quickly stepped forward while saying, "Please stay for awhile. You can fish if you like, and there's some ham sandwiches in the car if you're hungry."

Seeking to strengthen her husband's invitation, Mrs. Willard wasted no time in adding, "Oh, yes, by all means do stay. We'd like to become better acquainted with you."

Stopping in his tracks, Dwight felt his apprehension begin to diminish for a beautiful brief instant, just as it had on that day in school when Jana looked at him so placidly.

"Alright," he for that reason accepted their offer. "I haven't fished in a long time." He even found himself slightly smiling.

"Good!" Mr. Willard heartily stated. In approaching him he solidly placed his hand on his back.

Delighted that he was staying, Sandy reacted by hollering, "Yippee!" Then, focusing her attention on the conch, she grabbed it and held it up high. "Does anyone know how to blow this?" she asked. "I've heard it can be done."

"I've done it a few times," Dwight confided. Walking to her, he knelt down beside her. "It's been a long time, though." Grasping the shell firmly, he mentioned, "It's a good thing the tip of the spire broke off, or it'd be difficult to use. The lips have to be positioned just right to get the effect you're looking for." While recalling a day long ago in which his father taught him how to make sound with one of these shells on this very beach, he was inspired to lift it to his mouth and blow strongly and surely into it to create a resonant tone of much beauty. When he had finished doing so, he handed it back to Sandy and smiled with unusual ease. "You try now," he said.

"Alright," she complied. Yet upon attempting to replicate the sound, she found her efforts to be in vain, for no matter how hard she tried, she could not achieve a satisfying result. In near exhaustion she ultimately sighed, "Oh, how did you do that?"

"Don't feel badly," he encouraged her. "You did better than I did the first time I tried it. It takes time and practice. Just keep at it and you'll get it right."

"I will," she stated while fondly gazing at him. "I'll practice every day."

Dwight was quite touched that this child placed so much emphasis on his advice, for he was not accustomed to such a thing. Looking at her, he detected sincerity, and he knew in his heart that he had made a friend today, which in his estimation made this day special without doubt.

* * *

Dwight was pleased that he decided to stay amongst the Willards. And fishing turned out to be a lot of fun, even though he hadn't caught anything as of yet.

Standing beside Cybil and Bill, who were also fishing, he cast out his line and began to reel it in in the hopes that he would soon get a bite. Then suddenly his patience paid off as he felt a strong tug on the line.

"I think I've got something!" he yelled as excitement began to consume his emotions.

Drawing the undivided attention of Cybil and Bill, as well as the others, Dwight gave the fish some slack before beginning to reel it in.

"I think it's a big one!" Jerry hollered as he rushed forward beside him. "Wow!" he exclaimed as a large fish came into view at the water's surface a short distance out to sea.

"Just keep reeling it in," Mr. Willard anxiously spoke up as he, too, arrived on the scene. ... "You're doing just fine."

The struggle between boy and fish continued to take place until just when it seemed as though Dwight would succeed in his efforts to land it, the tension on the line died; and he knew that the fish had managed to break free.

Hearing the moans of disappointment from the people about him, Dwight drew inwardly, believing his efforts to be seen as a failure. So much he had wanted to impress everyone with an accomplishment, it being something he unfairly thought to be a constant necessity where humanity was concerned. In other words he felt that if he couldn't triumph in the things he attempted based upon the world's standards of success, then the world would scorn him as a failure. Thus both his self-esteem and his trust in people were tarnished.

"That's too bad it got away," Mr. Willard casually stated while patting him on the back. "There'll be other fish, though. Just keep at it." He talked reassuringly. "You did a fine job."

Dwight looked at the man in a very approving manner, relieved that he had been spoken to that way. In fact Mr. Willard gave him the distinct impression that catching the fish was irrelevant and secondary to the enjoyment of participation.

"That was entertaining," Mrs. Willard spoke up in a similar fashion. "Better luck next time." Turning aside, she leisurely strode back to where Sandy was sitting alone.

Inspired by their dispositions, Dwight reeled in the rest of the line to ready himself for another attempt. Contentment was winding its way into his heart once again, and so much he liked what he was feeling.

Minutes later, when he had resumed position with pole in hand, Bill struck up a conversation with him in an effort to be sociable.

"Do you come here often?" he asked.

"Ya, I do," Dwight was able to answer him with relative ease. "I like it here a lot."

"I can see why. It's so pretty," Cybil commented as she

awkwardly tried to handle her pole. ... "I wish Jana were here today. I think she would have enjoyed it," she eventually added, prompting Dwight to stand utterly motionless in thought, for he, too, wished she were here. Seeing her was all he ever looked forward to whenever he went to school.

"I should have asked her to come along," Bill determined. "She was so down after that incident yesterday with Scott. This may have picked up her spirits."

The information Bill had just imparted aroused a great deal of interest on Dwight's part, so much so that he wanted to ask what happened. *But no, I better not*, he told himself, not wanting to be thought of as prying, it not occurring to him that Bill and Cybil may have appreciated the concern he afforded their childhood friend.

"She still is upset, Bill," Cybil informed him. "This morning I spoke with her after church and she told me so."

"Then that makes me wish all the more I had asked her to come along," Bill told her. "It may have helped to take her mind off everything."

"I'm sure she'll feel better soon," Cybil predicted as Mrs. Willard approached from the right. "She's always struck me as resilient."

"Would anyone like a ham sandwich?" the woman unknowingly interrupted their conversation while standing in the distance. "There's still five left." Regarding Dwight, she added, "I'd like you to leave us with a full stomach."

"I am a bit hungry," Dwight admitted, grateful for the opportunity to feast on something he seldom had occasion to partake in.

"Come over to the car with me then," she advised him while raising an arm in a beckoning gesture. Looking to Bill and Cybil, they declined her offer.

Waiting in the background for the chance to try his skill at fishing, Jerry avidly rushed forth.

"I'll take the pole," he told Dwight.

"Okay." He handed it over to the spry youngster and grinned. Turning about, he walked to where Mrs. Willard stood waiting for him.

"Tell me, where did you learn how to blow a conch so well?"

she asked of him once they had begun walking toward the car.

"Ah... my father taught me," he so reluctantly informed her that he grew angry at himself over his inability to relax concerning such questions.

"It really was quite a nice sound." When he merely lowered his head in modest response, she commented, "I've never seen you here before. Do you live in Chism?"

"Yes, I've lived there all my life," he stated with increased discomfort, given that her topic of conversation centered too closely around his family life.

"And you're in what grade?"

"I'm a freshman now. I go to Fulton High," he told her, reminding himself of how dissatisfied he was about that aspect of his life.

"So you're in Bill and Cybil's grade!" she reacted in pleasant surprise. "Did you know them before today?"

"I'd seen them around but never talked to them," he stated as they neared the car. "I don't know very many people besides the ones from Chism."

"In time that'll change," she felt inclined to say. "Today you met us and it's a beginning."

Dwight said nothing in response to her belief. He simply looked at her and nodded his head in cooperation more than agreement, for to be cooperative, he had learned, was the easiest way to avoid questions and explanations he had no desire to address.

* * *

The ham sandwiches were delicious, so much so that Dwight ate two of them while seated beside Sandy. Very close to them the rest of the Willard family and Cybil talked about a few matters of interest that happened to come up.

It was shortly thereafter, while looking at his watch and seeing a time of four thirty, that Mr. Willard informed everyone the hour had come for their return trip home.

"Gee, Dad, can't we stay awhile longer?" Jerry urged him. "I wanna fish again."

"No, it's time we left," his father stood firm. "I intend to go to

Dolores Horton's to fix her steps when we get home."

"I was thinking about that myself," Mrs. Willard admitted. "But I knew I wouldn't have to remind you. You rarely forget such things."

By manner of how he cast his eyes upon her one could see that Mr. Willard appreciated her faith in his integrity. One could also detect the effect that their deep love was having upon their children. And yet given that personalities vary to such a large extent, the attainment of a relationship such as theirs will never be sought or acquired by all married people. But one thing is for certain, it being that it's of utmost importance for some measure of love and respect to exist between a man and his wife, because if it does not, it can be rightly determined that their marriage had not progressed on the positive note it could and should have.

Dwight was able to discern the value of what Mr. and Mrs. Willard had, and he was genuinely glad for them; but very soon after that it came to include envy. *They're really happy*, he thought. *It reminds me of my...* He quickly forced this sentiment from his mind, because he knew that it would only induce him to grieve for the mother and father he had once known.

"Do you like my parents, Dwight?" Sandy ironically asked him just seconds later from where she yet sat beside him.

"Very much so," Dwight could not help but admit. "I like your whole family."

"I'm glad," she said, her face beaming her delight. "You can come visit us then!"

Truly the thought was appealing, but he did not want to commit to something he might not live up to.

"Perhaps," he therefore stated while glancing away and rising to his feet. Out of courtesy he now forced himself to approach the others despite his recurring anxiety. "Thank you. I enjoyed today a lot," he told them.

"You're most welcome," Mrs. Willard wholeheartedly assured him. Putting out her hand, she touched his arm while adding, "I can't thank you enough for what you did for Sandy. Something very good came out of that. We got to meet you."

"I'm... glad you see it that way," Dwight somewhat hesitantly reacted as though he were afraid her demeanor would suddenly change. "Good-bye." Withdrawing from her presence, he began walking down the beach.

"Would you like a ride home?" she quickly asked of him. "It's on our way."

"No, I want to stay here awhile longer," he blurted out with his back to her. "Thank you anyway."

"Alright, good-bye. I do hope we'll see you again."

The desire to respond positively lurked within Dwight quite strongly, but he would not allow it to surface at this time. Instead he said nothing while proceeding onward, feeling in doing so that he needed to have some time alone in which to sort out his feelings.

"See ya," Sandy told him when he neared where she sat.

"Bye, Sandy." He forced himself to smile for her sake. "Keep blowing that conch shell."

"I will," she told him as he continued to depart, at which time everyone began to voice their farewells.

Turning slightly, Dwight waved a hand before continuing on his way down the coastline. Never would he have thought he'd come to be so welcomed by these people, so much so that already he was beginning to feel he should like to be amongst them again. The disappointment he felt in departing was proof of that.

Close to where he had come to Sandy's assistance he ceased his advancement to look out to sea. It had been a long time since he witnessed such love, a long time indeed; and so yes, truly he wanted to be amongst that love once again.

* * *

When Mr. Willard and Bill had finished gathering the fishing poles, they made their way to the car where everyone stood waiting for them.

"He certainly is a nice boy, isn't he?" Mr. Willard commented while placing the poles in the trunk. "But rather withdrawn."

"Yes," his wife concurred. "He also seemed tense at times." Turning to face Bill, she stated, "He said that he's in your grade at school. Do you know anything about him or his family?"

"I don't know anything about his family," Bill told her, "but I recognized him from gym class. Carl Barnet has been giving him a hard time. He purposely tripped him one day on the gym floor."

"Oh, no!" she lamented. "Are you certain he did it on purpose?"

"Yes," Bill told her. "I saw it with my own eyes."

"And Carl bullied him in the hall one day, too," Cybil informed her. .... Yet strangely a troubled expression suddenly came over her features, prompting Bill to inquire what was wrong.

For a few moments Cybil took the time to gaze at all present.

"I've got to be honest," she spoke up in words that seemed difficult to find. "I never taunted him, but I can't say I was concerned about him either. I knew he was being wronged, and yet I didn't feel for him the way I should have. ... But then today, after meeting him for myself, I found myself wanting to befriend him the way you people did."

Mrs. Willard was an analytical woman who desired to gain insight into the reasons why people thought and acted in a certain manner; and so she asked Cybil why she hadn't been concerned about Dwight.

"I really think there's varying reasons," Cybil confessed. "For one thing, I remember thinking that he should have stood up to Carl, and that since he didn't he only had himself to blame for his problem with him. I admit it was convenient for me to think that way, because I used it as an excuse to disregard the wrong that was being done to him. After all, if he refused to help himself, then what concern was it of mine? ... But now, since spending so much time with this family, I've come to realize that often we don't get involved because we're too self-absorbed, or self-righteous… or even afraid."

As one could well imagine, the Willards were quite moved by Cybil's assertion concerning their influence upon her.

"You made a fine point about why people don't get involved, Cybil," Mr. Willard commended her. "But by getting involved, I think we'll see a whole new side to Dwight. It'll take time, though. It won't happen overnight."

"You and ma always said good things are worth waiting for," Bill vividly recalled. "I'll make an effort to befriend him."

* * *

Dwight arrived home around quarter after six to assure he'd be on time for supper.

As he strode into the kitchen, the enticing smell of fried chicken made him glad he had decided to come home in a timely manner. Understandably, the three mile walk had aroused his appetite.

Seeing Clair with an apron on, he knew that today she had decided to prepare supper herself rather than endure another bland meal of their mother's. As he shut the door, she briefly turned to see who was there.

"I've been expecting you," she stated. "Supper will be ready in ten minutes. Today's meal should be a lot better than yesterday's." Briskly she began scooping golden brown chicken from a frying pan. "That is, if those chickens are at least tender. With my luck they're probably tougher than shoe leather."

At first Dwight passed off her all too frequent pessimism. But then a spark of interest took hold of his thoughts. She had cooked a chicken! Was it possible she had slain his pet? He just had to know.

"Do you mean to tell me you killed a chicken while I was gone?" he pressed her for information.

"I most certainly did," she sharply admitted. "Right after you left I killed a rooster."

Without uttering another word Dwight rushed outdoors in the sincere hope he was wrong in what he suspected had happened, yet before he was even able to reach the barn, he noticed a blood-stained block of wood off to the right of the door.

For a few seconds he stood motionless, reluctant to investigate the matter further. ... But then, when he finally did approach the area in question, he saw the lifeless, bloody head of his favorite rooster, Tecumseh, lying on the ground next to an axe.

Initially Dwight's face was blank and non-responsive. *Why did she choose him*? he wondered before eventually recalling that Clair had gone into the coop that very morning and saw him feeding Tecumseh some dried bread. A maddening thought now occurred to him. *She killed him because she knew he was my pet!* Certainly she was hateful enough to do just that.

Upset by her spitefulness, he darted back to the house with the intention of telling her some things he had the wherewithal to know he shouldn't say. And so for reason of fairness, he convinced himself to at least be tactful enough to give her the opportunity to explain herself.

"Why did you choose that rooster to kill?" he asked with forced restraint upon reentering the kitchen.

"Because it was the easiest one to catch," she told him. "What do you care anyway?"

"That rooster just happened to be a pet of mine," he reminded her as he took notice of the cooked bird on the table. "You saw me feeding him this morning."

"Yes, I know he was your pet," she declared without regret for what she had done. "But like I already said, it was the easiest one to catch." Abruptly she began to tend her gravy as a smirk made its way across her face.

In acceptance of her explanation Dwight turned to walk away. ... Yet then all of a sudden, in a burst of insight, he was inspired to stop short and say, "That rooster wasn't the easiest one to catch. It was flighty. It took me a long time to gain its trust." As Clair threw him a resentful look in response to the claim he was making, he freely added, "Tell me what I'm wanting to know."

"You're gonna believe whatever you wanna believe, just like everyone else does!" she flatly accused him. "It's the way of the world!"

For a few tense filled moments their eyes were firmly fixed upon one another, and in that period of time Dwight thought about how bitter she was with life.

"If you did what you did to hurt me the most, it has backfired," he told her straight from the heart, "because you hurt yourself the most."

"And how do you figure that?" her curiosity prompted her to inquire.

"Because trying to hurt someone else lessens a person's self-respect, and when that happens, you like yourself even less."

"What do you know of such things?" she interrogated him in a wave of guilt. "Nobody could hate themself more for what they are than you!"

"No, Clair, I may not like certain things about myself. I may even hate certain things about my life, but I don't hate myself,"

Dwight admonished her. "There's a very big difference."

"Are you insinuating that I, on the other hand, do hate myself?" she thus challenged his judgment.

"I think there's something about yourself you hate," he was compelled to say. "And it can lead to disaster if it worsens."

"And are you changing your own life for the better?" she shifted the focus upon him in an effort to avoid addressing the truth about herself. "Because if you think you are, I don't see it."

"I'm trying to head in the right direction, Clair, and it's certainly better than not trying." Turning to walk away at this time, he heard her loudly yell out, "Drop dead! You sicken me!" Her animosity had become that extreme. Yet it wasn't that she merely resented the fact that he had tried to evaluate how she felt about herself. No, most of all she was irritated because he was perceptive enough to see the truth that was, a truth which frustrated her, a truth which her hardened heart wouldn't allow her to verbally acknowledge.

Without responding to her outburst Dwight continued to depart in the hope that he could avoid any more of her wrath.

As he ascended the stairs he felt justified for the things he had said to her. Hearing her noisily clanging pots and pans in her anger, he thought, *She just can't go on like this much longer.* Indeed he wished she didn't feel so sorry for herself in regard to the past.

Back in the living room, their mother had not even stirred over that which she overheard taking place in the kitchen; but then again, she loathed herself even more than Clair did, and regretfully neither one of them seemed to care enough to amend that fact. Perhaps the day would eventually dawn, though, when they would begin to do something about their dispositions before the opportunity to positively change the direction of their lives was all used up through the passage of time.

CHAPTER 6

ORAL REPORTS

Certainly the encounter Dwight had had the day before with Clair was symbolic of his efforts to rise above adversity. This was not to say he was naive enough to believe his domestic problems were even close to being solved, but he had managed to be assertive without being resentful, and that he sensed was something worthwhile, something to be pleased about.

Clair appeared to be very depressed all during breakfast, so much so that Dwight got the impression she would not have lashed out at him or anyone else on this given morning, her mood being that subdued.

Later, when the bus picked the two of them up from their usual spot and Sara taunted him, he found that he wasn't as unnerved by her conduct this time around, not like he used to be. This was a welcome relief, a sign of impending deliverance from his insecurities. And it wasn't that he had become numbed or hardened by the abusive conduct of others. It was that he had learned to become increasingly mindful of the reasons why people lashed out at him in the first place. They themselves were misguided, angry individuals attempting to punish the world for the pain within themselves. They wanted others to suffer to avenge their own misery. Escaping their conscience was their envy. They actually desired to feel good about themselves, but they went about it the wrong way. In knowing this Dwight had begun to understand why people used him as a scapegoat. It was to draw attention away from their own poor self-image in a vain and desperate attempt to purge their emotions.

Once inside the school in gym class, Mr. Milter had the boys do exercises throughout the entire period, which pleased Dwight very much in that he always felt much more relaxed whenever he performed on an individual basis rather than team events. In that way people would be less apt to focus on his performance, because it wouldn't have a direct bearing on them. And if that be the case, he felt as though the likelihood of being the recipient of their criticism would be greatly reduced.

Next, in biology class, the instructor, Mrs. Arion, talked for the greater part of the hour about reptiles, and although Dwight was quite interested in the topic, he dared not answer any of her questions out of the fear he'd put his foot in his mouth. How aggravating it was to refrain from responding in the midst of wanting to participate. It was like being in a psychological tug of war. ... And then it happened. With about five minutes left in the period Mrs. Arion brought up the topic which disturbed him more than any other; the deliverance of oral reports.

"I would like your reports to be at least ten minutes long," she informed everyone with fluent ease. "And I'd like you to choose any subject of interest in biology. Your choices are many, dare I say." She smiled reassuringly, not realizing that no matter how convincingly her smile could have been displayed, it could never have alleviated the unrest Dwight was currently witnessing on the inside. No, short of telling him he would not have to deliver a speech, nothing would make him feel any better. Mrs. Arion would not do this, however, because she did not understand the reality of his world.

"Now class, are there any questions?" she inquired.

Cliff raised his hand and she bade him to speak.

"When are we gonna have to give these reports?" he asked.

"I was thinking we should start them two weeks from today," she informed everyone. "That should give everybody plenty of time to prepare themselves."

"How are you going to determine who speaks first?" Sara inquired.

"I'll put everyone's names on slips of paper and place them in a bowl," Mrs. Arion stated while looking directly at her. "That should be a fair way to do it." Making a visual sweep of the room to determine if there were any more questions, she became satisfied there was none. Then the bell happened to ring to signify the end of class. "Now remember to read pages one seventy eight to one ninety for tomorrow," she loudly concluded to penetrate the immediate bustle of students as they began to depart for lunch.

From where she was seated Jana could tell that Dwight was sorely affected by the mention of oral reports. She'd talk to him later, she told herself as she left the room, sensing that he would be receptive to another attempt at befriending him.

When the room had cleared of students, Dwight rose from his seat and walked towards Mrs. Arion's desk. Mustering all the courage he could, he said, "Mrs. Arion, could I ask you something?"

Looking up at him with attentive eyes, she responded, "Oh, yes, Dwight, what can I do for you?"

With a nervous quiver to his voice he uttered, "It's about the oral reports. I really don't want to give one. I'm not ready for that sort of thing yet."

"I'm sorry, Dwight, but everyone must give a speech," she firmly insisted.

"But I...."

"There's no buts about it," she quickly informed him with fading patience. "If you want to pass the course you'll have to give a speech. Besides, you're much too reserved for your own good. You've got to open up more."

In the moments that ensued Dwight became inclined to suffer his losses and state, "I guess I have no choice then." Turning about, he began to walk away feeling as though he had been treated unjustly, as though his feelings held no merit.

"Why didn't you raise your hand to inquire about this during class?" Mrs. Arion pressed on a bit puzzled before he was able to fully depart. "I asked if there were any questions."

Gradually turning to look at her, Dwight merely whispered, "Need you ask?" Then he exited the room.

Unaffected by his response, Mrs. Arion went back to what she had been doing as though the issue had been aptly put to rest. She was able to do this because she couldn't relate to Dwight's inhibitions. She, being insensitive in her ignorance, didn't understand why he was lacking in confidence. Her belief was that if he wanted to be outgoing, all he had to do was embrace that trait, as though wanting it was enough, as though it was as simple as drawing in a breath of fresh air on a spring day. What she failed to comprehend was that Dwight's state of mind had been engrained within him over the course of time, and that it would thus take time for that trend to be reversed. Yet with all due respect and fairness to her, it was not that the woman had zero empathy. Had she known the depth of his feelings she might very well have been moved to compassion and compromise. She was so convinced, however, that she was right in what she required of her students that an alternate method of report giving was not warranted in her mind... not yet anyway.

* * *

When Dwight arrived at his locker, there was a forlorn look about him. The oral report that he would be required to deliver was at least two weeks away, yet based upon his current bearing one might have thought he would be delivering it at any given moment. Anyone who experienced similar emotions would have understood the discomfort he felt over the thought of talking before people. And if thinking about it made him feel anxious, imagine what the real thing could do.

Placing away his books and grabbing his lunch, he made his way to the second floor where the lunchroom was located. Upon entering, he immediately noticed Jana and Cybil seated at a corner table with Bill and Scott; and briefly thought about approaching them. Too unwilling to absorb the risk of rejection, however, he proceeded to a vacant table set against an adjacent wall and sat alone. Then, as he began to eat his sandwich, he became perturbed by the hold that his constraints had upon his life.

"Oh, Jana, we had such a good time at The Gulf yesterday," Cybil in the meantime informed her. "I want you to come there with us the next time we go."

"Ya, so do I," Bill wholeheartedly agreed. Regarding Scott, he added, "You're more than welcome to join us. I know my family would extend the invitation."

"Maybe," Scott only half-heartedly responded, for what he really had on his mind was planning another party for the weekend. In fact, when he noticed Joe and a few other people seated at a nearby table, he quickly came up with an excuse to join them by saying, "I'll catch up with all of you later. I need to talk to Joe about something important." Then he darted away.

"Jana, I've got to admit I was somewhat surprised to see you with him this morning," Bill wasted no time in saying. "After what happened Saturday I thought the two of you might keep your distance from one another, for awhile anyway."

"At first I thought it'd be that way, too," Jana confessed, "but when I arrived at school this morning he acted as though nothing had happened. Anyway, I'm hoping he won't be the way he was Saturday any more. And I suppose I could have been more tactful that day to discourage his outburst." Yet indeed, in her heart she did not actually believe what she had purported.

"Don't you dare put any of the blame on yourself, Jana Rossi!" Cybil reprimanded her. "The way he behaved was in no way your fault. You said nothing wrong. You did nothing wrong. You told me last weekend that false guilt would do none of us any good, and now I'm saying it to you. He was determined to go to that party, and nothing you or any of us said was gonna hold him back."

"I know, but I don't intend to reject him for it," Jana told her. "I happen to believe he's in need of a friend."

"That may be so," Cybil acknowledged. "But that doesn't mean you should blame yourself in any way for his choices. You even tried to dissuade him, but he wouldn't listen to you." As Jana considered what her friend had told her, Cybil was daring enough to inquire in spite of how it might be received, "Jana, you're not continuing to associate with Scott because he's so popular, are you?"

At first Jana was somewhat astonished by Cybil's bold line of questioning. But she wasn't insulted by it and she didn't get angry, and this is why. She had the good sense to realize that a friend would be naturally curious about her reasons for continuing to associate with Scott, especially when that friend had seen a side to Scott which was resentful, defensive, and uncompromising.

"Cybil, if I'm that vain that I'm with him because he's popular, then I have a major character flaw," she pointed out to her. "I only want Scott and I to bring out the best in each other as friends. I'm hoping that'll happen, but if it doesn't, I'll survive." Solemnly she looked at her to lend credence to her claim.

Satisfied by what Jana had said, Cybil nodded her head. Then, looking off to her left and noticing Dwight sitting alone, she stated, "Hey, there's Dwight Enhart over there." She motioned toward him. "He was at The Gulf with us yesterday."

"Really, who invited him?" Jana inquired with unbridled interest.

"It happened quite differently than that," Bill informed her. "Ya see, my little sister Sandy hurt her ankle and he rescued her, or helped her anyway, so that's how we got to know him. ... You know something, he's friendlier than one might have expected. Up until yesterday I only knew who he was by name."

"How did he react to meeting everyone?" Jana asked.

"He seemed rather shy and uncomfortable with us to begin with," Bill told her. "But everyone seemed to like him. My mother even wants me to get him to come to our house for a visit someday."

"That sounds like something your mother would say," Jana noted. Rising from her chair, she added, "I think Dwight's really down today. I'd like to talk to him. Maybe I'll be able to help him feel better."

"Why do you say that?" Bill inquired with a puzzled look.

"I think he's upset over the oral reports we're required to give in biology class," she said. "You didn't see his reaction to it like I did, being that you're both in Mrs. Arion's other morning class."

With a nod of his head Bill stated, "I can understand why that would upset him. Actually I wasn't too pleased about it myself."

"What are you going to say to him?" Cybil asked, grateful that she was not miffed with her for what she had dared inquire about Scott.

"Something reassuring," Jana emphasized before walking to where Dwight was seated.

"Hello," she cheerfully spoke up. "How are you?"

"Oh... hi," he reacted in delayed response as she sat down adjacent to him. "I'm alright." But he betrayed his contention when he looked away from her in an unsettled manner.

"You didn't make it to the game Saturday," she continued in an effort to put him at ease. With a sudden burst of enthusiasm she added, "It was great! We won!"

"Ya, so I heard," he told her with a forced smile before resuming to eat the last few bites of his sandwich.

In a further effort to converse with him Jana stated, "You know something, I'm really undecided about what I should do my report on in biology." She shrugged her shoulders a bit. "Do you have any idea what you're going to talk about?"

"I... don't know yet," he stammered as he grew nervous over the thought of it. "Maybe it'll be about some kind of bird. I like birds."

"Well, I'm sure it'll be interesting no matter what it's on," she stated. Then, in a confession she thought he of all people could appreciate, she added, "You know something, I'm somewhat nervous about the oral reports. I don't particularly want to give one."

"Really!" Dwight incredulously spoke up while eying her squarely. "I never would have thought you'd feel that way. You seem so confident."

"But it really doesn't appeal to me," she admitted. "It's commonly felt, you know. A lot of people don't like to speak before a group. It makes them feel too self-conscious. And if the truth be known, there are people who aren't intimidated by speeches, yet they still dislike giving them."

Dwight gazed about at this time to make certain that no one was listening to their conversation.

"If you're wondering about me, I'm very nervous about giving this speech. I want freedom of choice. ... I'll probably do terrible at it."

"No, don't say you won't do well!" Jana was swift to admonish him. "Keep telling yourself that you'll get through this, and practice giving your report until you feel confident!" Quite unexpectedly she grew embarrassed over her outburst. "Oh, I'm sorry," she as a result stated. "I didn't mean to preach."

"No, no, don't be sorry," Dwight implored her. "I'm grateful that you think I can do it. It means a lot to me." Yet before Jana could respond to his comment, they both heard an all too familiar voice behind them.

"Well, well, well, what have we got here?" Sara spoke up with sarcastic overtones while striding to the front of the table.

"Hello, Sara," Jana said while suspiciously eying her. "What brings you here?"

"Oh, I just saw the two of you together and thought I'd say hello," she stated with obvious derision. Then, while fixing her gaze upon Dwight, who was now looking away in an effort to avoid her piercing stare, she added, "Aren't you going to even say hello to me, Dwight? I always make sure to it that I notice you."

Managing to look up at her, Dwight surprised her plenty when he politely said hello before turning his attention to Jana once again.

Sara was not able to comprehend the nature of Dwight's disposition. And yet despite this, she was somehow driven to admire it, which in turn induced her to become jealous of his ability to conduct himself in such a respectable manner.

"I certainly thought you'd say a little more than that, but I'm sure that'll change when you give your oral report," she sardonically pressed on in an effort to not only upset him, but degrade him. It was as though she was trying to tempt him to lower himself to her level of conduct to justify her verbal abuse.

When Jana heard a girl giggling at another table, she ordered Sara to leave to put an end to the unpleasant episode once and for all.

"You're not wanted here! Not when you act this way!" she further rebuked her.

"Of course, anything you say, Jana!" she was quick to retaliate. Yet in her ongoing defiance she made the comment, "Don't talk too much, Dwight. I wouldn't want you to learn how to communicate before your speech." And with that she walked away.

In a wave of exasperation Dwight sighed while shaking his head.

"Sometimes I ask myself what could have happened to her to make her that way," he openly declared. "It's pitiful, isn't it, to think that she hates herself so much?"

Jana was thoroughly amazed over his ability to express any

measure of concern for a person who had treated him so rudely.

"Try not to let her bother you," she advised him. "She's assuming you won't do well at your speech. Prove her wrong." Yet as though Dwight hadn't heard her words of encouragement, he solemnly predicted, "She's probably right."

Contemplating the situation for a few moments, Jana finally suggested, "I'll tell you what, if you feel that way, then why don't you ask Mrs. Arion if you could hand in a written report instead?"

"I already tried that," Dwight regretted to inform her. "It didn't turn out very well."

"Oh, I see," she relinquished. ... But then suddenly an inspiring thought occurred to her. "Why don't you look at me when you give your speech? Sometimes it helps to look at a friend. At least that's how it is for me."

Dwight was utterly astonished over her desire to assist him in some way. Eventually smiling, he told her, "Thank you. I'd like that."

"You're welcome," she warmly replied. Then, upon noticing how little time she had left in which to finish her lunch, she added, "I've gotta go now, but we'll talk again soon."

"Okay, bye," he said as she rose to leave. "And... ah, you can look at me also if you like when you give your report." Certainly he was plenty surprised by what he had just proposed.

"Thank you. I'll remember that. Good-bye," she concluded before walking away, satisfied that she was well on her way to gaining his trust.

She really does care about me after all, Dwight thought with a flood of contentment. He could hardly believe it was true, and yet it seemed to be so. Yes, her actions had proven to him that a budding friendship was in the making.

* * *

When Dwight was invited to eat lunch with Jana, Bill, and Cybil on a regular basis, his days at school became much less dreaded. He now had something to look forward to. And true as it may have been that he did not speak of his own family as they were inclined to do about theirs, he liked their company enough to eventually feel comfortable in their presence. Not everyone was pleased with this arrangement, however. Scott disliked it enough to completely distance himself from Jana during lunchtime. Yet even though this was something Dwight recognized and felt ill at ease over, the gratification of having friends to socialize with boosted his mental health quite significantly. Undoubtedly he felt so extremely engaged at times that he forgot for a moment or two the unpleasant reality of preparing and delivering his oral report, and the dire condition of his home life. ... But then in biology class, on the Friday before the speeches were about to begin, he again felt anxiety pervade his emotions as he listened to Mrs. Arion lecture for the day. In an attempt to alleviate his overwrought mind, he sought to imagine himself standing before the class delivering his report with fluent ease. But it didn't appease him, and it was because he knew deep down that the person he envisioned himself to be was not true to him at all. Surely if he was to be honest with himself he would have to face the fact that unless a miracle were to occur, it would take time and effort to become a confident speaker. And even then, in line with what Jana had previously alluded to, he might possibly never desire to deliver orations anyway. And what doesn't interest us we are not likely to master.

Seeking a different approach to his unrest, he slowly turned his head to look at his classmates in the hopes that it wouldn't upset him, but no sooner did he do this than he became increasingly nervous. *I'm just not meant for this*, he badgered his mind. Then, in a sudden change of moods, he thought not in grief but in anger of how inconsiderate it was for Mrs. Arion to force this upon him when it was not even remotely necessary. Truly he pitied her for her insensitivity. Yet as though his stressful thoughts were not enough to deal with at this time, Mrs. Arion now began to talk about the oral reports before class was dismissed for the day.

"When you deliver your speeches beginning next Monday," she said, "I want you to make sure that you ask if there are any questions when you're finished. If there are, well, I'm sure you'll be able to answer them." She spoke in her usual, self-assured manner, a manner Dwight sensed she took for granted.

Later, in the lunchroom, Jana immediately picked up on

Dwight's apprehension, but she did not have to ask about it. She knew. Even Bill and Cybil had an inkling as to what was on his mind, which is why Bill was all the more pleased that he had something to say which might help to soothe his worries.

"By the way, Dwight," he spoke up from where he sat beside Cybil. "My family is having a barbecue on Sunday afternoon, and we thought you might like to come. Everyone is looking forward to seeing you again, especially Sandy. She practices trying to get some sound from that conch every day." He smiled in recollection of her efforts. "She's still having problems with it, but she's determined she'll get it right."

"And both Cybil and I will be there," Jana added in an attempt to convince him to attend the gathering.

Dwight was grateful for their desire to include him in their plans, but he could not imagine himself participating in the event. Sunday was the day before the oral reports were to begin, and so never would he be able to relax and have an enjoyable time when this mentally disturbing occurrence was so close at hand.

"I'm sorry," he as a result spoke up. "I told my mother I'd help around the house that day." Just as he had done on other occasions, he resorted to lying to avoid admitting the truth behind his insecurities, because he didn't know if his feelings would be understood, and he neither wanted to be thought of as foolish, nor pressured to change his mind about attending the barbecue.

Expressions of disappointment were exchanged by Jana, Bill, and Cybil.

"I'm sorry you can't make it," Bill spoke up then. "But if you must stay home, I guess it can't be helped."

"Ya, I'm already committed," he again lied just as Scott arrived at the table to speak with Jana.

Scott was still irritated with Jana for associating with Dwight, but when he confronted her about it, she told him that she intended to continue spending time with him. "He needs a friend," she insisted in earnest. "I can't understand why that upsets you. We all can use a friend." But because of jealousy Scott was not willing to abide by her decision. That was why he decided to approach her during lunchtime. It was to try to sway her attention away from Dwight.

"Jana, there's going to be another party tonight at Hickory Lake," he confided in a whisper which was nevertheless overheard. "Will you come with me?"

For a few moments Jana eyed him in indecision. Then, despite her prevailing reluctance, she nodded her head in compliance.

"What time is it going to be?" she asked.

"Joe's gonna pick me up at seven, so we'll be at your place about seven fifteen," he informed her with a smile of victory. "It'll be great! You'll see!"

"I hope so," Jana forced herself to say for his sake, after which Scott sardonically glanced at Dwight before proceeding to walk away.

"I hope you're not making a mistake," Cybil told Jana shortly thereafter.

Meeting her gaze, Jana said in defense, "Everyone deserves a chance to prove themselves. I've got to make sure I give him that much anyway. Tonight will tell me a lot." Yet in her heart she also believed that her decision to go with him had been an unwise one.

* * *

When school was dismissed for the weekend, a cool, misty rain sent shivers up Dwight's spine from where he waited for the bus. Even on days such as this he preferred to linger outside rather than in the school's corridors so as not to risk encountering the people who scorned him.

While standing there, he thought about going home and grew a bit depressed. It seemed like the only place he desired to be as of late, besides the countryside of Chism, was in the lunchroom with his friends. Jana, Bill, and Cybil were becoming very important to him, and more and more through the passage of time he found himself looking forward to being in their company.

It wasn't until his bus could be seen off in the distance that Jana arrived at his side breathing a bit heavily from her dash outdoors. She wanted to speak with him about his reason for declining the invitation to the Willards' barbecue, because she felt as though he had not been straightforward with her in regard to it.

"Dwight, I'm glad I got here in time," she said just as he laid eyes on her. "I swear you must move like a jack rabbit sometimes!"

Wielding a brief smile over her figure of speech, he replied, "I'm sure you're just as fast yourself."

Jana too grinned. ... Then, as if sensing her motive for being here, Dwight lowered his eyes and turned his head in the direction of the oncoming bus.

"I'm beginning to get to know you, Dwight," Jana told him without delay. "And I got the impression earlier that you're still having doubts about the speech."

Even though Dwight did not want to admit his feelings, he trusted Jana enough to do so anyway.

"If you're referring to my excuse for not going to the barbecue, you're right," he acknowledged with a hint of embarrassment. "I really don't have to help around the house Sunday, and I suppose I should force myself to attend it, but I know the oral report would be on my mind, so I wouldn't be good company. I'd only put a damper on everything. Surely you can understand that." Quite earnestly he regarded her.

"But Dwight, you might find that you'd enjoy yourself a great deal," she stated with optimistic appeal. "You might even find it therapeutic."

"Jana," Dwight sighed as he tried to find the right words to express himself, "maybe some day I'll be strong enough to do things differently, but right now I'm still searching for the source of that strength."

"I'm willing to help you find it if you'll let me," she gladly volunteered.

With true interest Dwight stated, "I appreciate that." Then a curious thought occurred to him. "You know something, I imagine if Mrs. Arion knew how upset I was after all this time, she'd be amazed."

"What ever made you think of something like that?" Jana inquired.

"Oh, it just seems to me that she doesn't understand where I'm coming from." In focusing on Jana, he asked, "What makes you so understanding, so caring?"

"I've always been concerned about people, at least for as long as I can remember," she freely admitted. "But I don't want you to think I'm claiming to know how you're feeling. I'm quite sure I don't."

"Perhaps some day I'll try to explain it to you then," he suggested as his bus pulled to a stop before him. There was suddenly an unusual air of calmness to his carriage, her trustworthiness bringing out this trait in him.

"When you're ready, I'll listen," she assured him whole-heartedly.

By way of a simple look Dwight revealed his gratitude. Noticing some students making their way out of the school at this time, he quickly stated, "I had better go now. Bye."

"Bye," she told him as he proceeded to board the bus.

Walking down the sidewalk, she watched him head for the rear of the vehicle to sit down. When he had taken his place, he peered out his window to look at her. There was no mistaking the three words he saw emanate from her lips. "Practice your speech!"

Deeply moved by her determined effort to be of support to him, he could not hold back a smile. ... And for the moment he felt good again.

CHAPTER 7

THE DELIVERANCE

There had been no party at Hickory Lake that Friday night, for not only had the weather turned much colder, a steady rain fell even harder than earlier in the day to make things all the more uninviting.

Jana wasn't disappointed in the least when Scott telephoned to inform her of the party's cancellation. She actually found herself feeling quite relieved, for she had grown to increasingly regret having said she'd attend it in the first place.

Saturday proved to be even more inclement than the day before as the cold rains came down even harder. But then, by the time Sunday pulled around, a warm southerly breeze brought forth clearer skies.

Looking outdoors from where he sat in front of his bedroom window, Dwight welcomed the brightness of the day. In noticing feathery cirrus clouds drifting by, he realized that the ups and downs of life were a reflection of what the weather went through all the time. Sometimes there was gloomy lows and sometimes there was sunny highs. And yet, where his family relations were concerned, the gloom never seemed to cease in recent years, life having become this strained.

Forcing thoughts of his home life from his mind, he got up and walked to his dresser where he had laid his speech. In no way was he about to risk driving himself into a state of depression today. The future would be difficult enough to deal with without that added burden, especially in the wake of the nervous anticipation he'd likely be feeling as he lay in bed that night thinking of tomorrow. The past few nights had been bad enough, but tonight, oh tonight would be the worst of all. The next day was Monday, and that he could not forget in the least.

Gazing in the mirror, he realized that in some respects he groomed himself according to how he felt at any given moment. Glancing downward, he grabbed a comb from his dresser and ran it thoroughly through his hair in an attempt to look more presentable.

"There, that's better," he said out loud.

Taking position with report in hand, he began to recite it, suspecting as he did so that Jana had been right when she said this approach might help, for although it was far removed from the real thing, at least he was taking strides to prepare himself.

When he had finished speaking, he smiled and said, "Thank you, Jana. Thanks for caring." Then he began to recite the whole thing all over again, believing he could somehow handle the uncompromising demands that had been placed upon him by an unenlightened teacher.

* * *

Dwight was so upset as he boarded the bus the following morning that he could very well have turned around and fled to the safety of his room; but he did not. It took courage, but as always he knew deep down it would do him no good to try to run away from his problems. Additionally, he did not want to disappoint Jana, or himself for that matter, by taking the short term only, easy way out.

As the bus resumed rolling down the dusty dirt road, his aspiration to focus on positive things proved to be in vain, for his anxiety was so intense over the prospect of what might happen in biology class that his body actually began to twitch. Part of the reason for this had to do with the insomnia he had experienced the night before. Yes, he unfortunately had proven himself to be so correct when he predicted the previous day that he would undergo such an unpleasant episode. There seemed to be endless tossing and turning, and no sooner did he fall asleep than he awoke only to gaze at his alarm clock in the hopes that it was not yet time to get up for school. What a tormenting feeling it was to dread the ticking of the clock because of what the future held in store for him. Certainly he wanted to vanquish his fears, and yet he could not seem to prevent unsettling thoughts from bombarding his mind, all of which sorely affected his nerves. On top of that, he hadn't been eating right lately, either, which put an additional strain on his overall health. ... And so truly he was burdened in more ways than one.

All too soon the bus came within sight of the school. In a last ditch effort for sought after deliverance Dwight had only minutes earlier resorted to the empty hope that there would be a delay of some sorts, such as a mechanical breakdown, to keep him away from his classes. Yet it seemed as though his futile wish only made the inevitable arrive all the sooner. So often this seemed to be the way of things, he realized as the bus came to a complete stop. When you wanted to avoid what lay in the future, time went by so quickly, and when you were looking forward to some future event, time passed so slowly. It was all a matter of one's perspective, he knew. And yet being aware of this didn't help to lessen his discontent.

Forcing himself to leave his seat and walk toward the front of the vehicle, he felt a gnawing sensation in his stomach. It was in fact such a nauseating feeling that he honestly thought he might vomit. Then, upon exiting the bus and seeing Jana, Cybil, and Bill making their way down the road in his direction, he darted for the school in order to avoid them, for he did not want to face them at this emotionally wrenching time. Perhaps after biology class he'd feel differently, he considered as he proceeded along his way. But right now he couldn't seem to expect any more than that.

Entering the building amongst the stream of students, Dwight was painfully aware of the strain that his insecurities placed upon his human interactions. Then, to add to the pressures of his life, he saw Carl standing by his locker waiting for him to arrive on the scene.

At first Dwight stood motionless in a wave of indecision, wondering how he should respond to such a threatening situation. Yet then just as he was about to go to the extreme of fleeing to gym class with his lunch and books, he saw Carl step aside while encouraging him to advance with a sweep of his hand.

Noticeably distrustful of his intentions, Dwight did not take his eyes off Carl as he proceeded forward. Then, while opening his locker door, he asked him what he wanted.

"Don't look so suspicious," Carl urged him. "I'm here to apologize for the way I treated you." In an effort to convince him that he was serious, he extended his hand.

At this point Dwight grew somewhat relieved, even though a significant amount of apprehension still lurked within the recesses of his mind.

"Okay," he eventually replied, and sealed the handshake. "But why the sudden change?"

"Hey, I realize I haven't treated you fairly, and I wanna make up for that," he said with such a casual tone that credibility was not even slightly personified.

Although Dwight detected something amiss, he still accepted his assertion, more because he wanted to believe it to be true than that he actually felt it to be the case.

"I'd like us to be on friendly terms," he for that reason told Carl.

"Alright, I'll see ya around then," Carl too hastily stated while beginning to walk away, as though a mission of some sorts had been accomplished.

To further appease him Dwight nodded his head, not knowing that Jana had been observing them from afar. As she approached, she was determined to discover why Carl had spoken to him, for she was very wary of his intentions.

"Hello, Dwight," she greeted him from behind.

Turning to regard her, Dwight wished that he had already departed for gym class, for he felt that if she discovered he was still upset about delivering his speech, she would be quite disappointed in him.

"Hello... ah, did you have a nice weekend?" he stammered as he clumsily placed away his lunch and books.

"Yes, it was very nice, thank you. The barbecue was such fun." In reference to his absence, she stated, "I was hoping you might have changed your mind and come to it after all."

Lowering his head, Dwight stated with a hint of remorse, "I

really wanted to go, but I couldn't get my mind off today." With a shrug of his shoulders, he realistically added, "Getting a ride there would have been difficult anyway."

"Well, there'll be other barbecues, plenty of them," she said on a positive note. Then, in regard to what she had just seen, she added, "I noticed Carl Barnet talking to you. Do you mind if I ask what he wanted?"

Casting a thought consumed gaze in the direction of Carl's departure, Dwight told her, "Can you believe it, he actually apologized for the way he's treated me." Looking at her, he went on to say, "I must admit I find it hard to believe he really meant it."

"I can understand why you feel that way," Jana readily concurred. "It's going to take a lot more than apologies to trust what he says."

With solemn insight Dwight contended, "And yet it's not necessary that I trust him to bear him no ill will, is it, Jana?"

In light of his statement Jana realized why she liked him so much.

"No, I guess not," she had to admit.

Dwight recognized the good will she was so abundant in possessing, which led him to say, "You know something, I wasn't going to say anything to you, but I'm still nervous about my speech. I practiced giving it like you said, and I think it helped some, but still… I'm a wreck." In his burdened state of mind he shook his head.

Jana had expected his anxieties to be challenging to contend with, and so she was not at all surprised by what he had just revealed.

"Just remember to look at me when you're talking," she reminded him.

"I shall," he responded just as the first bell rang.

"I better go. . . ."

They both spoke at once, then stopped short of finishing, looked at one another for a few seconds, and laughed.

"See ya later," Jana lightheartedly told him as their humor subsided.

Dwight returned the farewell. Then, in watching her disappear from sight down the hall, he felt fortunate to know her. She was too good to be true, he honestly felt.

* * *

There was a great amount of chatter in biology class as students conversed with one another about the topics they had chosen to speak on. That is everyone except Dwight seemed to be partaking in conversation.

As he sat at his desk with his hands clasped nervously together, he could feel his body's natural defenses taking control of his inner being, as though he were readying himself for the fight of his life. There was adrenalin flowing through his veins in a physically triggered response to trepidation, and unfortunately for him, he couldn't seem to prevent it from happening. No, it was as if he were at the mercy of his emotions.

When the last bell rang, he cringed as he saw Mrs. Arion walk into the room carrying her grade book firmly to her breast. Making her way behind her desk, she faced the class and raised a hand in a gesture for silence.

"Quiet everyone!" As the noise had subsided, she said, "Today is the day for our oral reports to begin. I hope everyone is prepared." She gazed out at the many faces. "I've got a bowl with all your names in it." She opened her desk drawer and withdrew it. "If you're ready, so am I." Reaching into the dish, she removed a slip of paper. "Julie Kent," she stated and looked at her while smiling. Heading for an empty seat at the back of the room, she enthusiastically added, "You're on!"

Julie advanced to the front of the class and began to deliver her report in a manner Dwight found himself envying. Yet surely she, too, had to be insecure in her own particular way, he surmised, for no one was totally free from that bondage if the truth be known. Yet if this girl was ill at ease about facing her classmates, she certainly was doing a good job of disguising it.

As Julie continued to deliver her essay, Dwight could only wonder who would be next to speak. For that reason he hardly heard a word she was saying, for all he could concentrate on was the awful realization that he would soon be confronted with another bout of apprehension when another slip of paper was removed from the bowl on Mrs. Arion's desk.

Julie finished her oration in the required ten minutes and asked if there were any questions. How fast the time had seemed to pass. To Dwight it was as though she had just begun to speak, and now she had finished. But she had spoken well.

After answering a question that was posed by Mrs. Arion, Julie proceeded to head back to her desk, yet before she could reach her destination Mrs. Arion asked her if she would withdraw the next name from the dish.

"Of course," she complied and went back to where it was located. Mixing the names up a bit, she removed a slip of paper. "Dwight Enhart," she said.

At the sound of his name Dwight felt as though his heart had skipped a beat. The moment he had been dreading for weeks was at hand, and he would force himself as best he could to go with the dreadful flow.

Arising from his seat with papers in hand, he wished that he had been the first one to speak, because even though it would not have been any easier to be first, at least this terrible ordeal would be over with.

Walking uncomfortably to the head of the class, he turned to face everyone when he was standing behind Mrs. Arion's desk; at which time, as he noticed the many eyes fixed upon him, he was stricken by such an intense anxiety attack that he felt as though it would be impossible for him to speak. Truly words would not come to his lips, which brought him to feel even more self-conscious.

By the time a few moments had passed, it was quite obvious to those who were present that Dwight was quite shaken by what he was required to do.

"Dwight, you can begin any time," Mrs. Arion told him from where she sat. Yet still there was no change in his rigid stance.

"Dwight, please begin! You're wasting time!" she eventually spoke with fading patience. "You've only got ten minutes!"

Dwight forced himself to shift his gaze upon his classmates in an attempt to ready himself for speaking, but when he did this he inadvertently laid eyes on Sara and saw her smiling in sadistic delight, which prompted him to lose courage. Looking away from her, he noticed Scott grinning over his awkwardness, and grew even more defeated. Indeed it got to the point where the humiliation of it all was just about to induce him to give up completely and rush from the room, when all of a sudden it happened. With nervous, twitching glances his eyes fell upon Jana, sweet, wonderful Jana, the only person in the entire room who had faith in his capabilities in a way that was worthy of appreciation. ... And then, as she looked at him with warmth and reassurance and tender compassion, he saw the word "relax" form on her lips.

Filled with a strength he did not realize he possessed, Dwight picked up his papers from where he had laid them on the desk.

"My report is on the migratory habits of the mallard duck," he began while keeping his vision glued to the paper. Yet in reading along, he felt the symptoms of his nervousness sweep throughout his body so immensely that his knees began to knock and his hands began to shake so badly that he had to lay the report back on the desk in order to read the words he had written. ... But then, recalling Jana's advice in the height of his reaction to this stress, he drew in new hope. "Look at me when you speak. It may help you," she had said.

Taking a rest from his labored utterance of words, Dwight lifted his head to stare at the girl who was coming to mean so much to him. Reaping solace from her supportive face, he found the strength to continue talking by looking from his paper to her, and then back to his report once again in repetitive glances. ... And it helped considerably, for he felt his tension gradually lessen, which allowed his heart to calm its beat, and his hands to become much more stable. Even his voice took on a changed tone as some of the tenseness left it. Of course it was true that he was not suddenly transformed into a skilled speaker. One could see that, but at least he was delivering his essay, which was a major accomplishment for him. It was an example of how a person's feelings could be influenced by knowing that someone believed in their potential. The beauty of the bond that Jana had secured with him had helped to plant a seed of confidence in his soul, and if nurtured well, that seed could sprout and grow into a well-adjusted individual in the days which lay ahead.

When Dwight had at last completed his oration, it seemed as though a giant weight had been lifted from his shoulders. Relief never felt so good.

"Are there any questions?" he then asked in the hopes there would be none.

"Ha, even if we had any, you'd never be able to answer them," Sara belittled him, which resulted in suppressed laughter on the part of certain students.

"That's enough, Sara!" Mrs. Arion harshly spoke up, much to the satisfaction of Jana. Looking to the front of the room, she added, "That'll be all, Dwight. Would you please pick the next name?"

Gazing at the desktop, Dwight knew what his classmates thought about his performance. It did not seem to matter to them that he had done his best at that which was so difficult to see through to completion, only that he had not done so fluently. Forcing himself to reach into the dish, he removed a slip of paper with slightly wavering hands and drew it before his eyes.

"Jana Rossi," he stated in softly spoken amazement. And wouldn't you know it, the mere sight of her name compelled him to momentarily forget about Sara.

Walking back to his desk, Dwight longed for the moment when the attention of his classmates would be directed away from him. In fact it was not until he had sat down and faced the front of the room that he felt truly relieved. It was over, he thought, and tonight he could sleep in peace until another such incident arose. What a wonderful thing!

Listening to Jana speak on her topic, Dwight found that he could hardly wait to talk to her during lunch. He so wanted to thank her for being of assistance to him on this exacting day of days in his life.

* * *

Cliff Roberts had managed to finish his report by the time the bell rang. His speech had been the fifth one for the day.

"We'll continue tomorrow," Mrs. Arion informed everyone as she rose to her feet. "I've got grade cards made out for the students who've already given their reports."

As Dwight's desk was being neared he grew a bit uneasy over the possibility that he may have received a failing mark. And he was fairly close to being right, for when Mrs. Arion placed his card before him, he saw that he had received a letter grade of D+. He was more disappointed than surprised by it though, for he knew that he had not spoken with the articulation expected of him.

"I'd like to talk to you when everyone has left, Dwight," Mrs. Arion informed him then.

Eying her, Dwight concluded that she probably wanted to explain why he had received such a poor grade, as though he needed to be told.

When the room had completely cleared of students, Dwight got up from his seat and approached Mrs. Arion's desk. Without saying a word, he stood there waiting for her to address him.

"I'll be just a few moments longer, Dwight," she said without looking at him as she continued to write in her grade book.

"Alright," he responded. Then, in an effort to seek comfort for his weary mind, he thought, *I shouldn't really mind getting a D+. At least the report is over with.* Yes, to him that was the most significant aspect of all, a telling reminder that he had managed to attain liberation in the face of adversity.

In closing her grade book, Mrs. Arion frowned a bit before saying, "Dwight, first of all I must tell you that you really deserved a failing grade, but I gave you a D+ out of pure generosity. You didn't speak loudly enough, and you stammered quite a bit." She beheld him so austerely that he looked away in an effort to avoid her piercing stare. "Now I was thinking that perhaps you could give another report to try to do better. I'd give you extra credit."

At this point Dwight looked at her in sheer and utter disbelief. After all he had been through, after all the discomfort he had fought so desperately to overcome, she had the nerve to ask him to endure it a second time around. Why, it was beyond his desire to even attempt to fathom; and so, in self-defense, he asked, "This isn't required, is it?"

"No, it's not required, but I strongly recommend you do this. You need to communicate better. Sara won't bother you again. I'll see to that."

Dwight shuffled his feet in increased discontent. Then he said, "Even if Sara wasn't in this class I wouldn't wanna go through this again. I did my best, and yet I feel humiliated." He was sincere.

"Oral reports aren't meant for everyone."

"We obviously don't see eye to eye on this," she told him. "But it's up to you. Just remember this, though: unless you learn how to communicate better, you'll have a hard time making it in this world." There could even be detected a hint of resentment in her voice over his unwillingness to follow a course of action she believed to be wisely founded on her part.

Dwight stood motionless for a few moments in saddened dismay. Then, from the very depths of his being, he somehow found the ability to say in a burst of insight, "My confidence will take time to develop. The end doesn't always justify the means, though you seem to think that it does." With the completion of these words he fled the room to avoid listening to another comment on her part. Try as he may, his best effort was deemed insufficient in the eyes of some. The reality of his world had proven it to be so.

* * *

Jana grew both puzzled and concerned when Dwight did not show up for lunch. After all, why would he not meet with her in gladdened relief over the completion of his speech? His absence just didn't make any sense to her, so much so that she could not help but glance at each and every person who entered the room in the expectation it'd be him.

"Dwight's nowhere to be seen," she finally made comment. "I find it very strange."

"Maybe he went to the study hall instead," Bill suggested. "We've got some tests coming up."

"Perhaps," Jana skeptically remarked, "but I was sure he'd wanna sit with us after the report he gave in biology class. He must be so relieved."

"You mean he gave his report already!" Cybil exclaimed.

"Yes, he did," Jana responded without elaborating on what transpired, her concern over Dwight's absence disrupting her train of thought.

Waiting a few seconds to be filled in on the details, Cybil finally blurted out, "Well, what happened!"

Jana initially regarded her friend with a blank stare. Then she said, "Oh, I'm sorry. My mind was somewhere else. ... Ah, he did pretty well, I thought. He was a bit shaky on the start but that's to be expected, considering the way he felt." She paused briefly. "He picked up the tempo after awhile, though, and came through just fine. I was very proud of him."

"I'm glad it's over with for him," Bill emphasized.

"So am I," Cybil declared. "I'd like to congratulate him." She, too, began to conduct a search of the premises with a sweep of her eyes.

"I'd like to congratulate him myself," Jana told her just as she noticed Sara approaching their table. "Oh, no, look who's coming," she indignantly reacted. "I wonder what she'll have to say this time."

Heeding her words, Cybil and Bill looked in the direction she had indicated, in the event of which Sara was upon them.

"Hello," she casually spoke up. "Where's Dwight? I wanted to let him know what I thought about his report today." Her mannerism made it quite transparent what the nature of her comments would be.

Jana eyed her with a forceful glare.

"Sara, you know full well Dwight wouldn't want to talk to you," she told her straight out. "Just leave him alone!"

Annoyed by her reprimand, Sara said, "For the life of me I can't understand why you even associate with him."

"If you dislike him so much then why do you keep approaching him?" Jana cleverly asked of her.

Sara was caught off guard by a point well made.

"I... never really thought about that?" she as a result stammered. Then, in an attempt to shift the focus away from herself, she rebounded by inquiring, "What's your excuse?"

"I happen to like his company," Jana informed her. "Not like some people I know." Distastefully she ran her gaze up and down Sara's body, not realizing in doing so that Dwight would have greatly disapproved of this behavior on her part, seeing it as a detriment, a debasing, to one's own character.

"You really should start choosing better friends, Jana," Sara advised her with further resentment. "Otherwise you might run the risk of putting an end to important relationships such as those with popular boyfriends."

"Right now the only relationship I'm interested in ending is the one I have with you!" Jana sternly told her, "So kindly leave before I take the notion to force the issue!"

Sara was intimidated enough to heed Jana's warning, yet her intimidation wasn't the type that's the result of feeling a deep sense of shame and remorse for inappropriate conduct. In other words Jana had unknowingly reinforced the girl's bad behavior by treating her with disdain. She had inadvertently self-defeated her cause by contributing to the hardening of Sara's heart, a most common of mistakes. Putting a contempt-filled person on the defensive by way of contempt only backfires because contempt is thus returned. And so in spite of her good intentions, Jana had resorted to a method far removed from the best option available. She had allowed herself to become consumed by the very feelings she was seeking to conquer, which in essence is a losing battle.

"Her callousness astounds me!" Jana nearly shouted while shaking her head.

"Why does she resent Dwight so?" Cybil asked. "It's terrible."

"Yes, quite terrible!" Jana angrily noted. "She just tries to satisfy her sick ego! She's... sadistic!" With a self-conscious lowering of her voice so as not to maintain the interest of nearby listeners, she added, "Her and Carl make the perfect match! I'll say that much!"

"Calm down, Jana," Bill implored her. "Don't let her upset you so much."

"I can't help it!" she flat out told him. "You didn't hear what she said to Dwight after he finished his report today!"

"Oh, no," Cybil cringed at the thought of it.

"Oh, yes!" Jana decried. "When he was all through speaking and asked if there were any questions, only because he was required to, she said that he wouldn't be able to answer them. It was humiliating for him. I could have hit her!"

"She certainly is vindictive," Bill acknowledged. "But she has to be troubled to be that way. It makes me feel sorry for her."

"How can you feel sorry for her!" Jana protested. "What about Dwight!"

"I feel for him, too," Bill sought to assure her. "But I feel even sorrier for Sara. She pays a high price for the way she mistreats him." As Jana beheld him in an ever questioning manner, he emphatically added, "Jana, ya can't fight fire with fire in a case like this. My parents said that love always defeats hate in the tests of time, because it's the opposite of hate, and it's stronger."

Realizing the point he was trying to get across to her, Jana eventually stated in appeased emotions, "I never thought of it that way. Perhaps I should come to your house more often." She even slightly smiled. "Your parents have taught you well."

"I like to think so," Bill maintained while Cybil looked upon him with utmost regard.

Shortly thereafter Jana said with a return of resolve, "I'm going to look for Dwight." Getting up from her seat, she began to clear the remnants of her lunch from the tabletop.

"But it's getting late," Bill reminded her. "There's only twenty minutes of lunch time left."

"But I've still got to try," she decided while briefly eying the clock.

"Do you want me to help you?" Cybil offered her services.

"No, I'm sure I'll find him," Jana told her. "You stay here with Bill and enjoy your lunch." With the wrappings from her own lunch she proceeded toward the garbage can located near the doorway.

Ridding herself of the debris she carried, Jana darted from the room to make her way to the third floor where the study hall was located. Upon entering, she was disappointed to discover that none of the dozen or so students in attendance turned out to be Dwight. *Perhaps the library*, she thought in a determined effort to find him. Heading down the hall the short distance where it was located, she ultimately checked every table and every aisle of books only to once again know disappointment in her search.

"Where can he be!" she finally exclaimed in near defeat. Thoroughly perplexed, she happened to pass a window and notice him sitting all alone at one of the outdoor lunch tables that were used by the students in the warmer months.

"Why on earth is he out there?" she whispered as she stepped forward to obtain a better view. Though it was sunny, she could tell by his clenched fists and clasped arms that the air had to be on the cool side. In fact his body seemed to be shaking a bit in the chilly atmosphere of the day.

Staring no more, Jana rushed from the library and down the stairs, continuing to wonder why Dwight was behaving so strangely. The mystery of it all drove her all the faster so that by the time she arrived outside she was slightly out of breath. It was only in having reassured herself that he was yet where she had seen him that she advanced onward at a somewhat eased pace.

Because he was staring straight ahead in deep thought, Dwight did not notice Jana's approach from his right. When she was almost upon him, she stopped short to say, "Dwight, why are you here of all places?" Her voice conveyed both her concern and confusion.

Swinging his gaze upon her, Dwight experienced immediate relief in discovering who had spoken.

"Oh... hi... I just felt like being alone. That's all," he told her. "I can't blame you if you find that strange."

"I must admit I was puzzled by your absence in the lunchroom," she stated as she drew closer and sat down across from him. "But now I can see that you're upset over something, and I'm guessing it has to do with what Sara told you earlier."

"You're right about my being upset," Dwight let it be known, "but over Sara?" He shook his head before looking skyward and adding, "Even though she does upset me at times, I find myself getting over it quickly." He again regarded Jana. "You see, I know that she thinks very little of herself, and knowing that makes me feel sorry for her."

In an instant Jana's mind was filled with even more confusion than before, because even though she considered Bill's prior advice to be solid, she could not understand how Dwight, the recipient of Sara's taunting, could be so anger free. This so affected her that she was not about to let the topic remain undiscussed.

"Dwight, you do realize that Sara has no right to belittle you, don't you?" she for that reason found herself asking.

"Yes, I know that," he told her. "It's just that I understand her behavior." In recognizing the enhanced confusion on Jana's face, he sought to explain himself by adding, "You see, Sara is insecure. She dislikes herself a great deal and takes it out on other people. Carl does, too. They don't have me fooled." He had suddenly come to acquire a certain authority in his speech, given that he so strongly felt he was correct in what he was saying. "They bully people because their self-respect is lacking. Taking out their resentments on me gives them a false sense of security." With firm conviction he thereby noted, "I'll have you know, Jana, that hating people who think so little of themselves isn't the answer, and it never will be."

"Well then what is?" she beseeched him.

With a penetrating look he solemnly declared, "To reach such as they through the power of love."

"And if they refuse to be reached, what then?" Jana further inquired of him.

"Then I guess they'll have to bear the consequences," he soberly contended, "because we all have only so much time to see the light."

Understanding at last the message he was attempting to instill in her, Jana asked with delving curiosity, "How did you get to be this way?" She seemed to speak as though she were emotionally stunned.

At first Dwight briefly pondered the question. Then he straight-forwardly stated, "I have known much love in my life. In fact, it's the love I remember as a little boy that helps to prevent me from hating the world. ... To be truthful, though, I sometimes do have thoughts that aren't all that healthy, but I'm trying to improve that." In a most genuine of manners he regarded her.

Jana was by now so greatly astounded by his insight that she actually became speechless. Truly all she could seem to do was stare at him with great respect, for here before her sat someone whom she had discovered to be unusually strong, even though the world perceived him as being weak. Yes, a glimpse of his character had sprung forth for her to witness, making her all the gladder that she had decided to befriend him. With a feeling of indescribable warmth she thought she would begin to weep then, for she realized she had been correct all along concerning the integrity she sensed within him. It was in fact so reassuring that she even found herself wondering if God had inspired her to reach out to him right from the very moment she laid eyes on him.

"I appreciate your honesty," she finally was able to say with deeply moving conviction. "But tell me," she pressed on, "if Sara hasn't got you all that upset, then what is it?"

"It's Mrs. Arion," he informed her without delay. "After class she spoke with me and told me that my report wasn't very good. She even said she'd like me to give another one, but I told her I wouldn't. I gave that report today under duress, Jana, and it made me feel even worse about myself, not better. But Mrs. Arion," he shook his head, "she doesn't see things my way. Yet I'm not saying she has bad intentions. I really think she means well deep down. But more and more I'm beginning to see in life that good intentions aren't nearly enough."

The thought of what Mrs. Arion had said to Dwight did not rest well with Jana. After all he had been through she felt as though the woman should have congratulated him for his efforts rather than criticize him. In other words she believed that Mrs. Arion expected too much too soon from him, and that her reaction to his report was not conducive to self-confidence on Dwight's part.

"Dwight, I'm glad you told Mrs. Arion you won't give a second report," she said with conviction. "You've done your part. I for one think you did quite well today anyway, and I mean that from the bottom of my heart. I say that because you persevered. I think you were brave today."

On the positive side, Dwight specified with a note of optimism, "I did get a D+ for my efforts. It's better than an E."

Jana impulsively smiled.

"Yes, it certainly isn't the worst grade you could have gotten, and yet it's only a grade, isn't it? And a biased one at that I might add." With growing trust they looked into one another's eyes until she suddenly realized how chilled she was becoming by the cool north wind sweeping upon them. "We had better get inside now," she consequently suggested while rubbing her arms for warmth. "It's cold out here, and besides that, class is about to begin."

"Alright," he stated as they both stood up. "I hope you don't get sick."

"I'm sure I won't," Jana aimed to assure him; after which, in sensing a sudden inspiration within him, she asked, "Is something else wrong?"

Dwight looked away for a brief instant before saying, "No, I just wanna thank you for listening to me, and for helping me get through my speech. If it wasn't for you, I don't think I would have been able to do it."

"Dwight, after what you just told me, I think you're capable of much more than you realize," she said with moving persuasion. "I'm so glad we're friends."

"So am I," he freely admitted. "You help me feel better about myself."

In walking side by side into the school, it was sensed by each of them that theirs would be a relationship that would stand the tests of time. But it would not come easy for them. And perhaps they were better off not knowing just how difficult it would be.

CHAPTER 8

THE CHRISTMAS COMPROMISE

In the weeks to come, the bond between Dwight and Jana strengthened. It could even be said that for the first time in years Dwight was able to routinely take his mind off circumstances as they existed at home.

Jana drew so much enjoyment from her association with Dwight that she found herself looking forward to eating lunch with him each and every day at their usual table. In fact so satisfied was she with the general direction of her life that it hardly even bothered her that she and Scott were seeing less and less of each other through each passing week. She had found a friend in Dwight, and friendship was something she placed a great degree of value upon.

When the end of the football season arrived, Scott had already developed a reputation for being one of the best quarterbacks ever to come out of Fulton High. The fleeting glory of fame sadly went to his head, though, to compel him to become ever self-absorbed. Jana detected and disliked his pronounced vanity, but if Scott sensed her disapproval he did not seem to be bothered by it. He knew, however, that many a girl was anxious to be in his company. All he had to do was ask; therefore what Jana thought of him no longer mattered to him all that much.

Though distant in nature, Carl continued to conduct himself in a civil manner, which even though Dwight found suspicious, he accepted, for it certainly was better than the way in which he had been treated by him during the beginning of the school year.

When December arrived, the anticipation of Christmas could be seen on the faces of students and teachers alike. Dwight, however, was not looking forward to this traditional season of joy, for his mother did not involve herself in the true spirit of Christmas as she had in the past. If anything, she had become increasingly despondent over the years, a sure sign in Dwight's estimation that masked yearnings for days of yore were jabbing at her heartstrings.

On the last day of school before the arrival of Christmas vacation it seemed to Dwight as though virtually everyone was overflowing with holiday cheer, which induced him to long for some of the same. In direct contrast to feelings witnessed earlier in the school year, he found himself desiring to remain in school with his friends, the people who accepted him for what he was. Yet it was a desire in terms of balances, for both comfort and discomfort were in close proximity to one another whenever he attended school. He endured discomfort in order to be with his friends, but being with his friends was offsetting the discomfort of attending school. The scales had finally begun to tip in his favor. That was why he desired to remain in the academic setting. The conclusion: Ambivalence is often a part of our lives, simultaneously attracting and repelling us at any given moment.

In the lunchroom that afternoon Dwight felt a certain sadness weigh heavily on his heart as he listened to Jana, Bill, and Cybil converse about their plans for the holidays. Certainly he didn't begrudge them their cheer, for he wanted all people to be fulfilled. Yet it pained him to think that his home would not even remotely bear a reflection of the merriment he was in witness of.

Without saying a word, he continued to listen to what was being said, unaware that Jana was currently wondering, and had wondered in the past, why he never spoke of his family.

"What does your family have planned for Christmas, Dwight?" Cybil ironically asked him just moments later.

"Ah... nothing as of yet," he stammered before looking away in the hopes that no more would be said about it.

Cybil regarded Bill and Jana in a somewhat confused manner. But then suddenly she recalled a comment she had once heard concerning Clair's treatment of Dwight. *Perhaps his parents treated him the same*, she considered, suspecting it might be the reason behind his unrest.

"I'm sorry, Dwight," she as a result stated. "I didn't mean to pry."

"Oh, no, it's alright. You didn't say anything wrong," he tried to assure her as best he could so as not to risk hurting her feelings. "We don't have anything planned yet. That's all." But then he grew taciturn once again.

Later that afternoon, as Jana and Cybil were walking down the hall towards their final class of the day, Jana said, "Cybil, I'm curious why Dwight became so defensive earlier. I wanted to ask him about it, but it was obvious he didn't want to discuss it."

"I know," Cybil acknowledged. "There's something wrong with his home life I think. He never says anything about it." Her face took on an inquisitive look. "Do you think it's because he's ashamed of it?"

"There does seem to be evidence of a problem," Jana conceded. "And the thought of that really disturbs me."

"But I wish we knew for sure," Cybil told her.

"Me, too," Jana assured her, "but I want him to tell me on his own when he's ready." They were just about to enter the classroom when a thought suddenly occurred to her. Earlier in the week the Willards had invited her and Cybil to their home for a social gathering, including supper, on Christmas Eve. Why, she simply had to ask about Dwight.

"Cybil, the Willards often ask Bill how Dwight is getting along! Perhaps they'd like to have him over, too, on Christmas Eve!" The notion of inviting him to her own home did not rest well with her for obvious reasons.

"That sounds like a great idea!" Cybil wholeheartedly supported her. "I'll suggest it to Bill the first chance I get."

"Ya know something, I think this may be just what Dwight needs," Jana stated as a certain glow radiated from her face.

Entering the classroom to await the arrival of Bill, neither girl realized that a coincidence had just taken place, for Bill had been thinking along the same lines as them, which prompted him to call his mother in between classes to ask her if he could invite Dwight over for Christmas Eve. Needless to say the woman gladly welcomed the idea; and so when Cybil and Jana presented their suggestion to him, he in turn told them what he had been up to.

"Dwight might want to be at home on Christmas Eve, though," he made sure to stress. "But we'd get him back in plenty of time to spend most of the evening with his family. It'll depend on his plans."

Jana thanked Bill for what he had done. Then, upon learning that he hadn't had the opportunity to invite Dwight to the gathering yet, she went on to say, "I wish he was in this class so we could tell him about it. I'll rush outside to catch him before he boards his bus." She was suddenly inspired to laugh over the thought of it. "I seem to do a lot of rushing to catch up with him, don't I?" And Bill and Cybil laughed also.

Events took on a different course than the ordinary, however, for when the last bell rang, Dwight did not go directly to the bus stop. No, he wanted to wish Jana a Merry Christmas before going home; and so, upon retrieving a few books from his locker, he attempted to locate her amongst the many jubilant students in his midst, not knowing that Jana had just arrived outdoors expecting to find him there.

Noticing that the Chism bus had not yet arrived on the scene, Jana conducted a visual sweep of the school grounds in search of Dwight. When she became satisfied he was not outside, she rushed back indoors to resume her quest.

Dwight in the meantime assumed he must have already missed Jana; and so, in disappointment, he began walking down the hall with the intention of making his way outside, yet no sooner had he proceeded along his way than he heard her yell out to him from somewhere within the crowd. Unable to see her amongst the busy traffic of people, he stopped in his tracks to wait for the ranks to thin. Then, just as he heard her call out to him again, he finally caught sight of her.

"Oh, I'm glad I found you!" she exclaimed when she was at last standing before him. "Where were you?"

"I was looking for you by your locker," he told her in obvious pleasure over the sight of her while pointing in the direction from which he had come. "I wanted to wish you a Merry Christmas since

I won't be seeing you until after our vacation. And I'd like you to tell the same thing to Cybil and the Willards."

Jana smiled as she beheld him.

"You can wish me a Merry Christmas on Christmas Eve if you like," she stated before filling him in on the latest developments. "We'll sing Chirstmas carols and pop popcorn! It'll be great fun! And Bill said his father would give you a ride back home, so all you have to do is show up!"

Dwight undoubtedly experienced a good feeling over the invitation.

"Thank you for wanting me there," he spoke up without delay.

"Does that mean you'll come then?" Jana hopefully anticipated.

Dwight wanted so much to shout out yes, but he would not allow himself to do so.

"It really sounds enjoyable, and I really want to go," he told her to confirm his interest. "But I can't."

"But why not?" Jana disappointedly reacted. "I thought you'd say yes for sure since you don't have any plans made yet."

In a desire to supply her with an explanation, Dwight replied, "But even though I don't have plans, I'd need a ride there." He would not bring himself to admit that his mother would never give him that much needed ride. "Thank you anyway though," he quickly made sure to add. "Tell the Willards I appreciate the offer. Ah... I had better go or I'll miss my bus." Commencing to walk away, he slightly waved while saying good-bye.

Jana was upset over his behavior, so much so that for the first time since knowing him she felt a significant amount of frustration flood her emotions. After all, if he wanted good things to take place in his life, then he had to put forth some effort to bring that about.

"Dwight, please find a way to get there," she therefore implored him before he was out of hearing range. "Somebody could surely give you a ride. It isn't that far. People are coming and going all the time." Yet much to her dismay he did not seem to be encouraged in the least by her words.

"I'll try," he would only say, "but I really doubt if I'll be there. Have a Merry Christmas." Resuming his departure, he felt increasingly saddened the further he got away from her, for he had wanted to tell her specifically why he was behaving this way, but time wouldn't permit it. In addition, the setting, the school, wasn't the best place to attempt explanations. *Some other time*, he thought, at a location where there weren't any distractions.

Watching him leave, Jana wondered about the state of their relationship. She had thought he'd jump at the opportunity to attend a gathering at the Willards, and yet he seemed so uncompromising. She consequently began to wonder whether she could reach him after all. She lacked the necessary information in understanding where he was coming from, and it was that lack of understanding which influenced her in a way that tested her devotion to his cause.

* * *

In the ensuing days Dwight felt as though there was little to look forward to. Christmas was going to be disregarded in his household, which disappointed him in more ways than one.

By the time Christmas Eve arrived his emotions were so overwhelmed that he fled to the barn to be with the animals; whereupon, for the greater part of a half hour he stroked Hazel's neck in an attempt to gain solace for his heavy heart.

Entering the chicken coop, he scattered corn on the floor and watched as the birds swiftly devoured it with their usual appetite for the grain.

Standing there, thoughts of Jana nearly brought him to the verge of tears, for he knew he had disappointed her. *I try*, he thought in an even greater wave of sadness, *but I get so uptight over the thought of doing things. I never seem to know what to say.* Lowering his hand into the wooden barrel, he withdrew additional corn for the ready and waiting flock. Tossing it onto the floor where it was again consumed in haste, he could not help but think about the nature of their existence. They were creatures largely driven by the survival instinct, a feature which made their lives so much less complicated than his in that their behavior was governed by a set of inherited traits. ... And yet they, too, had varying temperaments, much of which was contingent upon their individual makeup and the environment to which they were exposed.

Exiting the coop and closing the door behind him, he thought about the price humanity had paid for intelligence, for the knowledge thus gained had not always been used to the benefit of society at large. Attitude problems ran rampant, and as far as his own outlook was concerned he knew that he had proven this to be true in his own particular way. To whom much was given much was expected. He had once heard that said, and had ultimately taken it to mean that because of the God given ability to reason, mankind was expected to promote peace and brotherhood. Yet these things so often were not put into practice in a world that was overly focused on the quest for material wealth.

Making his way toward the house on this chilly December day, Dwight saw Clair walk onto the porch with a broom in her hand. Briefly regarding him, she commenced to sweep the landing off.

At first he began to climb the steps with the intention of going directly to his room; yet then, in a yearning for change, he stopped short, looked directly at his sister, and said, "Clair, don't you wish we had a Christmas tree this year? We still have all the trimmings in the attic."

Clair momentarily stopped sweeping in response to his suggestion as a smile began to form on her lips. One could only imagine her reminiscing of a time when she enjoyed life significantly, for she seemed to have such a pensive bearing about her. Seconds later, though, as the grasp of the world she had come to know took hold of her emotions, she resumed what she had been doing as though she had not heard a word he uttered, as if attempting to recapture any semblance of the happiness she once knew was an insurmountable goal to aim for.

Discerning the meaning behind her behavior, Dwight said no more. Sauntering into the house, he saw his mother seated on the living room sofa. For a few seconds he gazed at her before walking tentatively forward.

"Mother," he eventually spoke up, even though she refused to look at him. "I was wondering if we could have a Christmas tree this year. I'd cut it down and trim it myself."

A cold glare was cast upon him posthaste.

"There will be no such thing in this house! What is there to be cheerful about! I can't think of one thing!" Yet eventually, in a somewhat subdued manner of sober resolve, she almost sadly added, "Now leave me alone."

In resignation Dwight lowered his head and walked away with the intention of trying to forget, for awhile anyway, the state of his life.

Ascending the stairs, he glanced at the wall clock between the dining room windows and grew rather distressed as he recalled that Jana would be visiting the Willards in a matter of hours. How he wished he, too, could be there, for he imagined it would be an enjoyable time for all concerned. Truly he hoped Jana never took for granted all that she had to be thankful for.

When he entered his room, he shut the door and removed his jacket before plopping on his bed, but try as he may he just couldn't seem to prevent longing thoughts from entering his mind. Ultimately deciding to get up, he walked to his dresser to try to locate a book of poetry. Poems he found to be very inspirational, particularly during those times when life seemed at its worst.

Opening a drawer, he was just about to lay hands on the book when he heard a car pull into the driveway. Curious as to who it might be, he approached the window and was pleasantly surprised to see Mr. Willard and Bill exiting the vehicle.

Hurriedly Dwight opened the window, hoping he was right concerning why they had come.

"Hi!" he yelled out to them while poking his head outside, strongly desiring to prevent them from facing any inhospitality at the front door.

Looking up at him, Mr. Willard and Bill smiled over his unexpected greeting place.

"We came to find out if you'd like to come over to our place for awhile," Bill shouted. "Jana told us you didn't have a ride. Do you and your family have plans made yet?"

"No, we don't," Dwight quickly informed him, "and I'd really like to go with you!"

"We would have called beforehand but you don't have a phone," Mr. Willard apprised him. "I hope this isn't inconveniencing you."

"No, not at all," Dwight so thoroughly maintained that all he could seem to do for the time being was stare at them in a trans-fixed state.

"Well, are you coming or not?" Bill eventually asked.

"I'll be right down!" he enthusiastically answered him.

Pulling his head inside, Dwight closed the window and darted to his dresser to get his best shirt and pants. Dressing in a flash, he threw on his jacket, raced out of the room, and flew down the stairs with an exuberance that was so unlike his disposition of only a few moments earlier.

Arriving outdoors, he made his way to the passenger side of the car, at which time Bill opened the door for him while saying, "Sandy's gonna be glad to see you again, Dwight. She wants to show you how well she can blow that conch shell."

"It'll be nice to see her, too," he stated as he got into the back seat and sat down.

"It has been a while since we last saw you, Dwight," Mr. Willard commented as he, too, got into the car. "How have you been anyway?"

"Pretty good," he told him for the sake of convenience as the man started the engine. "How about you and everyone else?"

"Basically fine," he responded while backing out of the drive-way. "Mary Ann had the flu a few weeks back, but she got over it quickly."

"I'm glad it wasn't too bad for her," Dwight said.

In the interim a few more words were exchanged, in the after-math of which a rather lengthy silence triggered self-conscious thoughts on Dwight's part, for he felt as though it was his obligation to converse about something. Interestingly, he didn't focus on the fact that when there is such a silence, no one is contributing to conversation at that given moment. And yet merely telling him the error of his logic would not alter his feelings. It takes time to insti-tute lasting change, as well as a better understanding of the things that drive a person toward bondaged thoughts to begin with.

Unwilling to tolerate the quiet any longer, Dwight finally said, "I wonder if Jana's at your house yet."

"I doubt it," Bill told him. "But she knows we came to pick you up. She'll probably be over by four thirty."

"You must be fond of her, Dwight," Mr. Willard assumed. "She's a wonderful girl."

"I do like her a lot," Dwight freely admitted as he thought about how anxious he was to see her. "She's been good to me."

Although there was again silence as they continued along their way, rather than dwell on it, Dwight thought of other things while observing the early winter landscape, things such as Mr. Willard's generosity in having driven fifteen miles one way to pick him up, and of how good it felt to be accepted and cared about. He was even inclined to be glad to be alive, which in terms of conscious awareness was a long-lost feeling.

Pulling into the driveway of the Willards' home, Dwight became engulfed with a combination of nervous anticipation and excitement over the thought of spending an evening with them. He believed that ultimately he'd feel relaxed in their company, for he had come to know this to be a definite possibility.

Entering the kitchen by way of the front door, the enticing smell of baked ham immediately stimulated his senses making him realize how hungry he was becoming. He would look forward to a full-course meal, for it had been quite some time since last partaking in such an indulgence.

"Everyone must be in the living room," Mr. Willard assumed while leading the way there with Dwight third in line.

They had almost reached their destination when suddenly, set against the furthest wall of the living room, Dwight laid eyes on one of the most beautiful Christmas trees he had ever seen. With a warm feeling he stopped short to view it from afar, thinking of Christ as he did so, knowing full well that Jesus should be placed first and foremost as the focal point of Christmas.

Mrs. Willard was the first person to notice Dwight standing behind the approaching forms of her husband and son.

"Dwight, it's so good to see you again!" she exclaimed while rushing forth to greet him. "I'm so happy you decided to come!"

"It's good to be here," Dwight modestly stated as Sandy, who had been seated on the couch, darted toward him with the conch in her hand.

"I've been waiting for you, Dwight!" she declared in earnest.

"Come outside with me to hear me blow this!" Holding up the shell, she took hold of one of his hands to lead him away.

"Oh, Sandy, he just got here," her mother humorously protested. "You can show him later." Previously the woman had told the child she did not want to be subjected to the confinement of loud noises in the house.

"No, it's alright, really," Dwight spoke up while smiling. "I'd like to hear how well she can do it."

Sandy shouted her glee while rushing for her jacket, which she conveniently had placed on the sofa so that she could ready herself to go outdoors.

Once in the backyard with Dwight, who was nearly brought to the point of running to keep up with her, Sandy stopped and turned to face him. Raising the shell to her mouth, she let out a steady sound of rhythmic precision.

"That's fantastic!" Dwight found himself exclaiming. "You do it better than me now!"

"I practiced until I got it right," she told him with high-spirited conviction. Smiling in her victory, she added, "I guess that's all it took."

"It appears so," he thoughtfully responded, deeply recognizing the commitment of her efforts. ... "Thank you," he felt disposed to add.

"For what?" the girl inquired with a puzzled expression. "I should thank you for listening."

"I don't happen to see it that way, Sandy," he told her in deep awareness of the underlying, symbolic meaning of what she had said to him.

For a while Sandy pondered his statement before grasping its significance. Turning about then, they headed for the house only to notice that the entire family was observing them from the porch.

"So you finally got to show Dwight how well you learned to use that conch," Mr. Willard commented as Dwight mentally embraced the concern this family held for one another.

"Yes, she sure did," Mrs. Willard concurred.

When everyone had reentered the living room, Dwight again focused on the Christmas tree. In doing so, he witnessed feelings far removed from tense.

"Do you like our tree?" Mrs. Willard asked as she approached where he stood.

"Oh, yes," he told her in a low tone of voice. "It's been a long time since I saw...." He suddenly stopped short of revealing anything about his past, and grew a bit nervous over his near slip of words. "It's very beautiful," he sought to cover up his unease, but it was to no avail, for Mrs. Willard plainly sensed it within him. She would say nothing in reference to it, though, considering it for the best to allow him to say what he wanted to say in his own due time to those whom he trusted.

"This ornament has been in my family for generations," she informed him while singling out a small silver horn. "My grandmother brought it here from Sweden."

"It's very nice," Dwight said with regained composure. "So finely detailed."

"It is at that," she stated while withdrawing her hand from it. "I always hang it in a conspicuous place on the tree so that I can easily see it."

For a few more seconds they continued to admire the tree's beauty before Mrs. Willard asked Dwight if he would like to sit down.

"Alright," he told her and made his way toward the couch to sit beside Sandy.

"Would you like something to drink?" Mr. Willard spoke up at this time. "We've got eggnog, lemonade, and soda pop."

Dwight chose eggnog, and when Mr. Willard had made his way into the kitchen to retrieve it, Mary Ann decided that she, too, would like a refreshment.

"Would anyone else like something?" she inquired while getting up, only to be bombarded with requests by most everyone. "Gee, I'm sorry I asked," she as a result laughed before petitioning Eliza for assistance.

"Oh, that reminds me, I've got to check on the ham!" Mrs. Willard suddenly recalled while adding another piece of wood to the fire. "I'd hate to overcook it." She started for the kitchen only to delay her advancement to again regard Dwight. "I can't tell you enough how glad I am to have you here," she stressed with motherly affection.

Dwight conveyed his appreciation by way of a look. Then, as she was walking away, he gazed across the room and saw Jerry and Bill kidding around with one another, which prompted him to smile.

"Do they always get along that way?" he asked Sandy.

"Most of the time," she told him. ... "Do you have a younger brother?"

"Ah... no, I don't," he stammered a bit. "I have one sister." In his quest to change the topic, he consequently added, "Tell me Sandy, do you have any hobbies other than shell collecting?"

"No, not really," she informed him. "I would like to raise some baby chicks next spring, but we've got quite a few chickens already."

"But couldn't you buy two or three?" he inquired. "I'm sure it wouldn't cost that much."

"I know, but my dad said you can't order any less than twenty five where we get our chickens, and he doesn't want that many next spring."

In the ensuing moments Dwight recalled a time when he had hatched some eggs in a small incubator he had gotten for his seventh birthday. Why it would be just the thing to suit Sandy's purpose.

"I'll tell you what, Sandy," he spoke up. "I could hatch you a few chicks." Telling her about his previous experience with incubating, he added, "It fits four eggs, so it'd probably be just right."

"That'd be great!" she reacted with wide-eyed interest. "You're sure you wouldn't mind?"

"No, actually I think I'd enjoy it," he convinced her.

Sandy smiled brightly.

"I like you," she told him with wholly believable emphasis, an emphasis that reflected the essence of her innocence, and touched Dwight's innermost feelings.

Moments later, when Mr. Willard, Mary Ann and Eliza returned with the refreshments, Dwight was handed his eggnog.

"Umm, it's good," he noted after taking a sip.

"I only wish I could take the credit for making it," Mr. Willard told him as Mary Ann handed Sandy a glass of soda pop. "Mary

Ann made it." When she was standing beside him, he put his left arm around her shoulder. "My little girl is getting to be good at making a lot of things."

"Oh, daddy, you're prejudiced," she giggled. "You say everything I make is good."

"And that's a father's prerogative," he told her with humorous overtones. "You've got to accept that."

"Oh, believe me, I have," she sought to convince him. "When your father thinks your burnt cookies are really good tasting, then you know he's trying to make you feel good." As everybody, including Dwight, heartily laughed over her comment, she affectionately turned to the man and added, "But I do love you for it." Gently she kissed him on the cheek.

Later, after everyone had finished their refreshments, Eliza and Mary Ann helped their mother set the dining room table for supper. Upon the completion of this task, Sandy asked the two girls if they would like to play a game of pinochle.

"Do you know how to play that game?" she then asked of Dwight.

"No, I never even heard of it," he notified her. "But I'm willing to learn," he quickly made sure to add, for it had been a long time since he played a card game with anyone, and he didn't intend to let the opportunity pass him by.

"We'll teach you," Mary Ann told him as she commenced to clear off the coffee table, while Sandy in the meantime darted off for the cards.

"Ya, you can't do much worse at it than Mary Ann," Bill teased her as he sat on the floor before the table with his legs crossed.

"Very funny," Mary Ann reacted by gently tapping him on the head with her forefingers, to which Dwight grinned.

It was only seconds later that Sandy came dashing into the room with a deck of cards, paper, and a pencil in her hands.

"I'll sit by you, Dwight," she said while making her way beside him, even though she knew it would mean being on opposite teams.

"I'm surprised you never heard of pinochle," Mary Ann announced. "It's a very popular game."

"My family doesn't like games very much," Dwight was honest

enough to say in defense.

"Gee, they're missing out on a lot of fun," Eliza told him.

"I'll tell them that," Dwight responded in the hopes that the direction of their conversation would come to an abrupt halt. Then, as Bill began shuffling the cards, he thought, *If they only knew.*

"I hope you're including me in this game," Jerry earnestly spoke up as he squeezed between Bill and Eliza, putting an end to Dwight's preoccupied thoughts.

"Of course we are," Bill convinced him. "This is six-handed pinochle, so we need you to make six."

As the game progressed, Dwight could feel himself becoming increasingly absorbed in the enjoyment of it, but he did not have to wonder why this was so. He knew from the depth of his being that it was because he was not concerned in the least about anyone lashing out at him in any way, shape, or form.

By the time four thirty pulled around, Bill, Sandy and Eliza were on the verge of winning the game. It was then that Dwight became aware of Jana and Cybils' voices in the kitchen.

"Dwight, you made it!" he soon heard Jana say as she walked across the dining room floor. Understandably, in light of her previous conversation with him, she had doubted his attendance.

"Yes, I'm really here," Dwight stated in a manner that led her to believe he, too, was surprised by that fact. "And I'm having a good time. I'm even learning how to play pinochle."

"And he's catching on quickly," Bill informed her as Cybil entered the room to greet everyone.

"Oh, what a beautiful tree!" she exclaimed. "When did y'all trim it?"

"We put it up last night," Mary Ann told her. "We wanted it ready for Christmas Eve."

"It is gorgeous," Jana agreed while nearing it. "It really puts one in the Christmas mood, doesn't it?" Turning to face everyone, she enthusiastically added, "You are still planning to sing carols later, aren't you?"

"Most definitely," Eliza reassured her. "It's a tradition here."

"Dwight, you don't have to leave any too soon, do you?" Jana now asked.

"No, I'm in no hurry at all," he spoke up with such spontaneity that his disinterest in returning home was easily sensed by her.

"I was hoping you could stay awhile," she responded with a soft smile, though she found his revelation to be essentially sad.

As everybody conversed, Dwight talked more freely than he ever expected to be the case, which was certainly a welcome occurrence. Then, at precisely five o'clock, everyone seated themselves at the dining room table in anticipation of the fine meal they were about to eat. There was the baked ham and baked potatoes along with fruit salad, carrots, sweet potatoes, and piping-hot biscuits.

Because Dwight had not eaten a meal of this size in such a long time, no one at the table appreciated it more than him. Therefore as everyone present gave thanks to God for the food set before them, it was he who reflected the epitome of what God likes to see within people, the humble and heartfelt gratitude.

"This meal is fabulous, Mrs. Willard!" he found himself impulsively blurting out shortly thereafter. "You sure are a fine cook!"

"I'm glad you like it. Eat as much as you want," she advised him. "I like to see growing boys eat well."

Dwight made it known that he fully intended to take her advice, in the event of which Sandy proceeded to tell everybody about his offer to hatch her some chicks in the spring.

"It'd be alright if I kept them, wouldn't it?" With hopeful expectation she directed her attention to both her mother and father.

"I guess we could feed a few more chickens," Mr. Willard consented.

"Oh, thank you, daddy!" Sandy ardently stated before turning to face Dwight. "I will take good care of them," she sought to convince him.

"I know you will, Sandy," he said, keenly recognizing their shared love for living things. "But you'd be well-advised not to count your chickens before they've hatched." He raised his eyebrows for the added emphasis and smiled.

"It was good of you to suggest such a thing," Mrs. Willard told him. "I'm sure we'll all enjoy having chicks around. They're so cute when they're little."

"Ya, they sure are," Jana spoke up from where she sat opposite

Dwight. "I imagine it's interesting to watch them hatch. I'd like to see it."

"Oh, but that wouldn't be possible," Dwight quickly stated. ... "Ah... we live too far away from each other is what I mean," he then sought to emphasize in an attempt to avoid offending her. But it was too late, for her feelings had already been injured over his abrupt reaction to her innocent comment.

"Oh, yes... of course," Jana disconcertedly stated. "It was just a thought."

Lowering his head a bit, Dwight relinquished any further explanation of his behavior and went back to strictly eating. As for Jana, she was convinced more than ever that he was hiding something, and she sincerely hoped he'd confide in her in the not too distant future.

When the time came for dessert to be served, Dwight had a hard time deciding between carrot cake, tapioca pudding, and pumpkin pie, given that he liked all three choices. Yet after savoring a piece of the pie, he felt it would be impossible for him to try anything else. He was going to burst, it seemed, and even though he knew it wasn't advisable to overeat, it was an unusually good feeling.

Later, after the table had been cleared and all leftovers put away, the caroling began with Mrs. Willard at the piano. They sang White Christmas and Dwight's favorite, Do You Hear What I Hear, along with many others; and Dwight participated with all the enthusiasm of a life loving philanthropist. Then, at precisely seven o'clock, everybody again seated themselves in the living room to take part in an exchange of gifts.

"Gee, thanks a lot," Jerry told Mary Ann upon opening a package that held a small red truck. "It's just what I wanted!"

As Mary Ann voiced her acknowledgment, Sandy thanked Eliza for a scarf she personally had knit for her.

In Dwight's estimation this was such a touching moment that he knew he would never forget it as long as he lived. It did not matter to him that he had not been handed a gift, because it was a special gift to be in the presence of these people to witness their love, a love which scaled the essence of healthy living. Hence he recognized that he was receiving something of great value from them, which is why, from where he sat beside Jana on the couch, he was suddenly inspired to say in a low whisper which only she could hear, "Thanks for seeing to it that I got here."

Jana did not verbally respond to his statement, but her eyes spoke a thousand words as she placidly regarded him and nodded her head.

"Here ya go, Jana and Dwight," Sandy suddenly captured their attention as she placed a package on each of their laps.

"It's just a little something from the family," Mrs. Willard informed them as they exchanged looks of surprise.

"You mean.... this is for me?" Dwight was prompted to say in near disbelief.

"Why, yes, of course," Mrs. Willard told him. "You needn't be surprised. We enjoy giving gifts to friends during the holidays."

"And we like you, too," Sandy added with such dramatic emphasis that laughter was thereby initiated.

"And you did come to Sandy's aid, and we wanted to let you know how much we appreciate that," Mrs. Willard pointed out in remembrance of that day.

Clearly moved by this expression of giving, Dwight gazed upon the red package and felt a wonderful sensation flood his emotions. *A present for me*, he thought. ... Yet then suddenly a troubling sentiment occurred to him. "I didn't give you anything," he regretfully brought to their attention.

"Oh, yes you did," Mrs. Willard quickly corrected him. "You came to share this day with us."

As Dwight regarded the woman he felt as though he could see into the very depth of her soul. And so much he liked what he saw.

By this point Sandy was so consumed by suspense that she anxiously exclaimed, "Open up your present, Dwight!"

"Okay!" he responded with a burst of enthusiasm and did as she suggested. "Wow!" he then said while laying eyes on a beautifully knit red and white sweater. Holding it up for all to see, he emphatically added, "It's really beautiful!"

"Mom made it for you," Eliza told him.

"And I picked out the colors," Sandy made sure to add.

"Well, it's perfect," he found it rather difficult to say in his overwhelmed feelings. "And red just happens to be my favorite color. It always has been."

"Dwight, it is beautiful," Jana made comment. "And it sure looks warm, too."

"Open your gift, Jana," Mr. Willard now urged her.

"Alright," she said and began to remove the wrapping with the same vigor as Dwight. ... "Oh, it's lovely!" she declared while holding up an attractive blue sweater. "Did you make this one, too, Mrs. Willard?"

"Yes," she stated while nodding her head. "I do hope you like the color."

"Oh, I do," Jana guaranteed her. "Thank you so much."

"Jana, look!" Cybil drew her attention as she held up the green sweater that she had just received. Turning to face Mrs. Willard, she exclaimed, "You must have spent hours making all these things!"

"It's something I enjoy to do in the evening."

"Ya, she's always knitting things for people, even when it isn't Christmas," Eliza pointed out. "Gee, I think we had better invest in some sheep for her, don't you, dad?" At the very thought of it she laughed.

Casually placing his thumb and index finger under his chin, Mr. Willard acted as though he was considering it. Then, with as much seriousness as he could muster, he said, "Perhaps we should at that. I can see her shearing one now." As he and everybody else laughed, his wife went along with the joking by saying with feigned support, "Now you know just what to get me this year." Noticing Dwight as a willing participant in the humor pleased the woman exceedingly. You see she believed in the benefit of healthy laughter, and where he was concerned, she saw this to be much needed therapy in his life.

Moments later, as the mirth subsided, Jerry asked his father if he could pop popcorn. When the man granted the boy's request, Sandy volunteered to assist him.

Turning his attention to Dwight, Mr. Willard stated, "I heard you're doing well in school. Jana told us that you gave an interesting oral report awhile back."

"Well, I got through it," he gravely acknowledged. "But I sure didn't like doing it." With a certain degree of conviction he confided, "Being required to give it made me feel so... oppressed."

"Jana told us your feelings about that, too," he stated. "And I'm inclined to think it's a point well taken."

"So am I," Mrs. Willard conceded. "I remember an oral report I had to give when I was in school." She seemed about to cringe. "I was so nervous that my legs shook and I got all sweaty. When it was all over, I felt so relieved." She sighed as though she were reliving it. "The memory of it is still vivid in my mind."

Considering the similarities where the deliverance of their respective reports was concerned, Dwight's curiosity naturally piqued. Rather insightfully he then said, "And yet despite what you went through, Mrs. Willard, you're so outgoing, which proves there's hope for me also." Irresistibly he could not help but smile at the very thought of it.

"Dwight, I see in you so much potential and more," she made her feelings known. "It's as plain as can be. And believe it or not, it's your humble opinion of yourself that will be your saving grace. I predict it will lift you up, unlike arrogance, which brings a person down."

Dwight was so touched by her generous opinion of him that he was compelled to wish he could be in her presence on a daily basis.

Not long after Jerry and Sandy had finished popping the popcorn, Mr. Willard looked at the mantel clock above the fireplace and told Dwight he thought the time had come to depart for Chism.

"I wouldn't wanna upset anyone by getting you home too late."

"Alright, I'll get my jacket," Dwight responded while getting up, making sure as he did so to shield his disappointment over the thought of leaving.

"I'll get it for you," Sandy accommodated him as she rose from where she had been seated beside him. How she did enjoy his company, proving that age, in some instances, is not a barrier to friendship.

"Don't forget your present, Dwight," Eliza reminded him while grabbing it from where he had placed it beside the couch.

Dwight thanked her and said, "I'd feel terrible if I left this behind." Turning his attention to Mrs. Willard, he predicted, "You know something, I think I shall hope for a spell of cold weather just so I can wear this often."

"I'm pleased you like it that much," she responded as Sandy got back with his jacket and handed it to him. "However, I must admit that when Jana said you wouldn't be coming, I wondered if maybe you didn't believe in celebrating Christmas."

"Oh, no, that wasn't it," Dwight sought to assure her. "I just needed a ride." Putting his jacket on, he felt inclined to inquire, "Why don't some people believe in celebrating Christmas, Mrs. Willard?"

"From what I understand, it's because they see it as a pagan rooted celebration that doesn't coincide with the actual birth date of Christ. They also feel that Jesus wouldn't have wanted his birthday celebrated, especially in the manner that it's done. And then of course there's also certain religions in the world that don't look to Christ, so its members don't celebrate Christmas for that reason."

At first Dwight stood motionless in contemplation. Then he prudently said, "It would seem to me that God would be pleased whenever we remember to celebrate the great gift Jesus was and still is to the world."

So impressed was Mrs. Willard by his viewpoint that it prompted her to add, "And whenever we give a gift to someone, we're really giving it to Jesus. Jesus himself said that whatever we do onto others, we do onto him."

"I'll try to remember that," Dwight solemnly asserted. "I guess if we weren't so distracted, we wouldn't need reminders of the people we should be." Gazing about the room, he said good-bye to all present.

Returning the farewell, Mrs. Willard made sure to emphasize, "Please return soon. You're welcome here always."

"I'll keep that in mind. Thank you," Dwight replied as he headed for the door with Mr. Willard.

"And we could play pinochle again," Sandy suggested.

"That'd be fun," Dwight told her. Looking affectionately at Jana, he had no trouble whatsoever detecting the satisfaction she felt over his decision to have come here.

Moments later, while seated in the car riding homeward, Dwight reflected on what had been said about Christmas. In witnessing a peaceful feeling enter his soul, he wondered if a compromise had been reached. The manner in which one celebrated

Christmas determined whether or not it was acceptable in God's eyes. So often people considered an issue on an all or nothing basis, not realizing that the proper view lies between the two extremes. ... And yet that wasn't to say one should feel guilty for nonparticipation in the celebration of Christmas, peace of mind and a clear conscience being the valuable things that they are. It's highly important, though, that the non-participant not expect everyone to be just as they are, that they not regard all forms of celebration as inherently inappropriate and incapable of moral value. Stated another way, wholesome forms of praise and worship are a distinct possibility where Christmas is concerned, and where Christmas is not concerned.

As a sign onto him that he was on the right path in what he was affirming, contentment began to permeate Dwight's entire being from head to toe like a warm wave of chain reactioned impulses. Such is the nature of what can be reaped when taking an interest in the will of God.

* * *

When Dwight arrived home, he was hoping that he wouldn't be confronted by either his mother or sister, because he wanted to retain for as long as possible the unusually good feeling which lingered within him.

Ascending the front steps after having thanked Mr. Willard for his generosity and bid him farewell, he reflected on the day in which he met the Willard family at the beach. He even found himself wondering if the timing had involved much more than coincidence.

It was a relief to discover that no one was to be seen when he entered the kitchen. Hastily making his way toward the dining room, he proceeded up the stairs with his gift tucked under his right arm.

When he arrived at the top of the stairs, he felt reasonably certain he had succeeded in avoiding an unpleasant encounter with his sister. Yet then just as he began to tiptoe past her bedroom, she flung her door wide open.

"Trying to sneak into your room unnoticed," she accused him while entering the hall. "Well, I heard that man saying bye to you."

She looked at the gift he was holding and bluntly added, "Did he give you that?"

"His family did. I spent the evening with them," Dwight informed her. "They're nice people who treat me well."

"Oh, is that so?" she disparaged his claim, for she was in fact jealous of his relationship with them.

"Yes, it's really so," Dwight would only say while turning to walk onward, strongly desiring to escape her negative comments.

"What makes you think those so called friends of yours can be trusted?" Clair swiftly asked in an attempt to plant a seed of doubt in his mind. "After all, look what happened to us."

With a composure that was unusually easy to maintain, Dwight turned to say, "No matter what goes on in this house I'll still believe there's virtuous people, and you'll never be able to take that away from me. The Willards are sincere, I assure you. If you personally knew them, you'd realize it was so." His mannerism, his confident tone of voice, convinced her that he was speaking from the heart.

"But you can't know that for certain," she nevertheless pressed on in her desire to shatter his confidence. "One of these days they'll turn on you, and you'll come home disappointed, and I'll say I told you so."

With an unshaken spirit Dwight was inspired to say, "Surrender, Clair. You're not going to get to me this time. I feel that good right now." Taking a confident step forward, he perceptively added, "Not everyone is a reflection of this house." With that having been emphasized, he entered his room.

Swallowing her anger, Clair stormed back into her own room, slamming the door shut behind her as she did so.

In being away from her Dwight felt a renewed sense of relief. Looking to the gift he was clutching, he walked to his bed and removed its contents.

"My present," he said while gazing upon the beautifully knit sweater. "And it's so nice." Putting it on, he went before the mirror. "It fits just right," he took note of. "This is one of the best days of my life. ... And I know Clair is wrong," he reminded himself while continuing to stare at his reflection. "I feel so loved whenever I'm around those people."

CHAPTER 9

THE TREACHERY

Pleasant memories certainly can be of therapeutic value to a person, and so the lack of Christmas cheer in the Enhart household did not weigh as heavily on Dwight's mind as he had expected to be the case. Choosing to reflect on the time spent at the Willards' encouraged him to feel optimistic about the potential for brighter tomorrows.

He was pleased that the weather was on the cool side as January ushered in, for it gave him good reason to wear his new sweater to school. Yet in all likelihood he would have worn it no matter what, because a gift from the Willards was symbolic of the love and affection he so yearned to have in his midst.

Boarding the bus, Sara made up for lost time by directing a snide remark his way. But he invariably ignored her while heading for his usual seat at the rear of the vehicle.

Once inside the school walking down the hall toward his locker, he was thankful to feel much more relaxed than usual. This, however, turned out to be short-lived, for in nearing his destination he grew uneasy over the sight of Carl and Ben awaiting his arrival.

When Carl saw him approaching, he said hello, and Ben did likewise.

Despite having sensed feigned goodwill on their part, Dwight returned the greeting in as calm and composed a manner as possible. There were two reasons for his having done so, and he was consciously aware of each of them. First of all, he was determined to be courteous to the two boys in spite of his mistrust of their intentions. And secondly, he knew that Carl would likely be angered if he realized how suspicious he really was of him, and he didn't want to run the risk of being forced to deal with the repercussions of that.

In an attempt at amiable conversation Dwight made it a point to ask Carl how his Christmas had been.

At the sound of these words Carl's face immediately took on a grim look. Then he stated, "The same as always," with a tone that was indicative of not having enjoyed it at all. "I'm here, though, to invite ya to a party," he was soon to add. "It's gonna be at a friend's house Friday night. His parents are gonna be out of town."

At first Dwight intended to decline the offer, and not merely because he didn't want to socialize with someone he distrusted and disliked, but also because the thought of attending a party at someone's home in the absence of their parents did not bode well with him. Meeting Carl's piercing gaze, however, he felt pressured to cave in to his reservations and accept the invitation.

"But I live too far away. I wouldn't be able to get there," he went on to say in the hopes that he had a convincing alibi for nonparticipation.

"Oh, that can be taken care of," Carl counteracted. "We'll pick you up at your place around seven o'clock. You do live along Kirkland Road, don't you?"

"Ya, I do," Dwight felt trapped into admitting.

"Okay, everything is all set then for Friday?" he eagerly sought to verify. Yet when Dwight said nothing, he persuaded him to recommit by reiterating, "Okay?"

As soon as Dwight nodded his head, a glint of satisfaction could be detected in Carl's eyes. It was then, and only then, that he proceeded to walk away with Ben.

In watching the two boys depart Dwight became increasingly unsettled. Then, while lowering his head, he thought, *Why would he want me to go to a party? We're not friends.* No, it didn't rest well with him for obvious reasons, so much so that he failed to notice Jana's presence.

"Don't look so serious," she lightheartedly spoke up with a smile.

"Oh, hi," he pleasantly reacted to the sight of her. "You seem to be in a good mood."

"I am," she told him. "I had such a nice vacation. And the time I spent at the Willards was especially enjoyable."

"I know what you mean," Dwight vividly recalled. "I felt so welcome there."

"It's their virtue to bring that feeling out in people," Jana told him.

"And what a virtue it is to have," Dwight explicitly responded as he began to remove his jacket to place within his locker.

"Oh, you've got your new sweater on!" Jana immediately made mention of.

"Ya, and it fits just right," he apprised her.

"I guess one could say then that Mrs. Willard really has a keen eye for sizing people up," she said on a humorous note.

Still preoccupied by thoughts of Carl, Dwight barely laughed over her play on words.

"By the way, how was the rest of your vacation?" Jana asked him then.

"Ah... not too bad," he stammered. "Tell me, where are Cybil and Bill?" he was quick to follow up with.

"They can't be too far away. I just saw them. Did you want to ask them something?"

"No, I just wanted to say hello," he told her while closing his locker door. Looking at her for a few seconds, he added, "Well, I better get to gym class."

"Okay, I'll see ya later," Jana replied as he began to walk away.

Watching him leave, she began to wonder if he would ever confide in her, for he seemed more reluctant than ever to do so. She didn't realize, however, that he was in a quandary over an invitation to a party he had absolutely no desire to attend.

* * *

After having played a rather exciting game of soccer, the boys headed for the locker room.

In the course of time Dwight's unrest had diminished during

gym class, but he was not inclined to wonder why this was so. He knew that it was partially due to the social acceptance he had come to know where Jana, Bill and Cybil were concerned. But mainly positive change was manifesting itself in his life because he was learning to approach life from a healthier perspective. Yet still, though he understood that it was possible to look forward to gym, he felt relieved each and every time it came to an end, for he tolerated much more than enjoyed it.

When he had finished showering and dressing, Dwight happened to notice Carl and Ben changing into their clothes not too far away.

"See ya," he felt outgoing enough to say while heading for his next class of the day.

"Ya, bye," Carl responded as Ben waved.

Dwight had barely entered the hall when he realized he left his wristwatch in his gym locker. Doing an about face, he returned from whence he had come only to stop short in utter dismay over that which he heard in the next aisle upon nearing his destination.

"What a fool he was to have trusted me," Carl derisively told Ben. "He's not only a coward, but he's dumb, too."

"I wonder how he'll react when you get him alone Friday night and he finds out there's no party and no one to help him. I bet he'll be scared outta his pants," Ben presumed.

"You can bet on that," Carl anxiously anticipated. "I can hardly wait."

Dwight was quite shaken by what he heard. *He tricked me*, he thought. *He still resents me very much! I've gotta get outta here!* Hastily he left without his watch, not knowing that Scott had happened to witness the entire incident from where he was changing not too far away.

Dwight fled down the hall and up the stairs to the second floor amongst the puzzled glances of people whom he brushed past. Then, upon arriving at his locker, he opened its door and leaned his head against it, sighing in his apprehension as he did so. *My suspicions were right*, he thought with grave disappointment. Jana had warned him about Carl, and had been justified in doing so. Now, if he chose not to confess what he overheard, he would have to come up with a pretext for nonattendance of the party Friday night. Even then he knew Carl would never leave it at that, his dishonorable intentions being that extreme. ... But of course there was the truth, always the truth. That could be told, but as a precursor to what? A vicious attack from a troubled boy who resented the thwarting of his cruel plan. Truly, sometimes, every course of action seemed to have its shortcomings, its potential for unpleasant results, where the frailties of man were concerned.

Later, in biology class, Dwight found it impossible to shield his anxiety from Jana's perceptive eye, because the more he thought about Carl's treachery, the more tense and upset he became. Consequently, in the hall afterwards, Jana neared him with pressing concern.

"Dwight, is something bothering you?" she inquired while walking beside him.

For a few moments Dwight stopped in his tracks to gather his thoughts. Then, as he made his way against the wall to avoid the rush of students, Jana followed.

"You were right about Carl," he regretted to inform her. "He's out to get me."

"Oh, no!" Jana sorely reacted, for she had hoped it would not have actually come to this. "How did you find out?"

Filling her in on what had taken place earlier, Dwight went on to say, "He sure is determined to hurt me."

"Which proves how despicable he really is," Jana was disposed to lay claim. "There has to be something I can do to help."

"You did warn me about him and that was something. I guess I didn't want to believe you were right," he told her. "And yet I'm not surprised. I never did trust him." With a lowering of his eyes he added, "Life sure can be difficult sometimes."

Jana was momentarily speechless as she continued to regard him. Indeed she could not help but wonder how much adversity he would be forced to endure at the hands of Carl.

"Come on, let's put our books away and go to lunch," she finally advised him.

Nodding his head, Dwight walked onward in sober resignation.

"Dwight, how do you plan to handle this?" Jana asked him

shortly thereafter in troubled thought.

"I guess I'll tell Carl something came up. I'll think of some excuse." All of a sudden he turned to face her. "Please don't tell anyone about this," he beseeched her. "It'd only make matters worse if Carl found out I was listening in on him."

"If you wish," she acquiesced, neither one of them realizing that it was soon to be a mute point.

It happened in the hall after the final bell rang to dismiss the students for the day. Dwight was walking toward his locker at the time, when suddenly, out of the crowd, Carl was upon him, in the event of which, without uttering a word of warning, he flung him around by the arm and slugged him so viciously in the left eye that he flew back against some lockers and nearly fell to the floor. Then, grabbing him by the sweater, he snarled, "You dirty little snoop! So you thought you could get away with spying on me! Well you can't!" His eyes were glowing with anger and resentment, a telling reminder of the feelings of inadequacy lodged deep within himself.

Initially Jana did not realize what was taking place, but in a matter of seconds she happened to catch a glimpse of the awful scene as Carl readied himself for what appeared to be another harsh blow.

"Leave him be!" she screamed as she desperately dashed forth and grabbed Carl by the hair, thrusting his head backwards with a quick jerk.

"Let go, you bitch!" Carl bellowed and elbowed her in the stomach, forcing her to release her hold on him as she stooped over in pain. Then, just as he turned his attention to Dwight once again with the intention of abusing him further, the principal, Mr. Tailor, who happened to be in the general area at the time, arrived on the scene after having penetrated a group of interested onlookers.

"What's going on here?" he gruffly inquired while grabbing Carl by the collar and forcefully bringing him to his side.

In the ensuing moments, much to the man's consternation, he discovered that neither boy was willing to say anything in response to his demand.

"Who's going to explain this?" he adamantly persisted in growing irritation over their refusal to speak up.

Dwight was aware of the position he held. Yes, he knew that

because Carl had a reputation for being a troublemaker, he could tell the principal what happened and probably be believed. And yet he chose not to do so for two reasons. First of all, he knew that Carl would likely resent him even more if he did do this; and secondly, he was humiliated enough to be silenced. Jana on the other hand had every intention of speaking her mind; and so, while gently rubbing her stomach to ease the lingering pain, she felt strongly compelled to say, "Carl's responsible for this, I can assure you! And it should come as no surprise to anyone!"

Reflecting on the various disruptions he was aware of Carl's involvement in throughout his grade school years, Mr. Tailor realized that Jana had probably spoken accurately. However, in an attempt to be as fair-minded as possible, he released his grip on Carl while inquiring if he had instigated the incident.

At first Carl said nothing as he contemplated his answer. Then he appalled Jana by alleging, "I had good reason for doing this."

"Stop your lying!" Jana shouted in her outrage. Then, motioning toward the group of gathered students, she added, "Just ask some of them, Mr. Tailor! They must have seen what happened!"

Turning his attention to the crowd, Mr. Tailor was met with only a slight murmur of voices followed by approaching silence, for no one was willing to assume the risk of arousing Carl's wrath.

When it became transparent that details would not be forthcoming, Mr. Tailor sternly told Carl, "There's no good reason for this to have happened, so let no more of this take place or there's going to be some serious consequences, including possible expulsions!" With that being said he commenced to depart, yet not before ordering everyone to disperse.

When Mr. Tailor was out of sight, a devoted Jana made her way to Dwight's side and looked upon his dejected form with great empathy. Noticing Carl glaring at her, she returned an icy stare, each of them thus reinforcing their contempt for one another.

"He hasn't heard the last from me!" Carl bitterly told her before striding to where Ben stood waiting for him down the hall.

When Jana was again looking at Dwight, she whispered, "I'm so sorry." There was so much compassion in her voice that it nearly quivered.

"I know you are." Yet in a commentary of sobering truth, he added, "But this isn't just my problem, is it, Jana?" He was referring to society at large.

"No, Dwight, it isn't," Jana sought to convince him, "because I care about you, and I'm upset, and so what Carl's done to you is my problem, too, because I won't be content until he stops treating you this way."

Though Dwight was displeased over his inaction, he had enough good sense to realize that violence was not the answer to what Carl had done to him. No, there had to be a better alternative, one which was capable of putting an end to the animosity Carl directed towards humanity in general. Perhaps that was why he felt driven to tell her, "What both of us should want then is to reach Carl's conscience for the sake of everyone." Considering this as the objective would assist him in overcoming any feelings of resentment that crept into his mind from time to time over how he was treated by others, for he, too, was capable of lashing out at society, he had the wherewithal to comprehend. Yet if he had compassion for the abuser, then scorn would be kept at bay.

Raising his hand to his eye, Dwight could feel the swelling that had already begun to take place.

"Does it hurt badly?" Jana asked.

"I'll be fine," he sought to convince her. "But what about you?"

"My stomach is a bit sore, but I'll be alright. As for you, though, I think you better put some ice on that when you get home."

"Yes, nurse Rossi, I shall," he somehow found the desire to humor her, his personality having developed this much resilience.

In response to his comment Jana tenderly looked upon him as Bill and Cybil in the meantime arrived on the scene.

"We heard what happened!" Cybil exclaimed. "Are you both alright?"

Both Dwight and Jana assured her that physically they were not badly injured, after which Dwight proceeded to pick up his tablet and books, which had been strewn about the floor in the commotion. Upon completing this much hurried task, he wasted no time in darting away, for all he really wanted right now was to be alone to sort out his feelings.

"He's been degraded," Jana asserted as she watched him disappear from sight down the hall, her sorrow in saying this being painfully evident.

"It's going to break my mother's heart to hear about this," Bill predicted.

"I just hope this doesn't defeat him," Cybil interposed.

"Take heart, Cybil. I don't think it will in the long run," Jana said with a solemn, though confident, tone of voice. "He's a survivor, and more and more I see positive changes taking place in him. One of these days his personality will rise to the occasion when he's wronged, and he'll take charge no matter what."

* * *

On the bus on his way home Dwight heard and saw students whispering while casting glances his way, all of which reminded him of the humiliating position of awkwardness he had been in. He would nevertheless vanquish the powerlessness he had a reputation of owning, and he would do it honorably. It was only a matter of time, for otherwise he would continue to live in bondage; and bondage was a condition he had no intention of enduring for a lifetime.

"Don't fight too much," Sara verbally assaulted him as he unboarded the bus. "You really shouldn't take advantage of people that way."

Without responding to her ridicule, Dwight proceeded to make his way toward the house. Yet then suddenly, in a desire for solitude, he ventured across the road into the nearby woods. Placing his books beside a tree, he trod onward, making sure to take his tablet with him. For a few moments every now and then he would stop to look at a scampering squirrel or a singing bird, because after what had been done to him in school, he was inclined to seek every available means of comfort.

When he arrived at the place he liked so much, he eased himself to a sitting position. Staring at the cascade of crystal clear water, he prayed for the strength to cope with the strains of his life, knowing full well that he couldn't escape from himself. ... And now, motivated by his surroundings to open his tablet and take hold of the pen within it, he looked upon the beauty around him and commenced to write a poem from the depths of his heart. It went:

THE SETTING SUN

If ever at the end of day, the skyline draws your gaze its way;
To see a sight of sheer delight, the colors of the dusk in flight.
Duration short, it's His design, to fade the beauty by resign.
The setting sun, it will soon wane; don't take for granted it won't rain.
The moments gone, the dark remains, recapture never will lay claim.

Upon completing this poem he felt a bit better, knowing he had succeeded in preventing himself from hating the world. This was more than an accomplishment. It was a victory, all of which made him more determined than ever to encourage honest self-examination on the part of mankind. Empathy thus flowed within him, and to such a large extent it was felt because he had intimately come to know that improving one's outlook involves struggles. So in a very significant way he fathomed that they who routinely wronged others were burdened to the greatest extreme of all, their harsh actions lending credence to that assessment.

And now lo and behold, while looking upward, he exclaimed, "Oh, please help me find strength to get through this!" Lowering his head, he wept as a sign that he would trust in God to be delivered of his terrible predicament, for he felt that in one way or another God always answered the prayers of they who earnestly sought his rescue. He had once heard it said, and had believed it to be so.

CHAPTER 10

ZUZUECA (Zoo-zoo-ay-chah)

Bill had been right. His mother did become heartbroken when she heard what happened to Dwight. Kneeling by the fence that bordered the front yard planting bulbs for the spring bloom, she would stop and sigh every now and then, wondering what she could do to alleviate his plight. But it wasn't easy for her, because she could only do so much. She didn't see him all that often to offer encouragement to, and even if she did, she couldn't act in the capacity of a parent. She would pray for him, though, she told herself. And she would do it often.

"Would ya like to talk, ma?" she soon thereafter heard Bill speak up. "I'm a good listener."

With a soft smile the woman looked up at her firstborn child and said, "Do I look like I need it?"

"I think so," he made his feelings known while leaning against the fence. As she went back to working the soil, he speculated, "It's over Dwight, isn't it?"

For a few seconds she seemed transfixed in thought. Then she told him with a nod of her head, "Yes, what's happened to him has upset me immensely. You see I want him to know, I think he needs to know, how much he's cared about."

"But I think he already does know that," Bill was swift to point out, "where we're concerned anyway."

Raising a hand to sweep a fallen tress of hair away from her face, she said with moving emphasis, "It's at times like this that a person can feel so helpless. I'm so attached to him, and yet I can't protect him, and I want to so much."

"Try not to worry about him, Mother," Bill advised her. "He'll overcome this. Jana says he's a survivor. She thinks he's gonna surprise a lot of people."

"Perhaps he will at that. She knows him better than I. ... Jana's good for him," she then determined. "She has a firm grasp of what a friend should be."

"So do you," Bill reminded her. "After all, you've been a friend to me for a long time."

Affectionately gazing at him, she thanked him for talking, letting him know she felt better for it. Then, as she resumed working the soil, Bill turned toward the house only to glance over his shoulder at her, thinking in doing so how grateful he was to have her as his mother. How thoroughly he did love her.

* * *

The thought of returning to school the following day turned out to be too much for Dwight to handle. Too many people would stare at his swollen, blackened eye, he presumed. So he stayed in his room for most of the morning, coming out only briefly to eat a little something and take care of Hazel and the chickens.

He had expected Clair to be critical of his decision to stay home, but she had surprised him by saying nothing at all one way or the other. This compelled him to wonder if she sympathized with him for what he had gone through. Yet whether she felt for him or not, he was displeased with himself for avoiding school, because he didn't like that he had surrendered to his inhibitions. ... But it was a learning experience, and wisdom could be reaped from it.

Later in the day, after having eaten supper, he found the strong desire to remove himself from the house. Taking a long, reflective walk, he drew comfort from nature's beauty, the beauty of Mississippi, the land he loved so much.

He was about a mile or so from home on his return from his outing when suddenly, out of what seemed to be nowhere, a beautiful chestnut colt darted onto the road and stopped in its tracks, visibly uncertain as to where it should run.

Without a moment's hesitation Dwight approached the animal in an attempt to pacify it.

"Calm down, boy, calm down. Everything is gonna be alright." He spoke in a manner the colt immediately sensed as being trustworthy. "You're a good boy. Yes, you are." When he got close enough, he gently began to stroke its neck, continuing to do so even after he noticed a husky, elderly man making his way onto the road carrying a rope.

"Get back, laddie!" he ordered Dwight while approaching, thereby inciting the horse to warily rear back.

"Please, let me try," Dwight quickly interceded while extending his hand for the rope. "I think I can help."

For a few moments the man, whom Dwight now recognized as Matthew O'Maley, viewed him with obvious skepticism regarding his ability to restrain the animal.

"Alright," he ultimately gave in with a nod of his head, and handed the rope over to him. "I sure can't seem to get anywhere with that blasted beast." He had a brogue which was unmistakingly Irish.

Gradually Dwight approached the leery colt in another attempt at pacifying it. Then, when he had succeeded in doing so, he gingerly slid the looped end of the rope over its head.

"Good!" Mr. O'Maley voiced his delight while striding forth only to once again upset the animal, nearly resulting in a loss of Dwight's grip on the rope.

"Whoa!" Dwight stated as Mr. O'Maley ceased his advancement.

When Dwight had managed to again calm the horse down, he volunteered to lead it back to Mr. O'Maley's farm.

"I dare say that sounds like a good idea, laddie," Mr. O'Maley responded with dramatic emphasis before commencing to walk in the direction of the narrow dirt road that led to his property.

At first Dwight trailed about twenty feet or so behind the man. But then, when he felt reasonably certain all was going well, he closed in on the distance which separated them.

The O'Maleys' home was invitingly plain, as most of the country homes around Chism were, and in much need of a painting, but its unadorned appearance appealed very much to Dwight as being attractive in its own particular way.

"You have quite a way with that horse," Mr. O'Maley told Dwight once it had been turned loose in the corral. As the colt's mother whinnied in a combination of relief and affection, he went on to say, "You must have some animals of your own."

"We have a cow and a few chickens," Dwight informed him, realizing that this old family friend did not recognize him. It had been years since he last set foot on the O'Maleys' farm, though, for in the aftermath of his father's disappearance all visitations came to an abrupt halt, and neighbors became as strangers. This had by no means been a conscious decision on his part. It was more or less a consequence of the grieving process. ... Yet now, unlike his not-too-distant past, he was interested in reconnecting with humanity.

"So tell me, lad, where do you live?" Mr. O'Maley now inquired, thus verifying that he did not know his identity.

"Just a short ways from here actually," Dwight said while pointing. "I'm Dwight Enhart."

"Oh, yes, of course!" the man exclaimed. "You used to come here all the time when you were just a wee lad!" Extending his arm outward, he lowered it toward the ground.

"Ya, I did," Dwight admitted while smiling over the man's way of expressing himself.

"And I remember so well how you used to like my livestock," he suddenly recalled. "You haven't changed, I guess."

"Well, not in that regard," Dwight told him as his bruised eye came under the man's scrutiny.

"Gee, lad, what happened here?" he asked while putting a finger to it. "It's mighty nasty looking."

"Something regrettable," Dwight would only say, for he had no desire to elaborate on the specifics of what had occurred and why.

"I see you caught the runaway," they now heard a voice call out and turned to see Mrs. O'Maley approaching. "Who's this?" she curiously asked of her husband when she was standing beside Dwight.

"It's Dwight Enhart, though ya might not recognize him with

that black eye. You remember him, don't you?"

"I surely do," she was quick to acknowledge. "Why don't you come here any more?" she almost sadly asked.

"Suffice it to say that my father's disappearance has been hard on the entire family," he divulged in an unusually forthright admission.

"Oh, yes.... I remember what took place," she pondered. "What a mystery it was."

"And still is," Dwight stressed with utmost truth.

"Perhaps the day will come when you'll have answers," she suggested. Seeing Dwight nod his head, she added after a period of silent reflection, "I hope you visit us from now on. We don't receive many visitors, and we've missed you over the years."

"Thank you. I'll keep that in mind, ma'am," Dwight graciously replied. Gazing out to pasture, he then asked, "Tell me, how did that colt get loose?"

"Old fencing," Mr. O'Maley informed him while indicating where the animal had broken through. "I've got repairs to do I'm afraid. Normally that colt's not unruly, but a garter snake scared him a few months back and he's been jittery ever since."

Recalling a report he had once written on the Sioux Indian nation, a people who faced much adversity, Dwight thought about the name for a common ground snake. It was Zuzueca, and he remembered it, he presumed, simply because he had been taken by the sound of it.

"Mr. O'Maley, does that colt have a name yet?" he as a result asked.

"No, I can't say that it does," he answered him. "Why do ya ask, lad?"

After telling him about the report, Dwight further stated, "Zuzueca is the name for a common ground snake. And since a snake scared him, and he doesn't have a name yet, I thought it might suit him. It's probably what the Indians would have called him after what happened. Their names had meaning and were often linked to an event."

"Zoo...."

"Zoo-zoo-ay-chah," Dwight carefully sounded it out.

"Zoo-zoo-ay-chah," Mr. O'Maley slowly repeated the word and

laughed. "I'll say one thing. It's surely not a common name."

"No, it surely isn't," Dwight had to agree as he and Mrs. O'Maley laughed along with him, after which Mr. O'Maley looked out to pasture and said more fluently this time, "Zuzueca... Zuzueca, it's a fine name for a horse. Yes, indeedy, a fine name for a horse."

Dwight felt honored to think Mr. O'Maley had allowed him to name the animal. It was almost as though he believed he had earned the right.

Moments later, Mrs. O'Maley asked Dwight if he wanted to go indoors for some cookies and a refreshment.

"No, thank you, ma'am. But I would like to know if you have any other animals besides these horses."

"It just so happens that we do, lad," Mr. O'Maley interceded. "We've got chickens in the barn, and some ducks behind the house near the creek. I'll take ya to see 'em myself."

Dwight and Mrs. O'Maley bid each other farewell at this point. Then Dwight followed Mr. O'Maley to the barn.

Making their way into the coop, which adjoined the main structure, Dwight became impressed by what he saw, for the poultry was of a variety of breeds and quite healthy looking.

"Boy, what a colorful flock!" he voiced his delight.

"Ya, it is at that," Mr. O'Maley concurred. "There's Rhode Island Reds, Lakenvelders, White Rocks, and Black Australorps mainly." He singled out each breed with his finger. "They're good to have for the eggs, but every now and then a hen decides to be in a motherly way, if you know what I mean. Especially that one over there." He pointed to a red hen that was sitting in one of the dozen or so egg laying boxes. "She tried having little ones around this time last year, too."

"You did let her hatch some, didn't you?" Dwight inquired.

"No, I always order my birds through the mail instead," he informed him.

"I see. Well, I think they're just great!" Dwight remarked, wishing he also had a flock like this one. ... *But Clair might kill them off one by one just for spite*, he surmised, and discarded the notion as being foolish.

When the two of them were at the back of the house looking at the ducks, of which there were both mallards and pekins, Mr. O'Maley told Dwight that by spring there would likely be little ones, which aroused his interest very much.

"Thanks for the tour," Dwight told him once they had returned to the front of the house. "I'll try to make it back here soon."

"You had better do that, lad," he urged him, "or me and the missy will have a bone to pick with you."

Dwight issued the man a smile. Then they bid one another adieu.

Walking down the narrow dirt driveway toward home, Dwight thought about the price he had paid for avoiding the O'Maleys over the years. They were not worthy of having been shunned, and in doing so he had denied himself what likely would have been a satisfying relationship. Sad as this was, better late than never to renew a former friendship. It was symbolic of brighter tomorrows. ... But take heed, for choice is not an everlasting thing, and opportunity does wane. Therefore benefit as best you can from the love that is within your reach.

* * *

In school the following day Dwight was self-conscious of his blackened eye, but Jana was such a supportive friend that she not only understood why he needed a day at home in which to be alone, she also made sure to it that she gave him any assignments he missed in the classes that they shared with one another.

Dwight didn't expect Carl to express any regret for what he had done to him; but ironically, when he caught sight of him later in the day, he noticed within him a look of subtly discernible shame that escaped the detection of most people. In understanding insecurity so well, he was able to see it in others. He thus knew that Carl had paid a very high price for the error of his ways, namely in that his self-respect and self-worth had suffered the greatest setback of all. The conclusion: His misguided choices had compounded his dislike of self, adding to his emotional woes.

That afternoon, as he and Jana were walking down the hall in between classes, Dwight told her about the previous day's happenings at the O'Maleys'.

"I hadn't seen them in such a long time that they didn't even recognize me," he ended up telling her.

"In more ways than one it was a good thing then that you stayed home from school yesterday," she maintained. "You got reacquainted."

"Ya, I've been thinking about that myself," Dwight told her, despite the fact that he had not met the school's requirements for an excused absence by obtaining a written explanation from his mother as to why he had not been in attendance that day. Yet in light of everything that had taken place, an unexcused absence was the least of his concerns.

Suddenly curious as to why he had not seen his neighbors for such an extended period of time, Jana asked him why this was so.

"Ah... we just lost touch over the years," he would only say, for he still viewed the school setting as an inappropriate place for deep confessions. Jana did deserve an explanation concerning the story of his life, though, he firmly believed. She had clearly earned it.

CHAPTER 11

THE CONFESSION

By the time spring pulled around, Dwight had made a habit out of visiting the O'Maleys on a regular basis. He found it reassuring to have friends so close to home, because whenever he felt the need to be around people who welcomed him with open arms, all he had to do was walk a mile or so down the road. And Zuzueca was there, and growing into a beautiful stallion. So much he enjoyed this horse, and whenever he approached the animal he made sure to it that he gave him a treat of some sorts such as a lump of sugar or piece of carrot or turnip, all of which was consumed with great relish.

It was late in the month of March when he searched the attic for his small incubator to hatch some eggs for Sandy. Upon finding it, he went into the coop and collected four eggs to place within it. Then, at school the following day, he told Bill what he had done so that Sandy would know he had not taken lightly his word.

"She's excited about it," Bill told him from where they sat at an outdoor lunch table. "She has a box picked out for them already."

"In that case I sure hope they hatch," Dwight commented.

It was during the fifth day of incubation that something disappointing took place, however. After having carefully turned and cooled the eggs, Dwight paid the O'Maleys a visit only to discover on his arrival back home that someone had entered his bedroom and unplugged the incubator. Immediately suspecting his sister of this foul deed, he took hold of the plug with the intention of reinserting it into the wall outlet. Yet just as he was about to do so, he heard Clair say from the doorway, "Mother doesn't want you wasting electricity."

Turning about, Dwight viewed her with obvious skepticism, for he found it hard to imagine being denied the small amount of electricity required to operate such a tiny incubator.

"Mother said you can use that incubator when you pay the bills," Clair went on to say in such a convincing manner that he was inclined to believe her after all.

In the ensuing moments Dwight felt so much chagrin enter his emotions that he knew it'd be for the best to distance himself from his mother. Otherwise he might say something he'd later regret. However, he did say loud enough for Clair to hear, "If I were doing this for myself, I wouldn't mind so much, but it's for a friend."

"Well then you should stop making commitments you're not sure you can keep," Clair bluntly advised him before turning away.

Walking to his bed, Dwight sat down on the edge of it and whispered, "She's right. I'll have to be more careful what I commit to from now on."

In the spirit of the belief that every problem has a solution, Dwight soon recalled that the O'Maleys had another hen that wanted to set; and so, in a burst of new hope, he darted back to their farm with some freshly laid eggs of the day.

"Oh, you're back," Mrs. O'Maley warmly reacted to the sight of him. Noticing the concerned look on his face, she added, "There's nothing wrong I hope."

"No, not really. I was just wondering if I could put some eggs under your hen," he stated, and informed her of the agreement he had made with Sandy. "I have an incubator at home, but it's just not working out."

"I think we can accommodate you," Mrs. O'Maley pleased him in saying. "Come on. Let's go out to the barn and check into this."

Making their way there, Mrs. O'Maley asked Dwight whether he wanted to take the hen home with him. But he was quick to decline the offer.

"I think she should stay in familiar surroundings so she doesn't get upset," he made a good point in saying, though his main objective was to prevent Clair from sabotaging his project.

"We're going to have to separate that hen from the rest of the flock so she won't be disturbed," Mrs. O'Maley told Dwight once they were inside the coop. "The question is where to put her?" In deliberation she placed her hand under her chin.

"How about if I fence off a small area in the corner," Dwight suggested while pointing to the left of the door. "She'd be alright there, I think."

"Ya, I guess that'd work," she went along with his idea. "We've got some old fencing in the back of the barn you could use."

"Great!" Dwight voiced his delight. "Oh, by the way, I brought some eggs with me." Carefully he began removing them from his jacket pockets. "This really means a lot to me, Mrs. O'Maley."

"Yes, I can see that it does," she responded with a lighthearted chuckle over his unique enthusiasm. "There's a hammer and some nails in the next room."

As soon as Mrs. O'Maley started back for the house, Dwight began working on the enclosure. By the time an hour had passed he managed to assemble it and place the hen within it with the eggs he had taken from home. To his delight he saw her settle in on the nest in a matter of minutes, which was a sign onto him that he would be able to fulfill his commitment to Sandy after all.

Looking upon the bird, he said, "I sure hope nothing goes wrong this time."

There's something to be said about taking the initiative to address a problem without harboring resentments. On Dwight's part it had been accomplished.

* * *

In school the following day Dwight once again resorted to lying by telling Bill his incubator had broken down. Yet even though Bill expressed disappointment over this unforeseen development, at least there was the good news of the setting hen.

One thing can lead to another. So it came to be about a week or so later when Jana approached Dwight at the bus stop to wish him a nice weekend.

"I suppose you'll be studying for Monday's biology test," she said.

"Oh, I forgot about it!" he exclaimed just as he was about to board his bus. "And I doubt if I have time to get my book either! ... Oh well, I guess I'll have to study all the harder for the next one," he ultimately concluded.

Jana would have given him her own book had she had it with her, but she had not yet retrieved it from her locker.

"I'll be right back, Dwight! I'm going for your book!" she suddenly decided and dashed away before he could even voice a response.

By the time Jana returned outside the Chism bus was already traveling down the road. She didn't know it, but Dwight had thought about asking the driver to wait for her. Not wanting to generate unwanted attention, though, he refrained from doing so.

Turning toward the school, Jana encountered Bill and Cybil on their way out.

"You're heading the wrong way," Bill humored her and laughed. "It's time to go home." Using his index finger, he pointed in the opposite direction. "Home is that way, remember?" Grabbing her by the shoulders, he turned her about.

"Very funny, Mr. smart guy," Jana told him with an inevitable smile before explaining what had just transpired. "I still wish I could get this book to him."

"Maybe you can," Bill apprised her. "My family might be going to The Gulf for a picnic tomorrow afternoon. Why don't you come with us if we do? We're planning to stop at Dwight's anyway to surprise him with an invitation."

"That sounds like fun!" Jana jumped at the opportunity. "I just hope the weather is nice."

"That's why we're not sure about going," Bill told her. "It's supposed to rain this weekend."

Sometimes it seems as though certain plans are meant to take place, for when the next day arrived, the skies were basically clear and bright.

Being the pleasant day that it was, Bill and Cybil decided at noon to walk the few blocks to Jana's home to inform her that the picnic was going to be held after all. It was Mrs. Rossi who greeted them at the front door.

"Jana just went upstairs to her room," the woman told them as they entered the foyer. "Would you care for a refreshment while you wait for her? It's rather warm today."

"That'd be nice," Bill spoke up as Cybil nodded her head.

"Would lemonade be alright?"

"Yes," they each replied.

"I'll have Alice serve you then," she stated while making her way toward the kitchen. "You can go into the living room to sit down if you like."

Bill and Cybil heeded her suggestion. Then, only seconds after being served their lemonade, Jana and her mother entered the room to join them.

"You're here about the picnic, aren't you?" Jana swiftly asked.

"We sure are," Bill told her. "It's still on."

"Good! I've got Dwight's book right over here." She made her way to the end table beside the couch and picked it up.

"Is that the boy we talked about before?" her mother anxiously inquired while seating herself.

"Why... yes, mother," Jana uneasily responded as she recalled the day in which she first spoke of Dwight to her parents. And then there was that day only a few weeks earlier when her parents revealed what they knew of her relationship with Dwight based upon what Cynthia had told them. "You must stop associating with him," they cautioned her in earnest. "He's not right for you." But Jana felt they were wrong in what they asked of her, and so ignored their advice.

"Oh... I see," her mother reacted with obvious disapproval. Then, after a brief silence, she said, "I've got to go to the kitchen to discuss something with Alice." Standing up, she nodded at Bill and Cybil before regarding Jana. "I'd like to speak with you alone, dear, and before you leave this house."

"Yes... of course, Mother," Jana said while lowering her eyes.

"Is something wrong?" Cybil inquired when Mrs. Rossi was no longer in the room.

Jana made her way to a chair that was situated close to where

Bill and Cybil were seated. As she lowered herself to it, one could see that she was in a state of pressing thought.

"I never wanted you to know that my parents don't want me to associate with Dwight," she relayed to them. "It's solely based on prejudice, so I'm not eager to admit it to anyone. You see, they think he's not good enough for me."

"But my family and Cybil's aren't as financially well off as yours, if that's what you're referring to, yet we remain friends," Bill pointed out.

"It's different for us, though," Jana sought to explain. "We met so young. We've been friends since kindergarten. Now that I'm closer to womanhood, my parents want control of my social life. Appearances mean a lot to them. They not only want to approve of my new friends, Bill. They want to choose them. And if I ever marry, they're going to want the man to be wealthy and of high social standing."

"Jana, in your description of your parents, you seem to be accusing them of high class snobbery," Cybil interjected.

"Indeed I am," Jana dared to acknowledge.

"But maybe your parents would feel differently about Dwight if they met him," Bill suggested. "If they liked him, it could make a difference in their outlook."

"Perhaps, but they're impressed by status, and since Dwight isn't from a family of prestigious standing, and believe me they know all the names, I don't think they'd approve of him. Or maybe I should say my father wouldn't. My mother seems to think it's her obligation to go along with whatever he decides even if she doesn't like it, though she'd be hard-pressed to admit it."

"Bill may still be right, though," Cybil optimistically pointed out. "Time could work a miracle. Circumstances have been known to change."

Regarding her warmly, Jana said, "I hope so, because I don't want to argue with anyone, least of all my parents."

Detecting the extent of her troubled bearing, Bill sought to cheer her up by saying, "I think it might do you some good to get away from Fulton. You'll love The Gulf."

"Oh, yes, I know I will," Jana rebounded in spirit. "It's so close, and yet I rarely get there."

"Then it's about time you changed that," Cybil urged her. Turning her attention to Bill, she stated, "I think we better get going. Time is ticking away."

"Ya, I told my parents I wouldn't be gone long." Getting up, he said to Jana, "We'll pick you up around two."

"I'll be ready," she assured him as they proceeded to make their way into the foyer.

Bidding her friends farewell, Jana barely had the opportunity to reenter the living room before her mother walked in to join her.

"Please sit down, dear," she spoke up with urgency.

"Alright," Jana said, and obediently complied with her request.

When Mrs. Rossi had situated herself adjacent to her daughter, she wasted no time in saying, "I guess you're just too young to see the error of your ways where that boy is concerned."

"Mother, please, let's not go through that again!" Jana pleaded in fast approaching exasperation.

"Oh, I'm sure you don't mean to upset your father and I when you go against our wishes." She reached out to grab Jana's hand. "But that boy just isn't right for you."

"How can you make that judgment!" Jana exclaimed while drawing away from her. "You haven't even met him!"

"Listen to reason, Jana," her mother beseeched her. "I do know you should be associating with people who are more your type. Surely you can understand that."

"No, mother, I frankly can't!" Jana rebounded with a disheartened sigh. "We've talked of this before, and I told you then that I fully intend to remain friends with Dwight. He's someone I enjoy being around. You should be happy for me instead of trying to tear us apart."

As though Mrs. Rossi had not heard a word her daughter uttered, she solemnly reminded her, "Your father will be very upset over this."

"I can't help that!" Jana cried out in near tears while standing. Ardently she proclaimed, "Dwight's got more character than you realize! You'd have to meet him to see that for yourself!" She breathed in deeply for the added strength to endure the conversation.

"Now if you don't mind, mother, I've got to get ready to go on a picnic!" Walking to the end table, she grabbed Dwight's biology book. "I'll see you later." And with that she headed for the door.

"Wait, Jana! Please don't leave like this!" her mother implored her while standing.

Jana delayed her exit.

"You aren't giving me much choice," she stated with her back to her. "Are you forbidding me to go on that picnic? Because if you are, I guess I'll be forced to stay home."

"No... of course not," her mother capitulated in a rush of guilt. "But I'm asking you not to go for the sake of all concerned."

Turning to face her, Jana boldly contended, "You know something, mother. You don't have me fooled. You're really not the person you pretend to be. I think you often speak father's wishes instead of your own. You believe it's your duty. I don't think you feel free to be yourself. I'll never live that way, because I know all too well what it does to a person. All I have to do is look at you to be reminded." With that being said, she tearfully exited the room.

Mrs. Rossi slowly lowered herself to a sitting position in response to her daughter's chastising words, for they were words which carried a stark element of truth. And yet even though she knew this, and even though she secretly respected her daughter for her ability to perceive what the truth really was, she had avoided the truth for so many years out of deference to her husband that it was to the point of becoming an established routine. ... But the price had been a high one to pay in that it was not conducive to rising above the dissatisfaction of living that way.

* * *

It was nearly two thirty by the time the Willards pulled into the Enharts' driveway.

"So this is where Dwight lives," Jana fondly stated. "It's a rather quaint looking little house, isn't it?"

"I think so, too," Mrs. Willard agreed.

"You really don't have to rush back to the car, Jana," Mr. Willard told her once she had exited from the back seat with

Dwight's book. "You'll be glad to know I've decided to wait for you." Broadly he grinned.

Jana laughed over his remark, for she did appreciate a sense of humor. Then, on a serious note, she said, "I only hope Dwight's home."

"So do I!" Sandy spoke up from the back seat. "Don't forget to ask him if he wants to go to the beach with us."

"I won't," Jana assured her.

Walking toward the house, Jana witnessed a sudden discomfort she could not fathom the significance of. As a result of this sentiment she momentarily delayed her knock on the door. It was Clair who confronted her as she entered the kitchen.

"Hello, my name is Jana Rossi," she quickly introduced herself while stepping forward.

"I know who you are!" Clair coldly responded, having recognized her from school.

Jana overlooked the girl's unfriendly attitude and said, "I'm here to give Dwight this book." She held it up. "He forgot it in school and we've got a test on Monday."

"Oh, how noble of you," Clair derided her. "Just put it on the table." With brazen disregard she turned around to finish some dishes she had been washing as though Jana were no longer there.

"Ah, excuse me.... I'd like to see Dwight," Jana pressed on with steadfast determination.

"Oh, is that so?" Clair retorted while swinging about. "Well, he's up in his room. If you wanna see him, you can get him yourself."

For a moment or two Jana looked at her with fast approaching irritation.

"Why do you resent me?" she asked her then.

"I've seen you with my brother in school," she purposely avoided the gist of her question, given that she had no rational reason for disliking her. "I suppose you think you know him pretty well."

"Where his character is concerned, yes, I like to think so," Jana admitted.

"But what of his past?" Clair pressed on. "Has he told you about that?"

"What are you getting at?" Jana asked, not knowing that

Dwight had overheard this last comment from the kitchen doorway.

"Jana!" he exclaimed at the sight of her. "I had no idea you were here, too! I just saw the Willards' car from my bedroom window!" Realizing the awkward situation he was in, he lowered his eyes.

"I came here to give you your book," Jana wasted no time in saying. Walking to where he stood, she handed it to him. "The Willards gave me a ride here. They're going to The Gulf for a picnic and want you to come along. I do, too." She regarded him so tenderly that even Clair sensed she had a concern for him which couldn't be shattered.

In a matter of seconds an expression of relief shone on Dwight's face. Yet then just as he was about to speak, his mother entered the room in her robe. Without even attempting to address Jana she made her way to the refrigerator and opened the door. Her appearance was unkempt, and a burning cigarette twirled smoke up into the air from where it rested between her fingertips.

"Looks like I'm running low on beer," she said while removing one of the few remaining cans and opening it. Then, just as she was about to leave the room, Clair stated, "Mother, wouldn't you like to meet Dwight's girlfriend? She's such a nice girl!" She stressed her words sardonically, inducing Dwight to again lower his gaze in embarrassment.

"Girlfriend?" She was hard pressed to stifle a ridiculing laugh. "I suppose you go to school with him."

"Yes... I do," Jana stammered as she became disagreeably astonished by the woman's rudeness. "I'm pleased to meet you," she politely stated nonetheless while extending her hand.

"Likewise, I'm sure," she indifferently replied without reciprocating the gesture. Then, while sipping her beer, she exited the room.

Perplexed by her untoward behavior, Jana momentarily looked to Clair before shifting her attention to Dwight.

"Now if you don't mind, I've got to do these dishes!" Clair suddenly blurted out while walking to the door and opening it.

Paying her no attention, Jana continued to regard Dwight.

"Well, are you going to come with us or not?" she asked.

Raising his eyes to meet hers, Jana had no trouble detecting within his glassy stare the shame he felt over his family's conduct.

"I'd like to go with you," he confided in a low tone of voice. "I'll take this book up to my room first." With a gait that mirrored an escape, he departed.

"Aren't you the persistent one?" Clair irately reacted by slamming the door shut.

Observing her, Jana felt justified in saying, "Now I'm beginning to understand why Dwight's so withdrawn."

"If you're blaming others for his personality problems, you've got a lot of nerve!" Clair retaliated. "He can blame himself for what ails him, nobody else!"

"I'm not talking about blame," Jana told her. "But it seems to me there's a lot of anger in this house, which isn't beneficial to anyone." As Clair rolled her eyes back in disgust, she went on to emphasize with eloquent conviction, "Don't you see, he's suffering because of it. And yet, despite that, he isn't bitter, which may well be his path to freedom."

Clair was not receptive to Jana's insight. In fact she was just about to utter something nasty when Dwight came rushing into the room with a summer jacket on.

"Let's go," he told Jana with an enthusiasm that amazed her plenty, given the scope of what happened just moments earlier. What Jana did not realize, however, was that he had acquired the ability to bounce back from adversity relatively quickly as a survival mechanism. Even Dwight found it difficult to recognize this trait within himself, the resilience salvaged from hardship.

"Yes, let's go," Jana replied in gladdened relief over his zeal.

Walking away, Clair jealously delivered a final look of resentment their way. Their prevailing hold on optimism she could see and envy, but not understand.

* * *

The Willards were pleased to once again spend time with Dwight.

Shortly after eating, while everyone was still seated on the beach, Mrs. Willard spoke of something the entire family had discussed the day before.

"We've decided to come to the beach as often as possible on nice weekends throughout the summer to see you," she informed Dwight with a smile. "I only hope you can find the time to be with us on those occasions."

In his gratitude Dwight observed all who were seated about him on the sand. To be so cared about; what a good feeling. How he was growing to cherish being in their company.

"I'll find the time," he emphatically stated. "Thank you." Looking to Jana, he could tell that she desired to attend the gatherings whenever possible, for her eyes conveyed her willingness to do so.

Now one might have thought Dwight would be able to relax on a permanent basis in the presence of these people, yet when they decided to play a game of volleyball, he felt a flood of unease enter his emotions. But the intensity of that unease paled in comparison to days gone by, a sure sign that he was well on his way to becoming a confident individual.

"You can be on my team, Dwight!" Sandy told him while her father and Bill set up the net a short ways off. Jumping up and down in her excitement, she added, "This is gonna be fun!"

Dwight could appreciate the girl's robust enthusiasm.

"Alright, if you wish," he obliged her. "I'll do my best."

"That's the spirit," Jana declared while tossing him the ball. Grinning with anticipation, she added, "We're going to be on opposite teams."

"Oh, boy, I think our team had better do a little practicing then!" Dwight stated with such dramatic emphasis that it sparked laughter on the part of they who heard him.

To begin the game, Sandy served the ball, and although Dwight was a bit edgy at first, it soon graduated into pure enjoyment. How good it felt to be genuinely at ease. It enabled him to understand that it was participation, free of constraints, which made a person a winner at this sort of thing, not their skill at the game or the outcome of the score. He would not speak of this to the Willards, though, for he knew they were already aware of it.

It was after the game ended in a victory for Jana's team that Dwight decided to take a walk down the beach, assuring everyone he wouldn't be gone long.

"I'll go with you!" Sandy volunteered. "Can I, mom and dad?" A hopeful glance was directed their way.

"I don't know. It's up to Dwight," Mr. Willard told her before looking to him for approval.

"Ya, she can come along," Dwight said, for he did not want to disappoint the girl.

Sandy jumped to her feet with an exuberance Dwight found appealing. She was therapeutic to be around, a reminder of the extent to which a person can savor life.

In the ensuing moments, as they walked along the shoreline, Dwight listened as Sandy spoke of how much she was looking forward to receiving the baby chicks, and of other things such as school and her friends. Every now and then he would speak up with a "That's nice," or "Is that so?" But in truth he was in no mood to converse with her right now.

"I think I'll sit for a while," he stated when they were nearly three fourths of the way to the place where they had met. Plopping down, he breathed in some fine fresh air. "I want to look at the ocean."

"Sometimes I like to do that, too," Sandy told him, "but right now I'd like to go down the beach to look for shells."

"Okay," Dwight complied. "But be careful. Remember what happened that other time."

"You should know by now that I could never forget that day," she related in a manner that was indicative of her enduring appreciation. With that having been so aptly mentioned, she proceeded on her way.

Dwight had not been seated very long when he noticed Jana approaching in the distance. He presumed she wanted to speak to him in private, for after being in the presence of his mother and sister, he could well imagine her curiosity regarding his home life.

"I hope you don't mind my following you," she said when she was nearly upon him. "But I thought you might like to talk."

"You know I don't mind," Dwight expressly told her. "Please sit down." He motioned to the side of himself with his eyes.

Doing as he recommended, Jana beheld him with a pensive look.

"I suppose you're wondering about a great many things," he noted.

"Just say whatever you want," she stated as a gentle breeze blew back a few tresses of her dark hair. "I came here to be of help in any way I can."

"I believe you," he avowed with a heartfelt gaze, after which he drew in a deep breath before imparting, "I do want to tell you some things about my life. I feel you have the right to know, because you've proven yourself to be my friend."

"Thank you," she responded. "I'm listening."

At first Dwight searched his mind for the right approach to his confession. Then he said in slightly labored words, "You saw how my mother and Clair were today, and I'm sure you didn't like it, but there is a reason for it."

"Maybe a reason, but it can't be a good one," Jana could not seem to prevent herself from asserting.

"Please, let me finish first," Dwight surprised her by saying with an unusual degree of authority. "You don't know all the facts."

"Okay," she humbly abdicated and kept quiet.

Dwight looked out to sea for inspiration. Then he spoke in a tone of voice that seemed to reflect a growing relief in the knowledge that he was confiding in her at long last.

"When I was a little boy my family was quite happy. In fact, the Willards remind me of what we once had." Briefly he looked in their direction before turning seaward once again. "My father was a fine man. He used to take me to this very beach and we'd laugh and fish and run in the waves. We had a very good relationship." Now came the difficult part to reveal. "But when I was nine years old, my father went to work one morning and never came home. We figured he may have had an accident, so my mother phoned the police that evening, but they never found him, only his abandoned car." A short interlude now ensued, one which involved the sound of the breeze, and the ripple of the waves upon the shoreline. Then he again continued speaking.

"After a while my mother's sadness changed to bitterness, especially when she heard rumors that my dad abandoned us. As the years went by she began to believe she could never trust again. She even encouraged Clair to feel as she does." Looking to Jana, he saw that her eyes had become clouded by tears. "My mother doesn't have faith, and it's destroying her life. She and Clair target me to abuse because of the anger they feel toward my father. That's why they despise me so much."

"I'm so sorry," Jana nearly whispered. "I hardly know what to say. ... Do you ever feel any resentment toward your family?" she soon felt compelled to inquire.

"I used to, but not any more," he confessed. "Where my father is concerned, I don't feel I have a right to draw any conclusions, because I don't even know all the circumstances behind his disappearance. Even if he did abandon us, though, I wouldn't hate him. I know God wouldn't want me to. ... And as for my mother and Clair, well, even though I don't like how they think, I know they're hurting, and that's what sticks in my mind the most. More than anything I feel sorry for them, because they don't seem to realize that my father's disappearance hurt them much less than the pain they've inflicted upon themselves needlessly."

At first Jana gazed at him in near disbelief.

"You're too understanding to be true," she found herself saying then. "Now I can see why you're able to overlook the way Sara and Carl treat you."

"It's because I know how badly off they are. But I could never get them to admit that of themselves, not now anyway. They'd just laugh in my face. Yet maybe some day, with the right approach, someone will get them to see the light."

"I think it just might be you," Jana felt disposed to predict. .... "Dwight, why do you think kids from the same family turn out so different?" she then asked of him. "You and your sister are like night and day."

Dwight thought about her question for awhile. Then he said, "I think it's a combination of things, but mainly I think it has to do with how we interpret what we're exposed to. Clair and I both have good memories and bad memories, and yet we drew such different conclusions about life." Regarding her directly, he added, "I sometimes wonder if Sara and Carl have any good memories. Maybe they don't." In the sobering thought of that prospect he lowered his head.

"Dwight, I've never known a person like you before. I know

that the Willards have positive attitudes, but they have a close family. I just want you to know how honored I feel to be your friend. I felt drawn to you ever since that first day I laid eyes on you." Ever so gently she touched his arm.

Warmly holding her in his sight, Dwight told her, "I remember so well the way you looked at me when Carl bullied me that first day of school. I felt then that you cared, really cared. It was rather amazing to me at the time because you didn't even know me." With utmost certitude he added, "I'll always value your friendship. .... And yet, I'm beginning to see that God is my best friend, my main strength. Without him I'm nothing."

"Dwight, I didn't realize how religious you are," Jana emphasized.

"I am, though I try to see beyond religion," he earnestly stated. "I see myself as an aspiring Christian. Years ago I think my mother was headed in that direction, but right after my father disappeared she began to turn away from God. Oh, I know no one's the perfect Christian. I mean who amongst us will ever attain the perfection of Christ? Yet her faith was so easily shattered, and she was bold enough to think it was God who abandoned her instead of the other way around." If ever a confession saddened the eyes of the revealer, this was the epitome of it. Truly it could be said his aim was not to disparage his mother.

"What an insightful way you have of looking at things," Jana remarked.

In the ensuing moments, as Jana reflected on the way in which her parents felt about Dwight, she grew a bit troubled. *Dare I tell him*, she wondered. *Yes, I must*, she then decided, believing the truth should no longer be avoided on her part either if additional progress was to be had in their relationship.

"Dwight, I just recalled an unpleasant fact I think you have a right to know about," she thus maintained.

"What is it?" he asked with keen interest.

At first Jana formulated her thoughts a bit further. Then she stated, "As you know, sometimes friends have to admit certain truths to one another, and since you've done so with me, I should do so also."

"Alright," he responded. "I'm listening."

"It's... my parents. They don't want me to associate with you," she said with difficulty. "They say you're not the type of friend I should have because.... well, they say you're just not right for me." Having made that revelation, she grew silent in her reluctance to admit the full extent of their prejudice, for she did not want to say anything painfully unnecessary to get her point across, her concern for his feelings, her empathy for him, being pronounced enough to prevent her from doing so. And yet Dwight was so wanting of a clearly defined reason for her parent's outlook that he inquired, "Is it because of social standing?" As Jana slowly nodded her head in her ongoing reluctance to admit the truth, he stated with grave acceptance, "Try not to be upset for my sake. I'm far from the only person who's been confronted by that sort of thing."

"But you don't seem to understand! They don't want us to associate with one another in any way, shape, or form!" she candidly announced.

"I know what you're saying, and I don't like how they feel," Dwight sought to explain, "but I can accept what I don't like. Sometimes you have to. Not only that, what you told me doesn't really come as a surprise. I suspected they felt that way for some time now."

"But how is that possible? You never even met them," Jana was quick to make mention of.

"That's why I felt that way. If they had wanted to meet me, you would have invited me over to your house by now," he astutely brought to her attention.

Impressed by his reasoning, Jana readily released a smile.

"You never cease to amaze me," she told him.

"Someone you know could say the very same thing about the girl sitting beside him," Dwight alleged with a returned smile. As Jana made it evident she appreciated his reference to her, he ultimately advised her, "Try not to worry about me. I think I can handle your parents' feelings. At least I hope I can."

"Maybe I can, too," she acknowledged with the optimism he had encouraged her to believe in. "And really, when it gets right down to it, our friendship can't be ruined by anyone if we're determined to prevent it from happening."

"How true," Dwight concurred. "But let's be sure to associate for the right reasons, you know, because we're friends, not in defiance of anyone who doesn't want us to be together. There's so many hardened hearts in the world, and I don't want us to follow in those footsteps."

"I'll try to remember that," Jana replied. .... "Gee, I'm glad you forgot your biology book in school Friday."

"Me, too," Dwight was quick to say. "Maybe this conversation was meant to take place after all."

"I like to think so," Jana inferred in her delight over the strides made in their relationship on this day.

So what was in need of being said had been said. And the truth had set them free. .... Therefore as the sun shed its golden rays across the calm ocean waters, the sight of two friends sitting side by side was a striking image to behold.

CHAPTER 12

CHICKS AHOY

In all honesty Scott was not a satisfied person, and even though it would have surprised a great many people to know he suffered in silence, it was indeed the case. Try as he may, his popularity in school, as well as the community at large, had not and could not abate his inner wants and needs. Least of all could his inflated ego, which had further complicated his life by triggering exaggerated expectations of what he should be in the eyes of the people.

Seated on the living room sofa, he reflected on his life and grew disturbed over his inability to feel content with his accomplishments. *I should feel great!* he pressed his mind. After all, he was a skilled athlete who had proven his talent. He was someone popular enough to attract most any girl he desired. And yet he felt so ungratified, as though always something was missing. Fulfillment had become an elusive dream, and it was because he knew not the limited value of earthly gains.

So wrapped up in thought was he that he did not even stir when his father entered the living room by way of the back door.

"Hi, son," the man sounded out as he placed his trench coat and briefcase upon the desk.

"Oh... hi, dad," Scott stated in delayed response. "How was your day?"

"Demanding as usual." Collapsing on a lounge chair, he loosened his necktie. "I'm bushed."

"You look it," Scott told him. "You've been really busy lately, though."

"That's for sure. ... But you've been taking it easy ever since the football season ended," he suddenly felt predisposed to focus upon.

"Maybe a bit," Scott was reluctant to admit. "But I do keep busy most of the time with chores and schoolwork."

"But that's no excuse, Scott, and you know it!" the man adamantly rebounded with an aroused sense of purpose. "I've been through this myself, don't forget, so I know you're not gonna stay in good shape year round unless you keep at it. As far as I'm concerned it's a must."

"But..."

"There's no buts about it!" he pressed on. "If you want to stay on top and dominate, you've got to stay in good shape! Remember that, Scott!" For the added emphasis he repeatedly slammed a clenched fist into the palm of his hand.

For a few moments Scott eyed his father in growing unrest, the benefits of training being understood and accepted, but not the non-relenting task of living up to impossible ideals. Deep-rooted misconceptions had become the strain of both father and son. Never, not once, did Scott ever recall his father telling him to participate in football for the sportsmanship of it. It was always that he must dominate, he must be a winner, or he'd be a loser at life.

"Okay, dad, I'll think of something to do, maybe running," Scott finally sought to appease him by telling him exactly what he wanted to hear, for he had learned that whenever his father ranted and raved, it was the only way to satisfy him.

"And exercises, sit-ups, push-ups, the whole bit!" his father insisted. "And you've got those weights I bought you in your room! Take advantage of 'em!"

"Sure, dad, anything you say," Scott obediently went along with the man's wishes.

"And don't ever forget, Scott, how important winning is," he continued in a most emphatic of manners.

Scott looked away in a wave of disconcertion, sensing something was ever so wrong. What was the proper perspective of things? He had a desire to know. He didn't realize it, but his father had not been comfortable either by similar demands placed upon him when he was a boy. Yet sometimes a disliked attitude is repeated when it's taught, a better way never having been presented or perhaps believed. We live in a world where constrained emotions are often camouflaged by a false sense of security? How does the incentive for discovering the truth about life come into play when one isn't even encouraged to seek that truth, when honest self-examination is frowned upon by a father? There is a thing called override, which beckons the heart of man. Through it we can open the door to enlightenment. We are not abandoned without hope.

* * *

Dwight had been known to get excited over the birth of a living thing; and so, upon his arrival home from school on the day that the chicks were to hatch, he rushed over to the O'Maleys' farm to survey the situation.

"Are there any little ones yet?" he eagerly inquired of Mr. O'Maley once he had reached the barnyard.

At first the man merely eyed the winded boy to allow the suspense to mount even further within him.

"I think I heard something this morning when I fed the chickens, lad," he told him then.

Without the utterance of another word Dwight headed for the barn, leaving Mr. O'Maley behind to delightfully laugh over his passion for life's simple pleasures.

Arriving at the chicken coop door, Dwight slowly opened it so as not to disturb the hen with any sudden movements. Then, upon peering inside, he caught sight of three of the fluffiest little birds he had ever seen.

"Oh, wow!" he voiced his satisfaction while making his way in. Eventually lowering himself for a better look, he said, "Can I hold one, mother hen?"

"I hope she doesn't get angry with you," Mr. O'Maley stated from the doorway as he watched Dwight pick one up. "Most hens are cross when they have young." Yet in truth he could tell that some measure of trust had already been established, for the hen did not appear upset in the least. Dwight's daily visits to see to her needs had apparently put her at ease in his presence.

"I don't think she minds," Dwight spoke the man's sentiments. While cuddling the chick to his face, he asked, "Do you think every egg hatched?"

"Well, lad, we'll soon find out," Mr. O'Maley stated, for the hen had just stood up to inspect the condition of her brood. "Well, I'll be darned. It looks like they all did," he determined. "She should be happy now. She has her family."

"Ya," Dwight said while wistfully looking upon them. "A happy little family."

It turned out that there were twelve chicks in all. Dwight had originally taken four eggs from home to place under the hen, but the O'Maleys, much to his gratification, had given him eight more to bring the total to a dozen. A general consensus gave rise to the increased egg count, it being that to deprive the hen of her entire brood would not be the humane thing to do. After all, she did deserve to raise some of her young after putting forth the time and effort to hatch them out.

Dwight was so pleased by the results of the hatch that the following day in school he quickly sought out Jana, Cybil and Bill to tell them what happened.

"We'll probably go to the O'Maleys Saturday afternoon to pick them up if that can be arranged," Bill informed him. "My ma and dad already have plans made for Sunday."

"Alright," Dwight stated. Looking to Jana and Cybil, he added, "You girls will be coming, too, I hope."

"I wouldn't miss it," Jana told him while Cybil nodded her head in agreement. "Just look at you, Dwight," she then made the observation. "You're so outgoing. It's almost as though you're a different person than the one you used to be."

"Sometimes I feel like I am," Dwight contended, hoping that positive strides would continue to be had.

The next day Bill confirmed that his family would be able to make it to Chism on Saturday after all. When the meeting time was set, and the appointed day arrived, Dwight headed for the O'Maleys' just past noon to await the arrival of his friends.

Because the day turned out to be quite hot, Dwight decided it would be a good idea to move the hen into the farmyard with her brood to escape the stuffy barn. It was in the immediate aftermath of having done so that he saw Mr. O'Maley approaching from the house. His dog, Laddie, a good-natured collie that was well-behaved around livestock, was walking ahead of him at a steady gait.

"You certainly got here plenty early, lad," Mr. O'Maley spoke up when he was within hearing range. "Your friends won't be here til two."

"I know," Dwight said as he began to pet Laddie, "but I wanted to see the chicks."

"I had a feeling that might be the reason," he chuckled. "It's nice to have ya here early anyway, my boy."

Dwight did not take for granted the hospitality shown him. Regarding the hen at this time, he asked, "Mr. O'Maley, do you think she'll be upset over losing some of her young?"

"Perhaps a bit at first," the man anticipated. "But animals seem to know it's a harsh world, so they're good at adjusting to losses."

"I think so, too," Dwight surmised without removing his eyes from the brood. "And besides that, she'll still have eight chicks left to take care of." Yet then, in his empathy for his fellow man, he became introspective as he thought about the losses people experience in life. For them recovery was never that easy. For them there could be grief for a lifetime. For them the circumstances behind the loss mattered greatly.

It was a few minutes after two when the Willards were seen pulling into the O'Maleys' driveway. Dwight was sitting beside the barn at the time fanning himself with a small branch he had stripped from a nearby hickory tree.

"It's a hot one today," Mr. Willard commented when he saw Dwight's attempt at relief.

"The thermometer on the barn says ninety three, and it's in the shade," Dwight informed him as Jana and the others approached.

"You look like you're gonna collapse," Jana good-naturedly told him as the O'Maleys exited the house.

"That just might happen," Dwight humored her while standing. "But if it does, I'll expect you to revive me with some cool water."

"And how would you like it administered, with a bucket over the head, or a cup to the mouth?" Jana inquired of him with a mischievous smile.

Dwight could not help but burst out in laughter.

"I'll leave the method up to you," he indulged her by saying.

As Jana inevitably smiled, Dwight pointed to his right near the shade of an old oak tree.

"There's the chicks," he said just as Sandy arrived where he stood. "There's twelve of 'em."

"Oh, Dwight, they're really cute!" she exclaimed while striding forward for a better look. "Can I hold one?" Anxiously she glanced back at him.

"I think so," he stated while making his way to her side. "But I better get it for you." Stooping over, he picked up a fuzzy black one much to the concern, yet tolerance, of the hen.

While Sandy nestled the chick to her cheek, Jerry asked if he, too, could hold one. Granting his request, Mrs. Willard thanked Dwight for what he had done.

"It was my pleasure," he sought to convince her. "I like doing this sort of thing." Noticing the O'Maleys standing in the background, he stated while stepping forward, "Please meet some good friends of mine, the O'Maleys. I wouldn't have been able to accomplish this had it not been for them."

After an exchange of the usual amenities, Mrs. Willard uttered, "We've been looking forward to meeting you. Any friend of Dwight's is bound to be of interest to us."

"We feel the same way," Mrs. O'Maley replied. "We're glad to have him back in our life." Before anyone could inquire what she meant by that, she added, "Would you like to come inside for refreshments? This weather makes one thirsty."

"That'd really hit the spot," Mr. Willard gladly accepted her offer. "I'm parched." On that note the others agreed.

Walking toward the house, Sandy made it evident she was enthused about the chicks. In fact she wouldn't even stay indoors to drink her lemonade. Instead, with glass in hand, she took to the barnyard to observe the hen and her brood as they scratched the ground for any food they happened upon.

About a half hour later, when everyone had returned outside, Dwight was assigned the task of selecting four of the chicks for Sandy to take home. Before doing so, he led everyone behind the house to see the ducks, followed by a stop at the corral for an introduction to Zuzueca, who ate up the attention given him with great relish.

When the four chicks had been placed in the small box Sandy brought along especially for them, Dwight handed the container over to her while stressing the importance of taking good care of them.

"Don't worry, I will," she wholeheartedly assured him as the hen clucked in agitation.

"Sandy is pretty reliable about such things," Mr. Willard vouched for her. "They'll be well taken care of, Dwight."

"Ya, I remember how she doted over those chicks we got last spring," Bill laughed. "She practically lived with them and probably would have if she had been allowed."

"Well, I liked them," Sandy mildly protested amongst the mirth.

"Gee, I guess I didn't have to tell you anything then," Dwight stated while yet smiling. "I'll try to stop by to see them some day. And hopefully soon."

"Oh, yes, you have to!" Sandy fervently insisted.

Considering everything she witnessed, Jana felt fortunate to be here, for her parents had not encouraged her to foster an appreciation for either domestic or wild forms of animal life. Hence she saw herself as being deprived. And yet, better late than never to become aware of these things, she told herself. Better late than never to be in touch with life as Dwight and Sandy seemed to be.

* * *

The thought of summer vacation had its good points and its bad points as far as Dwight was concerned. Certainly he would be getting a much desired reprieve from the pressures associated with school, yet he would not be seeing his friends nearly as often, which saddened him a great deal.

On the last day of school Jana sensed what Dwight was feeling.

She knew, however, that they would at least be able to see each other once in awhile, which helped to appease her.

"You know something, Jana, the past school year at times seems surreal to me," Dwight pointed out to her later in the morning in between classes. "It seems like I met you so long ago, and that I've aged four years in nine months."

"And yet it was only yesterday," Jana intimated. "Sometimes it's surreal to me, too, I guess."

"All I know is last September I never thought I'd be disappointed in any way to see this day come, and yet I am." Regarding her warmly, she so readily saw what he was revealing about their relationship that the use of additional words was not the least bit necessary.

Later, during lunch hour, Dwight seized the moment, noticing that no one was any too talkative. Yet more so than ever it applied to him in his poignant mood.

When the final bell rang to herald the beginning of summer vacation, Jana, Bill and Cybil made sure to it that they bid Dwight farewell at the bus stop.

"I'll look forward to going to the beach with you on Sundays," Dwight told them as his bus came to a complete halt a few feet ahead of him. "And whenever I'm able, I'll try to get to your house, Bill."

"You had better," Bill urged him. "My family expects it, especially Sandy."

In his appreciation Dwight nodded his head. Saying good-bye, he started for the bus, yet before he could even arrive at its door, he was pushed aside by Sara as she barged in front of him.

"Watch where you're going!" she hollered while turning to face him. "Can't you see, or what!"

"I'm sorry," Dwight unconsciously took the blame. "I didn't mean...."

"Oh, sure, sorry!" she boldly pressed on. "Who cares that I might have gotten hurt!"

"Just leave, Sara," Jana tersely advised her. "You're overreacting."

For a few moments Sara defiantly eyed Jana before focusing her attention on Dwight once again.

"Watch where you're going from now on!" she sternly concluded before boarding the bus amongst the curious glances of students passing by.

Without taking on embarrassment, Dwight watched her departure.

"She's so miserable," he felt justified in saying. "What's to become of her?"

"Try not to let her bother you," Bill encouraged him. "I think she's angry with the world."

"I'm not all that upset for myself," Dwight let it be known. "Not any more. You see I'm not about to let her defeat me, because if I do, I lose, and that's no longer acceptable." Once again gazing in the direction of her departure, he added with a seemingly serious overtone, "But I really do wonder sometimes if she could turn a herd of stampeding elephants by her very presence. I mean it might only take one look." He shook his head and widened his eyes for the added emphasis.

So caught by surprise were Jana, Bill and Cybil over his comment that at first all they could seem to do was stare at one another as though a bit stunned. Then they burst into laughter, a laughter which they tried, but failed, to stifle.

"Dwight, I didn't realize your sense of humor could be like this!" Cybil found herself exclaiming. "I would never have expected it of you!"

"What can I say? A person can only take so much," he responded with a clear attempt at coping. Yet on a sober note, he brought to their attention, "Don't get me wrong. I'll always find her behavior disturbing, but I remember once hearing that humor can be therapeutic, and who doesn't need therapy from time to time."

"How true," Cybil concurred with a lingering smile.

With good-byes once again being voiced, Dwight boarded the bus and waved to his friends from the window by which he sat. It was at this precise moment that Jana thought about his resilience, a resilience that enabled him to thwart the attacks of spiteful people through various methods, even humor.

"He really has changed, Jana," Bill spoke up as the bus began moving down the road. "You've done something for him."

"Only because he let me," Jana humbly acknowledged her limitations. Looking in the direction of the departing vehicle, she further stated, "Because you and I both know, Bill, that a person can't be forced to be what we think they should be. He's chosen to uplift himself." At the mention of that they proceeded homeward in high-spirited conversation, all three of them seeming to comprehend that a humanitarian interest in one's fellow man benefits all concerned in the long run.

CHAPTER 13

RUNNING SCARED

It was as early as the following Wednesday evening that Dwight was idly walking down Kirkland Road in a thought-consumed frame of mind. Already he found himself deeply missing the companionship of his friends now that school was no longer in session.

As he approached the road that led to the O'Maleys' farm, he contemplated paying the couple a visit before opting to head in the direction of The Gulf with the intention of taking a swim. How he was anticipating the arrival of next Sunday, for rain the previous weekend had cancelled the outing at the beach.

The peaceful sounds of the world around him did not escape his notice, sounds such as the distant tune of a songbird and the gentle rustle of leaves. Arrested by their soothing effects, his attention was not secured by a vehicle approaching from behind. The vehicle was filled, however, with a danger he hadn't anticipated would affect his life this far from school. No, he just didn't consider that Carl, in his obsession to hurt him, would take it upon himself to resort to lengths such as this.

"There he is!" Carl exclaimed from where he sat on the passenger side of the front seat. "Hurry and pull up beside him, Fred!" Anxiously he turned to regard the other boys whom he had asked to come along, namely Scott, Ben, and Sam Harris, the boy who had tried to carry on a conversation with Dwight in the locker room at the beginning of the school year. "The moment I've been waiting for is at hand!"

When Dwight realized there was a car slowing down behind him, he turned to see who was there. At first a mild form of curiosity could be noted on his features as he observed the group of boys pulling up beside him. But then, just as the car came to a complete stop, he caught sight of Carl's menacing stare.

Unable to fathom the amount of fear that swept throughout his body, Dwight stood in a frozen stance. The tension mounted to the point where he actually began to wonder if his life might be in danger.

"Let me at him first!" Carl adamantly told everyone before jumping out. "I told myself I'd get you some day!" he now said to Dwight with gloating arrogance. The distance between them could not have been any more than ten feet. "No one can help you this time!"

In a desperate attempt to dodge Carl's charge, Dwight managed to veer to his left and race into the woods as fast as his two legs would carry him. He ran faster and faster, yet even though he did this, it seemed as though he could hear the many footsteps of his assailants only a few feet behind him. Psychologically speaking, his emotions were overwhelmed by the fear factor, for he had no doubt whatsoever he'd be mercilessly pursued by the group of ill-intentioned boys.

When Carl realized that Dwight was escaping them, he ordered his accomplices to branch out to their right and left. "We'll circle around and trap him!"

Never had Dwight been as fleet of foot as he was on this day, which served him well, for he ruined Carl's strategy by keeping well ahead of everyone.

"Where'd he go!" Carl angrily bellowed when he and the others had united at the base of a gradual upsweep in the terrain. "How did he escape!"

"I guess he runs faster than us," Sam so obviously stated that it swiftly procured a perturbed look from Carl, who had assumed Dwight would never be able to outrun all five of them. "Let's split up and search the area again," Sam therefore suggested in an effort to assuage Carl's inflamed ego.

"Ya, let's just do that!" Carl hissed before darting off to his right in obsessive search of Dwight.

In the meantime, about seventy feet or so up the slope, Dwight sat crouched behind a large tree in fear. *Don't let them find me*, he prayed to God. *Please don't let it happen.* Yet then suddenly his foot slipped on a rock that happened to be lodged under his left shoe, causing it to roll away and alert the boys of his whereabouts.

"There he is!" Sam exclaimed while pointing upward. "Let's get him!"

In a matter of moments the boys were ascending the hill as fast as they could run, forcing Dwight to again take up flight. To his benefit he possessed endurance, in addition to speed, which gave him enough of an advantage to once again frustrate his pursuers, only this time he chose to climb a large oak tree and shield himself in its thick upper branches.

No sooner had Dwight assumed a stationary position in the leafy domain than he heard the advancing footsteps from below. Then suddenly, right before his eyes, stood Carl and Scott beneath him. He knew that if they discovered his hiding place this time around there would be no escaping. But to his relief they merely scanned the forest floor before dashing away to continue their quest elsewhere.

By now Dwight's heart was pounding so loudly in his chest that he wondered if one of the boys might actually be able to hear it. But he refused to move, unwilling to risk discovery and the beating that would subsequently follow.

"Blasted! Where'd he go this time!" he eventually heard Carl yell out in the distance. .... "Someone find him! Keep looking!" he angrily persisted, and spewed forth foul language.

"How on earth did he get away so fast?" Fred remarked in utter confusion. "We weren't that far behind him."

"Ya, but he knows these woods pretty well," Scott reminded him. "He must have a good hiding place."

"Well keep looking!" Carl strongly insisted in his refusal to give up. "I thought we had him for sure!" As a clear indication of the misplaced priorities he had so intimately come to know, he once more resorted to the use of foul language. While doing so, he clenched his fists repeatedly.

For the next few minutes the five boys thoroughly combed the woods, and in that period of time they walked directly below Dwight more than once. Then, finally, after what seemed an eternity in Dwight's estimation, the search was reluctantly discontinued.

"He escaped this time but he can't hide forever!" Carl bellowed as he and the others proceeded to make their way back to the car. "Do you hear me!" he yelled out quite loudly. "I'll be back! You can be sure of that!"

Despite the boys' withdrawal, Dwight still would not budge from his hiding place, for he feared they were lying secretly about just waiting for him to make a move. He, of course, didn't know it, but Scott and Fred were already witnessing pangs of shame and guilt for the part they had played in the foul deed perpetrated against him. Always there are consequences to our actions, and a toll was being exacted for choices made. Yet down the path of life it's far better to experience guilt for a moral transgression than a further hardening of the heart, for from the guilt can be reaped an improved disposition, whereas the hardened heart reaps additional disdain, and increased pain and suffering for the family of man.

Dwight remained in his awkward position for well over an hour. When he finally did muster enough nerve to descend from the tree, he walked cautiously to the road before dashing home to dwell in the safety of his room, feeling as though he was about to awaken from a terrible nightmare.

Sitting on his bed, he looked to the floor with tear-filled eyes. How it did cut like a knife to be so scorned. In his burdened state of mind he foresaw that he would be on guard nearly all the time while outdoors, and it was far from reassuring to anticipate living that way. Something of value, a zone of comfort, had been taken away from him, and so much he wanted it restored, recaptured, reestablished, so that he could again relax whenever he was amongst the territory long considered soothing to his soul, the countryside surrounding home.

* * *

The following Friday evening unveiled the first summer party to be held at Hickory Lake. At this gathering a considerable number of young people were in attendance, many of whom intended to consume the abundant supply of beer on hand. And yet even though at first glance it appeared as though they who were present were at ease in mind and spirit, it was symbolic of the facade that masks the discontent of the world in general, a world filled with individuals searching for fulfillment in ways which cannot possibly procure it.

From where he was seated beside Roberta, a soft spoken, likable girl whom he was with for the first time, Scott noticed the suggestive glances of Ginger, who was seated next to Joe not too far away. So enthralled was he over this girl that he was prompted to return her glances in spite of the presence of Roberta. Such is the way of infatuation, an infatuation that prevented him from seeing the error of his ways.

"Hey, Scott, do ya wanna play a game of volleyball?" Fred suddenly broke his train of thought. "We just put up the net!" He pointed in the direction of a small clearing off to the right of the parked cars.

"Sure," Scott jumped at the opportunity. Regarding Roberta, he asked if she desired to participate in the game.

"No, I don't think so," she responded in a voice which seemed to be that of a younger girl's. For her age, however, she was quite mature in the ways of wisdom. She was the type of girl who sought to determine as best she could the reasons for her choices, and whether those reasons were justified. She was that conscientious. Was it therefore ironic that a girl such as she would be here today? Definitely so, but was it not also understandable that Scott should be drawn to her in the first place? After all, a person sometimes gravitates toward an individual for reasons they cannot recognize. In other words, it may very well have been that Scott was attracted by some quality he saw within her, and that subconsciously he sensed she would be morally advantageous to be in the company of. In the corners of his mind a healthier outlook was the goal he desired, and he may have discerned that Roberta would steer him in the right direction in the attainment of that objective.

Scott anxiously headed for the group of kids who were readying themselves for the match.

"We've still gotta pick teams," Joe shouted just as he joined them.

"Ya, and I suppose everyone will wanna be on mine," Scott dared to assume and laughed.

"If you say so," Joe reacted with a forced smile. Addressing Ginger, who was standing beside him, he asked, "Are you gonna play, too?"

"No, I'd rather not," she told him. "I'd like to talk to Roberta instead to get to know her better."

"Alright," Joe freely accepted her wish, "but you're gonna miss out on a lot of fun!"

Ginger was jealous, so jealous in fact over Roberta's association with Scott that she wanted to injure her in some way. And so, by the time she neared the girl, she was in a very intrusive mood.

"So you're Roberta," she said while casually taking a place beside her on the grass. "It looks as though we're the only ones who aren't playing volleyball."

"So it does," Roberta responded while making a visual sweep of the area. "Don't you feel like playing either?"

"Oh, no, I'd just love to," Ginger overemphasized her interest in doing so. "I'm passing it up to get to know you better. That's all. In school we just know each other by name."

"Yes," Roberta said. "You do know Scott, though, don't you?"

"Why, of course!" Ginger exclaimed as though she were insulted. "Who wouldn't know who Scott is!" Her motive was to find any fault she could in Roberta's comments to get her to feel a false sense of guilt.

"Yes, I suppose most people do know who he is," Roberta had to admit. "But I meant on a personal level."

"Oh, yes, for me even personal," Ginger sought to assure her as best she could.

Intently scrutinizing Roberta at this time, Ginger wondered why Scott would even be seen with a girl as plain as she imagined her to be.

"Tell me, Roberta," she therefore continued, "how did you ever manage to come here with Scott?"

"He called me up and asked me," Roberta informed her in obvious discomfort over her bold line of questioning. "You didn't think

I asked him, did you?"

"No, not at all," Ginger told her with a look of thwarted intent. "It just surprises me that Scott would ask you here, that's all." Shrugging her shoulders a bit, she impolitely added, "I mean he can afford to be choosy."

"Maybe all that choice wasn't what he expected it to be?" Roberta was wise enough to suggest despite her instantly hurt feelings. Yet when Ginger, by way of her body language, expressed only disdain for her opinion, Roberta inquired, "Why are you doing this to me?"

"I'm just trying to let you know where you stand with Scott for your own good," she rudely told her. "You surely must realize you don't stand a chance with him in the long run, don't you?" It was her intention to discourage her from seeing him again by arousing feelings of unworthiness within her.

"You have no right to talk to me that way," Roberta managed to say in calm rebuke. "I happen to care a lot about Scott. I can see how troubled he is deep down. Maybe that's what makes me feel for him so much."

"What do you mean troubled?" Ginger swiftly counteracted with derision. "With his popularity what would he have to be troubled about?"

In response to her narrow view of Scott's life Roberta candidly stated, "He may seem to have it all to you and many other people, but did it ever occur to you that he's really not very happy. I think he's looking for acceptance aside from his achievements on the football field."

"You're crazy!" Ginger told her in growing contempt over the logic she was employing, a logic she didn't understand, and thus was not receptive to. Looking to the group of kids participating in the volleyball match, she added, "I think I'll go enjoy myself!" Getting up, she brusquely concluded, "You're a fool!" Then she began to walk away in her refusal to heed sound logic when she heard it.

Initially Roberta eyed Ginger's departure in mounting dismay. *How can she be so nasty?* she suddenly found herself wondering as she picked up a dry piece of wood that was lying beside her and threw it off to her right. How it seemed that people failed to see Scott in a true light. .... Yet perhaps someday he would see her as his friend, this girl who had his best interest at heart now and for always.

* * *

With the onset of nightfall everyone congregated around a bonfire. It was at this time that ale was consumed at a much faster rate than before darkness struck.

Sitting beside Roberta, Scott, in his obsession over Ginger, conceived a plan to be near her.

"I think I'm gonna be sick," he faked nausea as he got up and stumbled forward a bit in well acted out deceit. "What kind of beer are we drinking anyway?"

"Is there anything I can do for you?" Roberta beseeched him while dashing to his side amongst the humorous glances of kids who sadly did not see drunkenness to be the serious matter that it is.

"No, I just need to get away for a while," Scott sought to convince her in his quest for privacy. "I'll feel better after resting. Go sit down." With that he began to walk away before another word could be said to hold him back.

In the hopes of avoiding any suspicion, Ginger allowed ten minutes to pass before pretensing fatigue.

"Joe, I've got to go to the car to lie down for awhile. I'm so tired." She spoke up loudly enough to be overheard. While yawning, she added, "You don't mind, do you?"

"Are you kidding or what?" Joe reacted in near disbelief. "You always party to the end."

"But I'm serious!" she stated with fast-approaching impatience.

"Okay, I'm sorry," he relented. "If you want, I'll take you home."

"No, it's not that. I just need a nap," she so strongly emphasized that she momentarily wondered if she had inadvertently aroused his mistrust.

"Alright, if you feel that tired, then go ahead," he finally told her much to her relief. "But I must admit I'm surprised."

"I know, but last night I stayed up late. I won't be gone long." Standing up, she walked lethargically away so as to strengthen her contention that she was weary. And Joe believed her to be sincere, for that is exactly what he expected her to be.

* * *

As Scott made out Ginger's silhouette against the light of the fire, his heart sped up its beat.

"So you made it," he whispered when she was standing a few feet beyond him in the clearing. "I was wondering if you'd come."

"I had to be careful," she said while turning to smile in the soft light of the moon. "I've been waiting for this moment."

"Me, too," Scott conceded while walking before her. Gazing into each other's eyes for a few moments, he kissed her passionately.

Was their attraction inherently wrong? Or was it the way in which they went about being together? Their type of interest does not form healthy relationships. But what a common interest it really has been since the dawn of humanity, lust and the temptations of the flesh being what they are. One cannot find happiness at the expense of one's dignity. The distractions of the mind set hinder the fulfillment that can be.

* * *

As is often the case when people are preoccupied, they don't realize how much time has elapsed.

"I'm gonna check on Ginger," Joe spoke up after she had been gone nearly half an hour. Standing up, he gazed at Fred's overindulged form on the ground beside him. "Some people can't handle their drinks, can they?" But no one seemed to be paying him any attention as they conversed amongst one another.

Joe walked to his father's car and tentatively peered inside as though he were afraid he might disturb Ginger. But when he discovered that she was not there, he grew quite concerned. He knew she would not have attempted to walk home, yet as he made a visual run of the dimly-lit area, he could not imagine where she could be.

In his bewildered state of mind he was just about to yell out her name, when suddenly, he detected a slight rustling in the grass just off to his left. At first he barely heeded what he heard. But then, as he made out the sound of voices, his curiosity compelled him to investigate.

Entering the small clearing just beyond the tree line, Joe initially saw nothing. But then, with the light of the moon aiding his vision, he stopped short in utter disgust, for there before his eyes were Ginger and Scott embracing one another on the ground.

It was Ginger who first noticed Joe standing there glaring at them. As she drew away from Scott while letting out an audible gasp, Joe snarled, "Dirty cheating backstabbers! And I thought you were both my friends!" Pouncing upon Scott, he began to punch him in the face and stomach.

"Joe, please stop!" Ginger screamed while immediately getting up.

When it became obvious that Joe was not about to relent, Ginger desperately tried to pull him off Scott.

"Somebody help!" she yelled quite loudly when her efforts proved to be in vain. "Joe, please stop!" Sobbing uncontrollably, she fell to the ground in despair. "Please stop!"

It was only seconds later that Cliff arrived on the scene at a fast gait.

"Get him off of him! He's killing Scott!" Ginger hysterically told him, for by now Scott was unconscious and bleeding at the lips and nose, yet still Joe would not stop beating him in his intense rage, a rage which the alcohol in his system had played a part in compounding.

"That's enough, Joe!" Cliff hollered as he and Fred, who had in the meantime emerged from the darkness, raced over to him. Grabbing him by the arms, they dragged him with great difficulty from Scott's stationary figure.

"Let me at him!" Joe fought back with frenzied strength. "Let me at him!" Yet try as he may he was not able to break free from their detaining grip.

"Come back to the fire!" Cliff harshly reprimanded him. "You need to get a hold of yourself!"

In the ensuing moments Joe continued to try to fight his way free. It was not until he had surrendered his efforts, however, that his wish was granted. As he drew away from his restrainers, Roberta entered the picture.

"Oh, no!" she exclaimed while throwing her hand to her mouth at the sight of Scott's battered form. Rushing to his side, she frantically began to shake him in an effort to revive him.

Without saying a word Joe shifted a repugnant look from Scott to Ginger before trodding past the onlookers who had gathered about. Through each passing moment feelings of betrayal intensified within him. Yet he was far from pleased by his own conduct, for he had resorted to violence to deal with deceit.

Roberta was able to grasp the significance of what happened, yet being the caring girl that she was, coupled by the urgency of the moment at hand, she put her head to Scott's chest where with great relief she heard the thumping of his heart. Tearing a piece of material from her blouse then, she ran to the lake and moistened it with water before returning to Scott's side to dab the blood from his face.

While some of the kids mingled in the clearing, Ginger fled the scene. It was shortly thereafter, as Scott began to regain consciousness under the gentle touch of Roberta's hand, that the spectators proceeded to disperse.

Looking up at Roberta, Scott soon became aware of his surroundings, and in doing so felt ashamed. In his lowly position he realized that he had sacrificed his self-respect tonight. Roberta, on the other hand, had not done so. Indeed it could even be said her behavior was magnanimous.

"Why are you doing this for me?" Scott eventually asked, for in light of what happened, he did not expect benevolence from her of all people.

"Somebody had to do something," she solemnly responded while continuing to dab his face with the cloth. "Just because you're drawn to Ginger doesn't mean I don't care what happens to you."

Although self-centeredness had become rooted in Scott's personality, in the moments that ensued, as he closely watched this girl whose actions so perplexed him, he was persuaded to say with honest conviction, "I'm sorry, Roberta. I don't know what got into me. I thought I'd feel good about what I did.... but instead I feel humiliated."

Roberta did not immediately respond to his comment. Instead she gathered her thoughts before saying with biblical wisdom, "We all reap what we sow to one degree or another, and often learn valuable lessons the hard way." In sober acceptance, she added, "You made your choices." Handing the cloth over to him, she stated, "I think you can take over now. You'd better rinse this out in the lake first, though." Rising to a standing position, she felt an intense longing to be apart from him. "I think it'd be a good idea if I got a ride home with someone else," she therefore apprised him.

"I... guess that's understandable," Scott somewhat reluctantly told her in the realization he was disappointed over the thought of her leaving.

Looking upon him, Roberta felt compelled to say, "Maybe you never learned, Scott, that you can't find happiness in life at the expense of people's feelings, especially your own." With additional emphasis she added, "The irony of it all is that I never even wanted to be at this sort of party with all the drinking going on. My parents would be upset if they knew where I was. I only came here to be with you, but I won't make that mistake again." Hearing someone shout as to whether Scott was alright, she yelled back that she thought he was. Yet when she focused her undivided attention upon him once again, she softly said, "Or maybe on second thoughts you're not alright. Until you learn how a girl should be treated, please don't call on me again. I'm not willing to pay any price for the sake of being with you. You see, it just wouldn't be worth it, because I'd only end up feeling poorly, even worse than I do right now."

Scott was so greatly affected by her direct admission that all he could seem to do was stare at her.

"I'll keep that in mind," he stated then in admiration of her independent constitution.

So upon considering that only minutes earlier Scott yearned to be in the company of Ginger, what a contrast it was that in watching Roberta flee he was saddened in a way which even now he sensed could be of benefit to his emotional well-being. ... But would he feel that way in the long run? Would it be lasting? Would he even feel that way tomorrow?

* * *

Dwight's life took a disturbing turn for the worse. The added burden of living in a state of constant alertness when outdoors took a huge toll. He didn't sleep well and ate rather sparingly, and not merely in response to his robbed peace of mind, but also in the dire knowledge that there were people out there who desired to hurt him, as though he was unworthy of common courtesy and respect. His response to his predicament was far removed from embittered, though, for he was wise enough to realize that you couldn't find a solution to a problem down the path of resentment. That was a fact of life which so many people refused to accept the truth of in their lifelong journey, thinking instead that they could revile anyone who didn't do right by them and reap satisfying results. And yet clearly he required more than a loving attitude toward his fellow man. As an accompaniment to this he was in much need of acquiring assertiveness, for lingering in a state of oppression was a detriment to sound living. But try as he may to be free of the chains which bound him, he remained so traumatized by the recent assault against him by Carl and the others that his bedroom became his refuge for most of the hours of each day since the dreadful attack took place.

Sitting before his window the following Sunday afternoon, he wondered if it was going to be a summer of bitter truths, which disheartened him enough to trigger thoughts of suicide. Yet as he continued his listless gaze out the window, it soon hit him; guilt. After all the love and acceptance his new-found friends had sought to instill in his life, after God had been generous enough to allow him to live in the first place, he had the notion to abandon all hope. Thus he realized in growing humility that God desired he look beyond his despair to the light at the end of the tunnel. The light was there, ever bright, and the strains of this world really were always temporary. Realizing that at the time of tribulation made deliverance all the more foreseeable. But it wasn't easy to be brave enough to live when one was anxious enough to die, he saw to be the case as he made his way to his bed to lie down. No, adopting such fortitude in the midst of adversity was no simple task.

For quite some time Dwight remained on his bed before making his way to his dresser. Removing a Bible from the top drawer, he read from Luke by the light of the window, and felt better. Then, as though in direct consequence to his willingness to endure the burdens of his life, he heard a car pull into the driveway and was filled with gladness over the sight of the Willards.

"Hello!" he yelled out to them from his raised window. However before they could even attempt to respond, he removed himself from sight to grab a beach towel and a pair of shorts.

"I was hoping you'd come!" he told Mr. Willard once he was standing by their car.

"This good weather should be taken advantage of," the man noted while raising his head toward the sun.

In a squatted position Dwight looked upon everyone and addressed them with such cheerful ease that no one would have imagined the extent to which melancholy had consumed him in the past few days.

When all greetings had been returned, Mrs. Willard asked him if he was ready to go with them.

"Very much so," he assured her. Opening the car door, he squeezed into the crowded back seat between Sandy and Jana, whom he was so pleased to see present. "How are the chicks, Sandy?" he asked.

"Oh, they're doing great!" she gladly informed him. "They got so big that I had to get them out of the house a while back. But their being big wasn't the main reason. You see their poopoo was starting to smell too much." And she giggled while wrinkling up her nose.

"Oh, I see," Dwight said while laughing. "I think you did the right thing then."

"So do I," Jana humorously concurred. "It would either be that or drive the entire family out of the house."

"You're something else, Sandy," her father commented as he proceeded to drive down Kirkland Road. "Nobody can accuse you of beating around the bush."

"For sure," Eliza stated with mock disgust. "She's too truthful!"

"Well, I think she expressed herself quite well," Dwight let it be known. "After all, she did attempt to be delicate about it." As he regarded her, he said, "I wonder what your interests will be when you get older."

"Oh, probably something to do with animals," she swiftly told him. "You know, a veter...veterin..."

"Veterinarian," Dwight said. "And you'd probably make a good one, too."

"You wouldn't make such a bad one yourself," Jana pointed out. "From what I've seen you have quite a way with animals."

"I do like them a lot," Dwight had to confess. "I've found that once you've gained their trust, you don't lose it as long as you treat them well. But I guess that isn't so strange," he then went on to say. "It's like that with people, too." In a most intuitive of manners he regarded her.

"You're profound," Jana as a result emphasized with moving conviction.

Dwight allowed silence to ensue on his part. Then, from where she was seated in the front seat, Mrs. Willard asked him how he had been getting along as of late.

"Not too badly," he would only say, for he didn't want to risk putting a damper on the mood of the day. "I've been trying to keep myself busy."

"Good for you. Tell me, how are the O'Maleys?"

"They're doing well," he sought to assure her, even though he hadn't been to their farm since the day before he was attacked by the boys. "And Zuzueca is getting so big. I'm getting quite attached to that horse."

"I could see that when we were at the O'Maleys'," she acknowledged. "And that horse seems to be so good natured, which is always a plus."

As they continued along their way Jana could not help but wonder whether or not Dwight was preoccupied in thought, for she began to sense a certain distraction within him. She would speak of it later, she told herself. And speak of it later she did, for after everyone partook in the meal of the day followed by entertainment in the form of volleyball, fishing, and swimming, she, Dwight, and Sandy decided to take a walk along the beach to broaden their enjoyment of the day.

At first the three of them hardly spoke as they strolled along at a leisurely pace. But when Sandy decided to head down the coastline to scout for shells, Jana took advantage of the opportunity to converse in private with Dwight.

"Something's bothering you," she said without warning. "You're trying to hide it, but I can see that it's there." Her face reflected an elevated yearning to know the truth of the matter.

Looking upon her, Dwight felt comfortable over the thought of confiding in her, this girl who had proven her concern for him.

"I'm not surprised you know something's bothering me," he told her as they slowly continued onward, "but it's so disturbing that I don't think even you could imagine what it is." Looking briefly away, he gravely imparted, "And yet maybe it should come as no surprise to anyone, least of all me."

"My goodness, what happened!" she swiftly asked with an interest that bespoke urgency.

Momentarily Dwight closed his eyes in a wave of emotional unrest. Then he said while gazing upon her, "Last Wednesday, when I was walking down Kirkland Road, I was attacked by Carl. He had some other boys with him, including Scott, I'm sorry to say."

"Oh, no!" Jana gasped. "And Scott was there, too!" She shook her head in dire consternation. "I'm almost afraid to ask, but tell me everything that happened!"

"I'll try," Dwight complied, and as accurately as he could retold the entire incident. Yes, he spoke of how he was approached from behind by the group of boys and chased like his life depended on it. "Ever since it happened I've been so upset that I can't seem to get it out of my mind," he confided. "In fact for a while I even wanted to... die." He strongly stressed this last word with such clear meaning that Jana widened her eyes in stunned response. "Yes, I contemplated suicide," he let it be known. "Are you shocked by that?"

At this juncture Dwight ceased walking. Then, when Jana had advanced a few feet ahead of him, she also stopped. Turning to regard him, she said with difficulty, "Dwight, this may sound selfish to you, but I feel hurt to think you considered sacrificing our relationship."

"But Jana, I'm human and imperfect and at times weak," he readily affirmed. "Yes, I was ashamed by what I felt, because I

knew it meant self-destruction, but when I felt that way I was thinking of unpleasant things, and it seemed as though I would be better
off dead. You see, sometimes when a person's depressed it's hard to
see beyond the gloom. A situation can seem hopeless, futile. You
think you'll never feel good about yourself again, never see a
brighter tomorrow. And when you feel that badly it doesn't give
you much of an incentive to go on living. ... But then I realized that
feelings of hopelessness can pass in time, so I decided to try to be
more thankful for what I have... and to call upon God for the
courage to live. But I'm not aiming to criticize anyone who's been
depressed enough to take their life. In fact I can relate to them."
Slowly turning seaward, he was inspired to add, "But I wish they
had weathered it through."

Jana was struck by the depth of his insight.

"Dwight, I've never had to endure what you have, so I don't
realize how difficult it's been for you, but if you ever feel that
depressed again, please remember how much I care."

Walking closer to her, Dwight openly declared, "You're such a
good friend. Always remember how much I value that." As she
eyed him with warmth, he added, "Try not to worry about me. I
shall overcome. I know that now. Pain is a part of life, but God is
there for us through it all."

Regarding him with ongoing affection, Jana said, "I'm still
learning so much about human emotion just by knowing you. I
hope we've helped one another, because that's how a friendship
should be."

"I agree," he wholeheartedly stated. "When it works both ways
it's so.... mutually beneficial." Looking skyward now, he appeared
to be beseeching God for the added strength to retain hope as an
essential part of his personality.

As the two of them edged their way further down the shoreline,
Jana suddenly recalled the occurrence which had taken place
between Scott and Ginger that previous Friday night, an occurrence
which from what she had heard through the grapevine had been
most unpleasant. After filling him in on the details as she knew
them to be, she commented, "I actually feel sorry for Scott. And
now that I know what he did to you, I realize how troubled he has to

be. I wish I could help him in some way, but we've drifted so far apart it's not likely to happen."

"I don't think Scott likes that we're friends," Dwight made the assertion. "Sometimes I see it in his eyes." When he saw by way of Jana's reaction that he was correct in his view, he further stated, "What's so ironic is that there was a time when I used to envy Scott's outgoing personality, and now I, too, find myself feeling sorry for him. It takes more than the things of this world to satisfy a person." With keen insight he went on to determine, "You and I seem to think a lot alike, don't we?"

"I believe we do at that." In her gratitude over his involvement in her life, she softly smiled as a breeze blew in from the ocean to toss about her flowing hair.

It was only a short time later that Sandy was seen returning from her quest for shells.

"Find anything?" Dwight shouted when he and Jana were about thirty feet away from her.

"Not really too much today," she frowned. "Just a few small shells and a sand dollar."

"Can I see them?" Jana inquired as she and Dwight neared the girl.

"Sure," she complied while lowering her hand into one of her dress pockets.

"Oh, these are pretty, Sandy!" Jana delightfully reacted to the trinkets once they were in her hand. "I have a few shells like this in my bedroom."

"I've got some really nice ones at home, like that conch from last year!" Sandy said with a burst of enthusiasm.

"Oh, ya, I think I heard about that one," Jana said while wryly smiling at Dwight. "Didn't you get help with that?"

"Ya, Dwight...." Noticing the look on Jana's face, Sandy understood the meaning behind her expression. "Oh, you know what happened. Boy, I'd really like to find something like that again!"

"Well, keep looking and you will sooner or later," Dwight encouraged her. "It usually pays off." Yet at the utterance of these words an abrupt change overcame his features as he reflected on the past. "How well I remember searching for shells with my father when we took long walks along this very beach," he stated with nostalgia. "Those were good times."

"Dwight, it sounds like you and your father had a very close relationship," Jana replied. "I'm sure you must..." She stopped short of finishing, for it suddenly dawned on her that Sandy did not know the circumstances behind his life.

"What's wrong?" Sandy was quick to ask over the abrupt transition in Jana's bearing. "Did somebody say something wrong?"

Jana knew not how to respond to the girl's inquiry. Yet just as she was about to say something, anything, Dwight beat her to it by announcing quite candidly, "No, Sandy, nobody said anything wrong. You see, Jana wasn't sure I wanted you to know that my father hasn't been with my family for quite some time, but I do want you to realize that. I want your whole family to know it. It's nothing to be ashamed of, and yet even though I know that, I'm so tired of rumors about his disappearance that I'm reluctant to even talk about him with most people. I guess I don't want to be asked questions I don't have answers for, or listen to speculations about betrayal that have no evidence to back them up. If there was only some type of closure it'd help so much." Looking to Jana with earnest appeal, he added, "I'm hoping Jana will tell your family all that I've told her. I want her to be my spokesperson."

"I'd be honored," she stated. "I would have already done so had I had your permission. I'll tell them later after we drop you off at home."

"Yes, wait until then," Dwight advised her. "I'd rather I wasn't there when you said it. After what happened last Wednesday, I'm not up to answering questions about my dad right now." Noticing the spark of interest in Sandy over his reference to Wednesday, he said, "Jana can explain that to you and your family also if she likes." Shifting his attention down the beach at this time, he suggested, "I think it's about time to start walking back. I don't wanna keep the others waiting if they're ready to leave."

"I'll be there in a little while," Sandy informed him. "I'd like to stay here just a bit longer."

"Alright," Dwight responded. "See ya back with the gang." Freely he grinned at her, this sweet girl who so accepted him for what he was.

When Sandy had resumed her devoted exploration, Dwight said to Jana, "Ya know something, for her age she's more understanding than a great many people."

"I know," Jana assented. Leisurely strolling along their way once again, she eventually asked, "Your mother and sister, are they still the same, Dwight? I mean do they treat you the same?"

Thinking about her inquiry for a few moments, he eventually stated, "They're so consumed by negativity that they generate more of the same. I know it's a harsh world, and that many things happen beyond our control, but their attitudes are by their own choosing." Shaking his head, he honestly added, "So no, they don't treat me any better. They don't treat themselves any better, and until they change their way of looking at things, they're not going to treat life any better."

"I was afraid of that," she said. "It must be so draining on you."

"I'll get by," he optimistically predicted. "Remember, I've got positives in my life, and I know it." In a most telling of ways he cast his eyes upon her.

Jana nudged his arm in reaction to his comment. Then, in due time, she was inspired to say, "If you don't mind my asking, Dwight, how does your family survive financially?"

"My father managed to save up some money, plus he inherited a considerable sum from a wealthy uncle who named him in his will. And my mother worked for a while, but now she.... she does nothing," he said. "There's also a life insurance policy that my father had, but it stipulates that in the event that a claim is made without a body as proof of death, the beneficiary has to wait seven years before collecting the money. Right now it's been six so there's one more year to go, one more year before my father is considered .... dead." In the sober thought of that reality, he ceased his advancement.

"It's only a stipulation, Dwight," Jana sought to instill hope within him. "Your father may still be alive."

"Sometimes I think it'd be harder to accept his being alive and avoiding us than dead with no choice in the matter," he told her. With a note of sureness he added, "I can't imagine he abandoned us. I still trust him, Jana. He must be dead."

"Yet it could also be that he has amnesia," Jana inferred. "It has been known to happen."

"Yes, I know," Dwight stated. "I've wondered about that more than once. You see, I love him enough to give him every option I can think of, every benefit of the doubt."

Jana could feel so much emotion emanating from him that it prompted her to say, "You really do miss your father a lot, don't you?"

"When somebody is as good to you as he was, it's only natural to miss them. ... There's just so many unanswered questions about his disappearance."

"Perhaps someday you'll know the truth," Jana told him. "But just remember this, Dwight, whatever you happen to discover, I want to be there to share it with you."

"I'll remember that," Dwight stated as he firmly planted his gaze upon her. "I shall remember it well."

* * *

As he was being driven homeward, Dwight felt a burning desire to remain in the company of his friends, the people whom he had grown to trust so much. His time with them always seemed to pass much too quickly.

Listening as Mrs. Willard spoke of a bake sale she was organizing to raise money for the church, Dwight found himself commending her for her efforts, in the aftermath of which she asked him if there was a church he attended.

"No, not any more," he informed her as he thought of a time when his family had also been church going. "I look to God, though," he made sure to mention with a conviction that came straight from the heart. "I know he's there because sometimes I can feel his presence around me."

"There are people in touch with God without being in a church every week," Mrs. Willard told him. "I'm not recommending a person stay away from church, mind you, but going to church is certainly no guarantee one's walking the right path in life."

"I like the way you think, Mrs. Willard," Dwight complimented her, knowing full well that he, too, fell short of attaining the healthy outlook that could be. Quite willing to admit this of himself, he was just about to do so when he happened to look at an oncoming vehicle and notice Carl within it. There were other people in the car besides him, but the only one he made out for certain was Carl; which is why, in his dismay, words would not come to his lips. Instead a cold chill shot up his spine in great measure causing him to wince a bit. Looking to Jana, he eventually whispered into her ear whom he had seen.

With widened eyes Jana whispered back, "Just be careful. He can't reach you if you are." Feeling the need to ease his burden in some way, she added with a touch of humor, "Let him waste his gas."

Dwight briefly smiled over her comment before saying, "I only hope he doesn't run out of gas right in front of my house, though."

It should be noted that vexation was beginning to take hold within the very core of Dwight's being, and that anger was sure to follow if the issues of his life weren't handled in a befitting manner, a manner which freed him from the bondage of fearful living.

Soon afterwards, when he was standing in the driveway of his home, Dwight bade everyone farewell.

"Until next time," Mr. Willard told him.

"Okay," Dwight said. "I'll be looking forward to it."

Watching his friends disappear from sight down Kirkland Road, Dwight knew that they had helped to make this day a good one for him. In the spirit of that belief he was motivated to look in the opposite direction and say with moving conviction, "You won't be able to weigh me down forever, Carl Barnet, not if I can help it." Turning toward the house, he deeply sensed that his prediction would come true as long as he retained trust in God Almighty, for God never had and never would forsake the needs of an earnest supplicant in the tests of time.

CHAPTER 14

THE MISSING LETTERS

In the weeks to follow Dwight made it his mission to refine his outlook toward life. In the process of doing so he began to assist the O'Maleys with the care and upkeep of their farm. Of particular interest to him was Zuzueca, whose chestnut coat when seen in the sunlight set against a green Mississippi pasture was a beautiful sight to behold.

We cannot anticipate the entire impact that our decisions will have on the quality of our lives, yet to be consciously aware that a proper course of action has been decided upon is a most rewarding of feelings. Such was Dwight's sentiment in regard to what Jana had revealed to the Willards about his life.

"Dwight, I know you've had it difficult in many respects," Mrs. Willard said with the concern of a true friend as they headed for the beach one Sunday afternoon, "but we're willing to help you in whatever way we can."

"Don't you people realize how much you already have helped me?" Dwight was quick to bring to her attention. "Don't you realize that my scars are beginning to fade?" Undoubtedly it was a relief to know he wasn't concealing the truth from them any longer. Rather, he was trusting them with the truth.

It wasn't until one mid-July day, as he was making his way down Kirkland Road, that Dwight began to wonder what it would be like to return to school in September. Certainly he expected to feel ill at ease in the presence of certain people. After all, it had become a conditioned response. Yet even a conditioned response can be dealt a crippling blow in the passage of time. Adversity lurks within the shadows of our lives, but fear has no hold on the triumphant. And so until he conquered his fears, the victory he craved would elude him.

In some respects it was ironic that now, at a time in Dwight's life when he was struggling with emotionally-wrenching issues, that he should cross paths with a scorned individual. Little did he know there was a family moving into the very house his childhood friend, Timothy Crane, had once inhabited. The abandoned structure was shielded from sight behind some rather large pine trees, yet as he neared the road that led the hundred feet or so to its location, his curiosity was piqued by the sound of activity of some sorts coming from that general direction. *Could it be that Timothy's back?* he wondered for a brief instant before dashing down the road. Why, it would be a dream come true, for he often hoped he'd return to Chism. One of the really puzzling aspects about the whole situation was that Timothy had assured him he'd write as soon as possible, but a letter had never been forthcoming, making communication impossible. But Timothy, being the likeable person that he was, had probably made friends quickly in Chicago, thus losing his desire to correspond with him. Yet deep down this had never been seen as a likely scenario. Another unsolved mystery in the life of a boy who longed for answers.

Memories of a time when the world seemed fair now flashed before Dwight's eyes. It was a time when he and Timothy shared one another's childhood dreams and aspirations. This very road had been traversed on numerous occasions by the two of them. Why even after Timothy moved to Chicago, moments were spent staring at that empty house which seemed to have lost all joy and warmth, and all traces of Timothy.

Arriving within sight of the vacated homestead, Dwight was quickly met with disappointment, for it turned out to be not the Cranes at all who were responsible for what he heard. In the yard he saw two strangers, a man and a woman, directing moving men down the ramp of a large furniture-filled van. To their right, standing on the paint peeled stairwell, were two young men who appeared to be close to his own age.

At a distance Dwight observed what was taking place. Then, just as he was about to walk forward to investigate, the older man saw him and beckoned him to advance with an upswept arm.

"Do you live around here?" he asked when Dwight was within hearing range.

"Yes, I do," Dwight answered him. "I live down the road a short ways. My name is Dwight Enhart."

"We're new here as you can see," the man said while stepping ahead. "Permit me to introduce myself. I'm John Aimes and this is my wife, Elizabeth, but I call her Beth. And over there," he pointed to the two boys, "are our sons, Edward and Roarie."

"I'm pleased to meet you," Dwight stated while initiating a handshake. "Where did y'all come from?"

"Chicago," Mr. Aimes answered him and oddly began to smile. "Forgive me for acting this way," he then sought to explain himself, "but I find your accent very different. Don't get me wrong. I'm not criticizing it. I'm just not used to it."

"Oh, I see," Dwight replied, and invariably began to chuckle. "And to me it's you who have the accent."

"That must be true," Mrs. Aimes conceded, "because you're not the first one to tell us that. I suppose after awhile we'll sound like Southerners, too."

"That just might happen," Dwight told her with a smile.

"Where will we be going to school?" Roarie now spoke up. "I didn't see a high school when we drove into town."

"There isn't one in Chism. We have to travel to Fulton," Dwight notified him. "We'll be riding the same bus."

"Gee, that'll be a new experience for me," Roarie mentioned. "In Chicago I lived only two blocks from the school."

"What grade are you in anyway?" Dwight asked.

"Tenth. And you?"

"The same," Dwight answered him, sensing his willingness to gravitate toward friendship. "I only hope you won't miss Chicago too much."

As though a bombshell had shattered the mood of the moment,

Dwight suddenly saw Roarie look to his family members with a troubled expression on his face. It was a look he could identify with all too well, for it reminded him of all the sensitive topics he desired to steer clear from in the past.

"Oh, he won't miss Chicago," Mrs. Aimes interposed in an effort to dispel the tension in the atmosphere. Wrapping her arm about Roarie's shoulder, she added with seeming believability, "We got tired of the hustle and bustle of city living, so we decided to buy a house in the country. The main reason we decided on Mississippi is because we're friends with the former owners of this house, and they offered to sell it to us at a reasonable price. Perhaps you know of them. Their last name is Crane."

As one could well imagine, Dwight was immediately overcome with elation, for here before him stood a family who could provide him with some information at long last about a boy who had been a significant part of his life.

"Ya, I knew them well!" he exclaimed. "Timothy and I were the best of friends! When I came here just now I was excited because I thought he may have returned! Tell me how he's doing? Is he well?"

At these words the entire Aimes family exchanged puzzled glances. Then, finally, Mr. Aimes said in earnest, "I'm sorry, but Timothy was killed over two years ago in an automobile accident. It was quite sad and the family took it very hard." As Dwight's face imparted a look of crushed hope, he added, "That's why his family decided to sell this house. They didn't want to return here without Timothy. Too many memories, you understand."

"Yes… I guess I can," Dwight gravely acknowledged while lowering his head.

"I'm sorry," Mrs. Aimes attempted to console him. "It's plain to see you were quite attached to Timothy."

"Yes, I was," Dwight confided while reflecting on the last day he'd seen him. And it was a haunting thought, for on that day they vowed to forever keep in touch. Yet now he discovered they'd never be able to. "Did you know him well?" he inquired with a yearning for additional information.

"Not really," Mr. Aimes replied as his wife excused herself to direct the moving men. "But to me he seemed unhappy. I was never able to figure it out really. I believe he was treated well, and yet I sensed he found it a challenge to fit in." He paused to reflect on the struggles of his own son, Roarie. But Dwight, being so engrossed by thoughts of Timothy, did not notice this on his part.

"I never would have thought Timothy'd be that way," Dwight stated. Reflecting on his own life, he was quick to add, "But things can change. Maybe something was bothering him."

"That could very well have been," Mr. Aimes commented. "You know something," he then recalled. "Now that I think of it, Timothy's parents once told me he wrote several times to a friend of his back home, but that he never got a response. Did you receive any letters from him?"

"No, I didn't," Dwight specified with sole interest in what he was saying. "In fact it bothered me that I hadn't."

"It must not have been you that he wrote to then," Mr. Aimes presumed as the moving men reappeared to retrieve another piece of furniture from the van.

"I can't imagine who else it would have been, though," Dwight said in all honesty. "We were so close. .... How did the accident happen?"

"He was crossing a busy street and got struck down," Mr. Aimes apprised him. "It was such a tragedy."

Dwight could appreciate the man's concern, but no words would arrest what he was currently feeling. Timothy was dead, no longer able to be communicated with, and the thought of not receiving his letters disturbed him beyond measure.

"I must go," he therefore blurted out while commencing to walk backwards. "Thanks for the information." Swinging about, he left this place of many memories.

Mr. Aimes shouted farewell as he watched him leave. But Roarie merely looked onward, sensing in doing so that Dwight, like himself, was a burdened individual.

"He's emotional, isn't he?" he stated while stepping beside his father.

"Under the circumstances it's understandable," Mr. Aimes indicated. "It's unfortunate the way he found out about Timothy. He didn't see it coming."

"He had to be told, though," Roarie maintained. "You did the right thing."

"I guess you're right, son," his father agreed. "He knows the truth now and won't have to wonder any longer." Turning aside, he proceeded to enter his new home. But Roarie, because he remained focused on Dwight, continued gazing down the road in the direction of his departure. By all appearances there was something about him that had secured the boy's fascination for reasons he couldn't quite fathom.

* * *

Dwight did not go directly home. Instead he made his way into the woods until he reached that special place where sparkling clear water gushed forth from a small waterfall.

Lowering himself to a sitting position, he tried to imagine what happened to Timothy's letters. He was certain Timothy would have gotten his address correct, and yet where were the letters? *Lost in the mail*, he first had thought; *but no, not every one of them*, he then determined.

For quite some time he sat in deliberation before it suddenly dawned on him that it was usually Clair who got the mail. A cold chill now began to pervade his entire being over the awful notion that crept into his mind. "Could she have been that devious?" he whispered out loud, recalling that Timothy had relocated to Chicago almost a year after his father's disappearance, and that by then both his mother and Clair were well on their way toward bitter envelopment.

Awakened by the prospect of events as they may have happened, Dwight jumped to his feet and started down the gentle slope that blended into the pathway home.

Entering an unoccupied kitchen, he proceeded toward the dining room only to nearly collide with his mother, who was headed in the opposite direction.

"I'm sorry," he blurted out, "but I'm in a hurry to talk to Clair."

When the woman idly brushed past him without saying a word, Dwight resumed his mission by ascending the stairs and knocking upon Clair's door, not softly or timidly, but with brisk determination.

"Mother, is that you?" he heard her say.

"No, it's Dwight," he informed her. "I've got to talk to you."

"Go away! I'm tired!" she immediately yelled out. "We have nothing to say to each other!"

"Well, like it or not you're gonna listen," he firmly insisted while opening her door and entering the room.

"How dare you intrude on my privacy!" she angrily shouted while rising from her bed. "Get out of here this instant!"

For awhile Dwight regarded her in silent defense. Then he stated with somber conviction, "No, Clair, not this time." Walking to the center of the room, he turned to face her before adding, "I hate to falsely accuse you of anything, but I was told something today that upset me, so I've got to ask you something."

"Enough of this jibber jabber!" she cried out in annoyance. "Just spit it out plain and clear!"

"Alright, I'll try," he responded with sought after resolution. Yet in an effort to be as tactful as possible, he decided to start out by saying, "We're going to have some new neighbors."

"Now isn't that interesting," she sarcastically uttered with fake enthusiasm. "And who might they be?"

"Some people from Chicago, and they're moving into the Cranes' house. I was told by them that Timothy wrote some letters to a friend of his years ago. Do you know anything about that?" he asked while keenly observing her.

"Oh, now I see what you're getting at!" she bitterly retorted. As her face took on a rigid expression, she voiced the claim, "But I don't know anything about any letters!"

Dwight continued to study her for a sign she might be lying.

"Alright, that's all I wanted to know," he stated then despite his prevailing skepticism, knowing he had no concrete proof, and hence no right, to blame her for what happened. Turning to leave, he felt it his duty to stop short and add, "Thanks for talking."

"I didn't have much of a choice!" she harshly reminded him.

"No, I guess you didn't at that," Dwight was persuaded to admit, "but I had to know." Walking to the doorway, he was just about to depart when Clair casually asked, "And how are the Cranes doing anyway? Fine I take it."

"I don't know how they are right now," Dwight related, "but they lost Timothy through an accident a while back. I was told that's why they sold their house."

"Oh... I had no idea," Clair stammered in response to this unexpected news. "I guess one never knows." In her voice there was a hint of sympathy that Dwight was pleased to detect. However when she became consciously aware of the feelings she was allowing herself to experience, she suddenly grew ill at ease, just as the worldly person becomes ill at ease when speaking of God. It's a reflection of the dominant outlook, of routined thought patterns, familiar usage. That is what determines the direction of the soul. And because Clair had become so constrained, she found it challenging to express compassion for people. She had adopted the opinion that she would end up reliving the pain and disappointment of her past if she allowed herself to love again. Repeat rejection was the fear she harbored, her insecurities being that firmly engrained within her personality.

"Oh, well, I guess we'll never see the Cranes again," she thereby stated with apparent indifference.

"For quite a while now I didn't think we would," Dwight told her in all honesty. "They never communicated with us."

By way of the silence that ensued, Dwight viewed their conversation as being finished. Yet as he turned to leave, there was such a definitive look about him that it prompted Clair to become stricken with regret for what she had actually done.

"Wait," she impulsively called out. As Dwight heeded her suggestion, she self-consciously added, "I've got something for you." From the expression on her face he could tell she was feeling troubled about something, despite her efforts to avoid such a sentiment. Slowly making her way to the storage trunk beside her bed, she opened it and removed a jewelry case. Upon opening that, she withdrew three letters. "Here," she said while extending her hand to him with unusual gentleness. "I didn't read them. It never occurred to me he'd end up dying."

At this stage Dwight experienced a number of emotions, some of which were comforting, some of which were not. There was anger toward Clair for having been so deceitful, disappointment in her beyond words, relief that he knew the truth about the missing letters, yet sorrow in the knowledge that it was too late to answer any of those letters. Even frustration began to consume him, a nagging frustration which prompted him to say with utmost certitude, "Clair, even if Timothy were still alive, what you did was wrong." Shaking his head, he added, "How could you have done this to us?" Yet even now the sternness in his voice was not filled with contempt. Pity was instead the epitome of what he felt for her, this girl who so often made unwise choices.

"I don't know why I did it. I just felt like it at the time," she uneasily stated in an attack of remorse. "I don't know why I do a lot of the things I do." Yet in an effort to alleviate her guilt, she flippantly added, "But you have the letters now, so go to your room and read them." Turning her back to him, she found that she wasn't able to reap any satisfaction in what she had done after all.

"Clair, I think I can forgive you for this," Dwight told her at this time. "But that really isn't enough, is it, because I'm not God. Don't you think you had better consider that?" Having stated his position, he exited the room.

In view of current developments, Clair lethargically walked to her bed in an onslaught of shame, commencing to weep as she did so.

"Why am I this way?" she sobbed while lying down. "Why do I hurt him like I do?" Truly it was a wretched sight to behold.

For a brief period of time she remained where she was before rising to gaze at her opened trunk. Bending over, she lowered herself to the floor with the aid of the bed and began to fondle her childhood keepsakes. Softly smiling, she embraced a particularly sentimental one as a tear rolled down her cheek.

Moments later, in resuming her search down memory lane, a family picture was found that had been taken only one year before her father's disappearance. Studying it, she saw that the people posing within it looked happy, so much so that she was inspired to place her right hand upon it in the hopes of recapturing that moment in her life.

"I love you, daddy," she longingly whispered, and again began to cry.

* * *

Dwight anxiously opened Timothy's first letter, which was post-marked November, 1942.

Sitting in front of his bedroom window for the added light, he began to read it very slowly so that he would not miss one solitary word. It went:

Dear Dwight,

I hope you've been well. I'm fine. I know I should have written sooner but we've been busy settling into our new house. It's really nice, sort of like an old mansion. I think you'd like it.

I really miss Mississippi a lot. It's not easy leaving friends like you. I'm hoping to go back there for visits. My parents said we might.

At this point Dwight felt like heading straight back into Clair's room to give her a piece of his mind in no uncertain terms. Wisely, however, he reminded himself that it would be counterproductive to put Clair on the defensive, especially now that he had seen a glimmer of humility and compassion within her. These things were not meant to be discouraged, and if he chastised her, resentment would likely be the result. Therefore he decided to read onward instead.

School here is different. There's so many kids in my grade that I doubt if I'll ever get to know them all. It's going to take time for me to adjust, my mother says.

Have you heard any news about your father yet? Sure hope everything turns out well.

Do you still go to the beach a lot? I remember how we use to go there so much. There really has been good times for us, hasn't there?

The other day my cousins from Indiana came to visit. We all had a good time.

Well, I guess I'll say bye for now. Take care and write back soon.

Your friend always,
Timothy

P.S. My mother is planning a birthday party for me next week. Wish you could be at it.

Sitting there, Dwight was thankful that Timothy had valued their friendship after all, yet he was also saddened by the realization that he could not send him a letter in return. How puzzled Timothy must have been, he assumed. It was awful, so awful in fact that for an instant or two he felt as though he could in no way find the strength to endure the emotional repercussions of reading the next letter, which was postmarked January, 1943. ... And yet, upon staring at it, he realized that he would not be able to stand the suspense of putting it off until later either. With forced composure he therefore opened it. It read:

Dear Dwight,

I was surprised when I didn't receive a letter from you, but then I thought maybe my letter got lost in the mail. Let me know if you got it.

Dwight, I miss Chism a lot, and it's getting worse instead of better. What's the saying? You can take the boy out of the country, but ya can't take the country out of the boy. That's me I guess.

Do you still have Hazel? I remember how you always liked her so much. And what about those chickens of yours? I really miss all those animals. The only time I get to see any is when I go to the zoo. That's one thing I know you'd go ape over. Ha! Ha!

I've got a hobby now. I collect rocks and minerals. Do you have any hobbies?

Well, I've got to go now. I just heard my mother call me for supper. Write back soon.

And then he closed his letter just as before.

Dwight stared at the letter for a few moments before placing it back in its envelope and opening the third and final one, which was postmarked March, 1943. His face suddenly took on a smile as he recalled Timothy's clever play on words. "Go ape over it," he stated before centering his attention upon this last letter, which was very short. It went:

Dear Dwight,

I guess I'm forced to assume you aren't receiving my letters, because I think you would have written to me other-wise. Still though I had to make one more attempt to reach you, because you're the best friend I've ever had. I think of you often.

I sure hope you receive this letter. I'm beginning to wonder if you've moved away from Chism too. Take care of yourself.

Your friend always,

Timothy

Now one might have thought Dwight would suffer an emotional breakdown over circumstances as they stood; yet he did not. However he did say in regard to what he was forced to accept, "Oh, God, I'm still young, and yet I get so tired of living sometimes. Please forgive me for that." Feeling mentally exhausted, he replaced the letter in its envelope and laid all three of them upon his dresser before making his way to his bed to lie down. Quite interestingly, his mind became eased of its burden in no time at all as much welcomed slumber overcame him. He wasn't in a position to realize it of course, but God had taken such pity on him for what he was required to accept that he bestowed upon him the ability to sleep in the midst of his woes. Call it a heavenly sedative if you will.

* * *

The general store that Mr. Willard owned was small, yet still he managed to stock its shelves with most every grocery item in need by the public.

Cordially bidding farewell to his final purchaser of the day, his thoughts turned to Sandy. It was Saturday, only two days before her birthday, and he was to remember candles for her cake. Walking to the shelf where he stocked miscellaneous items, he picked up a box of them, smiled softly, and said, "My little girl is going to be ten. How time does fly." It seemed as though only yesterday she had been born, a child who turned out to be so vivacious, so loving, so overflowing with warmth.

For awhile he reflected on the times of his life, realizing in doing so that life had been good to him largely because he had put forth a conscientious effort to be good to life. There was a certain respect and appreciation expected of him for having entered into this world, a thing not to be taken lightly.

Making his way to the cash register, he placed its currency in a moneybag and left the store, locking the door behind himself as he did so. In heading down the sidewalk he felt content in where he was headed. A prosperous man he thus saw himself to be for harboring the desire to go home after a day's work.

Entering the kitchen by way of the front door, he saw his wife at the stove preparing supper. Jerry could be heard in the next room asking Bill if he'd play catch, pleading with an urgency that made it apparent he was not about to relent.

"How was your day, dear?" Mrs. Willard inquired with a quick glance in his direction before returning her attention to the pork chops she was frying.

"Just fine," he said. Walking beside her, he gave her a kiss on the cheek, which she made easier by tilting her head sideways for greater exposure. "I've got the candles." Withdrawing them from his pocket, he placed them on the counter to the right of the stove.

"Oh, good! Sandy's very excited about her birthday this year, much more than usual, mainly because of Dwight." She now began to scoop the browned chops from the frying pan onto a platter. "Suddenly she had the wonderful idea that he should be here for her party. I couldn't agree with her more."

"You know something, that is a good idea," Mr. Willard noted.

"As a matter-of-fact why don't we ask him to spend the night Sunday. After the party Monday I could take him home."

"Perfect," she smiled. "I think Dwight would like that." Gradually, though, the look on her face faded into an expression of solemn thought. "You know, when I think of what Jana told us about his life, I'd like to sweep him away from that house and adopt him."

"I know what you mean," he concurred. "Sometimes I feel the same way, but then I remind myself it's not that simple, and that it's possible to re-strengthen his own family."

"I realize that, but still..."

"Hello, daddy!" Eliza unknowingly interrupted their conversation. "I didn't hear you come in." She dashed to his side and wrapped an arm about one of his. "I've got a surprise for you after supper. I made one of your favorite desserts. I know it won't be as good as mother's, but I am trying."

"I'm sure it'll be most delectable," he assured her with a smile.

"Could you begin setting the table now, dear?" her mother wasted no time in saying. "Supper is just about ready."

When Eliza left the room, Mrs. Willard told her husband in a virtual whisper, "Make sure you're not critical of her pumpkin pie. I want her to feel good about her efforts."

"Ah, yes, pumpkin pie." He smacked his lips while rubbing his stomach. "I'm sure I'll be able to handle that."

"I... wouldn't have high expectations if I were you, dear," the woman rather tentatively gave him fair warning. "You see, I already sampled it earlier, and let's just say she must have done something very wrong." Holding one another's gaze for a few moments, they simultaneously broke out in laughter.

"I'll try my best to be tactful," he humorously sought to appease her.

In the following minutes, as they helped their mother place the food on the table, Mary Ann and Eliza spoke of new dress styles that were on display at one of the downtown shops. Seated in the living room in the meantime in his favorite chair, Mr. Willard began reading The Fulton Chronicle as he usually did around this time of day, whereas Bill and Jerry played catch in the yard. It was shortly thereafter that Sandy arrived home from an afternoon of play with some kids in the neighborhood.

"Daddy!" she immediately sounded out at the sight of him and rushed to his side. "Did mother tell you I wanted Dwight at my party?"

"Yes, she did, and I think it's a good idea. You're a very thoughtful girl. Dwight will be pleased by the invitation, I'm sure."

"I hope so," she only half-heartedly said, and slightly frowned, much to her father's bewilderment.

"Why the long face, sweetie?"

"It has to do with my friend, Amy. You remember her, don't you?" When he nodded his head, she added, "Well, anyway, I invited her to my birthday party, and when I told her about Dwight and my plan to have him here, she told me he was too old for my party, and that I shouldn't ask him. She said I should only have people my own age over for it. Was she right, daddy?" Imploringly she regarded the man for his insight into the matter.

At first Mr. Willard eyed his daughter as he searched for the right words to tell her.

"Come sit by me," he encouraged her then. After she had done so by squeezing in between him and the arm of the chair, he advised her, "No, Sandy, she wasn't right. You see, when a person gets along well with someone and they become friends, they shouldn't create barriers that'll put a strain on their friendship. We can't help how old we are, but we can control our behavior. Now I think you'd enjoy your birthday much more if you had all your friends over, including Dwight. And not only that, I'm gonna be there, too, and I'm your friend, and I'm a lot older than Dwight is." As the two of them smiled at one another, he further stated, "I was thinking of asking Dwight to come home with us tomorrow after the picnic to spend the night. In that way he could visit with us a while longer. Would you like that?"

"Oh, you know I would!" she stated in her delight. "I like him so much. And you know what else?"

"No, what?" Her father chuckled in response to her unending enthusiasm.

"He hasn't seen my chickens since that day we went to the

O'Maleys' farm. I know he'll be anxious to see them."

"I'm sure he will at that," he said just as Mary Ann announced that supper was ready to be served. "I guess we had better eat now, sweetie."

"Yes, and thank you, daddy!" She got up and kissed him without warning. "And I'm gonna tell Amy, like it or not, Dwight's going to be invited to my party." With that having been determined, she headed straight for the kitchen to tell her mother how happy she was about everything.

CHAPTER 15

JANA'S INDIGNATION

Something happened to fill Jana with such a combination of vexation and disappointment that she could not utter another word in protest, which no doubt would have been in vain anyway.

The incident had taken place in the library as the family awaited the stroke of six, that being the hour when their devoted maid, Alice, a black woman who had worked for the family for many a year, would serve their main meal of the day. Jana had been seated on the sofa with her father and sister at the time, whereas her mother had situated herself where she usually did on a lounge chair.

At first their conversation was incidental, concerning such things as the nice weather and an upcoming theatrical performance to be held in Jackson. But then a strong discomfort began to work its way into Jana's emotions as she listened to her father speak about money, and his contention that it was important to possess an abundance of it. More so than ever talk of this type troubled her, for she believed Jesus when he said no one could serve two masters, both God and money, for they would love one and hate the other. And yet even though she objected to and quite often became agitated as of late by her father's relentless quest for money, she couldn't deny that she was cloaked in a material world by way of the comfortable life style she had always known. The key, however, was to place one's emphasis on that which is of greatest value, the things of God; honesty, morality, the Golden Rule, the state of one's spiritual life. Therefore a noble cause it was to prevent money, a mere invention of mankind, from becoming one's personal god as her father had seen fit to do. He and so many other people in the world were so impressed by financial wealth even though it had never achieved for anyone that inner sense of fulfillment which can only be found through the ways of God.

When the topic of conversation shifted away from money matters, Mrs. Rossi asked Jana and Cynthia if they'd be willing to assist her in the making of a dress the following afternoon. It had not been the first time she requested such a thing of her daughters. How well both Jana and Cynthia recalled being instructed as very young girls in the art of dressmaking.

"I'd really like to help you, mother," Jana stated as Cynthia voiced her support of the idea, "but have you forgotten that I already have plans to go to The Gulf with the Willards tomorrow? Of course if it's rainy...."

"No, you're not going there!" her father abruptly silenced her.

"But why not?" Jana protested.

"Because I don't want you associating with that boy!" he told her straight out. "I know you've been seeing him there! Don't deny it!"

Jana was immediately distraught.

"Dwight's my friend! Why do you resent that!" she implored him. "There's just so much you refuse to understand!"

"I don't like hearing you speak to me in that tone of voice, young lady!" he rebuked her. "It's as plain as can be you've given me no recourse but to put an end to your escapades once and for all!" In a gesture of authority he so austerely cast his gaze upon her that she found herself barely able to withstand it. "Tomorrow you'll stay home to help your mother, and that goes for every Sunday from now on! I've given you plenty of time to mend the error of your ways, and my patience has run out! It's as simple as that!" Noticing that Alice had entered the room to inform them supper was ready to be served, he sternly concluded while standing, "Now let's go eat!"

At this juncture Jana was more than merely upset. She was outraged, for she had never been so extremely dictated to before, not even by this disciplinarian of a father who stood so oppressively before her. He had been strict in the past, yes, but never so final and unfair in the demands he placed upon her, which is why she felt as though she simply had to do something in retaliation. The only thing that came to mind, however, was to ask her sister her opinion on the matter in the hopes that she'd see her side of the issue and positively influence the man.

"You don't agree with him, do you?" she petitioned her before anyone was able to begin leaving the room.

"It doesn't matter how she feels!" Mr. Rossi irately informed her. "I've made my final decision! Let it go at that or I'll ground you for the remainder of the summer!"

"But I do agree with you, father," Cynthia nonetheless spoke up to let her feelings be known. Regarding the disappointed face of her sister, she added, "Don't think badly of me, please. I know you're upset over this, but I only have your best interest at heart. Really we all do. Trust father's judgment before it's too late."

"Too late!" Jana exclaimed while bounding to her feet. "Too late for what! You all seem to think I'm behaving like some simple-minded fool, when all I am is a friend to someone who's a friend to me!" Her eyes now felt the wetness of her tears. "Do you hear me? All I'm guilty of is friendship! How can you object to that!" In a wave of fatigue over her passionate outburst, her legs weakened and failed her so that she again found herself sitting on the couch.

Mrs. Rossi and Cynthia were nearly moved to tears by their own right, but Mr. Rossi remained unaltered by Jana's open display of conviction.

"Jana, you're making this much more difficult than it has to be," he sorely lamented. "You never used to be rebellious. What's come over you?"

Following a brief pause, Jana rather despondently said, "May I go to my room now? Suddenly I'm not very hungry."

"No!" her father refused her. "You're going to be at the supper table with the rest of us! It's the way we want it!"

"But I don't mind if she...."

"No, she'll be amongst us!" he adamantly interrupted his wife. "And that's final!"

Seeking to comfort her daughter, Mrs. Rossi walked to her side and said, "Come, come, dear, you must eat something. Alice has prepared a delicious meal for you. You'll feel much better after you eat." *As though eating would make everything better*, Jana thought in a fit of disgust. "Tomorrow we'll make that new dress and you'll forget all about this. You'll see. It'll be just like old times." With that having been so feebly predicted, she guided Jana from the room in the manner one leads a small child somewhere.

They were nearly halfway down the hall on their way to the dining room when Jana suddenly found herself questioning the motive behind her mother's request that she help her make a new dress on Sunday. Certainly she had known of her plans to be with the Willards, and yet she had still chosen to put her on the spot in the presence of her father. Any other time she would have been willing to help her with the project, but why Sunday afternoon? It had to be more than coincidence, which is why, in annoyance, she allowed herself to say, "You're becoming just like father!" Briskly breaking free of the woman's touch, she continued onward alone despite harsh words of protest from the domineering man trailing behind her.

Jana was a girl who was coming to know the stark reality of being in the midst of a circumstance she did not want to be a part of. A strain had been placed on her relationship with her family, and that strain would undoubtedly affect her relationship with Dwight. Truly she felt badly for all concerned, including her father, whom even though she loved a great deal, she disliked certain things about.

* * *

Jana tried not to let it bother her that her father glared at her during supper. Had she considered herself deserving of such treatment, she certainly would have reacted differently, but not out of caring about a fellow human being whom she had also grown to respect. To her that was not a valid reason for allowing guilt to consume her.

It was after requesting and being given permission to leave the table that she entered the kitchen by way of the entrance at the end of the hall. Then, as she had so often witnessed before, she saw Alice at the far end of the large room seated at a small table with a plate of food set before her.

Alice had what Jana considered to be an outstanding personality; and Jana knew her well, for she had worked for the family ever since Cynthia's birth. For the first few years of her employ she resided elsewhere, but eventually was encouraged to move into the Rossi's spacious home, where she remained ever since. Being of a nurturing disposition, Jana was naturally drawn to her. Yet because she was, it had always grieved her to think that she was required to eat alone in the kitchen. But that was the nature of the society in which they lived, and it had been that way for many a year. How vividly she recalled asking her father at the age of nine if Alice could join them at the supper table only to be told it was absolutely out of the question. Such a thing just wouldn't be proper, he had said. But to the unprejudiced mind of a nine-year-old girl it was Alice's separation that was deemed improper.

"Hi, chile," Alice greeted her with her usual warmth. "Ta what da I owe dis visit?" She had an accent which bespoke her Southern ties.

"I just wanted to talk," Jana solemnly informed her. Sitting down adjacent to her, she delayed the onset of any emotionally wrenching confessions by saying, "Supper was great as usual. You prepare food better than anyone I know."

"Thank ya, chile," Alice graciously responded. In noticing Jana's troubled bearing, she perceptibly added, "I kin see dat ya didn't come here ta talk bout my cook'n, dough."

"No, Alice, I didn't," Jana let it be made known. "As a matter of fact I couldn't eat all that well despite the fine food." In her pressed state of mind she added, "I know you couldn't help but overhear some of the things my father said to me earlier." When the woman nodded her head, she went on to say, "You recall what I told you about Dwight, don't you?"

"Oh, yessum, dat's the boy you's so fond of," she said with a smile. "I ramemba how happy ya was when ya spoke bout him." With a face that suddenly took on a somber bearing, she came to disclose, "But yer pa don't want ya ta see him, and ya doesn't like dat, does ya missy?"

"No, I certainly don't," Jana confessed. "Oh, what should I do, Alice?" she then beseeched her. "I'm at my wits end! I want to obey my father, and yet I feel Dwight needs me. ... But I'll be truthful.

I'm drawn to him." In a manner that confirmed her passionate point of view, she stated, "I enjoy his company so much. I can honestly say he enlightens me."

"Cheer up, chile," Alice sought to comfort her while firmly clutching her hands. "Strong friendships is diff'cult ta ruin, no mat'r who done tries ta do it."

"Perhaps," Jana conceded, "but my father doesn't give up easily."

"Yer mama and papa care bout ya more den ya real'ize. Iffin dey did'n dey would'n give a hoot who ya a'sociated with. It's jus dat dey're used ta a'sociat'n with da rich folks. Dey don't know much diff'rent, and dey feel as dough you'll only be happy iffin ya lead dat same kinda life. Da ya und'stand missy?"

"I guess so," Jana was reluctant to admit, "but they're wrong. I would never be happy following in their footsteps. They act like they're better than other people, and that really bothers me."

"But things ain't really so bad fer ya. You's bett'r off den ya real'ize. Just look round ya at all da pain der is in da world and ya kin see dat it's true."

"I'm not saying I don't have things to be thankful for. I know I do," Jana acknowledged. "But my father has such a difficult time accepting people for who they are. He either tries to mold everyone into being what he thinks they should be, or rejects them right from the very start, and it's so... bigoted." She nearly cringed at the thought of it.

"Oh, chile, you's such a good girl," Alice stated in all sincerity. "I reckon iffin dere was more folks like you we'd all be a whole lot bett'r off. But don't fret so much, missy. You's gotta try ta a'cept yer pa fer what he is. Don't ya know dat acep'n folks fer what dey are is da first step in help'n 'em change fer da bett'r." In saying this she meant that when Christian principles were put into sound practice, it was an incentive for wayward souls to acquire the beauty of what they were in witness of.

"That sounds like good advice," Jana assented, "but in the meantime I'm being treated unfairly because my father is too blind to see the error of his ways."

"But it's only temp'rary, missy," Alice pointed out with a smile that was symbolic of victory. "His rule over ya won't last ferever,

jus as da mast'rs rule over da slave comes ta an end." Putting a hand
to Jana's cheek, she enthusiastically added, "You'se gonna be set
free, missy!"

Jana could not help but be impressed by the woman's optimism
concerning the far-reaching scope of things as she saw them to be.
Specifically focusing then on her reference to master and slave, she
was inspired to ask, "Has it been hard for you, Alice, hard to accept
people for what they are?"

"Yessum, missy, it done has," she soberly admitted while
reflecting on her past. "I had ta learn dat even dough badness isn't
fergott'n, we kin see past it. It takes some folks years ta find dis out.
Some never seem ta. Dey jus don't seem ta real'ize dat we kin live
in a world a hate and be set free a it in our hearts."

By way of her thought provoking comments Jana gathered that
Alice had somehow suffered a terrible injustice in her life; and so
she asked her whether or not that was the case.

"Iffin ya mus know, missy, my past has had suff'rin in it," she
replied. "Ya see fear and prej'dice sets folks up ta do awful, hateful
things. Always ramemba dat. It done took me a long time ta figure
out dat da folks dat hate others hates demselves da most, and dat ta
wrong others is a sign a weakness." Gazing directly at Jana, she
added, "Da worst a what happened was ta my papa when I was a
girl." There was a brief silence, one in which she seemed to be
trying to find the right words to convey the essence of what she
wanted to say. "Ya see, chile, my papa was involved in many
campaigns ta help da black folks. And my God, chile, he was such a
good man. ... But he was lynched by some white folks one night. It
was da Klan, missy, and me a young girl not yet knowing dat much
bout da ways a da South. Well, I reckon dere ain't no way I kin let
ya know how I felt when I saw my papa dangl'n from dat rope." She
eyed Jana all the more intently before saying with a fervor that
really moved her, "It was den dat I began ta hate da white folks fer
da first time, specially when I heard my mama cry'n at night."

"Oh, Alice, I had no idea," Jana empathetically reacted. "I'm so
sorry." Gently she touched the woman's hand as tears came to her
eyes.

"I knows ya feels badly, Miss Jana," Alice sufficiently stated while eying her squarely. "But don't cry for my sake, chile, cause da hate is gone now dat I got ta know some fine white folks like you." She smiled tenderly. "You's pure a heart, missy, and ya cares bout people. Dat's really good. God done used ya ta help me. He done sent me a girl straight from heav'n ta get ta know."

Through her tear-filled eyes Jana managed to say, "You mean I've made an impression on you without even realizing it?"

"Yessum, missy, ya surely has," Alice contended as best she could while firmly yet gently cupping her hands about her cheeks. "Der ain't no doubt bout dat."

"I'm so glad, Alice," Jana responded, "because I love you. To me you're a member of this family."

"Thank ya, chile. I prec'iate dat." But then, as though she read Jana's mind from earlier, she made sure to add, "But ya do und's-tand dat dat don't mean I kin act any diff'rent den I do right now. Der'll still be rastric'tions on what I kin do with yer fam'ly."

"We as a people are so bound by our prejudices, aren't we?" Jana was quick to say in another bout of melancholy. "I wish we thought of ourselves as one race, the human race."

"Dat's a nice thought, chile," Alice affirmed, "but it's not likely ta happ'n til Jesus comes in glory."

In the continuation of that mode of thinking Jana said, "I wonder what advice Jesus would give me concerning my relation-ship with Dwight when my father wants it ended."

"I reckon he'd say iffin what yer pa wants of ya goes against God's laws, den ya don't have ta obey yer pa," Alice astutely told her. "But be das'creet bout it, missy, cause yer pa'd have my hide iffin he heard me tell ya dis!" With that having been so unre-servedly emphasized, she impulsively laughed in a manner Jana found herself following suit with.

Later, in her bedroom, Jana did not feel like laughing, however, as she made her way to her window to stare out. From her perspec-tive, the cast iron fence which surrounded the yard was symbolic of the prisoner she saw herself to be within the confines of her own home. She was as a captive, a captive who yearned to be set free from the shackles of her world's expectations.

"Oh, Dwight, how are we going to prevail in all this?" she softly uttered in her pronounced distress. "Do we have what it takes to conquer bias?" Recalling Alice's words from earlier, she somehow knew that they would prevail as long as they had faith and hope and love in their hearts. Only through this realization was she able to prevent herself from crying in despair.

* * *

On Sunday, when Dwight was picked up by the Willards, he was disappointed to discover that Jana was not with them; especially today, for he was quite anxious to tell her the facts, as he knew them to be, about Timothy's life. So grateful was he to again be with the Willards, though, that Jana's absence did not overshadow his optimistic resolve in the least. And besides, Jana would surely be amongst everyone next week, he thought, not yet knowing that she was no longer going to be a part of these outings. To the contrary, Cybil, Bill, and Mr. and Mrs. Willard were aware of the recent developments within the Rossi household. But where Dwight was concerned, everyone, including Jana, felt as though the truth was much too hurtful to come from anyone's lips except hers. She would be best able to articulate the way things were. So what was the nature of what was said to explain her absence on this day? Only that she wasn't feeling well, which even though meant to serve as a diversion, was far removed from a lie.

Riding toward the beach, Sandy was quick to inform Dwight of her upcoming party and her wish to have him there.

"That sounds like a good time, Sandy," Dwight stated. "I'll try to get a ride to it. Really I will."

"How about taking that ride today and spending the night," Mr. Willard suggested from the driver's seat. "We'd all like to have you over."

Dwight did not have to consider the offer very long before accepting it, in the aftermath of which Sandy predicted that it was going to be the best birthday party she ever had. She just knew it.

As the day progressed, everyone had their usual good time at the beach. Then, on their way back home, they stopped off at Dwight's so that he could inform his mother of his plans, pick up a change of clothes, and take care of the animals.

While the Willards awaited him in the driveway, Dwight found his mother seated in the living room. The drapes, as usual, were drawn almost completely to give the room a dark and dismal aura, a bleak reflection of her defeated attitude.

"Mother, I plan to spend the night with some friends," he wasted no time in telling her. "I thought I should tell you where I'll be."

"Suit yourself," she managed to say while reaching for her cigarettes. As she began to remove one from the package, Dwight turned for the barn. Yet just as he neared the stairwell, he was inspired to rush upstairs to speak to Clair. Arriving outside her door, he knocked rather tentatively upon it, then entered at the sound of her invite.

Seeing her lying in bed under the covers, Dwight could not help but wonder about her overall health. Certainly noticeable changes had been taking place within her since that day she gave him Timothy's letters. There seemed to be a shift toward repentance for past transgressions. Yet her guilt held the capacity of finalizing her self-destruction, he saw to be the case, for it was as though she was finally willing to admit the truth about herself only to conclude she couldn't live with what she discovered. Were desperate means being considered to put an end to her tormented existence? He was beginning to suspect that very thing. And yet it was her change of heart which compelled him to approach her right here and now with the expectation of civil treatment.

Clair revealed her depressed state by staring blankly into space as though she could see right past him.

"Whatta ya want?" she asked then in a tone that confirmed her dejection.

"I thought you might be willing to do me a favor," Dwight spoke up without delay.

"Really... what kind of a favor?" she curiously inquired while sitting up in bed.

"Well, the Willards, the people that I go to the beach with on Sundays, have asked me to spend the night with them in Fulton, so I was wondering if you'd take care of Hazel and the chickens today and tomorrow. They'll need fresh water."

It seemed as though Clair was about to smile. Yet when she grew awkwardly embarrassed over her spontaneous reaction, she said rather impatiently while turning away, "Yes, I'll do it."

Dwight was appreciative of her compliance. She had ended up being abrupt, yes, but no longer bitter. Indeed, for a moment or two, she even appeared pleased by his willingness to give her the benefit of the doubt. Perhaps she liked the idea of proving herself capable of trustworthiness after all. Perhaps she craved redemption.

"Thank you," he replied. "I'll return the favor somehow."

Clair realized that Dwight was willing to look beyond her trespasses, yet she had such a hard time seeing past them herself that she curtly stated with her back to him, "What's the point?" At issue here was poor self-worth, a most difficult thing to come to terms with when one is at odds with life.

Dwight knew that Clair was attempting to surrender her habitual ways. Yet because he did not want to run the risk of pushing her beyond her limits, he decided to leave the room at once without uttering another word. Once outside her door, he experienced a deep sense of satisfaction in having been able by the grace of God to approach her in the first place. So much he wanted her to find fulfillment in life, but he knew it would never come to fruition as long as she refused to address the root of what ailed her.

Moments later, as he called to mind that the Willards awaited him, he dashed away for a change of clothes, feeling certain as he did so that brighter tomorrows were always possible as long as one cultivated an attitude which was conducive to bringing it about, an attitude directed at God in faith and trust.

* * *

The hot afternoon sun was suffocating, so it was a relief to walk into the shelter of the Willards' two-storied home. In doing so, Dwight immediately reflected on the memory of last Christmas, for it had been a beautiful evening spent here.

"Dwight, it's been much too long since your last visit," Mrs. Willard declared while placing the picnic basket on the counter beside the sink. "We mustn't let it go on that way."

"I would like to come here more often," he openly admitted while heading in the direction of the living room with the others.

The opportunity to sit down had barely presented itself before Sandy asked Dwight if he was ready to go into the barn to see her chickens.

"Sandy, give him a rest," her father advised her. "There's plenty of time for that. He's spending the night, remember?"

"I know," she conceded, "but he must be anxious to see them."

Mr. Willard was about to admonish the girl for her persistence when Dwight ended up saying, "You're right, Sandy, I am." Getting up, the two of them made their way outside and proceeded across the yard to a small barn that sheltered twenty or so chickens. Adjoining it was a fairly large pen.

Entering the structure, it immediately caught Dwight's attention that one of the chicks given to Sandy turned out to be a Rhode Island Red rooster that looked a lot like Tecumseh.

"I had a pet rooster like him once," he wasted no time in saying. "His name was Tecumseh. That's an Indian name."

"Really?" Sandy responded with piqued interest. As he nodded his head, she went on to determine, "Then I think I should name him after him. He'll be Tecumseh the second."

Smiling upon her, Dwight said, "Okay, Sandy, Tecumseh it is."

"Whatever happened to your rooster?" she inquired.

At first Dwight did not intend to be truthful with the girl. But then, after a period of contemplation, he decided to admit, "My sister killed him for supper one day."

"But why did she do that!" Sandy exclaimed. "Didn't she know he was your pet!"

"Oh, she knew he was a pet of mine," Dwight told her. "That's why she killed him. You see, she feels the need to hurt me at times, so she did it one day when I wasn't home." Seeing the troubled look on the child's face, he was disposed to add, "You do know my family has certain problems, don't you, Sandy?"

"Yes, I've overheard things," she confessed. "You're different, though, and I'm glad. I think you'll be able to help them some day."

"I hope so," Dwight would only say in modest response.

A gleam of respect twinkled in Sandy's eyes concerning the

essence of what he stood for. Turning her attention to the flock, she made her way to a feed barrel and withdrew some grain. Handing a portion of it to Dwight, the two of them began to scatter it on the floor. To illustrate the value placed upon their friendship, a few extra grains were thrown in the direction of Tecumseh.

Not too long afterwards, upon returning indoors, Dwight saw that Bill was on the telephone. Withdrawing the receiver from his ear, he held it out to him and said, "It's Jana. She wants to talk to you."

Making his way to Bill's side, Dwight took hold of the phone while thanking him.

"Hello!" he addressed Jana quite cheerfully. "I missed you today!"

"I missed you, too," Jana admitted from where she secretly spoke to him in the library. "I'm glad you came to Fulton. Cybil told me the Willards were going to invite you."

"Ya, and I'm sure glad they did," he told her. "It feels so good to be back here again."

"Listen, Dwight, I haven't got long," she quickly divulged. "My mother will be in here any minute. I've got to meet with you in private so we can talk."

"Alright... where?" he obliged her as a sudden feeling of unease began to penetrate his emotions.

"Between my house and the Willards there's a small playground. I'll meet you there in a few minutes."

"Okay," he said.

"I can't talk any more," she hurriedly whispered, for her mother had just entered the room. "See you there."

"Who were you talking to?" Mrs. Rossi inquired just as Jana released her grip on the phone.

"Oh, just Cybil," she lied. "I'd like to go see her now. I hope you don't mind."

"No, not at all." Approaching her, she grasped her hands firmly within hers and proclaimed, "I enjoyed today so much, didn't you? Thanks to you and your sister I've got that dress I wanted."

"Yes, mother... it was nice," Jana literally forced herself to say while uncomfortably drawing away from her, for not only didn't she like her mother's facade, she resented the reasons why that facade had even developed in the first place. "Ah... I've gotta go now," she conveniently pointed out while heading for the door. "I'll be back soon."

Once off the gallery walking down the steps of her home, Jana reflected on the lie told her mother, strongly sensing in doing so that if she had it to do all over again, she would have done no differently. That's just how determined she was to retain her relationship with Dwight, for lying was not a dominant feature of her personality make-up by any stretch of the imagination. In fact, if the truth be known, she hated resorting to it. Such is the price paid for mismanaged scruples.

Back at the Willards, Dwight told Bill and Cybil what Jana had requested of him.

"I wonder what this is all about?" he curiously went on to say. "She seemed so concerned about something."

"You'll find out soon enough," Cybil would only mention.

Departing from the Willards' house with Cybil and Bill, Dwight sensed that something was about to happen to put a damper on his mood.

"I'll show you the way to the playground," Cybil volunteered as they neared the sidewalk. "I live close to it."

Dwight nodded his head in compliance. Then, upon bidding Bill farewell, the two of them proceeded along their way.

"You know something, Dwight, I never told you this before, but my older sister, Hannah, is in your sister's grade at school," Cybil said just seconds later.

"Really... I didn't know that," Dwight responded with only half-hearted interest, for lingering thoughts of Jana still occupied his mind.

"Yes, and she said she's gotten the impression more than once that Clair is battling with depression."

"Her noticing that doesn't surprise me," Dwight solemnly declared. "Clair is a troubled girl, that's for sure. But then again, is anyone really content?" As Cybil cast a disconcerted look upon him, he added with a pang of regret over the extremity of his comment, "I'm sorry. I don't mean to be a pessimist. I shouldn't forget that fulfillment can be had, though I do believe it can vary from day to day and even be lost." In a further attempt at explaining himself, he quite discernibly added, "Life can be so full of distractions and heartaches you see." As Cybil nodded her head in agreement, he felt motivated to say, "Getting back to Clair, though, she wasn't always the way she is now. I remember a time when she and I would be rewarded in some way for our efforts to do well. My dad was a firm believer in that."

"And how would he reward you?" Cybil asked of him.

"Sometimes he'd treat us to a snack of some sorts, or perhaps an outing at the museum, an afternoon at the park, or a day at the zoo. He said that he wanted us to always put forth our best effort. But that didn't mean we had to get straight A's in school, or be perfect by anyone's standards. He seemed to know when we were doing our best, and that was all he ever asked of us." Looking at her, he stated, "I think you would have liked my dad. He was fair-minded."

"I'm sure you're right," she conceded. "It's easy to see you thought highly of him."

"And still do," he made it a point to emphasize.

A short time later, when they were nearly to the playground, they stopped before a small two-storied home.

"See over there," Cybil said while directing his attention ahead and to their left. "The playground's there. You can't miss it."

"Okay, thanks," Dwight told her. "Where do you live anyway?"

"Just across the street," she informed him while pointing at a medium-sized green house. "Right smack dab between Bill and Jana."

"How convenient," Dwight replied with a smile. Looking onward, he somewhat apprehensively added, "Well, I guess I better not keep Jana waiting."

"Alright, see you tomorrow," Cybil concluded before walking away with a heavy heart over that which she knew Jana was going to be revealing to him.

As Dwight neared the playground, which consisted of a carousel, a slide, and a few swings, he laid eyes on Jana, who was sitting on one of the swings with her gaze cast to the ground. How distraught she appeared to be, he thought while approaching her, as though she were about to weep.

"You look like I always used to," he said in an attempt to humor her when he was nearly by her side.

"Oh, you're here already!" she reacted in surprise. ... "I was just thinking, that's all." With a forced smile she went on to say, "Gee, it's good to see you again. I hope you feel as well as you look."

"I had been feeling fine," he apprised her. "That is until I received your telephone call." As she eyed him with some semblance of difficulty, he continued, "So tell me, what's so important that we had to meet like this?" The look on his face reflected the depth of his concern.

Jana took on silence as she looked from Dwight to two small children that had just arrived on the scene to ride the merry-go-round. Their presence reminded her of her own childhood, of a time when life held so much less complication. The scope of it all was oh so fleeting, and in some respects she envied what she could no longer have.

"I suppose you were surprised when I wasn't with the Willards earlier today," she finally spoke up.

"I was more disappointed than surprised," he confessed. "I figured that something important must have come up to keep you away. Then I was told you weren't feeling well."

With the unenviable task of confession at hand, Jana stated, "I had them tell you I wasn't feeling well to mislead you, Dwight, and unless you considered my mind, you were misled." As he regarded her with a probing stare, she advised him to sit down on the swing beside her.

Grasping the importance of the moment at hand, Dwight heeded her request without uttering another word. Then, as he centered his undivided attention upon her, she began to speak without looking at him.

"It's my parents again, Dwight. They forbade me to go to the beach today because they don't want me to associate with you any more. I won't be able to go there from now on." In a desperate quest for a solution to their dilemma, she said, "But we'll find other ways to be together."

Even though Dwight was grievously affected by what was told him, he was honest enough to admit, "When you told me before that your parents didn't want you to associate with me, I tried to dismiss it. Well, since that time, after thinking about it a lot, I've come to realize that I was being selfish, because I didn't want to give you up, and I guess I hoped your parents would by some miracle change their minds about you and me... but since they haven't... I think it'd be for the best if we went along with their wishes." His concluding words were spoken with stinging difficulty.

"Oh, never!" Jana fervently cried out. "I'd never consider such a thing, and you mustn't either!"

Dwight had a distinct advantage over Jana, and this is what it was. Since he had been exposed to so much more disappointment than her over the years, he was better equipped to handle it, to cope with it, to accept it. That was why he was able to tell her, "I'm sorry if you're upset, Jana, but I meant what I said." When she nearly gasped in stunned response, he found it a necessity to add, "I know it's not what either of us wants, but I don't want to contribute to problems within your family. I want us to humble ourselves and admit defeat. It's important we do this." He stressed this last point with such emphasis that she knew he meant it with all his heart.

"I agree that it's important, Dwight," she acknowledged, "but that doesn't mean we should be forced to stop seeing each other completely."

As though sensing what took place earlier, Dwight stated, "Surely you must realize you'll have to resort to lying to be with me. That wouldn't be a good thing. You'd only end up frustrated." When he perceived she was not in total agreement, he imploringly added, "Don't you see! We've got to be willing to give each other up in order to benefit from this!" Yet at the sound of his own endorsement, tears began to well up in his eyes.

In a combination of hurt and confusion, Jana nearly shouted, "I can't understand you sometimes! I thought you valued our friendship more than this!"

"But I do value it!" he adamantly sought to convince her while rising to his feet. With his back to her he stated with a quiver in his voice, "Please try to understand that that's why I'm willing to let you go. I don't want to become a wedge between you and your parents. It wouldn't be right." Turning to face her, he noted with conviction, "You were born with the parents you have, and like it or not, you should respect their wishes in this matter!"

"Even if I know them to be wrong!" Jana exclaimed.

"Yes, in our case even then," he found it painful to say. "I'm just not willing to defy them. It'd only create more problems. Can't you see that if they're put on the defensive it'll harden their hearts even further!" With clear insight he dared to allege, "It'd self-defeat our reasons for being together. We could even end up resenting each other over the tug-of-war." With a lowering his eyes he related, "We'll part as friends, Jana Rossi, always friends. And no one can take that away from us. It's beyond their ability." With that having been so eloquently stated, a tear rolled down his cheek as a telling reminder of the appreciation he held for her involvement in his life.

Like an echo resonating down a canyon Jana recalled Alice's recent advice concerning accepting people for what they are, which brought her to realize that she had not only been selfish in her decision to retain her relationship with Dwight at all costs, she had also been closed-minded to think that her way of seeing things held the only possible solution to their dilemma. In other words she, unlike Dwight, had not taken into consideration a thing called surrender.

"I think I'm finally beginning to see what you mean," she thereby stated. "We've got to accept what we don't want to if we're to ever know deliverance." Yet when she found herself looking at him, she became so agonized over the thought of going their separate ways that she, too, began to cry. "I'm going to miss you so much," she as a result told him with a strained voice.

"I'll miss you, too," Dwight was barely able to tell her.

"It won't be for forever, though," Jana pledged as a ray of hope. "And we'll see each other in school. That can't be avoided."

Dwight wouldn't admit it, but he actually felt that seeing one another in school would only lengthen their period of adjustment. Yet perhaps by September they'd be better prepared to look at one another without suffering for it.

"And when the day comes, Dwight, that my parents no longer have a say in who I choose as friends, I'll be at your doorstep," Jana further professed.

Dwight was so humbled by all they were required to accept that he felt as if a great weight had been lifted from his shoulders, which served in evidence that sacrifice does have its intrinsic rewards when it's practiced with a noble purpose in mind. Gazing in the direction of the Willards' house then, he said, "I think I better let you get back home." Yet while he still had the opportunity to do so, he intently regarded her before saying with great depth of feeling and a fervor that truly moved her, "Thank you so much, so very very much for everything. Whenever I think of the definition of the word compassion, I'll think of you."

Jana was so overcome by emotion that she could no longer articulate words. Yet words were no longer necessary to convey the essence of what was felt, for in light of spoken sentiments, she knew they were proven friends. The tears they were shedding confirmed their regard for their relationship. So with the time for parting having come, Dwight did it in haste so as not to prolong the agony of going their separate ways. Though he was tempted to do so, he would not look back one last time, believing it would only enhance the pain of the loss, the pain of the moment.

So it came to pass that Dwight and Jana accepted her parents' demands, knowing in their hearts that the unfairness thrust upon them would not be enduring, as well it shouldn't, for time would not allow injustice to be a permanent situation for anyone. No, sooner or later one was always delivered from their bondage. And the guilty ones pay such a high price for the distress they inflict upon others, for it undermines their own satisfaction, thus vanquishing the oppressor.

CHAPTER 16

THE DESPERATION OF CLAIR

Even though the birthday party turned out to be memorable for Sandy, and even though Dwight enjoyed certain aspects of the affair, lingering within his mind was the disappointment he felt over that which had become of his relationship with Jana.

With keen insight Mrs. Willard noticed the ache in Dwight's eyes, because even though he tried his best to shield his anguish so as not to put a damper on the festive event, he found it challenging to exude happiness on the outside when he was crying on the inside. Could it be called a weakness that he was struggling with his loss? Was his emotional attachment to Jana an insecurity to be reckoned with? In the eyes of some it would be so considered. Yet if the truth be known, he knew that he'd be able to come to terms with his loss as long as he looked to God. His heartache was due to the fact that he had been barred from seeing a dearly loved friend. So it wasn't that he had become dependent on Jana's involvement in his life. Rather it was that he had acquired a deep and abiding respect for a girl whose companionship he would sorely miss. And so because his mourning was justified, he was not about to be defeated by it. In time his deprivation would be easier to bear. Rebounding was his for the choosing, and he knew it in the midst of his sorrow.

Later, while being driven homeward by Mr. Willard, Dwight wondered if Clair had taken care of the livestock after all. He did not experience a rush of guilt for questioning her word, because he knew he had good reason to doubt her credibility. In any event, he so hoped she had lived up to what she had said she would do.

Shortly thereafter, when Mr. Willard pulled into the Enharts' driveway, Dwight thanked him for everything while stepping out of the car.

"You stop by to visit us any time you get the chance, ya hear," the man urged him. "And try your best not to fret about Jana. Hope springs eternal."

"So I've come to believe," Dwight noted with half a smile before closing the car door and stepping back. Waving a final farewell, he approached the barn to investigate his suspicions concerning Clair. Suspicion was not his sole purpose in following this course of action, however, for he was anxious to see the animals. When he got close enough to the structure, he noticed that the back door was open and that Hazel was out to pasture. Making his way into the coop, he was pleased to discover that Clair had indeed kept her word, for the chickens had an adequate supply of both food and water.

"Well done, Clair," he said out loud in eased emotions.

Standing in the doorway, he, being the type of boy who possessed a natural curiosity, became fascinated by the flock's behavior.

It was scarcely an hour later that Dwight took a notion to head for the O'Maleys' farm to pay them a visit. As he approached in the distance, he noticed Roarie conversing with the couple by the corral. It appeared as though he was being shown the livestock, which consisted of Zuzueca, the young stallion's mother, and a few cows that Mr. O'Maley had recently purchased.

"Dwight, we were wondering where you've been," Mrs. O'Maley wasted no time in saying at the sight of him. "You haven't been here in awhile."

"No, I just got back from visiting with some friends in Fulton," he informed her as Roarie and Mr. O'Maley turned to regard him. "The plans came up suddenly."

"I see. Were you with those nice people who came here for the chicks last spring?"

"Yes, I was," he apprised her. "I spent last night at their house so that I could attend their daughter Sandy's birthday party today."

"That's nice."

"Dwight, I understand you already know our new neighbor," Mr. O'Maley interceded while looking to Roarie.

"Ya," Dwight acknowledged. "I met him and his family the day they moved to Chism. Good to see you again, Roarie. Are y'all settled into your new home?"

"Pretty much so, but it seems like there's always something to do," he updated him. "My dad even wants to raise some livestock. I do, too, even though I've never done that sort of thing before, being that I grew up in Chicago. But I must admit I'm looking forward to it. We're also thinking about planting some type of crop eventually."

"That sounds like a fine idea," Mr. O'Maley wholeheartedly supported him. "I've worked the land all my life, and though it's had its challenges for me and the missy, it's been rewarding, too, a labor of love." Broadly he grinned.

Mrs. O'Maley supported her husband's viewpoint with a nod of her head. Refocusing her attention on Dwight then, she said with compassion, "Roarie told us the news about Timothy. I'm so sorry. I remember him well."

"Yes, I was sorry, too, in more ways than one," Dwight related. "He was a good friend." With that having been imparted, he lowered his head in the memory of him, recalling that he never did get around to telling Jana what happened. But then suddenly her knowing this no longer seemed relevant. Perhaps losing his desire to inform her about Timothy was a coping mechanism. Perhaps it was a sign that he was taking the necessary steps to come to terms with her expulsion from his life.

Mindful of his sensitivity at the mention of Timothy, Mrs. O'Maley stated, "The death of a friend can be difficult to adjust to, but you've got friends in us to help you through this." As Dwight looked upon her with warm, appreciative eyes, she added with a note of sureness, "You'll feel better in your own time."

"Yes, in time," Dwight emphasized with a near whisper. "For death is hard on the living, and this, too, shall come to pass."

Roarie and the O'Maleys were so moved by Dwight's manner of expressing himself that a thought-provoking silence ensued, after which Roarie said, "Dwight, just before you arrived I invited the

O'Maleys to a housewarming we're having this Wednesday evening. We want all of our neighbors to attend it. Do you think you and your family can come?"

"I can," he said without delay, "but I wouldn't count on my mother or sister. I don't think they'd care to go. They aren't the sociable type."

"Alright," Roarie left it at that. "It starts at seven."

"That sounds fine," Dwight responded. In an effort to steer clear from further talk of his family, he cast his gaze in the direction of Mr. O'Maley and asked if there were any chores to be done.

"No, I can't say that there is," the man told him. "The livestock's been tended to already."

"In that case I think I'll go see the ducks," he decided. "Would you like to come with me, Roarie?"

"Sure," he gladly accepted the offer. "I've got to get used to being around animals."

"Just keep coming around here and you'll have plenty of that," Mr. O'Maley humorously advised him as the two boys headed for the creek.

It was when they were nearing their destination that Roarie uttered, "You know something, Dwight, Mr. O'Maley told me how you were with Zuzueca when he broke loose awhile back. He said you've got a way with animals he wishes he had."

"It's not impressive or complicated really," Dwight maintained. "You see, when an animal senses you can be trusted, it begins to relax. That's what's behind it all."

"That sounds reasonable enough," Roarie accepted his explanation. "Do you find it's the same way with people, too?"

"I suppose so," Dwight contended as they stopped before the creek, which was speckled with ducks of varying colors. In thinking of Clair, he added, "But sometimes even though a person may trust you, they find it difficult to relax around you because of the guilt they feel for having wronged you."

Sensing wisdom in Dwight's statement, Roarie was curious enough to delve into its source.

"Where did you learn these things?" he inquired.

"From the Bible," Dwight answered him. "I read from it often."

Seeing a look of surprise on Roarie's face, he asked, "Haven't you ever read from it?"

"No... it never even occurred to me," he was honest enough to say with a shrug of his shoulders. "My family isn't very religious."

Always aiming to make a valid point, Dwight told him, "Maybe some people would say I'm not religious either, because I'm not in a church every week, yet I still look to God." As Roarie took on a rather dazed look, he went on to say, "I've learned a lot about life from the Bible."

"What sort of things?" Roarie asked.

"Mainly how we should live," Dwight enlightened him. "I will say, though, that my time spent in church years ago did help to point me in the right direction."

Roarie regarded him in a manner that reaffirmed his willingness to be his friend. As Dwight crouched down then to get a better view of the ducks, it suddenly occurred to him that he was already coming to terms with the pain of losing Jana. Singling out a female mallard, he stated, "She had little ones last spring. See over there. That's one of them. And that one over there can actually fly because it's not too heavy. The others are, though. They're fed pretty well, probably too well." At the mention of that he looked up at Roarie.

"They're really nice," Roarie cited while smiling in reference to Dwight's closing comment. "Do they always stay out here?"

"They like to stay near the creek most of the time, but there's a small shack for them right over there in case the weather gets really bad." He pointed to the other side of the stream just beyond a decrepit wooden bridge, which consisted of no more than three or four boards.

"You really like these birds a lot, don't you?" Roarie remarked.

"Ya, they're entertaining to watch," Dwight replied. Digging into his pocket, he withdrew a dried piece of bread and began to break it up. "Here ya go," he called out while throwing the morsels into the water.

Watching the ducks consume their handout, Roarie felt confident he was going to enjoy having Dwight as his neighbor. Yes, there was something about him that made being in his company enjoyable.

Returning to the front of the house, the two boys were invited into the O'Maleys' home to partake in a light lunch of egg salad sandwiches and fresh milk. They talked of many things while they ate; the balmy weather, the ample supply of rainfall, and the work in need of being done to restore the Crane homestead to some semblance of its former condition. Mrs. O'Maley served some tasty pralines then, a family favorite, after which Dwight and Roarie departed for home.

Together they walked along the narrow dirt driveway that led to the main road. Then, when it came time to go their separate ways, Roarie invited Dwight to stop by his house the next day at one o'clock.

"Maybe we could take a walk to the ocean for a swim," he suggested.

Though unsettling thoughts of Carl bombarded Dwight's mind, he decided to cast aside his fears and accept the invitation, knowing full well there was a part of him which was beyond the grasp of mankind's depravity. Additionally, it might be of therapeutic value to be occupied rather than idle, particularly in the aftermath of what happened where Jana was concerned.

"Good, I'll see ya tomorrow then," Roarie concluded while commencing to walk away.

Observing his departure, Dwight wondered if theirs would be a relationship that would stand the tests of time. Issues would undoubtedly present themselves, he had come to believe. Always it was bound to happen in one way, shape or form. It so seemed to be the way of the world, the way of this life.

Once at home in the privacy of his room, Dwight reflected on what he told Roarie about religion. He knew that people defined religion in various ways, and yet he himself had discovered that a person could read the Bible in the privacy of their room and come to know Jesus Christ as mankind's wonderful link to God through the salvation he represents. So even though religion could be used as a stepping-stone to God, it wasn't enough in and of itself.

Suddenly wondering how Clair was getting along emotionally, Dwight began to center his thoughts around her, for he had not yet seen her since arriving back from the Willards'.

Placing upon his dresser a book about birds he planned to finish reading, he left his room and made his way down the hall to her bedroom door.

"Who's there?" he heard her respond to his knock.

"It's Dwight," he said, "Can I come in?"

"Alright," she bade him to enter.

Walking into the room, Dwight found her standing before her mirror with a forlorn look on her face. Her hair tumbled over her shoulders in an unkempt state.

"Clair, is anything wrong?" he intently asked of her.

Apathetically regarding him in the mirror, she told him with a note of humility, "I was just thinking about my life... and how I don't like who I am."

Dwight could appreciate her willingness to communicate her feelings, yet he grew strangely tongue-tied as he gazed at her reflection in the mirror, for he was uncertain how he should respond to her. Yet he believed something was in order; and so, after a brief deliberation, he stated, "Clair, I know you're upset right now, but try to remember that it's only temporary. It can be dealt with. I'll help you in whatever way I can, if you'll let me." There was tenderness in his voice and compassion in his eyes.

Clair beheld him in the mirror. Then she said, "That's a noble thought, but it's too late. I won't ever be able to come to terms with all that's happened since dad abandoned us."

"Clair, it was never proven what happened to dad," Dwight swiftly reminded her. "I think he deserves the benefit of the doubt, don't you?"

"But mother said...."

"She doesn't know what happened," he firmly insisted. "Unfortunately she's brainwashed herself to think the worst."

Turning to regard him directly, Clair asked, "Do you really keep yourself from hating, or do you just act out the part to hide the bitterness within? I've wondered about that more than once."

"I try to be honest in what I say," Dwight asserted. Compelled to focus his attention upon her once again, he stated, "I sense changes taking place in you, Clair."

"I want what we once had," she said with a distant stare.

Dwight realized that she was no longer inclined to lash out at the world. This very much concerned him, however, for if her surrender was only aimed inwardly, and not toward God, then it could lead to her self-destruction.

"Clair, try to be optimistic," he therefore urged her. "Feeling badly will pass. It's not for forever. I know."

Visually scrutinizing him, Clair found herself in envy of his ability to persevere in the world as she had come to know it.

"What motivates you to be this way?" she consequently asked with a spark of fascination.

Softly smiling, Dwight said, "The love of God." And he placed a clenched fist upon his chest to symbolize his meaning.

Clair was momentarily silent in thought. Walking to her window then, she peered longingly out.

"I'm so tired," she lamented. Drawing her head against the curtains, she eventually began to cry. "Oh, how I hate this house. I can't bear to live in it any more."

In the concern he felt for her Dwight happened to lay eyes on the family portrait she came across on the day she gave him Timothy's letters. Yes, there it was on her dresser in plain view, a token of her want for a better life.

"I guess good memories have a way of resurfacing," he made the claim as she continued to weep.

Turning aside, Clair saw what he was looking at and said, "Ya, they do, but so do the bad."

"True, but it's worse when a person is bitter," he dared to allege, "so never allow yourself to be bitter again. You'll be free of a terrible burden, and feel better for it."

"But I don't know if that's possible," she confided. Slowly walking over to the portrait, she clutched it to her breast. "I don't think I have the strength to go on."

"As long as you're still alive and wondering, there's still hope," he brought to her attention.

"It's easy for you to say. You've got friends," she told him.

"You've got to be willing to be a friend to attract friends, Clair," he felt disposed to say. "It isn't a one-sided thing. And more importantly than that, you've got to seek the love of God."

"I've searched for that love," she informed him in a yearning for comfort. "I just can't seem to find it, though. If it's there, why can't I find it?" Intently she regarded him with a probing stare.

Dwight thought about her question for awhile. Then he explicitly stated, "Unless you free your mind from distractions, the presence of God will elude you. Believe me, I've found that out the hard way."

Clair sensed that he had given her some good advice, but she was currently so depressed that all she could seem to do was nod her head and close her eyes while yet clutching the picture close to her.

As for Dwight, he felt as though she had heard enough for one day. Yet he did feel inclined to utter one last thing before leaving the room. It was, "Thanks for feeding the animals while I was gone."

* * *

The next day proved to be an eventful one for Dwight.

At about ten in the morning he decided to pay the O'Maleys a visit. Upon his arrival there he found Mr. O'Maley working on his car near the side of the barn.

"Hi, what seems to be the trouble?" he inquired of the man.

"Oh, hi, lad," he spoke up at the sight of him. ... "Ah, nothing serious. I'm just tuning the engine up a bit. It won't take too much longer. ... You know anything about cars, my boy?" he asked without tearing his attention away from his work.

"Not really too much," Dwight informed him while casually leaning against the fender. "But I wish I did. And I'd like to learn how to drive one even more."

"Well, you should have told me before. I'll teach you in a little while," he readily volunteered while looking up at him from under the hood.

"Are you serious!" Dwight reacted in apparent disbelief. Seeing the man nod his head, he added with enthusiasm, "Okay, I'll be right back after I collect the eggs!" Dashing away, he returned minutes later with Mrs. O'Maley following a fair distance behind him.

"I heard the news, so I came to be a spectator," she lightheartedly told her husband once she was by his side. "This might turn out to be entertaining."

"No, don't say that, Mrs. O'Maley!" Dwight mildly protested. "I want this to go smoothly."

"There, we're all set," Mr. O'Maley informed them while standing upright and slamming the hood shut. Withdrawing the keys from his shirt pocket, he briskly threw them at Dwight. "Get in the driver's seat, lad!"

"Okay!" he eagerly complied. When Mr. O'Maley was seated along side him, he added on an amusing note, "I do know enough to put the key in the ignition. But what now?" He regarded the man with childlike innocence.

"Well, to begin with, just think of the gear system in the form of an H. The upper left is reverse, the lower left is first, the upper right is second and the lower right is third, and in the center you have neutral. On the floor you have the gas pedal, clutch, and brake." He singled out the three of them while pointing. "Right now the car is in first so push the clutch in, put the car in neutral, then start her up with your left foot on the brake and your right on the gas."

Doing as he was told, Dwight tried to follow the man's instructions as best he could, but he ended up chugging and stalling the vehicle more than once in the process.

"Try again," Mr. O'Maley repeatedly advised him until finally he did manage to back the car up, only he did so too quickly and wound up going right through Mrs. O'Maley's flower bed, leaving most of her petunias and zinnias a trampled mess.

"Boy, this is harder than I thought," he consequently stated in a wave of embarrassment once he had stopped beyond the ruined flowers. "I sure hope you're not ready to give up on me yet."

"No, I'm not, lad," the man sought to assure him with a wide grin, "but from the look of the missy, I wouldn't ask her that." Joining him in gazing at the woman, Dwight saw that she was glaring at them with her hands placed firmly on her hips.

Awkwardly Dwight attempted to humor her with a smile. Then he rolled down his window and said in an effort to appease her, "I know you have every right to be mad, but you did come to see something happen, and it did."

"Those flowers were beautiful!" she shouted. "I think I should have stayed in the house!" Yet just as she was about to storm away, she saw the lingering smile on her husband's face, and inevitably sighed in resignation. "Oh, get on with the driving lesson," she subsequently announced with a forgiving toss of her hand. "I guess I can always grow more flowers."

In great relief Dwight told her, "When we get back, I'll help you salvage any surviving plants." Yet when he put the car into first gear with the intention of driving off to the right of them, he ended up misjudging the degree to which he had to turn the wheel, thus trampling them a second time.

"Oh, Mr. O'Maley, she's surely gonna have my hide!" he dramatically stated in response to what he had done as they proceeded to bounce along their way down the narrow dirt road.

"Ya, and I think you just might end up having mine!" Mr. O'Maley just as dramatically emphasized while clutching the seat for dear life. "Slow down, laddie!"

"Gosh, maybe I shouldn't even come back here after the lesson," Dwight seriously suggested with his eyes firmly fixed on the road and his hands firmly gripped on the wheel. "She might need some time to cool off."

"Yes, and maybe I, the instructor, shouldn't come back here to face her either!" Mr. O'Maley just as seriously stated.

When it nearly came time to pull onto the main road, Dwight was already experiencing a false sense of security concerning his driving abilities. But Mr. O'Maley knew otherwise, so he cautioned him to slowly begin working the brakes. Yet when he attempted to do this, he applied too much pressure to the pedal, resulting in he and Mr. O'Maley being thrust so violently forward that Mr. O'Maley nearly hit the dashboard.

"Gee, I never thought learning to drive would be so jerky," Dwight made comment once they had come to a complete stop, as though he couldn't imagine why things were so different for him compared to other drivers.

"Believe me, neither did I, lad!" Mr. O'Maley exclaimed in obvious relief that they were no longer moving. "I think it's that you need more practice."

"Ya, but already I feel myself improving," Dwight was quick to say while readying himself to continue onward.

"Ya, you're improving alright," Mr. O'Maley emphatically said. "But let's just take it slow and easy so that the only casualties are the flowers, okay?"

At first Dwight seemed somewhat bewildered by his comment. Yet as he held the man under his scrutiny, they simultaneously broke out in laughter.

Pulling onto the main road in the direction of the coastline, Dwight soon began to drive more skillfully, so much so that Mr. O'Maley told him he felt certain he'd only need a few more lessons after all.

Arriving at The Gulf and parking the car, Dwight walked to the shoreline to determine whether it would be comfortable enough for swimming when he returned later in the day with Roarie. Putting his hand to the water, he thought about what his relationship with God had come to mean in his life, comprehending that as long as he earnestly sought to accept those things which were in need of being accepted, he would triumph in the long run. Therein resided the treasure to be reaped. Therein resided the proof that surrender, when it's called for, has its hidden rewards, its intrinsic benefits.

Driving homeward, Dwight felt increasingly confident behind the wheel of the car, so much so that he was inclined to say out of the clear blue sky, "Thanks, Mr. O'Maley, thanks for everything. You don't know how much it means."

Firmly grasping him by the shoulder, Mr. O'Maley responded, "You're very welcome, lad," with the love that a father would voice toward a much cherished son.

* * *

Later, after having helped Mrs. O'Maley salvage what was left of her flowers, which wasn't much, Dwight went home, put his swimming suit on under his pants, grabbed a towel, and headed for Roarie's. In doing so he felt a measure of anxiety enter his emotions over the thought of associating with the Aimes, which stemmed from the way in which he departed from their company on the day they moved into their home. But this was another day, he prudently reminded himself; and so, upon arriving at his destination and being greeted at the front door by Mrs. Aimes, a feeling of mental ease had been secured by him.

"Roarie's upstairs putting his swimming suit on," the woman informed him. "I'm sure he won't be long." Cordially she invited him into her home.

Walking indoors, Dwight was immediately engulfed by thoughts of Timothy, for it had been many a time he entered this very doorway. Slowly running his gaze about the immediate area, he felt quite moved by the nostalgia of it all.

"There's many memories here for you, aren't there?" Mrs. Aimes found it easy to tell.

"There sure are," Dwight freely acknowledged. Eventually placing his full attention upon her, he added, "I do hope you'll like living here."

"I already do," she said with a smile. Yet when an expression of pressing regard overcame her features, she felt compelled to add, "Dwight, I'm glad Roarie is upstairs, because I'd like to speak to you in private. Won't you follow me into the living room?" With a rather graceful sweep of her hand she beckoned him to do so.

Dwight heeded her request by entering the attractively decorated room of blue and seating himself on the sofa.

"I'll try my best to be as brief as possible," Mrs. Aimes wasted no time in saying while situating herself adjacent to him. "Roarie has been looking forward to swimming with you today. In fact he's been quite fond of you ever since the day he met you."

Thoroughly confused by her revelation, Dwight responded by telling her, "But how is that possible? We spoke very little to one another that day. I was a stranger to him. Even now he hardly knows me."

"Sometimes you're just drawn to certain people," she maintained. "I think he wants you to be his friend because of the way you feel about Timothy. And he does need a friend right now, especially after...." Suddenly she clammed up over her near slip of the tongue concerning the guarded secrets of Roarie's past. Dwight, however, was quite perceptive when it came to the subject of guarded secrets, given that he had lived with them for so long. And so, when he deduced that she was trying to hide something from him, he said in an effort to appease her, "I assure you I'm willing to be Roarie's friend, Mrs. Aimes. And I'll try my best not to do anything to hurt him."

"It's not you hurting him I'm worried about. It's him hurting you... and himself, too, for that matter," she found herself confessing. "You ah... see, despite his good intentions, he's got a weakness, I'm afraid, and he doesn't always have it under control."

"You're looking at someone who's got his own share of weaknesses," Dwight pointed out to her without reservation. "I've got news for you, Mrs. Aimes. I don't expect perfection in relationships. Life is too imperfect for it to be possible. If Roarie offends me, I'll try my best to reach an understanding with him."

"And if that can't be accomplished?" she solemnly inquired of him with raised eyebrows.

"Then I suppose we'll go our separate ways, but with no hard feelings where I'm concerned." Noticing her pronounced skepticism concerning his ability to carry such an assertion through to completion, he made it his objective to affirm, "I've seen what bitterness does to people, Mrs. Aimes, and it saddens me. I've seen it lessen the quality of a person's life." With further insight, he told her, "And it's all for the choosing."

In response to his impressive outlook Mrs. Aimes said, "I can see why Roarie likes you so much." Yet when her face took on a look of grave significance, she felt compelled to add, "However, I must warn you to be careful of growing too fond of him. Keep some distance from him, please." Her eyes imparted a look of urgency.

Dwight found it difficult to imagine her reasons for speaking to him in such a crucial manner, for it was as though she was attempting to protect him from Roarie without divulging why. But he wanted to know what he was up against so that he could prepare himself to handle it. And he didn't believe it was an unreasonable request, which is why he inquired, "Mrs. Aimes, can't you tell me something more? I don't know what to make of this."

"Make of what?" Roarie interrupted them while entering the room with a beach towel in his hand.

"Oh... ah, nothing," his mother tensely spoke up. "Just chit chat."

"Don't wanna tell me, huh," Roarie good-naturedly reasoned.

"Must have been pretty secretive."

"Don't be silly," his mother countered with a hint of annoyance. "It was nothing." Yet her reaction only served to enhance both his and Dwight's curiosity.

Though Roarie was somewhat taken aback by his mother's strange conduct, Dwight was determined to prevent their conversation from escalating into something contentious.

"I guess you're ready to leave for the beach, hey Roarie," he consequently stated in an effort to change the subject.

"Ya... I suppose so," Roarie capitulated for Dwight's sake. "I've been looking forward to this. The other day I went to the beach alone and took a swim. I must admit I was nervous at first. I've heard stories back home of shark attacks."

"There is always that possibility I guess," Dwight conceded, "but I've only seen two sharks in my life."

"Really, tell me about it," Roarie encouraged him with wide-eyed interest.

"Well, the first time I was sitting on the beach and saw one break surface about two hundred yards or so from shore. That was unusual, though. The other time I was with my dad. We were in a boat and saw one about twenty feet from us."

"Was it big?" Roarie inquired as though his very safety depended upon his knowing this.

"Ya, it was a fairly good size," Dwight admitted while smiling over the extent of Roarie's fascination.

Noticing Dwight's response, Roarie inferred, "I guess you think I'm overreacting."

"Well, just a bit," Dwight told him while yet smiling. However, on a sober note, he went on to convey, "My dad did tell me, though, when I was a little boy that any person who took to the ocean had to respect it to reduce their chances of being consumed by it. But there's a difference between that and fear. A goal of mine is to be set free from fear." Looking upon him, he intently added, "We'll swim close to the shoreline, but out of respect."

Roarie marveled at Dwight's ability to articulate his thoughts so well. As for Mrs. Aimes, she was so grateful for the manner in which Dwight had handled their suspended discussion that she found herself asking him to return for supper later that afternoon.

Dwight took her behavior to be somewhat of an enigma. On the one hand it was an admission that she was receptive to his involvement in her son's life, yet on the other hand she had already told him she wanted his involvement with Roarie kept in check. Yet maybe it was also that she wanted to get him back here to resume their former talk in private, when and if the opportunity presented itself. These were the types of thoughts that crossed his mind. But despite everything, he still found himself desiring to be amongst this family, therefore he graciously accepted her invitation. Getting up then from where he was seated, he said to Roarie, "Shall we go?"

"Yep, all set." He held up his towel and headed for the door, at which time his mother and Dwight exchanged a look of ongoing appeal in regard to their unfinished conversation. Yet somehow it was even more than that, for Mrs. Aimes seemed to be warning Dwight to be mindful of today, he got the clear impression.

Just moments later, as they began to head towards The Gulf, Roarie asked Dwight if he wanted to go home to inform his mother he'd be eating supper elsewhere. In that way she'd know not to expect him.

"No, that's not necessary," Dwight replied. "I don't know if the O'Maleys told you anything, Roarie, but my relationship with my mother isn't what it should be."

"No, they didn't say," he notified him, "but I did sense something was wrong when I invited you and your family to our house-warming."

"Oh, ya," Dwight recalled his reaction to the invitation. "But let's not talk about unpleasant things, not now anyway. Let's just enjoy the day."

"Alright," Roarie acquiesced. Nevertheless, a short time later, when he and Dwight were nearly halfway to The Gulf, he was tempted to ask, "Dwight, I'm curious about what my mother said to you. Was it.... disturbing?"

"I'm not sure what it was," Dwight let it be known. "We never did get down to specifics. She was evasive, and yet she was trying to tell me something."

Realizing what that something may have been, Roarie inquired with gravity, "Was it about me?"

"Yes... it was," Dwight rather reluctantly admitted. "Does that bother you?"

"It might," Roarie was prone to concede. Glancing at him, he went on to say, "You see, I don't like it when my mother talks about me behind my back. It makes me feel betrayed."

"Wouldn't it depend on what she was saying?" Dwight wisely pointed out. As Roarie cast his eyes to the ground, he was quick to advise him, "Don't be so hard on your mother, Roarie. Whatever she was trying to tell me, she must have had your best interest at heart, because she loves you. That I saw in her eyes plainly, and it's something to be very thankful for. Don't ever take a mother's love for granted."

"I still wish she'd leave it up to me to tell people what I want them to know about my life," he spoke up in defense. "I might have a talk with her about that." Another troubling thought now occurred to him. "I bet you're curious about me now, but I'm not ready to tell you anything."

"Then I guess we had better leave it at that," Dwight recommended.

In thanking him for being so understanding, Roarie hoped he'd be able to refrain from developing a sexual attraction towards him, for there was in his past bitter proof as to what this would mean. Yes, he realized that not only would he be jeopardizing their friendship if he entertained inappropriate thoughts of him, he would also be contributing to disruptions within his family, as he had so painfully learned while in Chicago. Circumstances were different this time around, though, for the person he was drawn to in this particular instance was not a worldly man, but a virgin boy who greatly loved God and his principles. And so a direction he had never been inspired to pursue was about to present itself once his past was made known.

When the two boys arrived at their destination, they saw that the ocean was beautifully calm and glassy, a marvel to the naked eye with its many subtle shades of blue.

"I can't understand why there aren't a lot of people here,"

Roarie made mention of. "It's so nice."

"Sometimes there's quite a few," Dwight told him. "As a matter-of-fact it was here that I met some friends of mine." He slowly ran his gaze about the general area in memory of that eventful day. "I come here with them almost every Sunday for a picnic."

"Maybe I'll get to meet them some day," Roarie intimated.

"I'll see to it that you do," Dwight suggested while beginning to remove his shirt.

When Dwight was standing in his swimming suit, he ran to the ocean and dove in with Roarie following close behind. They swam out a short ways together and submerged only to resurface near the shoreline, doing this over and over again about five or six different times. And glad Dwight was to be spending time in a place he loved so much with someone who had befriended him.

Later, when they were seated on the beach drying themselves off, Dwight told Roarie about his jerky driving lesson from earlier in the day.

"Mr. O'Maley said he's never had such a ride," he laughed. "I'm sure I'll do much better tomorrow morning, though. ... How about you, Roarie, do you know how to drive?" he then asked.

"Ya, my dad taught me back in Chicago. It'll be great when I get my driver's license, though. Then maybe we can go to see a few movies in Fulton."

"That sounds like fun," Dwight responded. "And Bill and Cybil could meet us there. They're friends of mine."

"But let's keep coming here, too," Roarie made it a point to emphasize.

"Oh, ya, I'd never stop coming here," Dwight told him with certainty. ... "You know something, Roarie, it's good to have you around here to do things with. I'm glad you moved here."

"So am I," Roarie admitted. "I like it here much more than I thought I would." Gently they smiled at one another before lying down on their respective towels to drink in the warmth of the sun.

Moments later, Dwight found his thoughts drifting to what Mrs. Aimes had warned him about. Yet only briefly did he allow this to happen, for he had learned in life that attempting to draw conclusions based upon sketchy details was a futile game better left unplayed. The margin of error was simply too great concerning judgments reached. So he allowed himself to think of other things instead, things which he was certain of, such as how much he loved God and how much God loved him, not realizing in doing so that he would be of assistance to Roarie in discovering the truth about life.

* * *

Early the next morning Dwight partook in his second driving lesson and understandably did quite a bit better this time around. Immediately thereafter he paid Roarie a brief visit, assuring both him and his family before departing for home to be at their house-warming by seven that evening.

As he proceeded down Kirkland Road he did not realize the importance of his timing, yet for some reason he was suddenly stricken with an intense yearning to be in the company of his sister. As a result of this feeling he sped up his pace only to find himself nearly running by the time he arrived home.

Making his way into the house and discovering that neither Clair nor his mother were anywhere to be seen on the main floor, he darted up the stairs, stopping before Clair's bedroom door.

"Clair, are you in there?" he inquired while knocking upon it. ... "Clair, are you there!" he continued in a burst of urgency when she did not respond.

Still hearing nothing from within, Dwight stormed into the room only to discover that his sister was not present. With his curiosity now soaring to a new height, he felt as though it was absolutely essential he find her. But in rushing down the hall to the bathroom, he found himself confronted by a locked door.

"Clair, open up! I know you're in there!" he pleaded while fumbling with the doorknob. ... "Please, Clair, open up!" he yelled quite loudly; yet still all he heard was silence from within.

For a few moments Dwight was hindered by jumbled emotions. Managing to gather his wits then, he charged against the door with as much might as he could muster. Yet when this attempt at entry proved to be in vain, he earnestly appealed to God for additional strength while repeatedly kicking at it until it finally gave way.

It's difficult to assess each and every variable which compels a person to do what they do, yet there upon the floor lay an unconscious Clair with her slit wrists spewing forth her life-sustaining blood.

"No, Clair!" Dwight exclaimed in horror while rushing forward and kneeling beside her, too mentally jolted to do anything but stare at her in stunned response. Time would not permit a gradual absorption of the emergency, though, for time was of the essence. And so because he did not stand a chance of averting her death as long as he allowed his emotions to get the better of him, he took decisive measures by grapping the hand towel from the rack just a few feet away and tearing it lengthwise into strips. These pieces of cloth he used to wrap tightly around each of her wrists to arrest the bleeding. Rushing to his mother's room then with the intention of having her drive Clair to the hospital, he found her in such a deep state of sleep stemming from an overindulgence of alcohol the previous night that he was unable to awaken her no matter how hard he tried. Forced to give up his futile efforts, he ran back to Clair's side in the realization that it would be up to him to take further action. His driving lessons could not have come at a better time, he thought while taking his sister into his arms and carrying her down the flight of stairs with as much agility as he could muster.

Finding the keys to his mother's car exactly where he remembered them to be, Dwight carried Clair's limp body from the house and speedily drove away. Despite the timing of his lessons, he still found himself wondering if his sister might die anyway, for each and every time he glanced at her stationary figure in the back seat where he had laid her, she looked all the whiter with death. It reminded him of the day he saw her so depressed, for it had crossed his mind at that time that she might be contemplating suicide. Really, though, it hadn't been all that long ago that he himself thought about ending his life. Therefore yes, he could relate to feelings associated with suicide. But to actually attempt it! What a reflection of abandoned purpose and crushed hope.

Continuing along his way, Dwight cried off and on, reminiscing of life as it used to be.

When he arrived at Fulton General Hospital after what seemed an eternity, he carried Clair inside where the main floor staff was quick to respond to her dire condition.

"We'll do everything we can for her," a nurse sought to assure him as two orderlies hurriedly began to wheel Clair away on a gurney.

Dwight knew that God was there for him, yet to experience the fellowship of people who had proven their friendship, he found himself on the telephone calling the Willards. It was Bill who answered the phone, and after filling him in on what had happened, Bill told him that he and his parents would leave for the hospital as soon as possible.

Seated in the waiting room, Dwight witnessed such an intense longing to speak to Jana that he actually thought about calling her. Thus he grew ashamed of himself, for he knew that contacting her would be a violation of his commitment to obey her parents' wishes. In addition to that, she might be tempted to rush to the hospital to be with him, which would further complicate matters, thereby broadening their period of adjustment. Their decision to stay away from one another was meant to be unconditionally honored, unconditionally accepted, no matter what transpired. It was not meant to be reversed when times got tough. .... But oh how it did take strength to distance yourself from someone when you yearned for their fellowship so much, proving that life does have a way of testing our convictions.

It wasn't too much later that Dwight heard the voices of Bill, Cybil, and Mr. and Mrs. Willard as they made their way into the building. At first they did not notice him approaching from their right; but then just as Mr. Willard was about to speak to the nurse at the main desk, Mrs. Willard laid eyes on him.

"Dwight!" she exclaimed. "Did you hear anything about her condition yet!"

"No," he said with a quiver in his voice, for the sight of his friends had deeply affected his emotions. "She's lost a lot of blood, though. Oh, Mrs. Willard, I don't want her to die like this. I want her to feel good about herself before death comes her way."

"Then I think we had better have faith she'll recover," she stated while firmly grasping his hands within hers.

"I'm trying," Dwight told her with all the conviction he could muster, "but you didn't see how awful she looked." As everybody began to follow him into the waiting room, he solemnly added, "I thought she was going to do this."

"But how could you have known for certain?" Mrs. Willard begged to differ with him in an effort to ease his heartache.

"I recognized the signs," Dwight said while nodding his head to affirm that belief. "I tried to get her to think positive, but she was determined to hurt herself. I'm glad I tried to reach her, though, because even though this happened, it's right to try." Looking at the faces of the people about him, he gratefully added, "Thanks for coming. I'm glad you're here."

"We know you are," Mrs. Willard compassionately responded. "Is your mother with your sister?" she then inquired in the hope that she was.

For awhile Dwight was silent in thought. Drawing in a breath then, he said in serious admission, "She wasn't in any condition to be here. I couldn't even wake her up. It was obvious her drinking got the best of her last night." In the anguish he bore concerning that reality, he maintained, "I guess she's resorting to suicide, too, in her own way. The method may be different, but the intent's the same." With a lowering of his head, he made the determination, "She's lost touch with life over the years and forgotten what love is all about."

"And yet you have known a mother's love, haven't you, Dwight?" Mrs. Willard recalled being told by Jana, though suspecting as much all along.

"Yes," he let it be known, "but nothing has helped me more than the love of God. If it weren't for that love, I would have become bitter just like her. I might have even become a menace to society, taking my resentments out on others."

As everyone present became moved to tears by Dwight's confession, a doctor approached and asked if a member of Clair's family was amongst them.

"Yes, I'm her brother," Dwight was quick to state while rising to his feet and wiping the wetness from his cheeks. "How's my sister?"

"You can relax," the doctor put his mind at ease. "We've been able to stabilize her vital signs. She's going to make it."

"Oh, thank God!" Dwight exclaimed. "Can I see her?"

"Yes, in fact she's been asking for you," the man surprised him by saying. "But don't be too long. She needs her rest. She's in room 317." Turning to depart, he stopped short to conclude, "It's a very good thing you got to her when you did. If she had lost any more blood, she surely would have died."

Watching the man disappear from sight down the hall, Dwight felt a moving sensation engulf him, and he knew that the premonition he had had while walking down Kirkland Road was something more than coincidence. It was spiritual, and it was of God, for who but the true God would have wanted Clair to be spared from the grip of her own destruction? Certainly an evil source would not have wanted this, for that would have meant it was fighting against itself and what it stood for.

Turning to face everyone, Dwight said with utmost appreciation, "I guess I'll be alright now. Thanks again for coming."

"Do keep us informed," Mr. Willard advised him.

"I shall," he assured him. Looking upon all who were present, he made the revelation, "It's nice to have friends like you." Then he proceeded to walk away.

When Dwight arrived at room 317, he momentarily ceased his advancement to prepare himself to face Clair, for he fully expected her to be guilt-ridden for what she had done, and he wasn't looking forward to witnessing that guilt within her.

Entering the room and seeing tubes protruding from her body, he found himself questioning whether or not she was ready to receive visitors after all. ... But then suddenly she opened her eyes and beheld him with a depth of feeling her lowly condition prompted her to unveil.

"Clair," he stated while approaching the bed. "You really put a scare into me. I oughta be mad at you for that."

"I'm sorry," she barely was able to say, "but I... didn't think you'd find me in time to go through all this fuss. .... I thought I'd die first."

"Oh, Clair, will you ever come to believe your life is important?" he emphatically asked of her. "Is there no reaching you?"

"It seems not," she softly whispered. "If I felt there was, I wouldn't have tried what I did."

"I predict some day you're going to feel differently, though. You'll see," he stated while gently touching one of her hands.

Gazing up at him, she imploringly said, "But it won't ever happen at home. I can't bear the thought of going back there."

"But... Clair, I'll help you...."

"No, I can't go back there!" she interrupted him in obvious distress. "You must find a place to send me so that I don't have to go back there... please!" She was speaking so labored it concerned him it might be putting too much of a strain on her, for which reason he said in compliance, "Alright, I'll do what I can, but right now you need your rest, so I had better leave, but I'll return tomorrow. ... Try not to worry." Empathy seemed to radiate from his very being.

"Dwight"

"Yes, Clair."

"I'm sorry I upset you. ... And I'm sorry about Timothy, too," she weakly uttered before drifting off into unconsciousness.

"I know you are," he whispered as a flood of tears began to cloud his vision. "I know." And in that very moment he seemed to comprehend like never before why it was such a worthwhile ambition to rise above the scorn of the world.

Leaving Clair's room, Dwight happened to see the doctor with whom he had previously spoken walking down the corridor in his direction.

"Doctor, I'm glad you're here," he wasted no time in saying. "I need to talk to you about Clair." When the man nodded his head, he added, "She doesn't want to return home, and I guess if I'm to be totally honest, I have to admit it's the right choice. You see she needs to be in a different environment. To go home would be too depressing for her. She doesn't like it there."

"I see," the doctor responded. "I was going to ask you what course of action you thought should be taken, but I didn't want to say anything in front of your friends."

"I appreciate that," Dwight told him. "But I'm sure you know more about this sort of thing than me. Where do you think she should be sent for help?"

"Based on my experience I would suggest a psychiatric ward I know of in Jackson. It's a very reputable institution that's state and federally financed, so your family wouldn't have to pay the full cost of her convalescence."

"But it's so far away, over a hundred miles," Dwight swiftly made known his misgivings. "I'd hate to think of her that far from home."

"It really is the best place for her, though," he emphasized. "And who knows, she may be there only a short time. If your sister wants help, it's a sign she's already on the road to recovery."

"Alright then, if it's in her best interest," Dwight went along with his recommendation. "I'll let you talk it over with Clair to find out if she agrees to it. It's been a very trying day."

"I can well imagine," the doctor sympathized. "But before you leave, I'll get the necessary papers for your parents to sign. You can wait for me downstairs in the waiting room."

"Okay, but I had better tell you we only have our mother at home. I'll get her to sign them, though," he convincingly told him, even though he knew it might not be easy to accomplish.

"That'll be fine," he replied. "I'll see you in a bit then." With that having been settled, he entered Clair's room to check on her vital signs.

When Dwight arrived back in the waiting room, the only person there was an anxious man who told him he was waiting to hear word whether he was the father of a daughter or a son.

Sitting down, Dwight regarded the pacing man and thought about the gift of life, realizing in doing so that to thank God for that gift on the day of a baby's birth was a befitting way to celebrate that child's coming into the world. But what of birthdays in general, was it right to celebrate them, for they were not referred to very much in the Bible? ... And yet in a very genuine way there was a birth that was celebrated when he, the Messiah, came into this world and the shepherds came to pay homage to him. Therefore yes, life was meant to be celebrated after all if it was done so with thankfulness in mind, and a quest to be born in spirit. By virtue of that I say onto you that each and every day has the potential to be steep in lessons learned, and wisdom for the taking.

* * *

When Dwight arrived home, he parked his mother's car and made his way into the house to speak with her about Clair.

The living room was dim with its sun-faded drapes drawn almost completely, yet still he managed to distinguish her silhouette and the slow-moving spiral of smoke rising from the cigarette that rested between her fingertips.

At first he stood motionless at the entrance of the room staring at her stationary figure. Advancing a bit forward then, he gravely stated, "I put your keys back where I found them." When she did not respond to his statement, he added, "Did you even know I used the car, and why?"

With a blank stare she took a drag from her cigarette before saying, "I saw the blood and the razor blade. ... How is she?" The impression could be gotten she was attempting to quell her concern so that sorrow would be kept at bay, the hardened heart suppressing the caring heart lodged deep within.

"She's going to live," Dwight told her with clear relief. In noticing her seemingly nonchalant bearing, he went on to say, "To pretend that you don't care about her is beyond belief. You couldn't have become that unfeeling."

"I didn't wish her dead, if that's what you mean," she would only say in defense.

"But that isn't nearly enough," Dwight brought to her attention. "She wants to know that you care." In detecting her continued reluctance to amend her outlook toward life, he cried out while casting his face toward the heavens, "Oh, how I wish you had faith!"

"I used to go to church and look where it got me!" she harshly retaliated.

"A person can attend church without finding God!" he shouted in a fit of exasperation. "Attendance isn't nearly enough!" ... Eventually removing Clair's admittance papers from his shirt pocket, he stated, "I've got something for you to sign."

"What is it?" she suspiciously asked.

"Forms to have Clair admitted to a psychiatric ward in Jackson," he told her without reservation. "She doesn't want to return here. That shouldn't surprise anyone, least of all you."

"I won't sign them!" she protested while rising to her feet. "It'd be an embarrassment to have people think my daughter's crazy!"

Shaking his head over the irony of her statement, Dwight was bold enough to contend, "You've hurt yourself far worse than community gossip ever has. Instead of being concerned about what they think, you'd be better off thinking about what's in your best interest, and Clair's, or she may end up dead!" When it became apparent she was bent on remaining uncooperative, he stated while raising the papers in his hand for the added emphasis, "If you don't sign these for her, I will!"

At first a look of disgust developed on his mother's face regarding his daring claim. But when she realized he was not about to relent, she threw up her hands while exclaiming, "Alright, I'll sign them! Just leave them on the kitchen table!"

Filled with a sense of relief, Dwight said as she reseated herself on the sofa, "You'll be doing the right thing." Yet as he turned to depart, he was inspired to stop short and add, "On second thoughts, there's something even better you could do. You could express some love for her, because she could really use a dose of that medicine right now." Having made that suggestion, he walked into the kitchen feeling justified for what he had said for her own good. He of course didn't know whether or not his advice would be heeded in the long run, but at least he had spoken his mind in a fashion that befit the situation.

Later, at the approach of seven o'clock, Dwight forced himself to attend the Aimes' housewarming, assuring himself before departing from home not to put a damper on a gathering that was meant to be festive. ... As it turned out he was able to conduct himself quite well. However he did feel a sense of relief when the affair came to an end, for Clair had weighed heavily on his mind for the duration of the evening.

Lying in bed that night, Dwight prayed for humanity in general, knowing full well that the world was in much need of that. Focusing on Carl then, he foresaw that the time would come when he would have to stop running away from him, for living in the grip of fear was not a healthy existence. When Jana entered his mind, he reflected on how deeply he missed her companionship. Forsaking her had not come easy, but it had become an important part of his soul-searching. Truly, from the depths of his heart, he was bound and determined to salvage something of value from the pain and disappointment of losing her. And what might that be? The realization that it was wonderful to have been in her company while it lasted, and that he was enriched for having known her.

"Oh, God," he now whispered. "Help me feel you're all I need." Ever so effortlessly this boy in much need of resting his weary mind was carried into the realm of peaceful slumber. It had not been the first time he was assisted from above, and it would likely not be his last.

* * *

When Cybil informed Jana of Clair's attempted suicide, she became so sad to think she had not been of comfort to Dwight in his hour of need at the hospital that she withdrew to the privacy of her room.

Getting down on her knees at her bedside, she tearfully asked God for the strength to refrain from becoming bitter towards her parents for forbidding her to associate with Dwight. Only then did she feel prepared to go downstairs to face her mother, hoping in doing so that once the woman found out about Clair, she would sympathize with her wish to again see Dwight on a regular basis.

"I'm genuinely sorry for the girl," Mrs. Rossi stated in reaction to the news. "I hope she'll recover." Yet she was ill at ease at the mention of this, for Jana's disappointment in not having been at Dwight's side was blatantly obvious to her. But what was she to do, she found herself wondering, when she was married to a man who demanded that Jana stay away from the boy? She really did feel caught in the middle at times. And yet it was a position she had chosen not to challenge in the course of her marriage thus far. So in an effort to ease her conscience for the part she had played in circumstances as they were, she said as casually as she was able, "I'm sure that boy will be just fine. Try not to think about him so much." Making light of the situation was a coping mechanism, a vain attempt at feeling better about choices made.

Gazing at her, Jana succinctly stated, "You and father may be able to stop me from seeing Dwight, but you can't make me forget about him. I'll never forget him!" The tone in her voice echoed her conviction.

"But dear, you're only tormenting yourself," her mother conveniently dismissed her feelings. Placing an arm about her shoulder, she went on to say, "Now I suggest you ask your friends not to tell you anything more about that boy or his family from now on. They're only upsetting you needlessly."

There comes a time in life when due to circumstances beyond your control you admit defeat. Jana had just reached that point where her parents were concerned. Yet there was a very significant consequence to her defeat in that she was not now, nor would she likely in the any near future be, the cheerful girl her mother in particular wanted her to be. And so even though her parents had gotten their way with her, were they really triumphant? Actually no, and in essence it was because they were not living in accordance with the laws of God. The end result? A daughter whose spirit had been broken.

Without putting forth an effort to break free of her mother's touch, Jana seemed to drift unconsciously away from her. Ascending the stairs to her room, she felt so emotionally overwhelmed by her plight that she could not even cry. Such is the way it was for her right up until bedtime. Through force of habit she did manage to eat a few bites of her supper, yet she was extremely reticent as she did so. She didn't know it, but her mother was so affected by her mood change that she began to reevaluate her firm stand concerning Dwight, for if the boy meant so much to her, a girl who had always been level-headed, then perhaps it would be prudent after all to meet him for herself to obtain a firsthand impression of him. But how would she ever dare suggest such a thing to her husband, she found herself wondering, when she knew he'd be strictly opposed to the idea? For the time being she therefore discarded the idea rather than risk arousing the man's wrath. Each and every choice we make in our walk through life does have its consequences, though, so in the meantime she and her daughter would become all the more estranged as the days wore on.

Oh, where was comfort to be found for a girl named Jana? .... In the very same place it was discovered by Dwight.

* * *

Bright and early the next morning Dwight headed for the O'Maleys' to tell them what happened to Clair. He also wanted to ask them if they would be good enough to give him a ride to the hospital so that he could deliver to Dr. Braddock the admittance papers, of which his mother had been true to her word in signing.

Hearing a rooster crow as he ascended the front stairs of the O'Maleys' home, he wondered if he had arrived much earlier than he should have. But then he recalled Mr. O'Maley once saying that he always rose early, and so felt better about his timing.

Once inside the house, his speech was slightly labored as he told his friends the sobering news from the day before. But he refrained from making any mention whatsoever of his mother, for he did not want to reveal her drunkenness or general lack of concern. The O'Maleys sensed something was amiss, however, for if his mother had intentions of going to the hospital, then why would he not have gone there with her? In any event, they gladly consented to his request with no questions asked, their love and concern for him overriding their curiosity.

"How awful it must have been for you to deal with what happened," Mrs. O'Maley later told him when they were driving into Fulton. "It's a good thing you knew what to do."

"Actually it did take me a while to collect my thoughts," Dwight freely admitted. "But I was so upset. ... I discovered something about myself yesterday," he then went on to say. "I found out I was capable of much more than I realized."

"Many a person has made that same discovery, lad," Mr. O'Maley remarked. "Yes, indeedy, many a person."

Nodding his head, Dwight stated, "And for me it was symbolic of something, victory over my fears."

When they arrived at the hospital, Mr. and Mrs. O'Maley told Dwight they'd pick him up in an hour or so after having done some shopping downtown.

Dwight thanked them as he stepped out of the car, assuring them he'd watch for their return. Making his way into the building, he took the elevator to the third floor where he discovered upon walking into room 317 that Dr. Braddock was at Clair's bedside.

"I was wondering when you'd be coming," the man stated while glancing Dwight's way. "Do you have the signed papers?"

"Yes." Removing them from his shirt pocket, he placed them on the nightstand before advancing to the foot of the bed. "Clair, you look like you're getting your color back," he was delighted to make the observation.

"I do feel much better," she had to admit. "Dr. Braddock even said I can leave for Jackson tomorrow, as long as I remain stable today."

"Gee, that is good news," Dwight only half-heartedly responded, for he still hated the thought of her being located so far from home. "I really hope you'll be helped there, Clair."

Pondering his statement, Clair rather pensively stated, "Things are gonna be so different for me now. I'm not sure what to expect."

"You'll be getting some good care so don't worry," Dr. Braddock replied. Checking his watch, he added, "I've got a busy schedule today, so I had better get to it. I know the two of you would like to be alone anyway." Gazing down at Clair, he smiled and said in an affable manner, "You take it easy now, young lady, and eat your spinach to build up some good strong blood."

"Ugh, spinach!" she cringed and pleasantly surprised Dwight by laughing. "I'll take my chances without that!"

"Somehow I thought you'd say that," the doctor chuckled while commencing to withdraw from the room.

Since it was evident a meaningful change had taken place within Clair, Dwight was quick to comment on it.

"I think you're right," Clair concurred. In an attempt at intro-spection, she added, "Maybe I'm relieved I'm not going home."

"Maybe you are at that," Dwight would only say.

"Dwight"

"Yes, Clair."

"Did mother cooperate in signing the papers?" she took an interest in knowing.

"Yes, she did," he said in a desire to reveal only the final result.

"That doesn't sound like the mother I know," she declared in a wave of suspicion. "It was you who signed them, wasn't it?"

"No, it really was her," Dwight acknowledged with a direct gaze.

Determining that he was being truthful, Clair allowed a warm expression to overcome her features.

"Perhaps she still cares about me then... a little anyway," she accepted the possibility.

"In her heart I know she does," Dwight aimed to convince her; in the aftermath of which, out of the clear blue sky, Clair sounded out, "Do you plan to visit me in Jackson?"

"I'll try, but I don't know if I'll be able to get a ride there. It's so far away. I'll do my best, though." Gently he smiled in that assurance. "I hope you return home realizing you can have a good life, Clair."

"I had better," she replied, "or I'll end up just like mother. I could see that I was. That's why I tried to end my life. ... Poor mother," she then lamented with a distant stare. "What's to become of her?"

"Time will tell," Dwight solemnly reminded her. "I do know she can choose a different path. Pray that she does."

* * *

When Dwight and the O'Maleys arrived back in Chism, Dwight decided to accompany them to their farm.

Feeding Zuzueca a carrot from the garden, he reflected on a day a week earlier in which Mr. O'Maley told him of a breeder who wanted to buy the stallion. "I've sold my mare's colts before," he then went on to explain himself. "That's why I have her bred." Yet he was disinclined to sell this particular horse because of the attachment Dwight felt towards it. Therefore in consideration of that, not to mention the disappointment he easily detected in Dwight's eyes over the news of a potential sale, he ended up telling him he would in all likelihood retain ownership of the animal. Dwight, however, in laying no claim on Zuzueca, encouraged the man to feel free to sell the horse, since that was what he had originally intended to do.

"I'm gonna miss you if you're sold," he currently whispered into Zuzueca's ear from where he stood by the corral's edge. And as though sensing the implications of that occurrence, the horse whinnied in response and nuzzled ever closer to him.

A short time later, as Dwight watched the young stallion running in the open field, Mr. O'Maley approached from the house. From a window he had seen him stroking the horse's neck, which compelled him to call Mr. Zainer, the man who wanted to buy Zuzueca, and notify him he decided not to sell after all. Yet there was more behind his reasoning than Dwight's liking for the animal, namely Clair's attempted suicide, for after all Dwight had been through as of late in dealing with that, it somehow seemed incompassionate to deny him the continued enjoyment of having Zuzueca in his midst.

"He's growing into quite a beautiful stallion, isn't he?" the man alerted Dwight of his presence while taking a place beside him at the corral's edge.

Pleased by the sight of his friend, Dwight replied, "He sure is." Looking once more at Zuzueca, he made the claim, "But I think that horse would be beautiful to me no matter what he looked like." Suddenly remembering that Mr. O'Maley was in a quandary over selling the animal, he rationally pointed out, "But he's just a horse. I could get used to not seeing him any more if I had to."

"Ya, that's true that he's just a horse," Mr. O'Maley casually went along with Dwight's assessment. "In fact I reckon he's not much different than any other." Allowing a brief silence to ensue for the sake of leading up to the much anticipated moment, he utilized self-discipline to suppress his enthusiasm as he added, "But that horse isn't going to be sold anyway." As Dwight regarded him with a questioning look, he expressively went on to say, "It is my pleasure to tell you, lad, that Mr. Zainer has been duly informed there will be no transaction between himself and yours truly. After all, I can't very well sell him a horse that doesn't even belong to me, now can I?" Broadly he grinned with a satisfaction that was evident.

At first Dwight did not grasp the significance of what Mr. O'Maley was alluding to. But then, as he began to interpret the meaning behind the man's facial expressions, a look of astonishment came over his own features.

"Are you trying to tell me you're giving me Zuzueca?" he thereby inquired. Seeing a nod of affirmation, he exclaimed with a tone of great appreciation yet mild protest, "Oh, no, Mr. O'Maley, I couldn't! That horse is worth too much to give to me!"

"But you're worth more to me and the missy than the horse, or the money we could get for him," he assured him. Yet even then he could see Dwight was reluctant to accept such a generous gift, for which reason he was persuaded to suggest, "I'll tell ya what, we'll keep Zuzueca here a while longer until you're ready to take him home. And I won't take no for an answer!"

"But what if my mother refuses to let me keep him?" Dwight was quick to consider.

"Then I suppose we'll just have to keep him here forever!" the man persisted with resounding determination before winking at the boy.

Dwight was so touched by Mr. O'Maley's benevolence that he held him under his scrutiny for only a moment or two before impulsively hugging him.

"Thank you," he told him with heartfelt appreciation as tears came to his eyes. "Thank you very much." Gratitude was more than merely felt. It was exuded.

"You're welcome, lad," the man assured him while vigorously patting him on the back.

In the meantime, as though discerning the significance of what had taken place where he was concerned, Zuzueca trotted up to them and nuzzled them for some share of the attention. Separating from one another, Mr. O'Maley and Dwight began to laugh over the horse's unexpected, though intelligent, behavior. Then, as Dwight began to stroke the animal's head and neck to satisfy its whims, Mr. O'Maley smiled in the striking awareness of how much he had grown to love Dwight like a son. Surely the good feeling he was presently witnessing was the best reward he could ever have obtained in what he decided to do with Zuzueca. Surely it was much better than any money he could have generated from a sale.

* * *

Clair did in fact leave for Jackson the following day, yet before doing so by way of transportation that was provided by the hospital, Dwight called her from the O'Maleys' telephone to wish her well in her treatment.

"And please try to have a positive attitude," he told her in conclusion. "It really is the answer to getting better."

"I'll try," Clair would only say, still at times finding it difficult to fathom the extent of his concern for her.

Dwight thought a lot about Clair in the coming days, and prayed for her well-being on a regular basis.

When Sunday pulled around, he informed the Willards while riding toward The Gulf that Clair's attitude was much improved. Moments thereafter, he made the announcement that Roarie planned to show up later that afternoon to meet everybody.

Arriving at their destination, Dwight disciplined himself to keep Jana from entering his thoughts, and not because he wanted to forget about her, but because he didn't want to long for the pleasure of her company.

It was very soon after eating that Dwight saw Roarie advancing in the distance.

"Here comes Roarie now," he stated while rising from the sand to greet him.

When Roarie had made his way to Dwight's side and all introductions were completed, Mrs. Willard asked him if he was hungry for any of the leftover food.

"No, thanks, I ate before coming here," Roarie apprised her. "What I'd really like is to swim." Holding up a towel he had taken along, he asked if anyone else was interested.

As it turned out everyone went into the water to one degree or another, and when a game of water tag eventually ensued, it was discovered that Dwight and Roarie had to put forth quite an effort to catch one another, for they were both strong swimmers.

Not too long after drying himself off from his swim, Roarie left for home. In the aftermath of his departure, as Dwight was sitting on the shoreline looking out to sea, Mrs. Willard approached to speak to him in private.

"What are you thinking about?" she took an interest in knowing.

"Nothing in particular," Dwight stated while glancing up at her.

Lowering herself beside him, the woman said, "Roarie seemed like a nice boy. You must be glad to have him close by to spend time with."

"Ya, I really am," Dwight conceded.

"I can relate to that. As a girl I had a very dear friend who lived only two houses down from me, not to say we didn't have our differences once in awhile," she smiled in recollection, "but when you have someone to confide in and do things with, it can make for a lot of shared memories."

"I know," Dwight acknowledged. "I often recall the time I spent with Timothy before he moved to Chicago. ... And now I've since learned he's dead."

"I'm so sorry. When did you find that out?" she inquired with pronounced interest.

"It was when the Aimes moved here, right before Jana and I stopped seeing one another. I meant to tell you about him, but I was so upset over Jana, and then Clair tried to kill herself." Shaking his head, he added, "Everything overwhelmed me I guess, so I never got around to talking about it."

"Oh, Dwight," she sympathized. "You've had to deal with so much lately."

With a look of sheer acceptance Dwight said, "I once heard it said that hardships come in threes, but whether it's three or thirty-three, I don't ever want to become consumed by thoughts of bitterness or lost hope. That to me would be a very sad outcome, and I'd be defeated for it." With a penetrating look, he went on to say, "I guess as long as we keep an open mind we can find some hope to cling to even in the worst of times." As Mrs. Willard nodded her head, he changed the subject by adding, "I'd like to go to Jackson to visit Clair. The O'Maleys said they'd take me a week from Thursday. Mrs. O'Maley happens to have a sister living in that area that she'd like to visit anyway, so it should work out well."

"How good of them," she warmly replied. "I'm glad they're

there for you." Suddenly engulfed by an extreme measure of sentimentality, she found herself adding with deep emotion, "I hope Clair gets well soon, and I wish the same thing for your mother."

"So do I, Mrs. Willard, but my mother is bitter in a way that's harder to deal with than most people realize. You see, when my dad disappeared, Clair and I still had our mother, but my mother wanted someone to lean on, too, and she felt she had no one, when really, God was there for her. I think she felt abandoned. Maybe it would have helped to have some relatives close by, but my dad's an only child and his parents were already dead at the time. My other grandparents live in Michigan. That's where my mother is from. Then there's also Aunt Lorraine, my mother's sister, but she and my mother lost touch with one another after my mother's outlook began to deteriorate. It wasn't Aunt Lorraine's fault, though," he made certain to emphasize. "We got many letters from her when my father first disappeared, but my mother began to answer them less and less until finally Aunt Lorraine gave up trying to keep in touch." He momentarily stopped speaking, then softly smiled before adding, "Mrs. Willard, I liked my Aunt Lorraine. She was so enjoyable to be around, and whenever we visited her and my grandparents in northern Michigan, we had the best of times. I was only three years old when we first started making trips up there, and I remember that the autumns were really beautiful with all the brightly colored leaves. Once we went there in the spring, though, and I helped a man make maple syrup. He lived down the road a short distance from my Aunt Lorraine. I really liked doing that. ... So you see, I do have good memories from my childhood. It sure would be nice to see my relatives again, though, especially my Aunt Lorraine."

"Well, perhaps you can!" Mrs. Willard suggested in a burst of optimism. "And if that can't be arranged, you could at least write to each other."

"I used to think about doing that," Dwight told her, "but after my father was no longer at home, it seemed like there wasn't anything good to say." Looking at the woman, he soon felt inspired to add, "I think I'm going to take your advice. I wanna know how she is."

"Good!" she optimistically stated. "You'll be doing the right thing!"

Moments later, just as they stood up, Sandy rushed toward them and shouted, "Come play volleyball, Dwight!" She pointed to where the others had congregated by the net.

"Sure!" he eagerly complied and darted away without the least bit anxiety, so self-assured had he come to feel while in the presence of these people.

Mrs. Willard leisurely followed, gratified by the positive attributes she saw within Dwight, and perceiving him to be a boy with an outlook that was unusually thought provoking for his age.

* * *

In the days awaiting his trip to Jackson, Dwight felt inclined to examine both the person he saw himself to be, and the person he expected himself to be. He knew it was of utmost importance to keep things within their proper perspective, for how else could one recognize the limitations that existed. But when did one reach the ultimate of what they could and should be in the eyes of God? It seemed to be such a profound, elusive thing, something which only God himself can fully know and understand the depth of.

When the appointed day arrived, Dwight got up early to see to the needs of the livestock. Then, in anxious expectation, he awaited the stroke of eight o'clock before heading for the O'Maleys' farm.

Walking down Kirkland Road, he found himself wishing that Roarie was going with him on his journey. Believing the boy's father to be in need of his assistance on the farm, he had not even told him about his plans for the day.

Later, while he and the O'Maleys were driving toward Jackson, he tried to imagine what a psychiatric institute looked like, for he had never before seen one, and so could only speculate on the matter.

Arriving at their destination, Mr. and Mrs. O'Maley told him they'd return in about two hours or so to pick him up.

As he walked through the front door of the white, three-storied building, Dwight's eyes befell what he considered to be an arresting sight, for in chairs there were people with listless expressions on their faces, as though they were awaiting only one thing, that being impending deliverance from their present state, while in the distance in one of the rooms down a long, white corridor he could hear some-one eerily crooning. Stopping in his tracks to make a visual sweep of the area, he couldn't help but wonder if his mother might also end up here. Then he began to consider the people before him. Did they have family support of any kind? Why were they institutionalized? Were unresolved issues tormenting their minds? Certainly he saw there to be a great deal of unrest in the world. Yet surely there was also hope. Therein could be found the silver lining in the midst of the want and need.

Advancing forward, Dwight was greeted at the main desk by the nurse on duty for the day.

"I'm Dwight Enhart," he wasted no time in telling her. "I'm here to see my sister, Clair Enhart."

"Oh, yes, I believe she's in the recreation room. Go through the last door down the hall," she informed him while pointing a finger in that direction.

"Thank you," Dwight responded. "There's no time limit is there?"

"The afternoon visitation ends at three o'clock," was all the woman said as she hurriedly began thumbing through some papers.

Dwight proceeded to follow the directions given him, making his way down the corridor at a deliberate pace. Before he was able to reach his destination, however, he was approached by a confused looking young woman who had only moments earlier exited from the very room he sought to enter.

"Where's my mother?" she innocently questioned him, as though he had specifically come here to give her information in that regard.

"I... don't know," Dwight hesitantly replied. "Was she supposed to visit you today?"

At these words the woman's face took on a distorted look.

"You took her away from me, didn't you!" she harshly accused him. "Why did you do that! I needed her!"

"No, I didn't...."

"Yes, you took her away from me and now she won't be able to visit me any more!" In an outburst of tears she began running down the hall until two staff members came rushing toward her and forced her into an adjoining room while she kicked and screamed in frenzied resistance.

From where he stood Dwight regarded this scene in utter dismay. He had thought the people he initially saw when entering this ward were forlorn; but she, this irrational, crazed woman who accused him of such a bizarre thing, was beyond his expectations. It compelled him to wonder if some day it might be his own mother standing there saying, "Where is my husband? I want my husband. Why did he leave me?" Hence, this is what he was beginning to comprehend about the human condition; that perfect mental health is beyond the realm of possibilities, that no one has a flawless way of thinking.

As he continued along his way, he wondered whether another such incident might arise. In fact, it wasn't until he reached the door of the recreation room and peered through its window to see Clair leisurely sitting in a lounge chair reading a magazine that his thoughts took on a changed dimension.

Entering the room, Dwight discovered that Clair was not the only one present. In a corner a young man sat on a chair, while another man sat before a table that had a game of checkers on it, as though he were patiently awaiting the next player, whereas on a couch against the wall a fidgety woman kept twitching her hands while mumbling something in an incomprehensible manner.

Making his way before Clair, Dwight said as enthusiastically as he could, "Hello, Clair, I'm here!" As she looked up at him, he saw spontaneous approval in her eyes, which pleased him for what it represented.

"Dwight, I didn't know you'd be here today!" she exclaimed while standing. Becoming somewhat embarrassed by her outburst, she awkwardly added, "It... ah, feels good to see you." For the most part she was uncomfortable because of the transition she was yet going through in adopting an improved outlook. Guilt was still very much an issue in her life concerning past transgressions.

"I'm glad to see you, too," Dwight told her with an honesty she immediately sensed. Then, with firm yet gentle strength, he grabbed her by the arms and widened the distance between them so that he could get a better look at her. "You seem to be in good health," he was swift to point out. "But how are you doing mentally?"

"Alright," she replied with a clear level of doubt. Reseating herself on the lounge chair, she made the revelation, "My therapist says I've got deep-seated resentments to resolve, and that my self-esteem is in much need of repair, but he does encourage me, and is of some comfort." In recollection of her sessions, she went on to say, "I told him about you, too, and how you saved my life despite how I've treated you."

In earnestness Dwight proclaimed, "I think I had better tell you I didn't save your life that day, Clair." As Clair stared at him with a look of confusion, he added, "I may have come to your rescue. I may have delayed your death, but only God can save your life, and that takes place beyond this life." In humble admission he went on to say, "I had a premonition that day."

Clair saw in his acknowledgment what made him so uniquely intriguing.

"I'll remember that," she somberly stated. In a wave of curiosity she then noted, "So you believe God gave me a second chance to change my ways."

"I'm convinced of it," Dwight told her.

In the moments to come, as each of them became increasingly aware of the jabberings of the woman, Clair looked at her and said, "I was afraid of some of these people when I first came here, but not any more. You seem to get used to them after awhile to the point where their strange ways seem normal." Shaking her head a bit, she dared to consider, "But what really is normal anyway? I don't even know the answer to that question."

Thinking about it for awhile, Dwight stated, "Our view of normal varies from society to society and home to home, but the laws of God remain unchanged."

Struck by his comment, Clair eventually confided, "Sometimes when I'm lying in bed at night, I find myself wondering what made them this way."

Nodding his head, Dwight asked if they received many visitors.

"I was told by someone who's been here a long time that most of them don't. But some of them probably don't even have family members nearby."

"I suppose not," Dwight acknowledged. "And you're one of them."

"And yet you came here anyway," she thoughtfully pointed out. "Despite the distance, you came."

"Yes, because of some good friends who cared enough to help me get here," he said of the O'Maleys.

Clair was still in the initial stages of acquiring a healthier mind set. Withholding Timothy's letters and consequently learning of his death had affected her significantly. It had been a turning point in her life. Yet even then there was more to it than that. Dwight had not held her misconduct against her. He had taken an interest in coming to her aid in her time of need. He was visiting her now, and if he cared about her well-being that much, then certainly she should take an interest in helping herself.

Do any of us really know the extent of God's love? Can it actually be discovered in an imperfect world? In Dwight's estimation it simply mattered that there was love to be had, love to be given. And so, even though he was in no way certain what the outcome of his efforts would be, especially after what had taken place in the hall earlier, he decided to approach the confused woman and ask what she was trying to say. When she did not respond in the least, he knelt before her, looked her directly in the face, and added, "What's the matter?" Yet still she remained in her own world of thought.

Eventually standing, Dwight happened to lay eyes on a piano situated in the corner of the room.

"Maybe you'd like to hear some music," he suggested while making his way to it. Sitting down, he placed his hands upon the keyboard and began to play a song he had learned as a young boy while taking lessons from an elderly resident of Chism, Mrs. Penrite.

At first the woman seemed totally unaffected by the softly played tune, though the two men and Clair were quite receptive to the melody. Yet as Dwight neared the conclusion of his selection, she suddenly stopped twitching, stood up, and neared the piano with a look of captured delight on her face. When he ceased playing, she said in an appreciative manner, "That was nice."

"I'm glad you liked it," Dwight told her. "Would you like to hear more?"

"Yes, more," she eagerly responded. "You play more."

Dwight smiled at the woman, believing in his heart that it was often the simplest of pleasures which achieved the most satisfying of results. Therefore as he resumed playing the piano, he felt as though this day had been rewarding indeed, for touching the life of another individual, even in the smallest of ways, verily made it so.

CHAPTER 17

FOR THE BETTER LIFE

By way of resignation Dwight became more and more accustomed to not seeing Jana, he was pleased to discover. It did help considerably to be liberated from the guilt of their forbidden association. Yet most reassuring of all was the knowledge that his relationship with God couldn't be taken away from him by anyone.

Jana in the meantime found herself pondering an all-important question. Could her character be enhanced by the disappointments of her life? Certainly so if she was of a disposition to allow it to happen, if she reaped valuable knowledge from the sum total of her experiences. Still heartbroken, though, over the loss of Dwight's companionship, she did plan to socialize with him in school, telling herself mainly because she wanted it to be so that the academic setting was an acceptable place for interaction. She was grasping at straws, yearning to talk to him from time to time. Surrender was yet to be adhered to on the all encompassing basis expected of her by her parents.

As for Mrs. Aimes, she never did finish telling Dwight what she had begun to disclose about Roarie. Dwight strongly suspected it was because Roarie had asked her to say nothing more about him behind his back. The entire Aimes family did seem to be adjusting quite well to country living, though, which perhaps was an incentive in and of itself to refrain from further mentioning the topic.

While summer drifted along, Dwight looked over his shoulder

more than once in fearful anticipation of Carl's return. On several occasions as he was walking down Kirkland Road a vehicle was observed approaching in the distance which turned out to have Carl within it. But concealment behind a tree had always been exacted before the ill-intentioned boy was seen driving by.

When September ushered in, it brought with it the arrival of the first day of the new school year.

Naturally Dwight had mixed emotions over the thought of returning to Fulton High. Yet his misgivings were not as pronounced as they had been last year at this time. No, now he felt one hundred percent better, and slept that much better, too.

As he dressed, he foresaw that he would be forced to use the alarm clock gotten from Clair's room the night before to wake himself up every morning. In fact, he felt reasonably certain that if he did not assume this responsibility, his mother would allow him to sleep all morning long if he opted to do so.

Centering his thoughts on the day he visited Clair at the psychiatric hospital, he recalled telling her he would in all likelihood be unable to return for quite some time, if at all, but that he would surely keep in touch by writing at least one letter a week, which she in turn pledged to do. As it so happened those letters were mutually looked forward to, and whenever he received word from her, he made it a point to tell his mother, even though she appeared disinterested.

It was after having seen to the needs of Hazel and the chickens that Dwight's attention shifted to his Aunt Lorraine. Seated on the porch awaiting the bus, he softly smiled as he recalled a day two weeks earlier in which he received a most welcome of mail deliveries, it being an answer to a letter he had written her. In her response she indicated how sad she was to hear of his family's difficulties. Where her own family was concerned it was learned that her daughter, Rachael, had married, and that her son, Richard, had gone away to college at the University of Michigan and was majoring in law. Indeed, everything she made mention of reminded him of her concern for people, and he so wished he could see her in the not-too-distant future.

Pleasant memories of his Aunt Lorraine seemed to last for only a few moments before the Chism bus was seen coming into view down Kirkland Road. Standing up, he was relieved to feel a certain calmness overcome him, yet he quickly figured it out. In the gradual process that it involves he was defeating his phobias. Certain life altering discoveries had been made in recent weeks and months, largely because he had taken the initiative to seek them out.

Walking down the driveway, Dwight wondered how he would handle being in close proximity to Jana, for sooner or later it was bound to occur. With utmost resolve he hereby decided to keep his nearness to her at an absolute minimum, for if the two of them were in one another's company for any length of time, he knew that they would be tempted to speak, and possibly socialize, on a regular basis. Then word of what they were doing would no doubt reach the ears of Mr. and Mrs. Rossi and irritate them even further, which in his estimation would self-defeat all reasons for being together.

When the bus pulled to a stop near the mailbox and Dwight saw Sara sitting in her usual place, he did not fear a taunting remark as he had in the past. Yet still, as he boarded the vehicle, he hoped she would refrain from being unpleasant. But once again it turned out to be a futile wish.

"Dwight, I heard Clair isn't living at home any more. What'd ya do, push her to the brink of suicide?" she badgered him in an act of inconsideration that silenced the other passengers.

Dwight stopped in his tracks in stunned response, for of all the things she had ever tormented him about, this was the absolute worst. Truly she was a hateful girl, he thought in a combination of pity and anger.

"The fact that you would even say such a thing proves you have a very disturbed mind!" he thus told her for her own good. With a penetrating gaze he felt compelled to add, "I strongly suggest you try to remedy that!"

As Dwight proceeded to walk onward, looks of approval could be detected on the faces of students and bus driver alike. After seating himself, all eyes turned to Sara to discover what her response to his reprimand would be. Without a doubt she looked surprised, even humiliated and embarrassed, before turning forward to brood in silence. Yet before having done so, in a vain last attempt at retaliation, she did cast a final look of resentment Dwight's way. It was then that Dwight began to wonder if he had finally secured an end to her harassment. But then all of a sudden he decided not to fret about it, because if need be he would speak his mind again at some later date.

So what was the lesson learned? That sometimes a person is in need of a verbal chastisement to point them in the right direction.

* * *

"Why did that girl treat you that way?" Roarie inquired of Dwight while taking a seat beside him on the bus.

In an honest attempt at insight, Dwight said, "She treats me that way because she thinks it'll do her some good, ease her own misery." With further discernment he went on to say, "Her dislike of herself far outweighs her dislike of me."

"I wouldn't know about that," Roarie told him, "but I liked what you said to her. I think it needed to be said."

"Hopefully God sees it that way, too," Dwight remarked with utmost concern.

Caught off guard by his statement, Roarie uneasily noted, "Ah... like I said before, I'm not used to thinking about God."

In the heartfelt manner he was known to present himself, Dwight looked at him and stated, "I hope the day comes when you are." Then they ceased speaking for the remainder of the ride to school.

When the time came to unboard, Dwight and Roarie walked indoors along with the other students. Catching a glimpse of Carl, Dwight was relieved to discover he was not as uptight over the sight of him as he had been in the past. Wondering why this was so, he concluded that his faith in God had uplifted him. He had knowledge that he wasn't alone in his struggles against his tormentors. He had a means of defense, and it was the best weapon available. It was a weapon of love, not hate; peace, not violence. It was a defense that diminished fear and increased self-confidence, often reaching into the very soul of the enemy. So in the spirit of they who utilize this defense is a strength that a wrong against them can't destroy. This is what Dwight had come to realize. That was why he no longer felt alone whenever the world reviled him.

Entering the auditorium with Roarie and sitting toward the back of the room, Dwight quickly noticed Jana, Bill, and Cybil a few rows ahead of them, which brought him to ascertain that although a part of him yearned to be in their company, he was doubly determined to distance himself from Jana for the sake of his convictions.

Later, after having listened to the principal give a speech similar to the one of a year before, everyone went to their respective classes. As they did so, Dwight wondered whether or not there was a maladjusted individual, such as the one he had been last year at this time, walking nervously about. If there was, he hoped in his heart they would meet someone as compassionate as Jana, someone who held a genuine interest in seeing them through their difficulties.

Ironically, as Dwight's classes turned out, he shared four out of five of them with Jana, a fact which did not rest well with him for obvious reasons.

As for Jana, she could tell that Dwight was reluctant to speak to her, for she had not seen him so much as look at her throughout the day. This was an occurrence which greatly disturbed her, particularly in view of the fact that he had not been in her presence for such an extended period of time. Therefore to satisfy her whims in that regard, she decided to approach him the following day at lunch time to find out why he was avoiding her within the school setting, though in her heart she knew the reason why.

Roarie was seated with Dwight at the time, and although Jana was disappointed to discover that Dwight was not alone to converse with, the intensity of her desire to be in his company was pronounced enough to compel her to approach him anyway. Her hello was forthright.

Dwight was rather taken aback by Jana's presence. Yet Jana, in noticing this reaction within him, hoped she could reason it out of him.

Tentatively returning her greeting, Dwight introduced her to Roarie, after which Jana stated, "Dwight, I'd like to talk to you in private. It's important."

Looking upon her, Dwight suspected her motive for being here. To spare Roarie the inconvenience of having to move elsewhere, he immediately took it upon himself to stand up without warning and stride to a vacant table in the corner of the room. Jana was quick to follow suit.

As Dwight sat staring at the tabletop in strained emotions, he knew he was on the verge of saying what neither of them wanted to hear. Another unpleasant reality in need of being addressed, yet better now than later, for later would only enhance the pain of the inevitable.

He had that certain look about him, the look Jana recognized so well. Therefore to dissuade the onset of what she believed would be coming from his lips, she said, "Please tell me how you've been, Dwight. I've been concerned about you."

Though he saw through the strategy she was employing, Dwight indulged her by saying, "I'm adjusting. ... How about you?"

"I'm getting by," she confessed from where she sat across from him. As he again lowered his eyes, she brought to his attention, "I was disappointed when you didn't eat lunch with us yesterday."

At the sound of these words Dwight immediately became stricken by vexation, an extreme vexation that prompted him to firmly declare, "You know why I wasn't there! Surely you remember what we agreed to!" Seeing in her eyes the hurt over his candor, he imploringly asked, "Why are we together, Jana! It's only making things all the more difficult for both of us!"

"But I don't want us to drift apart," she eagerly pointed out. "I don't want us to lose interest. Time has a way of doing that to people."

"Only because people allow it to happen!" he strongly suggested to be the case. Drawing in a breath in preparation for what he believed should be said, he sorely continued, "We decided not to associate with one another any more, and that should include school. It doesn't rest well with me to do otherwise."

One could see that Jana was aware of the extent of his resolve. Yet as tears began to well up in her eyes, she asserted, "I didn't think it necessary to carry things that far."

"Well to me it is," he said in no uncertain terms. While she sadly beheld him, he maintained, "I'm just not willing to put you at odds with your parents. And don't say they won't find out about us, because we both know they will." With a widening of his eyes, he emphasized, "And even if they didn't know we were spending time together, I'd know it, and it'd bother me, just as it does now." When she did not respond, he asked, "Wouldn't it bother you, too?"

Jana wouldn't answer his question one way or the other, for she knew that if she said it wouldn't bother her, she'd be lying, whereas if she said it would bother her, it'd lend credence to Dwight's contention that it was for the best to distance themselves from one another at all times, which in her way of thinking was a no win situation. She really didn't have to say anything further, though, for with all the conviction he was able to muster, Dwight forced himself to convey one of the most difficult things he had ever been motivated to tell anyone. He said, "Please don't seek me out any longer. It makes me feel guilty." And with that he disregarded her.

Jana did not seem to comprehend why Dwight was able to give her up completely. By allowing her emotions to get the best of her she hadn't foreseen that he desired to release her from a heartrending situation because he loved her. In fact so greatly did he love her that he earnestly hoped their separation would be easier for her to bear than it was for himself. Would this serve him well? Would it be part of his deliverance, his saving grace? Time would tell.

With the pain of their reality solidly etched in her eyes, Jana stood up and searched her mind for a different approach to their dilemma, only to conclude there wasn't one to be had. All that seemed to be left was accepting that which she didn't want to. .... And so finally, at long last, she surrendered to the notion that she and Dwight had to totally shun one another, which was such an agonizing thought to absorb that she darted away without even saying good-bye.

Having watched her departure, Dwight returned to the table from whence he had come to spend the remainder of the lunch hour with Roarie. In light of his tendency to be uncommunicative, Roarie refrained from asking any questions, it being obvious to him that his conversation with Jana was weighing heavily on his mind. ... Yet on a positive note, here is a truth that should be emphasized. Duty had been put into practice. Pleasure had been put on hold. The benefits were yet to be reaped. The sowing had just been completed.

* * *

That evening, upon his return from a visit at the O'Maleys', Dwight asked his mother if he could have Zuzueca, for Mr. O'Maley had told him the time was right to separate the stallion from its mother.

"It's up to you," she surprised him in saying. "You'll be the one taking care of him, not me."

"And I intend to do it well," he told her. "Thank you." Turning about, a smile of satisfaction made its way across his face.

Heading in the direction of the O'Maleys' farm, Dwight realized that ever since Clair's brush with death subtle changes had been taking place within his mother. And now, on top of that, she had granted him ownership of a horse that meant so much to him. It was a refreshing change, a ray of hope; and in light of what had recently culminated between him and Jana, it could not have come at a better time.

While continuing along his way, Dwight reflected on a letter gotten the day before from Clair. In it he learned that a bond of trust had developed between her and a man who worked as an orderly in the psychiatric hospital she was at. This man, it was sincerely hoped, would aid his sister in coming to terms with her emotionally upheaved past.

Why does anyone become mentally ill? That question now began to occupy Dwight's thoughts. Certainly he recognized mental illness to be a complex issue, yet he also believed one's fears quite often played a major role in its unfolding. Personally he defined mental illness as a state of mind that interfered with healthy living. The degree to which one experienced it varied from person to person, it was true, but even in its slightest expression a consequence was felt. That's why it's of utmost importance to try to deal with a psychological issue in its early stages so that it does not escalate into a severe behavioral problem. No one is immune from mental illness. He himself had firsthand knowledge that this was so, for in his thoughts, in his words, in what he had done, and in what he had failed to do, he was lacking in complete mental health. ... But alas, he also knew that the day would eventually dawn when the shortcomings of this system of things would be no more, and all ill health would cease to be.

* * *

At the beach that Sunday, after participating in a refreshing swim, Dwight and Sandy decided to take a walk down the shoreline toward the place where they had met.

"You know something, Sandy, you could cover a wall with all the shells you've collected," Dwight stated as she bent over to retrieve a newfound specimen. "Many people would have long since given up looking for them."

"Well not me," she was quick to insist. "There's so many different sizes and shapes that I never lose interest."

"Oh, so that's what motivates you," he commented with a chuckle. .... "By the way, how's Tecumseh the second?"

"Just fine," she gladly informed him. "He's almost full grown now, and really beautiful."

"Does he crow a lot?"

"Mostly in the morning," she told him. "I often wake up to the sound of it."

"And is it music to your ears?" he inquired of her with a smile.

"Only if I feel like getting out of bed," she pertly replied, after which they simultaneously broke out in laughter before continuing onward, neither one of them realizing that it was the last time they would ever share fellowship in this life.

* * *

This school year was different for Jana in more ways than one, for she lost all incentive to be a cheerleader. It had never really interested her all that much to begin with; but now, in light of recent developments in her life, she found it to be even less appealing in the scheme of things.

Glancing at the clock which rested on her dresser and seeing a time of quarter to five, she decided to pay Cybil a visit before supper. Surely she must have gotten back from the beach by now, she presumed while getting up from her desk and closing the book she'd been reading.

In leaving her room and making her way down the long, sweeping spiral of stairs that ended in the foyer, Jana wondered how difficult it would be for Dwight to stay away from her in school, for she surely knew she meant something to him. Yet what she still didn't fathom, even after all this time, was that Dwight was much better prepared than she to adapt to life's less than desirable circumstances.

Jana was just about to leave the house when her mother happened to exit from the family room to see her reaching for the doorknob.

"Where are you going?" she suspiciously questioned her, wondering if she might be planning to meet in secret with Dwight.

In knowing she wouldn't be socializing with Dwight any longer, school included, resentments began to resurface on Jana's part. Yet why had her mother even assumed she might be meeting with Dwight in the first place? It was because she had never informed the woman of the decision made at the playground weeks ago. What were her reasons? Besides finding the topic much too unpleasant to talk about, she was reluctant to give her parents the satisfaction of knowing their unreasonable demands had been met. At one time she had planned to humble herself and tell them exactly what they wanted to hear, mainly because of the sound advice Alice and Dwight had given her. But then her feelings alternated in the aftermath of Clair's attempted suicide. From her perspective her parents became worthy of her disdain when they deprived her from being at the hospital with Dwight during a difficult time in his life. Conflicting emotions she felt on a regular basis. She leaned toward surrender one minute, then relapsed the next, at times wanting to be forgiving, at other times wanting to get even. ... So herein lies a distinction which will prove unconditional surrender had never been adhered to by Jana right from the very start. If her capitulation had been legitimate, she would not have had a change of heart. If her submission had been genuine, it would never have reversed itself. She used emotionally wrenching issues as an excuse for noncompliance, yet life is full of that. True surrender remains constant no matter what. ... But Jana, despite all her beautiful qualities, was a girl who was not used to doing without, and the indulgences of her world had transcended other areas of her life. That was her major weakness. That was why she refused to thoroughly give in to her parents' demands, even though Dwight had seen fit to do so. It was a reflection of her upbringing, of good intentions gone awry.

In a wave of exasperation Jana turned to face her mother.

"Sometimes I feel like a prisoner in this house! I'm just going to see Cybil! That's all!" she cried out.

Though in her heart Mrs. Rossi still at times wanted to side with her daughter, out of deference to her husband she was prompted to say, "I certainly hope you're not about to disobey us, Jana."

"No, mother, I'm not disobeying you, not even in school!" Jana blurted out. Noting the look of surprise on her mother's face, she went on to say, "You'll be glad to know Dwight and I have decided to go along with what you and father want. We've ended our relationship. I hope you're satisfied." In the pain that the release of these words caused her to feel, she lowered her head in remorse.

Mrs. Rossi was so pleased by Jana's revelation that she refused to see beyond her own appeasement into the dejection of her daughter.

"Jana, this really will make things so much less complicated for all of us! You'll see!" she exclaimed while attempting to embrace her.

"I doubt that!" Jana told her flat out while rejecting her advances. "I think you and father have made life much more complicated than it has to be through your hypocrisy!" Observing her mother's stunned reaction, she went on to say, "I think we've all lost over this, but most of all you!" Holding her in her gaze in a most denouncing of manners, she eventually fled the house without even closing the door behind herself.

Mrs. Rossi knew deep down that she would never get Jana to forget about Dwight. As in the past she would say nothing of this to her husband, though, for unless a dire set of circumstances drove her to the brink of rebellion, she would persist in the status quo.

Leaning against the door, the woman began to weep in mounting guilt for the part she had played in bringing about such unrest within her daughter, whom she did so love. This served in evidence that sometimes we unwittingly hurt the ones who are nearest and dearest to us because we aren't willing to admit that what we think is in their best interest actually may not be.

* * *

As she continued down the sidewalk Jana also cried, uncertain as to whether she'd be able to endure circumstances as she saw them to be. She realized that her plight was temporary, yet so much she wanted her parents to wake up and see the light. Wishing would not accomplish that goal, however; and so, for now anyway, it would behoove her to abide by their demands once and for all, for they were at times domineering, yes, but not abusive, a very relevant distinction.

The smell of freshly baked pies now filled the air, drawing Jana's attention. Mrs. Carlyle must have prepared some of her locally famous pastries again, she presumed. How vividly she recalled visiting the woman as a small child to taste a sample of her delicious treats. Some day she would surprise the woman with a knock upon her door, she now decided, but she would have to feel a whole lot better than she presently did to ever be inclined to do so.

Moments later, she saw evidence that the Willards had indeed returned from their outing, for in nearing Cybil's home she happened to notice Sandy and a few of her friends playing catch with a red rubber ball on someone's lawn. Never would she have imagined she was about to witness a terrible sight, but in what seemed to be an instant she saw the ball bouncing across the street with Sandy in heavy pursuit; in the event of which it could be determined that a rather fast approaching truck was about to collide with the girl.

Jana urgently yelled out for Sandy to cease her advancement, but her effort proved to be in vain. The child's sprightly body was struck down upon the hard pavement with a sickening thud.

"Sandy, no!" Jana shrieked in horror while running to where she lay motionless. .... "Call an ambulance!" she frantically added as the driver of the truck rushed to her side in great distress.

Without saying a word the man ran for the nearest house.

Jana was nearly reduced to a state of shock as she regarded

Sandy's ashen countenance. It was difficult for her to grasp the extent of the emergency at hand. Blankly staring at the faces of the gathering children, she vaguely made out the sound of Cybil's voice from the other side of the street.

"Jana, what happened!" she exclaimed as she and her parents arrived on the scene. ... "Oh, no, it's Sandy!" she screamed, and got down on her knees beside Jana.

"Yes, Cybil, it is, and I think she's dead," Jana was hard pressed to say in her bereaved emotions.

"No, Jana, she can't be!" Cybil painfully denied her contention. Yet upon further observation of Sandy's broken, bleeding body, she knew it was likely true. Placing her head upon the girl's chest to listen for a heartbeat and discovering that one could not be heard, she raised her head and wailed, "Oh, how are her parents ever going to take this! She just can't be dead!"

Jana was not able to utter anything else at this time. Yet as more and more people began to congregate in and amongst the general area, she hung her head low and wept over what this child's death would mean to those who knew and loved her. Undoubtedly she foresaw that Dwight would be greatly affected. In fact she fully expected him to be one of the most grief-stricken people of all regarding the untimely death, by worldly standards, of this sweet girl.

* * *

Because the Enharts did not have a telephone, Jana decided to call Roarie from the hospital to inform him that Sandy had died.

"And please tell Dwight," she begged of him with a quiver in her voice while looking into the lobby at a family in mourning. "I want him to find out about this from a friend."

"I'll go to him now," Roarie assured her. "Please tell the Willards how sorry I am."

"I shall," Jana told him. "Whenever there's a break in the crying that is."

Within minutes of hanging up the phone, Roarie started walking in the direction of Dwight's home to reveal the dreaded news. When he arrived at his destination, he found Dwight coming out of the barn in what appeared to be a lighthearted mood.

"Oh, hi, Roarie," he casually reacted to the sight of him. "To what do I owe this visit?"

Roarie stood silent in the time it took Dwight to notice the grave look on his face.

"What's wrong?" he consequently inquired, realizing that Roarie wasn't here on a social call.

"I've got something to tell you," Roarie reluctantly acknowledged.

There was by now such an unsettling mood in the air that it prompted Dwight to say in the onset of fearful anticipation, "Roarie, you're upsetting me! ... Please tell me what's wrong!"

Meeting Dwight's stare, Roarie at last found the wherewithal to say, "Sandy was in a terrible accident this afternoon. A truck hit her."

"An accident!" Dwight exclaimed. "Then I should be with her family!" Hurriedly he turned in the direction of the O'Maleys' farm, that is until he was stopped in his tracks at the sound of Roarie's piercing words, "Sandy's dead, Dwight."

The feelings which engulfed Dwight were not easy to put into words. It really wouldn't be accurate to say he was shocked by what had been told him, for in knowing and accepting that these things happen in life, he had already resigned himself to potential tragedy. Yet it was nonetheless as though a knife had been thrust into his heart, so unwelcome was this news about a girl whom he had grown to love in a purely genuine way.

"Dead," he almost whispered while looking back at Roarie.

With a nod of his head Roarie confirmed it was so, after which Dwight asked how he had come to know this.

"Jana called me from the hospital. She was at the scene of the accident. She witnessed it. .... I'm sorry. I know how much you liked her."

In the ensuing moments Dwight revealed virtually no emotion at all. Rather his face took on a blank stare. .... Yet then slowly but surely, tears began to develop in his green eyes and roll down his suntanned cheeks.

"Roarie," he then said, "it seems that when a person is repeatedly saddened, they begin to weary." Staring at the nearby woods, he was prone to add, "I think I'd like to be alone now."

"I understand," Roarie replied and watched as he walked out of view amongst the trees.

Heading for home, Roarie felt very badly for Dwight. He wondered how Dwight, a compassionate person, might react to the truth behind what had happened in Chicago if the day ever dawned that he found out about it. Yet then suddenly he concluded that Dwight, of all people, could be expected not to spurn him as the world was apt to do.

* * *

On his way to the funeral home with Roarie and the O'Maleys, Dwight found himself thinking about how terrible it must have been for Jana to witness Sandy's death. Yet even though he had not been exposed to the same mental trauma as her, what a strain the previous two days had been. Moments in which he desired to be set apart from humanity, and thought consumed nights, were his only remembrance. Going to school and concentrating on his studies turned out to be challenging to say the least. And even though walking to the place he had met Sandy only seemed to compound his grief, he lingered there anyway for hours on end. Did his actions reflect a lack of faith in the spiritual realm? After all, what purpose would it serve to dwell on the past when the future offered the only hope? Or was it that his pleasant memories of Sandy held the potential of soothing his mourning over her loss? Whatever be the case, his primary objective was to see beyond the sadness of today.

Pulling into the parking lot of the funeral home, Dwight wondered how he'd react to seeing Sandy's family and friends. Speaking to Mr. and Mrs. Willard over the telephone the previous day from the O'Maleys' farm had been difficult enough, let alone facing them imminently, he pondered while entering the building with his companions.

Hearing the low pitched sobs of people in mourning, Dwight's eyes quickly felt the wetness of tears. Briefly regarding Roarie, he forced himself to enter the room where Sandy was lying in a casket. To avoid looking at her, he gazed across the room only to be confronted by Jana's heartbreaking stare. Never had he seen her project such a subdued image, which compelled him to yearn for the freedom to speak to her.

On the opposite side of the room he now saw Mrs. Willard seated on a couch. To his astonishment she looked quite composed, almost her usual self, which initially he did not understand. He had expected her to be crying profusely, yet she wasn't, nor were any of the rest of the immediate family. Dampened cheeks were visible, yes, but as of yet no other outward signs of grief. .... But then suddenly he realized that their faith in God was sustaining them in their hour of need, which encouraged him to adopt an eased presence. When Mrs. Willard turned her head in his direction, he proceeded toward her. Making eye contact, there was such a free flowing exchange of emotion between them that he actually began to imagine life without Sandy for the first time since her death.

Rising to greet him, Mrs. Willard gently took hold of his hand before saying with a whisper of strength and stability, "Come with me to see Sandy for the last time until we have the privilege to join her."

How healthy can an outlook be? Dwight did not know the answer to that question, yet he surely believed Mrs. Willard was headed in the right direction. Heeding her suggestion, he and she cried in a side by side embrace while looking down upon the once energetic young girl lying motionless before them. Yet their tears were not in vain, for they were being shed for worthy reasons. Neither of them would ever harbor bitterness in their heart over what happened to this child, for they understood that one's physical life was both fragile and fleeting. Their crying simply meant that they loved Sandy immensely, and would miss her deeply.

Noticing how at peace Sandy appeared to be, Dwight wondered if God was aiming to reassure him that she was in a place of contentment. A soothing sensation thus overcame him, and he knew that the stage had been set for coming to terms with her tragic death. Sandy had left this world for the better life, the life which her earthly experience had paved the way for. ... But the intriguing aspects of today did not end here, for a significant occurrence was in the making. Unbeknownst to Dwight, he had been observed by someone who arrived at the funeral home directly behind him. She was a woman who found herself wondering if he was her daughter's friend. She was the mother of a girl who greatly missed his companionship. Touched by the manner in which he conducted himself, this lady couldn't seem to draw her attention away from him right up until the time he walked past her to make his way homeward to pick up the pieces following another milestone in his journey through life.

* * *

The birds seemed to be singing a mournful tune on the day of Sandy's funeral, Dwight keenly took notice of.

Standing at the cemetery with they who had gathered for the graveside service, he was thankful for the realization that his melancholy was temporary.

Distancing himself from Jana on this solemn occasion had been no accident, for the temptation to converse with her was far too great to be tampered with.

So what was the sought after goal? Long-term satisfaction. ... And the method of the quest determines the quality of the outcome.

* * *

When Scott broke his leg during a football game and was unable to finish the rest of the season, Ginger immediately lost all interest in him. To add insult to injury, his own father seemed more concerned about getting him back on the field than he did about his physical and psychological well-being. This was particularly disheartening for a boy who was constrained to begin with. And so sometimes he cried when he was alone in his room, wondering if he would ever feel free to be the person he longed to be.

Hence it. had come to pass that Scott's popularity couldn't shield him from the repercussions of improperly placed priorities. Where was the love, the love he so yearned to find? It seemed as though an elusive dream.

* * *

Visiting the Willards two weeks after Sandy's funeral was a sobering reminder for Dwight of the period of adjustment that's in need of taking place when a loved one dies, particularly in that it was the first time since the girl's death that he was amongst her family in their home.

Walking indoors, he felt an absence which would not likely go unnoticed for some time. Reminders of Sandy were all around him, and those reminders, he well knew, would at times pull at his very heartstrings.

Later, after everyone had eaten a fine supper, Mrs. Willard made her way upstairs only to return moments later clutching a box close to her breast.

"Dwight, I've been meaning to give you this," she said while approaching where he sat. "I don't know of anyone who'd appreciate it more than you." Gently she placed it within his receiving hands.

With a curiosity that was slight enough to reveal an awareness of its contents, Dwight opened the box only to lay eyes on the conch that symbolized the beginning of his and Sandy's friendship. As wistful thoughts began to rush through his mind, he raised his head to regard Mrs. Willard.

"I'm touched," was all he could bring himself to say.

"Let it remain a symbol of your undying friendship with Sandy," she urged him.

"Yes, I shall," Dwight assured her before allowing his gaze to fall upon the shell once again. Carefully closing the box, he was of an inspiration to add, "You know something, I had a hard time accepting Sandy's death at first. It seemed so unfair that she died at her age. I don't see it that way any longer, though," he then went on to say. "How can any of us be sure how long we'll be here? Sandy's death is proof of that." With a nod of his head, he additionally stated, "To focus on the love I've found in God, that's the main reason I'm able to accept her death and go on."

The Willards of all people could appreciate his way of looking at things, so much so that they were overcome by pensive thoughts.

It was seconds thereafter that Mrs. Willard said, "Dwight, it might interest you to know that the man who struck Sandy down paid us a visit to tell us how sorry he is for what happened. He said he's been racked by guilt ever since that day, because he thinks he was driving too fast. I told him he needn't torment himself, but that's easier said than done, because to come to terms with past regrets can be very difficult."

"Isn't that the truth," Dwight so emphatically remarked that one got the stark notion he had known this to be the case for quite some time now.

It wasn't too much later that a lighter mood ensued on the part of everyone. Was this a sign that coming to terms with Sandy's death was another step closer to completion? The clear-cut answer was yes.

* * *

That evening, when he arrived back in Chism, Dwight decided to saddle up Zuzueca and take a ride to the Chism cemetery to pick some wild flowers for the grave of a baby, a baby who was his younger sister.

Arriving at the outskirts of the graveyard, he dismounted the horse and tied it to the limb of a nearby tree before making his way to the opposite end of the cemetery. There he found the tombstone he was looking for. It read:

SHIRLEY A. ENHART
Nov. 5, 1933 - Jan. 13, 1934

Sitting before the stone, Dwight was inspired to reflect on what he had recently deduced concerning his sister's death. He believed that when she died, his mother became overprotective of him in her fear that he would be the next one to perish, which encouraged him to become too emotionally dependent on her. Then, when she rejected him in later years, he found it difficult to trust humanity. ... Yet in discovering that he would never be viewed with such inconsistency by God, he began to experience a much improved self-worth.

Aware that his spiritual mindedness had enabled him to under-stand certain aspects of his life, he began to pick flowers from the surrounding landscape, realizing in doing so that he was bound and determined to feel love, rather than scorn, for his mother.

* * *

As Roberta drove up to Scott's home in her father's car, inde-cision racked her mind as to whether she should carry her plans through to completion. After all, perhaps Scott would be perturbed at the sight of her, particularly if he had come to judge all girls based upon the actions of Ginger. Yet if that be the case, certainly it would be appropriate for her to set him straight in that regard, she now decided while knocking upon the front door with intent purpose.

Because Mr. Weston was not at home, Scott took the initiative to get up from the living room couch and maneuver his way to the door with the aid of his crutches. Standing face to face with Roberta, he was taken by surprise by her presence.

"Hello... what brings you here?" he found himself asking in delayed response.

"I wanted to know how you're doing," she informed him. "And I thought maybe we could study together if you like." She held up the few books she had taken along.

Scott scrutinized her for a few moments before rather expec-tantly saying, "Your being here, is it out of pity for what I've been reduced to?" Self-consciously he glanced down at his crutches.

Shaking her head, Roberta said, "I have news for you, Scott Weston. I had pity for you before you were using those crutches, not afterwards." Taking note of his bewildered reaction, she came to declare, "Oh, Scott, needing to use crutches is nothing to be ashamed of. I did wonder, though, if you might be down on yourself after what happened on the field." When he lowered his head, she went on to say, "I came here in the spirit of friendship, and it'll remain that way even if you never play football again." In her voice there was an echo of truth.

Though Scott longed to believe her, he suspiciously replied,

"After the way I chose Ginger over you, how can you expect me to believe that?"

"Because if people stopped caring about one another based on disappointment, who would be left caring for who?" she made a valid point in saying.

In an open desire to explore the depth of her character, Scott allowed himself to see into her unadorned beauty.

"I think I could use a friend right now," he thus said. "We never did get to know each other all that well, did we?" As she shook her head, he felt motivated to add, "I'd like to change that, and.... I'm sorry about everything." His words were quite labored as he said this, for sorry was a word he found difficult to verbalize.

Roberta could appreciate his humbled demeanor.

"I think I'm beginning to realize why I'm so drawn to you," she as a result told him. "I must have sensed something I liked about you right from the very start, an inner redeeming quality." At this point she gently smiled.

Though Scott was glad she had come here, he found himself wondering if he might feel differently once his injury healed. Roberta did not have unreasonable expectations about relationships, however. Nor did she intend to try to mold him into what she thought he should be. She did find him handsome, but there was nothing wrong with that as long as her main interest in him superseded the physical; for really, when it gets right down to it, the very essence of any healthy relationship is friendship. Make no mistake about it. It's not status, not money or power, and not the attractions of the flesh. The sought-after goal for they who are truly wise in their human relations is friendship. .... And Roberta was a girl who knew this.

Scott was already feeling better from an emotional standpoint, so much so that he was able to humor her by motioning to the interior of the house and saying, "Well, are you gonna come on in, or make a cripple stand on his leg all day long?"

Inspired to laugh over his lighthearted comment, Roberta entered the doorway with books in hand to try to convince a boy named Scott that some girls really could be trusted after all to have his best interest at heart and do right by him.

AN UPDATE

Could it be that God expects us to unceasingly attempt to reach the non-receptive of heart? Dwight thought about this more than once in days gone by, wondering if it would ever be deemed appropriate to walk away from his mother with the knowledge that he might never again be returning unto her. After all, did he not have the right to seek and attain a life of better quality, a life in which he did not have to endure the rejection of an embittered relative? This was a question that begged for an answer above and beyond a simple yes or a no. .... And he humbly sought the counsel of God in his quest to know what was expected of him at any given moment in his walk through life.

Through her continuing letters, Clair revealed that she was growing in her relationship with the man she had met at the psychiatric ward. She also let it be known that at her present rate of recovery she was soon to see a completion to her treatment at the facility.

In school Carl not only glared at Dwight, he often made threatening remarks. Yet Dwight managed to exchange eye contact with him from time to time in an unspoken desire to convey onto him the scars suffered of him.

Scott and Roberta began to spend more and more time together. In her company Scott had found a girl who was true to him, which helped him recognize the vanity of his and Ginger's previously held interest in one another.

Sara did in fact stop harassing Dwight on the bus following his firm rebuke of her crude remark. How he appreciated not having to endure her sarcasm any longer. He had learned a valuable lesson in this. He had learned that to stand up to people, when it's called for, has its inherent benefits.

Without abandon, Mr. and Mrs. Willard were as positive as ever about life, their faith in God not wavering in the least over that which had happened to Sandy. There was no guarantee to a long physical life, and they had known this to be true for some time now. Without a doubt they were determined to see beyond the pain of a place called earth, a place not timeless as it currently stands.

CHAPTER 18

TWO SEPARATE ILLNESSES

By way of the classes they shared with one another, Dwight became aware of Jana's hacking cough. And in the time that it took for her symptoms to subside, it went without saying that he was quite concerned about her. However the body can appear to be recuperated from an illness without it actually being the case, for when school was dismissed the following Monday afternoon and a cool rain drenched her to the skin as she walked home, she suffered a relapse. Then pneumonia set in to deteriorate her health even further, which resulted in a home visit by the family doctor with a verdict of complete bed rest until such time that he stated otherwise.

When Dwight discovered that Jana was absent from school, his curiosity prompted him to seek out Cybil for any information she might be able to provide him.

In the spirit of friendship, Cybil revealed everything she knew about Jana's infirmity as relayed to her that morning when she stopped by the Rossis' to walk to school with her as she usually did.

In hearing what transpired, Dwight felt an ache enter his heart over the possibility that Jana was dying. With a grievous lowering of his eyes, it almost broke Cybil's heart when he said, "How I wish I could see that girl. What a test of my convictions this is." Indeed it appeared as though he was on the borderline of depression.

Cybil had no doubt he'd be good medicine for Jana, but she wouldn't allow herself to say it, for she saw no benefit in bringing this to his attention.

"Oh, Dwight, I wish you could see her, too," she instead bemoaned. "It's just not fair."

* * *

By that evening Jana's condition had gotten dire enough to call for another home visit by Dr. Eshlon.

Dr. Eshlon was a compassionate man who exhibited a genuine interest in the physical as well as the emotional well-being of his patients. As a consequence he had acquired the keen ability to detect whenever a person's illness went beyond the physical realm into the psychological. And where Jana was concerned he did consider this to be the case, for she was so despondent, so withdrawn, so unlike the girl he remembered her to be throughout his years as the family doctor.

In the aftermath of examining her, he solemnly stated, "You don't seem any too willing to fight this malady, Jana."

"Maybe I'm not," she would only say while turning her head away from him.

Seating himself on the side of her bed, the kindhearted man gently placed one of her hands within his.

"Please take an interest in fighting your illness, my dear," he was earnest in suggesting. "Whatever is bothering you will pass in time. You'll see."

For the sake of the caring man's feelings, Jana forced herself to say she'd try with as much believability as she could muster. Yet as she cast her eyes in the direction of the window, Dr. Eshlon knew that her desire to live had faded for some reason. He had seen this in people before; the defeat, the surrender, the lack of enthusiasm.

"I'll be back tomorrow morning," he subsequently seen fit to relent, for the time being anyway. "Rest easy."

Walking down the staircase, Dr. Eshlon deliberately slowed his pace to organize his thoughts when he observed Jana's family peering up at him from the banister.

"How is she, Dr.?" Mrs. Rossi wasted no time in asking as he neared the bottom step.

Shaking his head, he said while holding up his medical bag for the added effect, "I'm afraid I have nothing in here that'll cure that girl of what's really ailing her." Noticing the troubled expressions in his midst, he gravely went on to say, "It's very apparent to me that Jana is suffering from two separate illnesses, one physical and one mental, and that her physical health will be slow to improve unless her outlook changes." Detecting a hint of unease in Mrs. Rossi's bearing, he asked if she had any idea what might be bothering the girl.

Glancing at her husband, she was just about to speak when he interjected by saying, "Jana may be upset about some boy we've forbidden her to see." In an effort to make light of the situation, he flippantly added, "But it's only a matter of time before she comes to her senses."

Dr. Eshlon knew from past experience that Mr. Rossi routinely forced his views upon his family. So in an aim to make him aware of the price one paid for domineering over people, he said while placing his left hand under his chin for the added emphasis, "You've always been one to get your way, Clayton, and yet I wonder if you'd be satisfied with that if your daughter died. For your sake I hope so."

An arrogant person is easily put on the defensive when unsolicited advice is offered them. Yet before Mr. Rossi could even hope to respond, Dr. Eshlon continued, "If Jana hasn't improved by the time I return tomorrow, I'm going to advise she be hospitalized." Heading for the door, he turned to face everyone before concluding quite matter of factly, "I sincerely hope you address the reasons for that girl's depression, and come up with a solution you can live with, because if she doesn't pull through this, you may wish you could turn back the hands of time to do things differently." His reasons for speaking this way were twofold; number one, he had always found Jana to be a girl of advanced maturity for her age, and number two, he didn't want her parents to live in guilt if she didn't recover from her illness, for he knew that if they required things of her which were not warranted, they would reap mental unrest as their ill-gotten recompense.

To one degree or another everyone remained focused upon Dr. Eshlon's strong recommendation in the aftermath of his departure.

"Well, even though he's blown this out of proportion, I suppose he means well in his own way," Mr. Rossi eventually stated with brazen indifference before heading for the library. However his wife was not inclined to react as he had in this particular instance. Rather she was persuaded to ascend the stairs to her daughter's room with pressing motherly regard.

Quietly making her entrance, she walked before Jana's bed and sat down in the very spot Dr. Eshlon had only moments earlier been seated. Gazing at her second born child, she became all the more distressed to see that the look on her face was one of enhanced paleness since earlier in the day.

Having felt the bed slightly move, Jana weakly opened her eyes. "Oh... it's you, mother," she said.

"Yes, dear, it is," she whispered with tender compassion. "Is there anything I can do for you?"

"What I want... you and father won't give me," she struggled to tell her in a low tone of voice.

Driven to the advent of tears, Mrs. Rossi implored her, "Does that boy mean so much to you that you'd cease to want to live!"

Feebly nodding her head, Jana replied, "I don't like avoiding him, mother. It... hurts me so... and... I can't see myself going through high school living that way. ... The thought is unbearable."

"But dear...."

"I'm so tired," she faintly interrupted her while closing her eyes. "So tired." And in her frail condition she drifted into a state of unconsciousness.

At this point Mrs. Rossi was struck by the realization that she had to do something to come to her daughter's aid, for by all indication the situation was desperate. From the depths of her soul a feeling of authority thus overcame her to direct her to the library where she found her husband casually seated in a lounge chair reading a book as though all was fine and well.

"She really is getting worse, Clayton!" she fretfully spoke up to make her presence known. When he did not so much as look at her, she firmly alleged, "We're killing her more than the pneumonia is!"

Startled by her outburst, and angered by her contention, the man retaliated by exclaiming, "What's gotten into you! I only want what's best for her! How many times must I say it!"

Shaking her head in ardent disagreement, she announced, "No, I don't think either one of us has really been thinking about what's best for her! We've ignored her feelings for so long we've lost sight of the truth, but I intend to change that! Dr. Eshlon and Jana have gotten through to me! I now know what has to be done!"

"What exactly do you mean?" he suspiciously questioned her.

With clear conviction she apprised him, "At noon tomorrow I plan to go to the school to take that boy home with me. I think he'll be good therapy for Jana."

"Over my dead body!" he adamantly defied her while rising to his feet. "If I have to, I'll come home from work to order him out of this house!"

"If you care about your daughter's well-being, you'll allow her to see him without interfering!" she fervently counseled him. When he all the more intensely glared at her, she went on to passionately add, "If you refuse to cooperate and Jana dies, I don't think I could live with you any more! I wouldn't be able to stand the sight of you, knowing what you've... what we've done to her!" In noticing the shock that developed on his face over her acquired assertiveness, she further declared, "I don't think I'd be able to live with myself either if I stood by and watched her get worse and worse without doing anything about it! Every time I looked in the mirror I'd feel like smashing it! So there's going to be some changes around here, Clayton, if you want me to remain in this house, because if there isn't, I'll go to Vicksburg with the girls to live with my mother!"

The woman had certainly stated her case. So with that having been done, she left the room, not realizing in doing so how important she was to her husband, for through her tenacious challenge of his authority he was genuinely worried he might lose her. Up until now this had never concerned him, for she had always yielded to his demands. Therefore because he was in actuality a repressed man who feared the thought of being abandoned, it did not take him long to decide that he would not defy his wife on this issue after all, for in knowing she meant what she said, he was not about to run the risk of pushing her beyond her limits, and forfeiting her companionship for good.

* * *

Dwight didn't realize as he rode the bus to school the following morning that reclamation was soon to be had where his relationship with Jana was concerned. Was there symbolic significance in this? Absolutely so, for at no other time since he had known her did he feel so saddened by their separation. He was disappointed beyond words, beyond tears, beyond all those times in the past few weeks when their eyes met in a way that reflected a yearning to converse with one another.

In light of what Cybil had disclosed the day before, Dwight fully expected Jana to be absent from school for quite some time. However he refused to ask for an update, instead choosing to believe that no news was good news. .... Then, while he was seated in his third class of the morning, he was surprised to hear it announced over the sound system that he was wanted in the main office.

Advancing down the empty corridors, Dwight couldn't imagine what this was all about. In entering the area just outside the principal's office, he informed the secretary of his identity, at which time she directed his attention to a lady seated to their left, telling him she desired to speak with him regarding some important matter.

Dwight was perplexed by her statement, even more so as he saw the woman get up and walk toward him, for he did not recall ever laying eyes on her.

"Permit me to introduce myself," she swiftly spoke up to allay his concerns. "I'm Eunice Rossi, Jana's mother. I'd like to talk to you about Jana if I may."

"Why... yes.. of course," Dwight replied in stunned response, in the event of which the secretary offered to give them privacy in conversation, telling them she was just about to leave for lunch anyway.

Mrs. Rossi thanked the woman for being so accommodating. Then, just moments later, when she and Dwight were seated alone, she said, "My being here has taken you by surprise, I know." As he nodded his head, she conveyed, "I'm very concerned about Jana's health."

"So am I, Mrs. Rossi," Dwight endeavored to assure her. "Cybil told me how bad off she is." Holding her in his gaze, he wound up confessing, "It's been hard to accept staying away from her, especially now that she's so ill. I care about her so much." His manner of speaking was thoroughly convincing.

For the part she had played in bringing about such a disturbing situation, Mrs. Rossi lowered her head in a rush of remorse.

"I respect that you've been obeying my husband and I," she told him then. "But I now feel we've made a mistake with you and Jana. I know my daughter. She's bright and perceptive, and good, and... well, I should have trusted her choice in friends enough that I asked to meet you before it ever came to this, but..."

"But you and your husband assumed I wasn't good for her," Dwight dared to interrupt.

"Yes," she felt pressured to say. "I'm afraid my husband is an opinionated man who has a hard time connecting with people. He's very set in his ways." Turning aside, she introspectively determined, "And if I'm to be totally honest, I'm forced to admit his attitude has rubbed off on me throughout our years of marriage."

By way of acquired insight, Dwight told her, "What we're exposed to can influence the way we look at things. I've seen it within my own family." Having disclosed that, he freely asked, "Jana, how is she?"

"Not all that well," she regretted to inform him. "Dr. Eshlon stopped by this morning to check on her condition. He wanted to hospitalize her, but I told him about my plans. .... You see I'm here to give you permission to socialize with Jana again." In detecting his immense interest, she went on to say, "Won't you come see her during your lunch hour? I could have Alice prepare something for you."

Dwight was initially so overjoyed by her offer that he nearly shouted out yes. But he self-disciplined himself to hold back on his acceptance as a wave of mistrust consumed him.

"I can see something's bothering you," Mrs. Rossi was quick to note. "I was hoping you'd be more receptive to my invitation."

"Oh, you don't know how much I long to be," Dwight enlightened her. "But I'm not sure what your motivation is. I mean are you telling me this because Jana is so sick, or is it that you truly regret what's been demanded of us? I don't want Jana or I to go through this again. This type of pain we can both do without."

Initially a look of delving thought was in evidence on the woman's face. Then, by nature of her mission, she pointedly remarked with moving emphasis, "My daughter is wasting away before my very eyes, and it's breaking my heart! Yes, I'm here because she's so ill, but through her illness I've come to regret what's been asked of her! Can't I come to you for both of those reasons!" Having captured his undivided attention, she was quick to add, "Jana told me she couldn't endure high school avoiding you." With pleading eyes, she therein concluded, "I want her back. Please help me get my daughter back if you can... before it's too late."

Dwight was astonished by the extent of what had been told him, for he had not expected Jana to be so deeply and permanently affected by their disassociation.

"I guess she's hurting even worse than I realized," he consequently stated.

"So you'll come with me then?" Mrs. Rossi anxiously anticipated.

"Will your husband make it unpleasant for us?" Dwight had to know.

"I told him he had better not, but it's the first time I've ever demanded anything of him, so I can't be sure he'll cooperate." In reference to that which was of primary importance, she brought to his attention, "Jana really does want to see you, though, so please, for her sake, cast aside your reservations and go to her as a friend... a trusted friend."

Because the thought of reaching out to Jana so greatly appealed to him, Dwight stated with cautious expectation, "Alright, I'll go with you, Mrs. Rossi."

"I'm so pleased," she responded with a sigh of relief. As she rose to her feet, she was of an inspiration to add, "I understand that you and Jana have been staying away from one another even in school."

"Yes," Dwight informed her in solemn remembrance. "And I can tell you why if you'd like to know."

"As a matter of fact I would," she conceded while reseating herself.

Gazing at her, he related, "There's a commandment, Honor thy mother and father. I felt it was our duty to obey it even if we didn't like what was being asked of us, even if we thought it unfair."

Impressed by his respect for her parenthood, Mrs. Rossi hardly seemed able to say, "How commendable." Mildly regarding him, she allowed a few seconds to pass before adding, "I think I should tell you I didn't let Jana know I was coming here today. She'll be very surprised to see you. I only hope she doesn't faint."

Willing to find humor in her comment, Dwight suggested, "Shall we find out then?" His statement actually induced a smile on her part.

Now that Mrs. Rossi had finally met Dwight for herself, she felt certain she had done the right thing in coming here, for it was plain to see he cared about her daughter's well-being in a very genuine way.

Riding the short distance to the Rossis' home, Dwight got a feel for the wealth they were accustomed to, for the car in which he rode was quite lavish. As they pulled onto the property, he deemed it unusual for a girl of Jana's background to even reach out to him, for her world was so material, so extravagant; and yet, in spite of it all, she remained in touch with her fellow man. Truly he admired her for that, and wondered if God was looking with favor upon her for having seen beyond her worldly influences.

"Mrs. Rossi, has Jana always lived here?" he inquired of her once they were standing in the foyer amongst the opulent surroundings.

"Yes, she was born two years after we moved into this house. Why do you ask?"

"I just find it unusual that a girl who grew up in a house like this would befriend me," he apprised her. "It's not what I would have expected." ·

Mrs. Rossi knew what he was getting at, so she informed him that Jana had never been a strong adherent of the material world. Going back in time, she noted, "When she was five years old, Clayton asked her what she desired for her birthday, expecting it to be something he could buy with his money. Yet all she wanted was a party with her mommy and daddy at it." With a distant gaze she attested, "We could have learned a lot from that little girl if we had taken her outlook to heart, but instead Clayton bought her an expensive toy which she lost interest in in less than a day."

"What a message there is to that story," Dwight asserted. "Thank you for telling it to me." Insightfully he then added, "I have the feeling you gave Jana much love, Mrs. Rossi."

"Yes, that she was given," the woman concurred. "Maybe you can get away with more mistakes as a parent if your child has been given that.... unless of course you've carried things too far and lost their affection."

"Don't despair," Dwight encouraged her. "You haven't run out of time yet." Surely he was referring to the likelihood that there would soon be an improvement on the horizon.

"I do believe I should take you up to Jana's room now," she graciously told him with unmistakable warmth. "Please follow me."

Ascending the stairs, Mrs. Rossi hoped she had effectively discouraged her husband from showing up on the premises to make an unpleasant scene. Barely had they spoken to one another that morning before he left for work, she now recalled. The after effects of their opposing views had yet to be reckoned with.

Entering Jana's room with her mother, Dwight immediately noticed how pallid she looked. Yet despite her appearance he saw her as nothing less than beautiful, so thoroughly engrained was his love for her. .... Then, just as he sat on the edge of her bed, she opened her eyes to see him staring at her.

"Dwight... is it really you?" she surreally whispered, as though she felt she could only be dreaming.

"Yes, it really is," he tenderly replied as Mrs. Rossi stepped into view at the foot of the bed. Beholding the woman, he added, "Your mother was generous enough to invite me to see you."

As one could well imagine, Jana was nearly overwhelmed by this welcome news.

"Oh, Dwight... my prayers have been answered then!" she was hard pressed to say. ... "I can scarcely believe it! It's... like a miracle!"

"Yes, a miracle," he avidly professed with a glow that was soothing to her soul. "But surely you must have known before today, Jana Rossi, that miracles really do happen... all the time." His final words were spoken with a soft, free-flowing ease.

Never had Jana been known to smile so sweetly. Staring up at her mother, she said with a heartfelt sigh, "Thank you. ... Thank you so very much."

"You're most welcome," she found it difficult to state in her joy over her responsiveness. "Enjoy your visit with your friend." Gently she touched the girl's hand and kissed her on the forehead. Glancing appreciatively at Dwight, she left the room to give them the privacy they so richly deserved, wiping a tear from her eye as she did so.

A mutual exchange of great affection now took place between Jana and Dwight as they began to cry over the extent of what their perseverance had come to mean in their relationship. Surely words were not easy to come by as they sought to take in the splendor of the moment.

"You mean we really can be together again, Dwight?" Jana eventually secured the means to express.

"It appears so," he was pleased to announce. "And what a good feeling it is." Being this close to her, he could see how physically challenged she was, for her breathing was terribly labored. "Oh, Jana, please take an interest in getting well," he as a result implored her. While she warmly beheld him, he added, "Really, it's much more than that I don't want to lose you in my life. You see, whether you realize it or not, the world can use more people like you. I of all people should know that."

Jana could not help but delight at the release of such generous words.

"What a beautiful thing to say," she duly responded. "But reaching out to you came easy. I was drawn to you right from the very start." Uplifted by the love within him, she added, "I do feel myself getting better already."

"I'm glad," he was quick to impart. ... "I think I should let you rest now, but I'll come back tomorrow."

"Yes, come back soon," she softly concluded while closing her eyes.

Standing up, Dwight lingered in honor of their friendship, noticing in doing so that she seemed to radiate a glorious inner peace. When he finally left her room, he made his way downstairs to eat the lunch awaiting him, aware of how circumstances could change in the course of time. A wonderful thing had taken place, for yesterday he had been denied the company of a girl who meant so much to him, whereas today he was once more by her side. How strongly this reinforced his contention that standing by his principles had been the correct thing to do all along.

* * *

Considering that Roarie had only recently gotten his driver's license, when his father asked him to head into Fulton after school to buy some paint and brushes so that they could begin painting their barn a bright red, he quickly took advantage of the opportunity to drive by proceeding down the road with the family truck.

Arriving in downtown Fulton, he parked on the main street and walked into the hardware store where he was greeted by the clerk on duty for the day.

At first he did not notice the glances directed his way. But then, as the clerk was filling out his order, he saw the man leering at him and returned a look of discernible interest.

Shortly thereafter, when the bill was all tallied and paid for, and the supplies had been carried to the truck in two separate trips, Roarie sat in the driver's seat waiting for the man to leave the store. Not only was he troubled by his behavior, but disturbed over his lack of understanding as to why this was so. Somehow he sensed there was no satisfaction to be gained by the offerings of the moment, yet temptation beckoned him to remain. A changed way of thinking was in order to free him from his worldly chains.

When the man exited the building and saw Roarie seated in the vehicle, he intentionally dropped his bag so that its contents would scatter upon the sidewalk. Then, just as he had hoped, Roarie approached to assist with picking up the items.

"It appears as though I'm growing clumsy," he commented just as Roarie bent over beside him. When Roarie said nothing, he inquired, "Do you live around here? I've never seen you before."

"I just moved to Chism this summer," Roarie apprehensively

responded as they neared the completion of their efforts. "Aside from school, I don't get to Fulton very often."

"Oh, I see. Then you probably don't know too many people around here." When Roarie shook his head, he added while standing, "Would you... ah... care to visit me for awhile? I live close by." And with a tilt of his head he indicated the direction without even the slightest regard for Roarie's youth.

Though Roarie was reluctant to follow through with the invitation, he unwisely decided to accept the offer anyway.

"But only for a little while," he emphasized.

"I won't keep you long," the man aimed to convince him while suppressing a smile of anticipation. "Just follow me."

Heeding the man's suggestion, Roarie found himself standing in the kitchen of his home just moments later.

"Do you live here alone?" he asked while running his gaze about the room.

"Yes," he told him. "Up until a year ago my mother and I lived together. She passed away quite suddenly, though, so I'm alone now." Retrieving some dirty dishes from the table and carrying them to the sink, he vividly recollected, "She didn't approve of my every preference, particularly the ones concerning intimacy." Desiring to discover Roarie's initial reaction to his words, he turned abruptly about.

Roarie paused only briefly before saying, "I, too, know how it feels not to be approved of." Though under the influence of the man's intense scrutiny, he managed to add, "But I don't want what happened in Chicago to happen here. I like it here, and I'd hate to ruin that."

"Then why are you in my kitchen?" the man casually inquired of him with a probing stare. When Roarie lowered his head in a loss for words, he added, "No one has to know if we're careful." Walking before the impressionable teenage boy, he put his hand to his cheek and lightly began to stroke it, that is until Roarie happened to glance at the kitchen window and see Carl Barnet staring at them through one of the panes. He had a contemptuous look upon his face.

"I've gotta go!" he thus exclaimed in fearful response. Abruptly heading for the door, he shouted, "I shouldn't have come here!"

"What's wrong!" the man voiced his dismay. Rushing forward, he yelled, "Come back if you change your mind!" Making his way onto the porch, he was disconcerted to see Carl walking away from the house while casting scornful backward glances at him. It was then that he was able to speculate what had taken place. Carl, in knowing he had a questionable reputation, had seen him with Roarie and decided to investigate whether the rumors he had heard would be verified, which they ultimately had been.

When Roarie got behind the wheel of the truck, he hastily sped away, hoping in doing so that what had just happened would not come to haunt him. For two reasons he doubted if Carl would keep quiet about this, though. First of all, he knew he had witnessed the man's lustful touch; and secondly, he had to conclude, based upon the repulsion he had seen in Carl's eyes, that he would promptly apprise all who would listen what he had been in observance of.

In his disappointment for having allowed himself to cave in to his desires, Roarie eventually began to cry. But it wasn't only for himself that he was shedding tears. No, he was also weeping for his family, for he knew they would be forced to address the repercussions of his actions. Even Dwight, in some respects, would be required to do so, and as each of them well realized from past experience, people could be cruel.

Arriving home, Roarie darted indoors to seek out his parents. Finding them in the kitchen, his mother immediately took notice of his overwrought bearing, and asked what was wrong.

Seating himself, the boy looked downward before announcing in labored words, "I've done a foolish thing. I've brought shame to myself and the family once again." Raising his head to regard the disheartened faces of his parents, he added, "I did try to fight it, though. I even left before anything happened... but it was because someone saw me through the window, someone who'll spread the news I think." His look was one of dread.

Mr. and Mrs. Aimes exchanged worried glances.

"Are you trying to tell us that the only reason you left was because you were seen, Roarie?" his mother beseeched him.

After a brief deliberation, Roarie had to admit, "I probably would have stayed. .... I feel so out of control sometimes. ... Dwight has to be told about this before he finds out from someone else. Otherwise he might not let me explain."

"I think you're right about that," his mother replied. With regret she then bemoaned, "Oh, Roarie, I wish you hadn't done this! You told your father and I that you wouldn't!"

In the strain of the moment everyone was driven to silence. Did the members of this household ever think about God? Certainly so, but something very important was missing, something which would aid them considerably in understanding what was expected of them. There's a tug of war taking place between the forces of good and evil, and we as a people are influenced by each of those forces. If we do not look to God for guidance and strength on a continual basis, we are left ill prepared to deal with the challenges that come our way. But within they who are receptive to the truth, there is hope, always hope. .... And within this family there were receptive minds.

* * *

It was nearly dusk by the time Roarie developed enough nerve to walk up to the Enharts' home. Standing before it, it suddenly dawned on him that aside from coming here to tell Dwight of Sandy's death, it had always been Dwight who visited him, never the other way around. Yet because of Dwight's poor family relations he had always sensed he preferred it remain that way.

Ascending the front steps, he had to literally force himself to knock upon the door. Then, in entering at the sound of Dwight's response, he saw him seated at the kitchen table with a sandwich and a glass of milk set before him.

"Hi, Roarie, what brings you here?" he stated while standing.

"I've got something important to tell you," he solemnly spoke up. "But you can finish eating if you like."

"No, that's alright. The food can wait," Dwight told him in a desire to not only be accommodating, but expedite the amount of time they remained in close proximity to his mother. Pausing only briefly, he asked, "What is it?"

To be assured they'd have complete privacy, Roarie proposed, "I'd rather we talked somewhere else, maybe the barn."

Because Dwight considered the suggestion to be both welcome and warranted, he promptly left the house with Roarie following close behind.

Once inside the structure, Dwight wondered what an unusually silent Roarie planned to tell him, for he seemed so deep in thought. Slowly walking to where Hazel stood by the corral's edge just inside the back door, he began to gently stroke her neck. Glancing in the direction of Roarie, he stated with sought-after preparedness for whatever might be told him, "I'm listening."

Uncertain as to how his revelation would be received, Roarie started out by saying, "Dwight, you're one of the best friends I've ever had... but I haven't told you certain things about myself." Making his way to the opposite side of Hazel, he leaned against the corral and added, "I guess I hoped there wouldn't be a need for it, and I guess I was afraid to lose you as a friend." At this point he also touched the animal's broad neck to stroke it.

"Roarie, don't you realize by now that I'll always be your friend?" Dwight strove to convince him. "You can tell me anything."

"But this is something... shocking," Roarie seen fit to state while eying him squarely. "And I felt I couldn't expect even you to come to terms with what I am."

"Roarie, what do you mean by the way you are?" Dwight inquired. "You didn't get in any serious trouble back in Chicago, did you?"

Seeking to expose the inevitable at last, Roarie related, "Yes, I did, if being involved with a man is considered trouble." Detecting the alarm in Dwight's eyes, he went on to say, "Yes, Dwight, it really happened."

"Oh... I see," he was slow to reply.

"But please believe me when I say I only wanted you to be my friend," Roarie swiftly brought to his attention. "The day I first met you I felt you were someone I could trust, and it drew my attention. ... I hope that doesn't upset you."

"No, Roarie, I'm not upset that you trusted me to be your friend. I should be grateful for that. .... I must tell you, though, that I don't like what you did in Chicago. In fact it makes me feel very sorry for you."

"Could you tell me why?" Roarie requested, given that he valued his insight so much.

Regarding him directly, Dwight upheld, "I think it's because what you did distracted you from what's really important in life, which is a disappointment to God." With an imploring overtone, he inquired, "Why did you do it, Roarie? What benefit did you ever hope to gain from it?"

"Why do so many people do the things they do?" he responded with a shrug of his shoulders. "Sometimes I wonder if I'll ever know what'll make me happy." In honest self-examination, he further revealed, "I guess I'm searching for something without knowing what that something is."

"You and the world," Dwight dared to maintain. "And if it's what I think it is, I wonder if God is any more disappointed in you than he is by the man who lusts after women." Even then he dared to suggest, "To all of you he might say the same thing, that you've searched for love in all the wrong places." As Roarie looked at him in utter amazement over his insinuation that a man lusting after women was just as unwholesome as what he had done, Dwight told him, "But if I'm truly your friend, I'll leave your judgment to God." By saying this he in effect meant that it would be wrong to draw any conclusions about Roarie's salvation based upon what he had done in his life thus far, for not only didn't he know what the future held in store for him, he also did not know what God's judgment toward him would ultimately be. .... Therefore the fact that he believed Roarie had committed a moral transgression did not mean he wasn't his friend, nor did it mean he couldn't continue to be his friend, for he was coming to know that whenever a person set out to acquire the qualities of Jesus, their character would be put to the test.

Roarie liked Dwight. He liked him a lot. He liked his way of looking at things. As it turned out, he even found himself liking that he was confiding in him, which is why, as he looked out to pasture by way of the back door, he was persuaded to say, "After Sandy's death I was going to tell you about my past, but somehow the time never seemed right."

"But now for some reason the time is right," Dwight perceptively stated. "Why is that?"

Slowly making his way across the floor, Roarie gathered his thoughts before explaining, "I had an unpleasant experience when I went into Fulton earlier. You see I happened to encounter a man who's like me. I even went with him to his home, and while I was there, Carl Barnet snuck up to his window and saw him touching me in an intimate way. By tomorrow the word will probably be everywhere, and I don't have to tell you what people are going to think about me.... and maybe even you."

In painful understanding Dwight looked away before saying, "It was an angry individual who found out about this, so don't be surprised if he stretches the truth to make things look even worse." Breathing deeply, he shuddered at the thought of what might culminate.

Considering the implications of what he had done, Roarie said with remorse, "I'm afraid I haven't been the friend I meant to be, Dwight."

Dwight had no desire to add to Roarie's heartache, for which reason he changed the focus by asking, "How do you plan to deal with this?" When Roarie made no reply, he predicted, "You'll see through this in time."

With a look that bore his skepticism, Roarie contended, "I'm not so sure about that." Walking to the door, he added with solemn acceptance, "You do realize our relationship will likely be torn apart over this, don't you?"

In response to his negative expectations, Dwight made the claim, "It appears you won't allow it to be any different than that.... for now anyway."

Uncertain as to what course of action he should follow, Roarie impulsively rebounded, "Maybe it'd be a good idea if we stayed away from each other from now on. It'd probably be easier on both of us." Disappearing from sight without warning, he stood outside the door with his head held low, attempting to fathom the seriousness of the situation.

As for Dwight, all he could seem to do was stare blankly into space in dire disappointment. Turning to Hazel, he put his face to her neck, and prayed that God would somehow assist Roarie, so concerned was he about his well-being, so sincerely was he his friend. Truly he did not dare, nor in fact did he desire, to condemn or punish or reject Roarie for what he had done, even though he honestly felt in his heart that he had behaved immorally. He knew, however, that in cases such as this, there was a fine line which was not meant for mankind to cross over, even though it was a line which many people took upon themselves to cross over anyway, believing they had the right to chastise a person who had done something depraved in their eyes. If only they realized their conduct was not sanctioned by God, they might not be so self-righteous. If only they knew that by trying to play the part of God they were very much rejecting God and convicting themselves in the process, for it is written, "As ye judges, so shall ye be judged in the same measure."

* * *

When Roarie would not so much as look at Dwight as they rode the bus to school the following morning, Dwight wondered if he was attempting to protect him from people's suspicions as best he could. Yet if that was his strategy, it did not serve its intended purpose, for as soon as they arrived at Fulton High each of them became aware of the low pitched whispers and accusatory stares converging upon them from all directions.

Experiencing this unpleasantness, Roarie longed to return home. The only reason he had not stayed there to begin with was that he knew it would only make matters worse if he refused to address the consequences of his actions in a timely manner. And really, all things considered, he did want to put this behind him once and for all.

Walking a few feet behind Roarie, Dwight felt as though they were about to run the gauntlet. Then, just as they began to go their separate ways, Dwight saw Carl, Ben, and a few other boys obstruct Roarie's advancement by way of a human line.

"You've got a lot of nerve coming here!" Carl sneered. "You've either got guts or you're just plain stupid!" Glancing over his shoulder at the gathering spectators, he scornfully added, "I think you need to be taught a lesson!" In a gesture of support, an egg was thrown from the crowd, splattering against Roarie's forehead and running down his face between his eyes.

As Roarie withstood this abuse, resentment began to take root within him. Never had he felt so despised. Then just as Carl stepped forward, Dwight intervened by exclaiming, "That's enough!" As all eyes turned to him in utter amazement, he boldly went on to say, "So this is how you choose to act! I was hoping you'd be different, but apparently it was expecting too much!" Running his gaze amongst the assembly of people, he advanced to Roarie's side before adding, "For all of you who approve of the way he's being treated, just remember, it's easy to think wronging someone is right when you stand amongst the majority." With absolute justification, he thereby concluded, "May God forgive you."

At the completion of Dwight's reprimand some of the students began to murmur amongst themselves, because even though they had initially thought themselves to be vindicated in condemning Roarie, his words had planted within their minds a seed of doubt. Why even Carl's closest followers were struck with speechless apprehension, so much so that when Carl saw this within them, he fought back by bellowing, "Don't let him scare you! He's probably just like Roarie!" But there was no use fighting it, for the crowd had already begun to disperse.

Staring at Dwight, Carl could not help but marvel at his ability to induce everybody to scatter.

"You're different!" he therefore scowled in a fit of frustration. Shaking his head confoundedly, he, too, proceeded to walk away.

Equally amazed by what had taken place, Roarie turned to face Dwight while wiping the egg from his face with the back of his hand.

"Why, Dwight, why did you get involved that way?" he inquired of him.

"I really don't think that should be a mystery to you, Roarie," he responded in grave disappointment, "so I'll let you figure it out for yourself." On that final note he headed for his locker in the hopes that Roarie would gain a grasp of certain truths, truths which were intended to be of benefit to him.

* * *

So as to spend as much time as possible with Jana during his lunch hour, Dwight ate while walking down the road towards her home. In the course of doing so he found himself wondering how much additional persecution Roarie would suffer at the hands of misguided people. In any event, he certainly wanted Roarie to realize that it was possible to heal even the deepest of wounds with a gradual fading of the scars.

Minutes later, as he stood at the Rossis' doorstep with a wild flower he had picked along the way, he was greeted by Alice.

"Hello," he warmly reacted to the sight of her. "I'm here to see Jana if I may."

"Oh, yessum, Mist'r Dwight. We's been expect'in ya," she politely bade him to enter. "Miss Jana's been look'in forward ta yer visit." In noticing the flower in his hand, she said, "Dat was right nice a ya ta bring me dat flow'r, Mist'r Dwight."

"Oh... I actually intended it for Jana... but I'll pick one for you soon," he stammered in response to her comment. "You can...." Suddenly he saw a grin develop on her robust face, which compelled him to stop short and laugh before saying, "Ah, Alice, now I know you have a sense of humor, and I want you to know I like that in a woman. You suspected all along it was for Jana, didn't you."

"Yessum," she conceded with a lingering smile. "But I'se gonna be expect'in dat flow'r from ya jus ta same."

"I'll remember that," Dwight told her. As his thoughts turned to Jana, he anxiously asked how she was getting along.

"Oh, she's much bett'r," Alice eased his concerns. "She done got 'er app'tite back. Why dis morn'in she done ate mos all 'er breakfas."

"That is encouraging," Dwight stated in obvious relief. "I've been praying for her." Gazing at one another for a few moments, Alice declared, "I kin see how good ya is fer Miss Jana. She done tole me dat, but now I kin see it fer myself."

While he smiled, Dwight heard footsteps down the hall and turned to see Mrs. Rossi approaching.

"It's good to see you again, Dwight," she hospitably welcomed him. "I'm sure Alice told you the wonderful news about Jana." As he nodded his head, she went on to reveal, "That isn't the only good news. My husband has assured me he won't interfere with your coming here."

"I feel better just knowing that," Dwight freely admitted.

Still focused on his inspiring outlook from the day before, Mrs. Rossi made it a point to say, "I simply had no idea what I'd discover in you." With that having been maintained, she wasted no time in adding, "Jana's anxiously awaiting you in her room, so I suggest you get on up there, because precious time is ticking away."

Dwight pleased the woman by the satisfied manner in which he regarded her. Then he headed for the stairs.

Arriving outside Jana's room, he knocked ever so gently upon her door. Then, in being given permission to enter, he noticed how much healthier she looked in the matter of just a day.

"I heard you were much improved," he commented while approaching her bed. "You're a quick healer."

"I've got good reason for wanting to get better," she enthusiastically said. Seeing the flower in his hand, she was quick to inquire, "Is that for me?"

"It sure is. It's from nature's flower shop." Rather dramatically he handed it over to her. While she put it to her nose, he unexpectedly determined, "And with my budget, Jana, the price couldn't have been any better."

Spontaneously laughing, Jana told him, "Well, it was sweet of you anyway. It's the thought that counts." As he took on a grin, she asked, "How has everything been going for you?"

"I'm doing fine," he replied while sitting on the edge of her bed. .... Yet as his thoughts turned to Roarie, a solemn expression overcame his features.

"What's wrong?" she sounded out. When he did not respond, she somewhat hesitantly added, "Is it... over Roarie?"

Intently looking upon her, Dwight made the assertion, "News of this sort travels quickly, doesn't it?"

"Yes," she acknowledged. "Cybil told me what happened when she stopped by to see me on her way to school."

"What exactly did she say?"

"That Carl saw a man making advances toward Roarie, and that Roarie didn't resist him. .... From what you know, is that the way it really happened?"

"I'm not certain of all the specifics," he informed her. Recalling what took place earlier, he eventually stated, "Roarie was harassed today."

"I expected he would be," she related. "In fact I was wondering if he'd even attend school."

"I think he felt he should face everyone now rather than later. ... But it was so unpleasant for him," he vividly recalled.

Pondering the situation, Jana conveyed the presumption, "You must be very disappointed in Roarie."

"I must admit I am... but you know something, I'm even more disappointed by what I witnessed this morning." With ongoing concern, he considered the question, "Why would anyone treat someone in a way they'd never want to be treated themselves?" In answer to his own query, he made the claim, "I think it's because they're discontent deep down, because let's face it, Jana, people who feel good about themselves don't behave that way."

"I think you're absolutely right," she stated. .... "What exactly did happen earlier, anyway?"

"To begin with, somebody threw an egg at Roarie. And if that wasn't bad enough, Carl seemed about ready to beat him up. ... I ended up saying a few things in Roarie's defense."

"And what was that?"

"Mainly that God wouldn't like what they were doing." Getting up and walking over to the window, he gazed out before adding, "I've only known about Roarie's past since yesterday. He was afraid to tell me about it. But now, after what happened, he knew there'd be no hiding it, so he paid me a visit." Without hesitation he went on to say, "Last night I was awake for the longest time thinking about the meaning of friendship." Turning to regard her, he leaned against the wall to voice the opinion, "I don't think being a friend to someone means you've got to like everything about them, Jana." Advancing toward her bed, he alleged, "I think some people have been wondering if I have a sexual interest in Roarie, but God knows the truth."

Nodding her head, Jana specified, "If it's any consolation, I never doubted you for even a moment."

Dwight appreciated her faith in his integrity.

"Oh, Jana," he consequently uttered, "getting to know you has been such a privilege. How can I ever thank you enough for reaching out to me in my time of need?" Clearly he saw it as more than coincidence that he had crossed paths with her. "I've thanked God for you often. I want you to know that." Yet as he pondered the various strains of his life, he walked back to the window and pensively added while peering out, "Just once, though, I'd like to go to bed at night like I used to as a little boy, you know, with a clear mind free of disturbances. How wonderful it'd be, a dream come true really." In saying this he meant that there always seemed to be some unforeseen occurrence challenging his ability to experience that peaceful, easy feeling.

"Yet as you yourself would say, your condition is temporary," Jana so aptly reminded him, though in her heart she felt like weeping over his sad revelation.

Affectionately casting his eyes upon her, Dwight asked, "When do you think you'll be returning to school?"

"By the middle of next week," she surmised. "I should be strong enough by then."

"You seem like you will be," he was pleased to acknowledge. "In fact you really do strike me as quite a survivor, Jana Rossi."

"I guess I am at that," she somewhat introspectively noted.

"And now, after all that's happened, your father said he won't try to keep us apart any more."

"I know, and I'm so relieved, which for me is my dream come true. ... It's rather sad, though, isn't it, that we were forced to go through all that we did?"

"But in the end we triumphed," Dwight avowed. "Therefore I think I'm going to appreciate our friendship like never before." The look on his face shed light on the essence of his feelings.

"I, too, have gained a greater insight into what we have," Jana apprised him. "And I have come to know that tomorrow really does offer new hope after all."

* * *

When Dwight arrived home from school, he immediately took a leisurely walk in the surrounding countryside. While doing so, he nourished a frame of mind which was conducive to answered prayer; which is why, that night, while lying in bed, he realized what was in need of transpiring to encourage Roarie to feel better about life, of things that should be said and done, of things that were absolute truths. ... Hence, early that morning, about an hour or so before the bus was scheduled to arrive, he headed for the Aimes with a small Bible in his back pocket.

Arriving at his destination, he was greeted at the front door by Mrs. Aimes, who obviously was very surprised to see him this early in the day. When she bade him to enter, he was confronted by the baffling sight of packed boxes and crates strewn about the general area.

"Mrs. Aimes, what's going on here?" he was swift to inquire.

"I think I had better let Roarie explain everything," she solemnly replied. As he stepped into view, she added, "Please don't be too long, Roarie. We've got a lot of packing to do." Having said that, she headed for the kitchen.

It was with some measure of difficulty that Roarie regarded Dwight.

"Maybe we should go outside to talk," he suggested.

"Alright," Dwight cooperated and anxiously followed him onto the lawn, in the event of which Roarie turned to say, "We're leaving."

"But why!" Dwight beseeched him. "I thought you and your family liked it here enough to see this through!"

"We do like it here. ... At least we used to," he stated his position with oncoming distress. "But you and I both know I can't live here any more, not after what happened yesterday in school."

"No, Roarie, I don't know that," Dwight spoke his true feelings. "People can be harsh, I know, but this is still your home."

Roarie looked briefly away in a wave of indecision. Then he conceded, "You may be right about that, but nobody wants to live where they're so despised things like that happen." Pointing at the living room window, Dwight turned to see that it had been broken. "It happened last night. Somebody threw a rock through it while shouting obscenities. It even had a threatening note attached." In his dismay he looked skyward before continuing, "I'm filled with such shame and guilt, and I don't even understand why! Do you know how awful that is!" Yet before Dwight could even attempt to respond, he went on to say, "I avoided you yesterday for your sake. I've caused enough hurt, and now I'd like to leave it behind me. I hope you can understand that, just as I hope my family can."

For a few moments Dwight was silent in thought. Then he said, "But leaving is no solution, Roarie, unless you realize what's expected of you, because the same mistakes made here and in Chicago can be made elsewhere, too." Focusing on his reason for coming here, he asked, "Would you like to know what's expected of you, even if it's something you might not want to hear?"

"I like to think so, if it's in my best interest," he asserted. "I do know I don't want to hurt my family any more. I've put them through enough as it is." At this point tears began to cloud his vision.

In the midst of the compassion he felt for him, Dwight weighed his options. Then he stated with gentle urging, "Roarie, look at me." As the boy obliged him, he made the observation, "This doesn't concern your actions alone, because the thought is the father of the deed." Detecting his obvious confusion, he was quick to add, "You just don't seem to realize what can be done for you. All this time you've given me the impression you've only had two choices, either hide your desires or express them, but there is another choice, a choice that'll ease your mind, and set you free in the long run."

"But Dwight, you don't realize how strong my feelings can be," Roarie sought to convince him. "They're so strong I can't imagine them ever changing."

Grateful that he was confiding in him, Dwight continued in carefully chosen words, "Roarie, I believe you when you say you have strong feelings. I really do, but it doesn't have to remain that way for a lifetime. Feelings can change. I found that to be true when I began to evaluate my own life." Recognizing his heightened skepticism, he earnestly insisted, "Don't you see, a changed outlook and changed feelings go hand in hand. This applies to all of humanity, from the man who lusts after women, to the woman who lusts after men... and to the boy who lusts after men." When Roarie lowered his gaze in reference to him, he added, "Anyone who thinks about doing something long enough is bound to act on their thoughts sooner or later. It's only a matter of time."

As usual, Roarie was captivated by Dwight's way of looking at things.

"So I've got to change the way I think to change the way I feel," he stated with probing thought. As Dwight nodded his head, he inquired, "And how long would it take for this to happen?"

"It'd depend on the person and what they were up against, I imagine," Dwight answered him. "But with God victory is always possible."

"I wish I could believe that," Roarie replied. "It would be so wonderful to be set free from what torments me."

"You can believe it," Dwight told him. "For your sake I pray that you do." In saying this he meant that deliverance would never be had as long as he refused to turn to God, for if that be the case, he would always be dissatisfied within himself to one degree or another.

At this point Roarie candidly made the confession, "I guess I find it hard to believe there really is a God who loves me."

Sensing that the timing was right to do so, Dwight reached for the Bible within his pocket, handed it to Roarie, and said, "Give this a try. You have no idea what it can do for you, but I do. As your friend I'm asking you to read it."

For the first time since the incident in Fulton had taken place, Roarie felt a glimmer of hope envelop him. It was as though he was finally beginning to see past the pain of the present.

"Now I know why I wanted you to be my friend," he had the insight to comprehend. Gazing at the Bible for a few thought-filled moments, he made the determination, "I think I will read this."

"Then you're one step closer to being comforted," Dwight predicted. As Roarie beheld him in the hope that he was, he added, "Where will you be moving?"

"To Virginia. My father has an uncle there. We'll be leaving tomorrow."

"Tomorrow," Dwight barely was able to articulate before Mrs. Aimes appeared on the porch to tell Roarie his father was in need of his assistance with something.

Assuring her he wouldn't be much longer, Roarie looked to Dwight and said, "It's been so good knowing you. I want you to know I'll never forget what you tried to do for me. I'll think of you often." His sincerity was self-evident.

"I'll think of you, too," Dwight echoed his sentiments. ... "We'll see each other before you leave, though, won't we?"

"I think it'd be for the best if we said our good-byes now," Roarie found it heartrending to say. "I don't like dragging out good-byes. It's too unpleasant."

"Alright... as you wish," Dwight acquiesced. "But no matter what, write to me, hey, when you get settled into your new home. I'd like to keep in touch."

"I just might do that," Roarie made the assumption with a forced smile, in the event of which they found themselves impulsively hugging.

"I love you, Roarie," Dwight told him as they separated to regard one another. "And I think you know exactly what I mean by that."

"Yes, I believe I do," he had to admit. In as composed a manner as possible, he advised him, "Have a good life, the life you deserve." Turning abruptly about, he ran into the house in the futile hope that it would erase his sorrow in leaving.

Though Dwight still longed to persuade the Aimes to remain in Chism, he slowly headed for home. He didn't know it, but Roarie had availed himself to taking a position by the living room window to observe his departure.

"I wish I could stay, Dwight," he struggled to say as tears dampened his cheeks. "I really do wish I could stay." Yet deep down he knew they would be going their separate ways. But they were parting as friends, friends who were striving to see beyond their differences into the broader scheme of things, a mind set in much need of being emulated by the throngs of humanity.

So given all that had recently occurred, how could Roarie possibly foresee that the day would eventually dawn when he would be quite fulfilled in his manhood? Consider it therefore significant that as a tear rolled off his cheek, it fell upon the Bible that he held within his hands.

* * *

The Aimes had already left for Virginia by the following after-noon.

In the days to follow, in an effort to come to terms with their unexpected departure, Dwight frequently saddled up Zuzueca to take long, solitary rides in the Mississippi countryside. Yet even then there was more to it than that, for he wanted to isolate himself from humanity so that he couldn't be asked any questions about Roarie. Despite everything, though, there was a very bright side to his life in that each and every time he visited Jana, he saw a girl whose health was fast improving. .... Then one evening after school, as he was doing his homework in the privacy of his room, he heard a car pull up to the house and saw Clair step out of it.

As fast as he could, he darted down the stairs. Then, upon arriv-ing outside, he ceased his advancement to watch his sister approach the house in the pretty blue dress that she wore.

"Clair, you're back!" he enthusiastically stated. "You didn't tell us you were coming home today!"

"I decided to surprise you," she stated as Dwight noticed a man in the driver's seat of the car. "How have you been anyway?"

For the sake of spared explanations Dwight told her he was fine.

"And you seem to be doing well," he made it a point to empha-size. "You seem content. Has he contributed to that?" With a tilt of his head he motioned towards the man.

"To a large extent he has," she acknowledged. "You see he's gained my trust, so much so that we're going to be married."

"Married! When!" Dwight exclaimed.

"Next Monday in Jackson. You can be there if you like. We'll come get you," she was quick to volunteer.

"You know I'd like to be there. But are you sure you're ready for marriage?" he felt inclined to ask, for he couldn't help but wonder if she was grasping at an opportunity to avoid returning home.

"Knowing Stuart the way I do, I'm sure," Clair sought to convince him. As they proceeded to ascend the porch steps together, she added, "I told him to wait in the car until I spoke to mother. I wanted to find out what her disposition was like first." There was a certain degree of apprehension in her voice.

"She doesn't say too much these days," Dwight informed her.

"But she did let me keep Zuzueca!" he saw fit to add on a bright note.

"What's that?" Clair confusedly asked.

"My horse," Dwight chuckled. "Don't you remember? I told you about him in that last letter I wrote."

"Oh, yes," she recollected, and pleased him by also laughing. "I didn't know how to pronounce his name on paper either."

Moments later, as the two of them neared the dimly-lit living room, Clair recalled life as it used to be.

"Mother, I'm home," she eventually spoke up while approaching the chair on which she sat. "I'm well again."

"So I see." As she ran her gaze up and down her attire, she noted, "And it looks like you've been shopping." Without the slightest hint of gladness over her return, she merely reminded her where her room was.

"No, mother... I won't be staying here any more," she took her by surprise in saying. Gazing at Dwight for an instant, she uneasily added, "I've met a man. He works at the institution I was at. That's how we met." Seeing the woman's face take on a look of unmistakable reproof, she stood her ground by proclaiming, "I love him, mother. He's a good man and I'm going to marry him."

"You do whatever you want!" she told her with fast approaching disgust, "but mark my words, you'll be sorry some day! You might even end up back in that hospital again!"

"No, mother, you're wrong," Clair admonished her. "A marriage can work. I believe that now. Stuart helped me to believe it, and I feel fortunate to have met him." She began to cry a bit. "But you encouraged me to be negative about life." Looking to Dwight, she complimented him by saying, "He was stronger than I realized. I only hope my character can equal his some day." Regarding her mother once again, she duly advised her, "Please surrender before it's too late. You could enjoy life again." Yet because only resistance could be detected within her, she subsequently told her with a sigh of acceptance, "I'm going upstairs to get a few of my things." And with that she walked away.

When Clair was out of sight, Dwight boldly stated while striding forth, "Can't you see you're driving her away from you again! Tell her you're happy for her, wish her well, anything! Just give her something good to remember from this visit!" Yet when there still was no change in her hardened demeanor, he continued in a fit of annoyance, "For her sake I'm glad she's leaving so that she doesn't have to put up with your miserable attitude any more! It's bad enough that I have to!" Turning aside, he made his way into the kitchen, plopped himself down on a chair, and shook his head in mounting aggravation over the unending challenge of reaching her. Yet despite circumstances as they stood, he wouldn't stop hoping for satisfying results, even as his heart ached, even as he realized that sometimes your desires were not to be forthcoming. Time would reveal the final outcome, and whether or not there'd be reason for celebration after all.

* * *

In her room Clair witnessed nostalgic feelings concerning a time when she enjoyed living in this house. Eventually using the inner strength she had acquired since her near death, she brushed these thoughts aside so as not to become all the more saddened by what had become of her mother.

When she finished packing the things she wanted the most, she departed from the room without looking back and made her way down the stairs only to stop at the living room entrance to peer inside one last time.

"Good-bye, mother," she stated. "Take care of yourself."

Spurned by a derisive glance, she eventually walked away in the acceptance she felt it necessary to adhere to. Finding Dwight seated at the kitchen table, she was prone to wonder, "How will you ever endure living here? She's beyond hope."

"Yet I remember a time when you were becoming just as her, and look at the turnaround you've experienced," Dwight was quick to bring to her attention. As she lowered her head in somber acknowledgment, he further said, "My life isn't as bleak as you may think, so don't fret. ... Does Stuart know much about us?"

"I've told him quite a bit," she confided. ... "Would you like to meet him?" she inquired on a cheerful note.

"I surely would," Dwight anxiously anticipated. "After all, he is going to be my brother-in-law." Reaching for her suitcase, he followed her from the house to where her fiance stood waiting for her by his car.

"Stuart, this is my brother, Dwight," Clair introduced them just as Dwight released his grip on the luggage.

"I'm pleased to meet you," he said as they proceeded to exchange handshakes. "Clair's told me a lot about you."

"And she just told me of the wedding plans. Congratulations!"

"Thanks, we're looking forward to spending our lives together." Putting an arm around her, he drew her to him and stated with a gleam in his eye, "I love this girl, and I intend to be very good to her."

"I like hearing that," Dwight told him. "I wish you both much happiness."

Looking up at Stuart, Clair commented, "I think you'll be very pleased to know he's got a moral outlook, Dwight."

"You're right," Dwight replied. "That does please me." Yet in truth he had already sensed a salubrious quality within the man.

Following a further exchange of words, Stuart placed Clair's suitcase in the trunk of the car and got into the front seat with her. It was then that Clair rolled down her window to say with an emotion-filled candor that truly moved him, "Dwight, I want to thank you for all you did for me. Thanks for caring even when I didn't." In stark awareness of the life altering implications of his actions, she then began to cry.

"As I told you before, I was given the proper timing to come to your aid that day," Dwight yet maintained in a desire to give credit where credit was due. "But I know exactly what you're trying to tell me, and you're very welcome." The look on his face bore his modesty through and through.

Nodding her head, Clair waved farewell as her soon-to-be husband backed out of the driveway. While they drove away, she could not help but think about the love she had for her brother after all, a love which had temporarily been lost because of shortsightedness.

Watching them disappear from sight down the road, Dwight felt rewarded for his involvement in giving Clair a second lease on life, so much so that he was no longer disheartened by his mother's disposition.

"Thank you, too, Clair, for proving I was right about people," he was thus inspired to whisper before returning indoors to resume his schoolwork. Yes, Clair had reinforced his belief that a better tomorrow for the mother he could not help but love was conceivable after all.

* * *

Dwight zoomed in on the positive aspects of what recently occurred. Roarie had indicated he'd read the Bible. Clair was on the road to recovery in every sense of the word. And Jana had returned to school in what appeared to be vibrant health. All things considered, he actually began to believe the day would eventually dawn when he would go to sleep at night like he used to as a little boy, you know, with a clear mind free of disturbances.

When the day of the wedding arrived, Clair and Stuart were true to their word in seeing to it that he got a ride to Jackson; and although their wedding was kept plain and simple, he thought it was beautiful just the same. ..... Then one Friday evening something noble happened. It concerned Scott, whose injury was nearly healed, and whose attitude was much more conducive to healthy living. Was this due to Roberta's influence in his life? To some degree it was, yet true peace of mind is never really attained to the extent that's possible unless there's an honest attempt to come to terms with one's past. ... And so finally, after it had eaten away at him long enough, he felt morally obligated to apologize to Dwight for past abuses he had participated in against him. He even said unto Roberta one day out of the clear blue sky as they were doing homework together, "I have unfinished business." Then she, in learning what he had done, urged him to make amends for the sake of all concerned.

"Go to him," she specifically had said. "After all, it is the right thing to do, and tomorrow may be too late."

The goal of initiating private conversation consequently became Scott's mission, because if he was going to apologize, he wanted to say more than that he was merely sorry. Many times he rode past Dwight's home in the hopes that he'd see him alone, but when that proved unsuccessful, he decided to knock upon his door. This turned out to be more emotionally wrenching than he anticipated, yet his guilty conscience prodded him onward. To his disappointment, though, when he was greeted at the front door by Mrs. Enhart, he was told Dwight was not at home.

"Do you know where he is?" he anxiously inquired.

"No, he doesn't tell me where he's going," she somberly related as he took note of her unkempt appearance. "Check the barn if you like. .... You a friend of his?"

The question caught Scott off guard, so much so that he became momentarily tongue-tied. Finally, however, he had the wherewithal to say in a flood of sobering truth, "No, ma'am, I couldn't be called his friend, not in a million years." But what really was telling was when a thought-consumed look developed on her own face, and she openly confessed, "I couldn't be called his friend either."

Scott felt a tremendous sadness engulf him in hearing a mother say such a thing about her son.

"Then maybe it's time we both tried to change that, ma'am," he dared to tell her.

Following a few moments in which their gazes were riveted, Scott headed for the barn. He didn't know it, but he remained under the woman's scrutiny from behind the living room curtains. Yes, there was something about him that held her interest. Could it have been the unpretentious, forthright manner in which he admitted to not being a friend to her son? Had his confession shed light on her own shortcomings, as though she saw herself through him?

Entering the structure and discovering Dwight was not present, Scott drove toward The Gulf in the hopes of finding him there. While doing so, he happened to catch sight of him walking down the narrow dirt road that led to the O'Maley farm. Thankful for having noticed him, he turned onto that road and parked only a few feet beyond him.

In the meantime Dwight froze in his tracks over the sight of the stopped vehicle. To appease any apprehension he might be experiencing, Scott requested to speak to him as soon as he was in a position to do so.

"I won't keep you long," he made it a point to stipulate.

Though Dwight had ample reason for not trusting him, he felt surprisingly unthreatened by his presence. He took this to mean he was not in bondage to his fears to the extent he once had been. There was a part of him that was untouchable, beyond the grasp of anyone, solely because God ordained it to be so.

"I'll listen to whatever it is you have to say, Scott," he told him then.

Though Scott was reasonably assured Dwight wouldn't spurn him, he was by no means convinced, for he didn't know him all that well. And he certainly didn't know what was going on in his mind. So in an effort to ease his way into conversation, he started out by saying, "I was at your house looking for you. I'm glad I found you." As Dwight merely stared at him, he got down to the gist of his intentions by adding, "I've been feeling very troubled lately."

"And do you believe you deserve to feel that way?" Dwight inquired of him for the sake of honest revelation.

"Yes... I have to admit I do," Scott conceded with a glimpse of the shame he bore.

"And are you expecting me to help you feel better about that?" Dwight asked.

"I only know I feel the need to apologize to you for what I've done," Scott enlightened him. "Whether you forgive me or not, I must say I'm sorry."

"I appreciate that," Dwight told him, "and I harbor no ill will toward you, but I'd still like to know why you treated me that way, Scott." His request was made in the firm belief that delving into the reasons why people behaved badly could be of benefit to all concerned.

Initially Scott was at a loss for words as he struggled to provide Dwight with an adequate explanation.

"I was jealous of Jana's interest in you," he then felt prevailed upon to admit. "And I wanted to punish you for it." Yet suddenly he gave Dwight the definite impression he was not seeing things in the proper perspective when he theorized, "If we had only started out as friends, things wouldn't have been carried that far."

Why did Dwight take issue with his statement? Why was he so intellectually repulsed by his reference to friendship? It was because he saw it as a diversion from the truth that dwelled within, for which reason he felt strongly compelled to say, "No, Scott, with all due respect, friendship wasn't the problem between you and me." As Scott beheld him in a disconcerted manner, he adamantly insisted, "Please, let's be completely honest. It wasn't necessary that we be friends. The problem was you didn't have goodwill toward your fellow man, just as those other boys didn't." As Scott cast his gaze to the ground in the onset of shame, Dwight continued, "Any person who has goodwill toward their fellow man would never attempt what you did. The fact that you didn't catch me is beside the point. You abused me mentally."

"I know!" Scott painfully cried out in an aim to accept responsibility for his actions. Raising his face as if to God, he struggled to say, "A part of me knew it was wrong, but I was so angry at the time! .... I didn't feel good about myself for doing it! I really didn't, and I found that it got worse and worse as time went on!"

"So now you're here," Dwight pointed out. "And I want you to know I respect you for that. Many people have regrets but do little about them. You, on the other hand, took action, and did the right thing."

"And would that still be true if you didn't accept my apology?" Scott asked of him with held back tears.

"Yes, I think so," Dwight voiced the opinion without delay. "You can only control your own actions, not mine."

Regarding him, Scott felt as though a great weight had been lifted from his shoulders.

"I never thought I'd feel so relieved in coming here," he divulged.

With a look of profound awareness, Dwight said, "The future holds more than we know, Scott."

Sensing the spiritual significance of his comment, Scott assuredly replied, "I'll remember that." Focusing on where he had come from, he continued, "I don't think your mother recognized me when I stopped by your house. She hadn't seen me in a long time, though."

"Sometimes I think she wouldn't even recognize herself from years gone by," Dwight brought to his attention. "She's not at all like she used to be."

"I did get that impression," he imparted, and briefly considered revealing what had been said about not being a friend to him. ... "Well, I guess I had better not keep you any longer. Thanks for talking." Taking advantage of the opportunity to do so, he stopped short to make the assertion, "If it's any consolation, I'm glad you outran us that day. I know I'd feel even worse if we had caught you."

Holding him in his gaze, Dwight made the claim, "You didn't think I could outrun you, did you?" When Scott was again left at a loss for words, he carried it one step further by adding, "Admit it, Scott, you didn't, you really didn't."

Thrust into a state of submission, Scott acknowledged with a slight grin, "You're right. I didn't. Your speed took me by surprise."

"And was it humbling?" Dwight inquired of him with a probing stare.

"Yes, it was humbling," Scott acquiesced. "You really took the wind out of my sails." When the lighthearted nature of his comment subsided, he seriously added, "Thank you. I think I just might sleep better tonight."

"You deserve to," Dwight maintained. "So long." As he turned aside, Scott was quick to ask, "By the way, I'm curious; where did you hide that day?"

At first Dwight merely regarded him in memory of how he avoided detection. Then he aptly replied, "Let's just say I've never been so thankful for trees with thick upper branches."

"How resourceful!" Scott exclaimed.

"I thought so at the time," Dwight purported before again turning in the direction of the O'Maleys', in the event of which Scott blurted out, "Do you think it's possible we could ever be friends?"

With his back to him Dwight pondered the question. Then he announced while looking over his shoulder, "I'm not sure we'd be compatible as friends, Scott. I'm not even sure I like you. ... Give it some time." Having said that, he began to walk away.

Scott felt deserving of Dwight's misgivings, as well he should. Getting into the car then and backing to the main road, he saw Dwight turn to view his departure. As they simultaneously waved, he began to drive away.

So it came to pass that something worthwhile had been salvaged from an unpleasant incident because two boys allowed it to be so. Could that be why they were going their separate ways with smiles of satisfaction upon their faces and feelings of satisfaction within their hearts? .... The answer was obvious.

CHAPTER 19

THE JITTERS AND JIGGLES
OF THE JAMBOREE

Never had Jana exuded so much exuberance, and here is why it was so. She had grieved for a friend. She had lingered in an illness. And she had triumphed through it all. Therefore a heartfelt appreciation for the many blessings of her life became the core of her outlook. So intimately she had come to know love, feel love, and radiate that love, much to the satisfaction of Dwight. ... Then one Monday during their lunch hour, she asked him whether he planned to attend the Fulton Jamboree the following Saturday evening.

"I wouldn't mind going," Dwight reinforced her belief that he was willing to be there, "but I don't know how to dance."

"Well, I'll teach you!" she quickly volunteered. "Tomorrow we could go to my house during our lunch hour. It'll be fun. You'll see."

"I guess if you're willing," he complied. "But only if you'll go with me."

"Oh, but I can't," she regretted to inform him. "You see Ted Stevens asked me weeks ago. We've gone with one another for the past two years." In light of his obvious disappointment, she optimistically added, "Why don't you ask Kathy Trent? I talked to her this morning and as far as I know no one's asked her yet."

"Alright," Dwight said in the hopes of improving his social skills. Yet as far as his inhibitions were concerned, the thought of asking Kathy for a date did not engulf him with a fear of rejection as it would have in the past, for he knew that even if Kathy refused to go with him, as long as he felt secure in his standing with God, he would not be crushed. It was all so beautifully reassuring, so much so that he discovered he was able to approach the girl with relative ease; whereupon, to his delight, she accepted his invitation. What he didn't realize, though, was that Kathy, along with a number of other students, admired the moral stand he had taken regarding the harsh treatment of Roarie.

The next day at noon, while he and Jana were on their way to her home to begin their dancing lessons, Dwight asked if she truly believed he could learn the basics in time for the jamboree.

"Don't worry! I'll have you ready!" she confidently told him. "When time is of the essence, people learn quickly!"

Once in the family room, a snappy record was placed on the phonograph. Then, turning to face Dwight, Jana stated, "The trick is in the timing. Now come here and I'll show you." Doing as he was told, she placed his hands in the proper position. "Now just follow me, one two three, one two three." They began slowly and awkwardly at first, but eventually quickened their pace as Dwight's skill grew more apparent.

"You see, it's really not all that hard to catch onto," she pointed out to him just minutes later.

"I guess not," he noted with a smile. "Tell me, how'd you learn to dance so well?"

"I've been to quite a few events where there was dancing," Jana informed him as they continued to keep in step to the music as best they could. "I just picked it up, a little through watching others, but mainly through participation."

"Yes, that does make a difference, doesn't it?" Dwight felt inclined to say with a hint of frustrated desire. "And if it'll help me break free of my chains, I want to be a participant, too, because I'm tired of feeling their weight."

"Believe me, you're breaking free. I see it in you more and more every day," she told him as the record came to an end. Walking to the phonograph, she proceeded to play another tune. Then, when they had finished dancing to that one, they made their way into the kitchen to have a snack in the company of Alice before returning to school.

While he ate, Dwight listened with keen interest as Alice spoke of her past, of a time when she picked cotton until her fingers bled, of a time when Mississippi was younger. Taking in her words, he recalled being told of the murder of her father by Klan members, which encouraged him to reflect on the fact that Mississippi and his country had a history of shameful oppression. Yet despite knowing this to be true, he loved his country. He loved it for its potential. Yet never was his love as enhanced as when he invited the love of God to cloak him. From that day forward it was unrivaled, which resulted in this sobering reality. Never would he disregard a moral wrong, whether it was sanctioned by his government or not, for to do so would only contribute to societal decay. ... But often we do not see things for what they are when he seems so wholesome by outward appearances. Yet it's part of the deception, part of the ploy. But don't hate him. Don't lower yourself a rung on the ladder of morality. Pity him for his ethical shortcomings. Rest assured that in the final result justice will prevail. He cannot escape the judgment of God. It's only a matter of time, and time is running out for him, and they who are akin to him.

* * *

When the day of the jamboree arrived, Dwight experienced the normal jitters that a young man feels when dating a girl for the first time.

Having recently gotten his driver's license with the help of the O'Maleys, he was encouraged by the couple to use their car, for he had gained their undivided trust.

Driving to Kathy's home, he found himself focusing on the transition of his childhood into manhood, and that which interested him in the way of a career. Yet it wasn't a yearning for material wealth that engaged him, for although he thought the Rossis had a beautiful home with comforts to offer, he was determined to keep God close to his heart so that he wouldn't covet what they had. It was a different type of wealth he longed for, the type that comforts the soul.

Arriving at his destination, he walked up to the front door where he was greeted by Kathy's mother, a woman with a pleasant smile.

"Kathy will be ready shortly," she told him as he entered the foyer. "Please come into the living room to wait for her."

Following her there, Dwight saw Mr. Trent seated in a lounge chair reading a newspaper. In nearing the sofa, he took note of the simple decor of the room, and mentioned that he found it appealing.

"Thank you," Mrs. Trent responded. "We've got repairs to do, but then again, most anyone could say that. I'm just glad to have a home." Her manner of speaking led one to believe she was content with her surrounding. "This is Dwight... Enhart, as I recall," she told her husband then while regarding Dwight for confirmation.

"Yes, that's right," Dwight acknowledged.

"Pleased to meet you," the man stated while extending a hand towards him.

"Likewise," Dwight replied as he returned the gesture.

"Kathy told us you're from Chism." As Dwight nodded his head, he added, "That's where I grew up, near the Moriah farm."

"Oh, ya, I know where that is," he said with a spark of interest. "I used to play there often while growing up. It's gotten pretty run down."

"I imagine it has," Mr. Trent remarked. "It's been abandoned for years."

"I wouldn't mind living there some day, though," Dwight let it be known. "It'd be worth fixing up, and I think it'd be a good place to raise some livestock, which is something I'd like to do."

"At one time there was plenty of that there," the man recalled. "It was a beautiful farm, and with hard work could again be."

"And I can see it now," Dwight thoughtfully envisioned. "My horse, Zuzueca, running in a green pasture with a mare by his side."

Granting him a look of amusement over the imaginative way in which he expressed himself, Mrs. Trent took it one step further by saying, "I think I'm beginning to hear hoofbeats already." As Dwight and her husband laughed, she asked if he desired a refreshment while awaiting her daughter.

"Oh, no thank you, ma'am," Dwight answered her. "We'll be leaving shortly."

"Alright, just make yourself comfortable," she cordially stated and walked away. "Kathy, Dwight's here!" she hollered up the stair-well before heading for the kitchen.

"Dwight, I'd like Kathy home by eleven thirty," Mr. Trent informed him at this time. "No later."

"Yes, sir," Dwight was quick to answer.

Minutes later, the sound of Kathy coming down the stairs drew the attention of both Mr. Trent and Dwight.

"You look wonderful," her father complimented her as she entered the room wearing a bright yellow dress. Rising to his feet, he declared, "You'll be the belle of the ball."

"Oh, daddy, you're making me blush," the girl coyly reacted. Regarding Dwight, she wasted no time in adding, "Are you ready?"

"Yes," he said in anxious expectation.

Saying good-bye to her father, Kathy walked over to him and gave him a kiss on the cheek.

"I'd tell you not to wait up for me if I thought it'd do any good, but I know you too well for that."

"That's right, so save your breath," he humorously advised her as her mother entered the room carrying a shawl.

"Don't forget this, Kathy. You know how chilly the night air is this time of year. And do have a good time, dear," she stated while placing the garment about her shoulders.

"I'm sure I will, mother. Don't worry." Turning to leave, she suddenly heard her two younger brothers giggling just outside the room in the hallway.

"Mother! Please do something about them!" she firmly insisted while turning to the woman in a fit of annoyance. "This happens every time I go out with a boy."

Heeding her daughter's request, Mrs. Trent shooed the spirited youngsters away, in the event of which Kathy looked to Dwight and said with dramatic emphasis, "They can be so embarrassing!"

"Don't let it bother you," Dwight urged her. "Some day you'll look back on this moment and smile."

"Well, unless you want a repeat performance, we had better get out of here," she emphatically told him while glancing in the direction of her departed brothers, thereby inciting Dwight's laughter.

Voicing their final good-byes, Dwight and Kathy left the house and drove the short distance to the community building where the jamboree was being held.

While he parked, Dwight noticed from the number of vehicles situated about that the turnout for the event was quite good. Unaccustomed to being at gatherings of this size, he began to feel a bit apprehensive as he walked around the car to open the door for Kathy; yet still, in the midst of his unrest, he did manage to retain a functional degree of composure.

Approaching the building and hearing the sounds of revelry within, it became apparent to Dwight and Kathy that the people were enjoying the music and dancing immensely. Once entering the large structure, they began to edge their way through the crowd just as a break came in the entertainment. Noticing Bill and Cybil walking off the dance floor together, Dwight waved to get their attention.

"We were wondering when you'd be getting here!" Cybil exclaimed as she and Bill arrived at his side. "I'm glad you made it!"

"So am I," Dwight told her, which for the most part was true. "This looks like quite a get-together."

"It always is," Cybil recollected. "I guess dances will never outlive their popularity in these parts."

"So it would seem," Dwight supported her contention. "Ah, tell me, is Jana here yet?" he wasted no time in asking.

"Ya, her and Ted are somewhere around here," Bill informed him while scanning the immediate area. "Would you like me to find them?"

"No, that's alright. I'll see her later," Dwight told him. "Right now I think I'll get some of that drink they're serving over there, whatever it is."

"It's called punch," Cybil teased him.

"Ah... right, punch," Dwight stated in reaction to his naivety. Turning to face Kathy, he asked if she, too, wanted some.

"Yes, that'd be nice," she responded.

Dwight slowly maneuvered his way through the crowd. Then, just as he got through filling the punch glasses, he noticed Carl standing beside him.

"I see you're trying to get up in the world. Out with a girl," he derided him. "Miracles never cease, do they?"

Staring at him, Dwight said with unmistakable resolve, "You're right. Miracles happen all the time." Then he strode away leaving him with an awkward expression on his face. Try as he may, he never seemed able to weigh him down no matter what he said or did to him.

Shortly thereafter, as Dwight and Kathy drank their punch while observing the dancers, Dwight wondered if he'd perform as well as them, as though it really mattered. Then, just as he was about to ask Kathy to dance, he heard a familiar voice and turned to see Jana.

"Oh, hi, I was looking for you earlier but with all these people I couldn't find you!" he reacted in obvious delight at the sight of her. "Are you having a good time?"

"Very much so! I've been dancing nearly every number!" she stated before addressing Kathy and telling her how nice she looked, it being a statement which encouraged Dwight to focus not on Kathy, but her, for in his way of seeing things she had a beauty beyond compare because of her proven inner attractiveness.

Kathy returned Jana's compliment. ... Yet strangely, as Jana beheld her, she was stricken by a feeling which prompted her to say mainly to Dwight, "I ...ah... told Ted I'd only be a minute or two. I did want to say hello, though. I'll see you both later perhaps." Rather abruptly she then commenced to walk away.

For a few seconds Dwight studied her departure. She was ill at ease over something, he had to conclude, for he knew the look all too well. Eventually turning his attention to Kathy, he inquired, "Would you like to dance? I'm still a beginner, but I'll only improve with practice."

"Yes, I'd love to," she so eagerly responded that the feeling was gotten she had been anticipating the request all along.

Taking her by the hand, Dwight led her onto the dance floor where in no time at all he found himself fitting right in with the rest of the crowd, so much so that when the song ended, he asked her to dance the next number also.

Later, when they were back at the sidelines, Kathy told Dwight he really was a much better dancer than he gave himself credit for.

"I had a good teacher. It was Jana," he said in the memory of those lessons. Looking to his left, he caught sight of Scott dancing with Roberta and spontaneously waved, which ironically turned out to be highly warranted, given that only moments earlier Scott had come to his defense. Timing can make all the difference; and so when Carl, in discovering he was at the jamboree, came up with a spur of the moment plan to attack him when he was away from the crowd, something relevant transpired. As events would have it, Scott became immediately suspicious when he went outdoors for some fresh air and happened to see Carl talking in low-pitched conversation to some boys in the parking lot. In order to investigate his misgivings, he approached them and asked what the big secret was in the hopes they'd confide in him.

Carl was eager to inform Scott of his intentions, because he did not know that he had experienced a change of heart in recent weeks.

"Would you like to be in on it?" he then wound up asking in the presumption he would.

"Not only don't I want to be in on it," Scott firmly told him and the other boys, "I'm not about to stand by doing nothing to stop it!"

Carl stared at Scott with an astonished look on his face.

"You're not challenging me to a fight, are you Scott?" he inquired then with a glimpse of the intimidation he sought to instill within others, proof enough that what goes around comes around, and that right from the very start a poor self-image had consumed him in great measure, possibly the greatest measure of all.

"No, there's a better way to handle this than fighting," Scott apprised him without delay. "I intend to go back into that building to tell people there might be trouble, and if we have to challenge you, you're going to find there's strength in numbers. Someone recently told me that to be a bully is to be a coward. Would you like to be looked at that way by all those people?" he cleverly asked of him while glancing over his shoulder.

"Gee, Scott, don't get your dander up," Carl made light of the situation. "I'll lay off him tonight if that's what you really want,.... but what's come over you?" His confusion was clearly evident.

"I finally woke up!" Scott startled even himself by shouting. As all eyes held him in captured arrest over the sheer forcefulness, the sheer volume, of his outburst, he took it upon himself to further say, "You can wake up, too, while there's still time! Think about what you're becoming and maybe tomorrow morning you'll get out of bed with a new lease on life!" Through the humble awareness he was coming to experience, he rather softly concluded, "I know I have." Turning aside, he proceeded for the building in full view of the speechless boys, not realizing that Carl was so filled with consternation over his moving words that he left the premises posthaste; yes, he along with the other boys. ..... So later, in returning Dwight's wave, Scott realized that he was well on his way to redeeming himself with not only Dwight, but humanity in general, which was a most rewarding of feelings. .... Therefore by virtue of that it could be concluded that good citizenship had taken firm hold within Scott.

When his attention was no longer focused on Scott, Dwight asked Kathy if she desired additional punch, to which she said yes. Walking away from her, he felt content with how the evening was progressing. ... Yet then suddenly he started thinking of Jana, even when he had returned to Kathy's side, which cast such a pensive bearing about him that Kathy asked if something was wrong.

"No, it's nothing," he sought to convince her, since he didn't have a solid grasp on his feelings. The time for revelations came sooner than expected, however, for it was only moments later, when the band announced it was going to play a slow tune and that the guys and gals should choose their partners, that he turned to face Kathy only to discover he was not comfortable with this arrangement. No, for some reason he couldn't relax dancing so close to her, which very much concerned him in that he found her to be a very nice girl. ... But then, as he gazed about the room, his eyes suddenly fell upon Jana and Ted's dancing embrace, and he figured it out. .... Then lo and behold Jana was gazing back at him; and they both experienced an intense longing to be dancing with each other instead of whom they were with. ... Sentiments bordering surprise rose within each of them; and yet, at the same time, it was so understandable they should come to feel this way, given the bond that had developed between them since the day they first met, given a friendship successfully nurtured in spite of social barriers, given a relationship which set the stage for their ongoing concern for one another's well-being.

When Dwight and Kathy left the dance floor, Dwight found himself trying his utmost to determine Jana's whereabouts. Then, to his intrigue, he saw her leave the building alone, and longed to follow her. *But what about Kathy?* he conscientiously told himself, realizing that to forsake her was a self-defeating alternative, since he would never be able to reap gratifying results at the expense of her feelings. ... Yet ironically, just as he resigned himself to forcing Jana from his thoughts so as not to risk slighting Kathy, he was rather surprised to hear Kathy say, "Go to her, Dwight."

Looking at the girl, Dwight intently asked, "Is it that obvious?"

With a gentle nod of her head, she smiled and said, "I've seen you and Jana together many times in school, not that that's so telling, but when I saw how your eyes lit up when she spoke to us earlier, I knew you had deep feelings for her. ... And then just now when we were dancing, I saw Jana glancing our way, and I knew she wasn't looking at me." Again she smiled in a way that conveyed freedom from offense. "You go to her," she urged him while giving him a slight nudge. "Find out where you stand with one another."

To say Dwight was appreciative would be an understatement.

"You're a very nice girl," he complimented her, "the kind of girl who'd make a good friend." Following an exchange of genial looks to verify they were on good terms with one another, he stated, "I won't be gone long. I think I'd like to dance with you again, and I do insist on taking you home."

"But I know many people here," she brought to his attention. "Finding a ride won't be a problem."

"That's beside the point. I told your father I'd take you home by eleven thirty," he reminded her. "I should be responsible about that, don't you think?"

"Since you put it that way, yes, I guess it is the right thing to do," she acquiesced.

Walking away from her, Dwight greatly anticipated what his encounter with Jana would come to mean in their relationship. When he arrived outside, he saw her standing by a small water fountain clutching her arms close to her for warmth in the cool evening air. Approaching her from behind, he removed his jacket and gently said, "You're cold," while placing it about her shoulders.

"Thank you," she whispered while regarding him in an approving manner. Staring into the distant night, she asked, "Your being here, does it mean what I think it does?"

Dwight allowed some time to pass as he gathered his innermost thoughts.

"Yes, I believe so," he answered her then. "You see, when I saw you dancing with Ted, I wanted it to be me." As Jana swung about to look at him, he saw that she was pleased. "Yes, Jana, it's true. I really wanted it to be me. I even envied him, as selfish as that may seem."

"Oh, Dwight, when I saw you with Kathy, I felt the same way," she readily admitted.

"So our feelings are mutual," he rather introspectively stated. ... "Did you tell Ted how you feel?"

"Yes," she acknowledged, "and he understood, but really, we came here in the spirit of companionship. ... What about Kathy?" she in turn inquired.

"Can you believe it? She sent me out here," Dwight was quick to inform her. Drawing towards her, he peered into her eyes before adding with depth of feeling, "What's happening to us, Jana? I never thought we'd feel this way about each other."

"Neither did I," she solemnly professed. "In the beginning I simply wanted to befriend you, but now... now I've discovered that it's gone beyond that. I only hope this doesn't create a problem for us, though, because something like this could put a strain on our friendship if we're not careful."

"Are you hinting we might allow our emotions to get the better of us?" he inquired of her.

"It is a common occurrence you know," she was quick to remind him.

"And yet if that happened to us, I think I'd be forced to conclude we were never really the friends we claimed to have been all along," he insightfully pointed out. "When people have a friendship that's headed in the right direction, they don't complicate it with bad choices." Putting out his hand, he barely touched her arm before adding, "For the most part, loving people has come easy for me, Jana, despite my disappointments in humanity, but you, you're someone I both like and love, and that's not something I feel about everyone. You represent everything I could ever possibly want in a girl, and I doubt if I shall ever love like this again." Drawing ever nearer, they looked into one another's eyes with enormous affection.

"I love you, too, Dwight," Jana stated then; in the aftermath of which he felt tempted to lower his lips upon hers. But he would not allow himself to do so, and he freely told her why.

"Jana, let's not move too quickly. I want us to focus on getting to know one another better. Why complicate matters?"

"Are you saying you'd rather get to know my mind, Dwight Enhart?" she rather discernibly asked of him.

"Indeed I am," he duly admitted, for which reason she intimated with sought-after compromise, "You wouldn't see a hug as too suggestive, would you?"

Looking upon her, Dwight smiled with absolute ease.

"No, I think a hug would be just right. After all, it is what good friends sometimes do, is it not?" Having settled that, they fell into an embrace of mutually acquired trust.

Neither Dwight nor Jana knew it, but from the entrance of the building Ted had been watching them for some time. Turning about, he searched the room until his eyes fell upon Kathy. Walking over to her, he asked if she wanted to dance.

"Yes, I'd like that," she stated while taking hold of his arm. "I wouldn't want to disappoint my mother. She's always telling me to make sure I have a good time."

Returning indoors a short time later, Dwight and Jana noticed Ted and Kathy on the dance floor together, which gave them the good feeling all was well.

To be prudent is to be wise; and Dwight and Jana certainly had demonstrated prudence on this day. Therefore as they began to dance, it seemed to be a foregone conclusion that no matter what, they would always wish each other well in life for the rest of their lives as long as they both shall live.

* * *

In the lunchroom the following Thursday, when Dwight saw Scott seated with Roberta at the other end of the room, he wondered how he was doing, for other than a few hellos they had not spoken to one another since that day along the roadside. So in an effort to change that, he approached the two of them towards the end of the lunch hour and exchanged greetings. Sitting down across from Scott, he asked how his leg injury was coming along.

"It's getting better every day. It hardly bothers me any more," he gladly informed him.

"That's good to hear. You did seem to be physically fit when I saw you spinning your way around the dance floor at the jamboree." He said this while rapidly twirling his index finger.

Both Scott and Roberta burst into laughter over his unexpected comment. Then Scott indulged him by saying, "Roberta did keep me on my toes. She must have thought it'd be good therapy to have me circle the floor as many times as possible." As all three of them laughed all the harder, Roberta was inspired to maintain, "Yet I was the one who ended up winded." Indeed her witty remark brought their laughter to a new height.

Swept by a feeling of ease, Scott was motivated to say when their mirth had subsided, "You know something, Dwight, Roberta and I are planning to go to the beach Saturday afternoon if the weather is nice. Why don't you come along?"

After a brief deliberation, Dwight replied, "Alright, I think I'd like that. But would you mind if I asked Jana to join us?"

"No... I wouldn't mind, but she might not wanna be around me," Scott felt obligated to point out. "She didn't like my attitude back when we spent a lot of time together." Glancing from Dwight to Roberta, he was honest enough to admit, "It was with good reason, I have to say."

"But that was then and this is now," Dwight was quick to remind him in an effort to encourage him to look to the future. "She may surprise you. I'll let you know if she's interested." Noticing that it was almost time to return to class, he got up to leave. "It was nice talking with you. I'll see you both around." Walking away, he was glad that he had taken the initiative to approach them.

When Jana found out about the plans for Saturday, she was reluctant to be included in them; yet when she voiced her reservations, Dwight advised her to think positively.

"People can change. I think Scott's done that." Recognizing her lingering doubts, he made the recommendation, "If you don't feel like going, there's no point in pressing it. I plan on being there, though. I feel I should be, because despite what happened last spring, Scott is gaining my trust."

Dwight was soon to realize just how meaningful his comment really was, for later in the day Jana approached him regarding that which she had heard through the grapevine, namely that Scott had stood up for him at the jamboree. As it turned out, one of the boys who was with Carl that evening spoke of what had taken place, which in reaching Jana's ears led to a decision on her part to go to the beach after all.

"Scott must be different," she earnestly reasoned in light of what she had just learned. "If what I heard is true, he has to be."

"I would say so," Dwight stated while reflecting on the conversation he had had with him near the O'Maleys' farm. As his face took on a certain glow, he said in a most delving of manners, "I think I should like to talk to Mr. Scott Weston about this."

When all is said and done, actions speak louder than words. Dwight knew this to be true, which is why he viewed Scott's conduct at the jamboree to be especially intriguing. So in anticipating Saturday, he was grateful when the day proved to be a pleasant one for an outing. That was an incentive in and of itself to walk the few miles to the beach ahead of the appointed meeting time.

Scott and Roberta arrived on the scene about a half an hour after Dwight. Walking to where they had parked, Dwight heartily greeted them.

"I hope you're hungry," Scott wasted no time in saying. "Roberta brought a lunch along."

"That sounds inviting," Dwight responded with a grin.

"Where's Jana?" Roberta asked. "I do hope she's coming."

"Ya, she plans on being here," Dwight informed her. "She should be here any minute. Her dad is letting her use one of his cars. He's got two."

"Two cars!" Roberta gasped. "They must be rich!"

Slightly nodding, Dwight stated, "Maybe so, but I think you'll find when you get to know Jana better that she's rich in a far better way than that. The girl I've come to know realizes what true riches are."

Scott and Roberta took him at his word. Then all three of them made their way to the ocean to wade in the cool water, after which they took part in collecting wood for a fire. It was during this period of time that Jana arrived on the scene in her father's car.

Tentative would best describe the meeting between Scott and Jana as they greeted each other on the beach. Such is the emotion often felt in not knowing where you stand with someone, in not knowing if resentments prevail.

Dwight attempted to be as facilitating as possible in mitigating any uneasy feelings between them, believing that in time their discomfort would subside.

When the fire was lit and everyone was seated around it, they talked of school, and the jamboree, and coming attractions at the Perinon. Shortly thereafter, when it came time to eat, Jana offered to give Roberta a helping hand with the intent purpose of allowing Dwight to speak in private with Scott, for she knew he desired to do so.

Taking his gaze away from the dying embers of the fire, Scott watched as the two girls made their way towards the car. Then he said, "Ya know, Dwight, I thought of something the other day when you asked me about my leg. It made me curious if there was any sport you ever wanted to get involved in."

"For me it never seemed enough to want to be involved," Dwight willingly told him. "My fears always got the best of me."

"And what were you afraid of?" Scott inquired with a great deal of interest.

"That if I didn't do well, people wouldn't allow me the luxury of having a second chance." Noticing the perplexed look on Scott's face, he sought to explain himself by adding, "You see, I used to believe that I got one chance to do well at something, and that if I used it up, it was all over, the end, no more chances."

"Whatever made you think that way?" Scott all the more confusedly asked of him.

"I felt I wasn't entitled to make mistakes. I felt I had to be perfect," he solemnly told him. "Feeling unsure of yourself tends to make you think that way. I was always expecting harsh criticism, and one should never expect the worst from people because it'll become a self-fulfilling prophecy." Yes, he knew that negative expectations resulted in a negative attitude of crushed hope, tarnishing the very essence of oneself. So after a brief pause in which he searched for the right words, he made it a point to emphasize, "I've seen how addictive negative thinking can be. It poisons the mind." Indeed, though he wouldn't say it, he believed such a mind set could lead to murder in some instances. ... "So I finally realized I don't have to be perfect. I only have to be me. That's why I've begun to throw myself back into life, instead of trying to run away and hide from it." Following a sigh of relief, he added ever so effortlessly with the inner freedom he had come to know, "And it feels so good to be headed in a positive direction. I'm actually beginning to feel at peace with myself again."

"Wow, Dwight, you make it sound like you've won a victory of some sorts!" Scott exclaimed.

"I feel as though I have," he openly admitted. "But don't assume I don't have relapses every now and then, because I do. Old habits die hard."

"I imagine that's something any one of us could say." Looking downward, it was commendable to hear Scott confess, "I also know what it's like to feel insecure. It seems like everyone expects me to never falter, from the coach, to the fans... to my dad." With a shake of his head, he added, "Is there no one who wants me to participate for the right reasons?" Then he answered his own question by humbly contending, "Maybe no one except God."

Mutually the two boys became silent in thought. Then, in the aftermath of their reflection, Dwight stated while he still had the opportunity to do so, "Scott, I heard something about you that I wanted to ask you about." As Scott beheld him, he wasted no time in adding, "I heard that you came to my defense at the jamboree."

Briefly looking out to sea, Scott said, "Obviously somebody's been talking." Again regarding Dwight, he voiced the opinion, "Someone had to do something, and I happened to be the one."

"What exactly did you do?" Dwight questioned him.

"I told Carl that people see bullies as cowards, and that I'd stand up for you and ask other people to do the same." After a rather long pause in which he and Dwight held eye contact, he divulged, "And I told him I finally woke up." Looking away in a wave of resurfacing shame over his past conduct, he continued, "It's no wonder he thought I'd approve of his scheme after I was with him that other time."

In an effort to lessen Scott's emotional woes, Dwight pointed out, "Remember the other day when you mentioned how Jana felt about you, and I told you that that was then and this is now?" Observing him nod his head, he made the comparison, "The same thing could be said about your being with Carl that day, because as it turned out, you stood up for me at the jamboree." As a look of appreciation emanated from Scott's eyes, Dwight told him straight from the heart, "Thank you for what you did. You helped spare me from an awful experience." Quite befittingly, he was persuaded to take on a look similar to Scott's.

"It was the least I could do," Scott sought to assure him as he noticed the girls returning with the picnic basket. "I knew I had to redeem myself. .... But it was also that I wanted to."

"And you have undoubtedly prevailed," Dwight so convincingly told him that in the afterglow of his comment they locked gazes right up until the time Jana and Roberta rejoined them.

Scott had made an interesting discovery on this day. He learned that both he and Dwight had been plagued by insecurities concerning sports; Dwight having thought he was never worthy of another chance, and he himself having thought he should never need another chance. ..... And so in a very real sense they could identify with one another in that regard and offer moral support. In fact this was something Scott seemed to comprehend as he regarded Dwight with a look of discernment Dwight easily recognized within his body language, for body language was a language he had learned to interpret quite well.

* * *

Shortly after eating lunch, Dwight and Jana informed Scott and Roberta that they were going for a walk down the shoreline.

While they leisurely strolled along, Jana broke the silence that had in the meantime ensued by saying, "Dwight, I was thinking about Clair the other day. How is she anyway?"

"She's fine. In fact she just wrote me a letter saying she likes married life. It did hurt her not to have mother at the wedding, though. She said that when a few of Stuart's relatives asked her where her parents were, she made up excuses."

"Life does have its awkward moments, doesn't it?" Jana would only say in her empathy over Clair's predicament.

"Yet I see it as more awkward when we live our lives hiding from the truth," Dwight suggested to be the case. "I think she'd have been better off telling his relatives her mother is ill, and her father is a missing person. She wouldn't have had to go into specifics."

"What ever made you conclude that?" Jana asked.

"Because I've lived it, the shame, the embarrassment. When I think of all those times I, too, shunned the truth." He almost cringed at the memory of it. "It's such an empty feeling." Looking upon her, he frankly added, "We often avoid the truth, and it doesn't solve anything. I'm not living that way any more. Whenever the truth is called for, that's what people are gonna hear from me from now on." Indeed there was an admirable undertone to his allegation in that he had spoken it free of wrath. Optimistic resolve was his sole purpose.

In nearing the location he met Sandy, he and Jana ceased their advancement to look out to sea, realizing in doing so that if their relationship was to grow and mature to their mutual satisfaction, it was in need of being nurtured on a continual basis. ..... Time stands still for no one.

* * *

When Dwight took a walk to the O'Maleys' farm the following day, he found Mr. O'Maley behind the barn working on his tractor.

"You haven't been around in a couple of days, lad. What have you been up to lately?" the man asked after bidding him hello.

"Last Thursday I studied for a test, and yesterday I went to The Gulf with some friends," Dwight replied while casually propping an elbow on the tractor. "What exactly are you fixing anyway?"

"Oh, I'm just changing spark plugs," he informed him while standing upright. "I've got a favor to ask of you, lad," he told him then.

"Really, what is it?" Dwight eagerly welcomed the thought of assisting him.

"It just so happens that last Thursday we got a telephone call from Mrs. O'Maley's sister, Maybell, in Natchez. We haven't seen her in nearly a year now, so she wants us to visit for a week. And ya know, Dwight, my boy," he continued in his striking Irish brogue, "when a person can do something about it, they shouldn't keep putting things off until tomorrow, because ya really don't know how many tomorrows ya have left." With a touch of the humor he bore, he stated, "Maybell never was one to take no for an answer anyway. Why if I told her I wasn't of a mind to go there, she'd probably threaten never to cook me another fine meal, and she sure has come a long way since learning how to boil water, if ya know what I mean." As Dwight openly laughed, the man expressively added, "I dare say she might even tar and feather me if it tickled her fancy." In a last minute attempt to be serious, he noted, "Anyway, we're going to call Maybell back tonight to let her know if we can make it."

"Well, after what you just told me, I think the choice should be obvious," Dwight said in prevailing mirth. "A woman like that isn't to be taken lightly."

Inclined to agree with him, the man robustly laughed and said with a grin, "And that's where you come in, my boy, because somebody's going to have to look after the farm. We'll pay ya for it if you're willing to do it."

"Are you kidding! I'd love to!" Dwight enthusiastically responded. "And I already know where all the grain supplies are and how much to give the animals, so it should come easy. But really, Mr. O'Maley, I don't want any money for it."

"No, you deserve to be paid," he firmly insisted. "Provided you do a good job, of course, which I'm trusting you will." Raising an index finger, he professed, "An honest day's work deserves an honest day's pay. It won't be a fortune, but you'll be able to buy yourself a little something." Promptly he winked with the affection he had come to harbor in his heart for him.

Dwight reluctantly gave in to the man's wishes. Then he inquired when he'd be leaving.

"Why don't we go in the house to discuss that with the missy," Mr. O'Maley suggested while wiping his hands on a nearby grease rag. "And if ya haven't eaten yet, you can stay for supper. We're having chicken and dumplings, and Mrs. O'Maley makes 'em as fine as they come."

"I can't very well say no to that, now can I?" Dwight wholeheartedly jumped at the offer.

Heading for the house, Mr. O'Maley briskly patted the boy on the back.

"The missy's gonna be mighty glad to hear the good news," he was disposed to point out. "She'll have the guest room ready for you in no time at all."

"You mean you want me to stay here!" Dwight was surprised to learn.

"I'd really like you to, lad. I want somebody here at night to keep an eye on things."

"Okay," Dwight consented. "And when I'm done with the chores here in the morning, I'll go home to take care of our animals before catching the bus." But he wouldn't admit that this would in a sense be a vacation for him, too, a vacation away from his mother.

* * *

The O'Maleys left for Natchez the following Tuesday afternoon; and so, upon arriving home from school, Dwight immediately darted over to their farm to perform his duties, realizing in doing so that the O'Maleys trusted him to be dependable; yes, dependable, that trait which is typically respected and appreciated whenever it is recognized within the people who earn the right to be called it.

As he went about his business, he reflected on the day Sandy picked up her baby chicks, and wondered if perhaps Jana would like to see the livestock again. Certainly she had seemed to enjoy that day, he vividly recalled; therefore, yes, tomorrow he would ask her to return, he decided as he headed for the creek to feed the ducks some corn.

In the course of our experiences in life we often discover something telling about our character, our concerns, ourselves; and Dwight was about to make one of those discoveries in stark reality. It happened with the dawn of the coming day in the immediate aftermath of his arrival at school. He was making his way indoors at the time when he happened to look to his left and notice a girl crying by the wall off to the side of the main entrance. Moved by her plight, he approached her and asked if there was anything he could do for her; but when she did not respond in any manner whatsoever, he specifically inquired why she was in tears.

The girl, whom Dwight estimated to be in the eighth grade, at this stage studied his face for awhile. Then she said with a note of certainty, "You wouldn't understand. You... couldn't understand."

"Don't be so sure about that," Dwight sought to convince her. "Try me."

Briefly the girl looked away as though she were not going to say a thing. But then all of a sudden she managed to tell him with a tone of painful acceptance, "I'm crying because I just overheard a boy tell another boy he thought I was ugly. But you wouldn't understand how that feels. You're far from ugly."

As though struck by a bolt of lightning, Dwight appeared to be transfixed in time, for he had not expected, and consequently was not prepared, to respond to her comment. He felt cornered, put on the spot, and for the time being tongue-tied, for of all the things he had ever dealt with in his life, being criticized about his looks had never been a torment for him as it obviously was for this girl who stood before him. And though it was true he had concern for her, he couldn't relate to her feelings, and he knew it. ... Yet he also believed that in the eyes of God her looks were irrelevant, which is why he eventually told her, "The heart is all that matters in the end. Besides, beauty is in the eye of the beholder."

Walking a few feet along the side of the building, the girl turned to face him before stating in a combination of anger and frustration, "It's people like you who find it so easy to say looks don't matter, because you don't have to endure the insults." Indeed she was implying that in the eyes of society a person's outward appearance was exceedingly important.

As Dwight watched the forlorn girl edge her way along the wall, he honestly felt helpless to offer her additional words of encouragement. .... But then suddenly he realized that his faith held the potential of guiding him along in his endeavors. And so, making his way to her side, he attempted to reach her by candidly admitting, "You're right. I haven't been treated as you have. And I do like to look at a pretty girl named Jana, but really, when it gets right down to it, if I got to know a girl who was pretty and found her to be unattractive on the inside because of the way she thought, and the way she treated people, she'd no longer be as pretty to me." As she intently gazed at him, he concluded, "If a person discovers what's really important in life, they'll feel more attractive, and no one's good looks can guarantee that." With that having been so eloquently expressed, he left her alone to reflect on the advice presented as food for thought, hoping in doing so that her self-image would thereby be strengthened, aiding her in becoming a more satisfied person. .... And though he didn't know it, the girl began to sense deep within herself that there was truth in his words after all, for he had spoken in a way she never before witnessed, in a way which was quite convincing in fact.

* * *

Jana boarded the bus for the O'Maleys' farm after school the following day.

Seated with her, Dwight reflected on the events from the day before and wondered why anyone would disparage someone's looks. Did they realize how hurtful their comments could be? Did they feel poorly about themselves and aim to punish others for it? Was their behavior a manifestation of the self-assurance they were lacking in? All things considered, he realized that it was quite easy to become self-absorbed. And yet despite knowing this to be true, he was glad for the looks he had inherited, looks which had spared him an additional avenue of criticism. But was he vain to be glad about this? He knew that in some respects the answer to that question was a resounding yes; and he was not at all pleased to discover this about himself.

Jana could tell there was something weighing heavily on Dwight's mind; so when they unboarded the bus and began walking down the narrow dirt road that led to the O'Maleys' farm, she asked him what it was.

"Something that happened yesterday," he told her with gravity.

"Do you wanna talk about it?" she inquired.

"I think I had better," he stated with a glance at her. "I can't seem to stop thinking about it." Formulating his thoughts, be began to fill her in on the details of the previous morning. When he had finished doing so, he went on to reveal, "So many times it's seemed as though people couldn't relate to me and my pain, but this time around it was someone saying that of me." In the irony of that transition, he told her, "I guess nobody can totally identify with someone else's pain. We're not them. If the truth be known, sometimes I feel like a hypocrite for what I said to that girl, because.... because my own feelings don't completely support what I told her."

"Oh, Dwight, you really are too hard on yourself sometimes," Jana mildly reproached him. "You told her some good things. You at least cared enough to do that."

"But as I was trying to reason with her I was glad for my looks," he felt the need to point out. "And it's disturbed me to find out I'm that vain."

"Are you suggesting you're supposed to wish yourself homely?" Jana asked of him in a strategy of reverse psychology.

"No, I'm not saying that," he told her as they stopped walking. She could see that he was attempting to find the right words to express himself. "I'm saying that if my outlook towards life was what it should be, I'd be indifferent about whether I was handsome, average looking, or homely, and yet at that very moment she told me I couldn't relate to her, I remember being glad that I couldn't."

"But Dwight, it's only natural to want to be physically attractive," Jana alleged to be the case.

"Is it!" Dwight bluntly challenged that presumption. "Or is it insecure!" Surely he was alluding to the spiritual perspective, the belief that when all is said and done our physical attractiveness will count for nothing, whereas our inner attractiveness will count for much.

"Oh, Dwight, call it what you may, but I have something to confess to you. When I first laid eyes on you, I found you attractive, and was drawn to you in a way I couldn't describe. Then, when I got to know you, I discovered you were attractive on the inside, too. Had I not liked your character, my interest in you would have faded. So I do realize looks aren't nearly enough." In hearing her say these words, he warmly smiled, in the advent of which she good-naturedly added, "But I did always hope you found me attractive, too, even if it was just a wee bit." Holding up her hand, she spread her thumb and forefinger barely apart while regarding him.

Dwight could not help but laugh over her mannerism.

"How dramatic you can be!" he told her then. As she, too, was driven to take on laughter, he eventually said with earnest appeal, "I assure you, Jana Rossi, that I find you most attractive in every way possible." But he would not wander from the progress they were making in their relationship by stealing a kiss, for he knew that a mere kiss was not always as innocent as it seemed to be, and that a mere kiss could complicate their lives greatly if it led to other things. The risk just wasn't worth the pleasure of a fleeting moment. Their relationship was far too precious to be experimented with, far too precious to be distracted from.

Moments later, as they continued onward, Dwight felt impressed upon to say, "Perhaps as time goes by, Jana, I'll over-come my feelings of yesterday. I do know it can be done. It's been proven. I'll have to work at it."

With concern for his well-being in mind, Jana said, "What more can be asked of you than that?"

Dwight barely made eye contact with her before turning his thoughts to the supper he was looking forward to preparing with her on this day. Together they would then care for the O'Maleys' live-stock until the time came when her mother stopped by to drive her home.

* * *

Lying in bed one night, Scott realized that he and Dwight shared more than an insecurity in sports. They also shared feelings of dissatisfaction regarding a parent's attitude. True, Dwight's mother demanded little of him in her pessimistic view of life, whereas his father demanded much from him in his vicarious quest for worldly achievements; yet both situations were quite disappointing, even at times disheartening, in that their parents were not of the healthy persuasion they could and should have been. So in his quest to be a person who strove for the pursuits of this world with his heart in the right place, Scott reached for the Bible that he only recently brought to his room, comprehending in doing so why Dwight's outlook was what it was. ... And it's all so relative.

* * *

Mrs. Arion taught tenth-grade science class, and though Dwight expected her to require oral reports, when the dreaded topic came up, he felt shivers go up his spine in great measure.

As the woman stood there telling the class what she expected of them, Dwight knew that she had not been of assistance to him in his walk through life. The fact that he was better prepared to deliver a speech this year was beside the point. Any progress made had come about in spite of her, not because of her.

Later, in response to the fair weather, many students took to the outdoors with their lunches. It was after having eaten with Bill and Cybil that Dwight and Jana decided to go for a walk on the school grounds before classes resumed.

"You probably thought of me when Mrs. Arion mentioned oral reports," Dwight stated as they neared a large oak tree a fair distance from the building.

"Yes, I did, but I think you'll do just fine this year," Jana predicted. "You're much more confident now."

"I do feel better about myself," Dwight had to admit, "but I sure do hate the thought of giving another speech. I feel so burdened whenever I walk into her classroom. Maybe I should refuse to give a report even if it means a failing grade."

"Would you really dare carry things that far?" Jana earnestly asked of him.

"Sometimes I think I should," he flat out told her, for he was tired of his mental strains. "There comes a time when you should stand up for your beliefs, not just say the words." After some additional thought, he added, "I'm not saying Mrs. Arion doesn't wanna do right by me, Jana, but she doesn't understand the right approach. I see her as insensitive, not cruel. .... Whatever be the case, I probably frustrate that woman. Sometimes I wonder if she might end up pulling her hair out over me, just as I might end up becoming a gray teenager over her." In hearing him speak this way, Jana broke out in laughter, which urged him to follow suit. However, when their mirth had subsided, he specified on a sober note, "I realize Mrs. Arion has to have certain rules in her classroom, but last year I took biology from her and this year science, not speech. I'm concerned about the people who'll follow us."

"You mean future students who fear oral reports?" Jana asked of him.

"Yes, I want things to be better for them. I want them to have what I was denied, choice!"

"Perhaps the day will come when that'll happen," Jana suggested to be the case. "Maybe it'll become a trend of the schools."

"I hope so," Dwight responded. "For the sake of a lot of people, I hope so, because I know firsthand just how hard it can be to concentrate in your classes when you're distracted by your fears."

* * *

The following Tuesday evening, when the O'Maleys returned from Natchez, Dwight was right there to welcome them back home.

"How was your vacation?" he enthusiastically asked as they got out of their car.

"It was quite nice," Mrs. O'Maley told him. "I do believe I've put on a few pounds, however. My sister's become too skilled a cook for her own good and mine." She frowned to expand on the point she was making. "I believe a jog around the farm is in order, if you know what I mean."

Dwight smiled in response to her comment. Then Mr. O'Maley said, "The old place is good to be back to. Being away made me realize how much I love it here. How was the weather while we were gone, lad?"

"A few nights ago we got rain. It was quite a soaker," Dwight informed him while nearing the trunk to assist with the luggage. "It'll provide moisture for the next planting."

"That's splendid news," he remarked. "A farmer's crops are his bread and butter."

"I know," Dwight acknowledged, realizing that growing things helped the man thrive.

"By the way, we bought something for you, lad," Mr. O'Maley announced as he closed the trunk. "We're hoping you'll like it."

"Really! What is it?" Dwight's curiosity prompted him to inquire.

"By the sound of your voice I can tell you like surprises," he indulged him as they headed for the house. "But you'll find out when we're inside. Just hold your horses." Quite heartily he let out a guffaw.

Moments later, when the three of them were seated in the living room, Mrs. O'Maley opened one of the suitcases and withdrew a small package. Handing it over to Dwight, she said, "We both wanted to bring back a little something for you."

"Thank you," Dwight told her and swiftly unwrapped a beautiful leather belt. "Oh, wow, it's really nice!" he exclaimed while examining it. "I'll wear it often." Gratitude was written all over his face. "And it's just what I needed. My old belt's worn out. Maybe you noticed that." Getting up, he removed it to put on the new one. When he had done so and was again facing them, he said with conviction, "You people sure are good to me!"

Mr. and Mrs. O'Maley regarded him with sheer delight.

"I'm glad you're pleased," Mrs. O'Maley noted. "We thought you'd like it."

"Oh, I do," Dwight reassured her while feeling how well it fit. "I really do."

In the ensuing moments the O'Maleys spoke of their trip, after which Mr. O'Maley decided to go outdoors before darkness struck. He missed the farm, and was anxious to get back to the routine of his workday. It was at this time that Mrs. O'Maley asked Dwight if he had enjoyed spending the week on the farm.

"At first I found it very relaxing, and soothing to my soul... but I must admit I eventually wanted to go home," he confided. "Be it good or bad there, it's still my home and she's still my mother. I can't help but be concerned about her."

"I think that's a good sign," the woman bolstered his attitude while gently nudging his arm. "It's got to mean something."

"I like to think so," he replied. Walking towards the doorway, he added, "I guess I should go home now. I'll see you soon."

"Yes, and thank you again for everything. Come back tomorrow and Mr. O'Maley will pay you. He has to go to the bank first."

Dwight knew that to again say he didn't want to be paid would not serve its intended purpose. So instead he emphasized, "Make sure it's not too much. I'd feel guilty if it was."

Mrs. O'Maley assured him the amount would be appropriate. Saying good-bye then, Dwight departed from her midst. Optimism verses pessimism, geniality verses petulance, love verses hate; that was what his going home represented. And because he knew there was a God, he also knew that within the recesses of his mind love would be the victor as long as he sought to keep God close to his heart. .... Therefore certainly it was a foregone conclusion that hoping and believing in a brighter tomorrow was always better than brooding over a gloomy past.

* * *

No one but God completely knows or understands why we are what we are. There are the experiences of our lives, the values we are taught, our God-given potential, our response to pain. All of this makes a difference in the person we come to be.

Walking along the shoreline of the ocean after school the following day, Dwight thought about this only to feel a rush of loneliness flood his heart, for he knew that no matter how much he was loved by others, Jana included, he would never be able to articulate the very essence of himself. No, there just didn't seem to be the right words in the English language to do it thoroughly; and even if there was, certain aspects of his existence were beyond his comprehension, beyond the grasp of his finite mind. .... Yet it was his lack of understanding which held the potential of keeping him humble in his place within the universe, for if he knew too much, he might place his faith and trust in his discoveries rather than God, which results in empty satisfaction. ... The tests of time are not meant to be squandered.

CHAPTER 20

SOME IMPROVED RELATIONS

At times Dwight prayed for strength concerning the oral reports that were about to begin, for he knew that sooner or later prayers were answered in one way, shape, or form when they came from the depth of the beseeching heart. But should he give an oral report or not? Though he believed he was under no obligation to do so, morally or otherwise, he opted to deliver one anyway in the hopes of initiating a healthy change. And how did he expect to bring this about? By reaching Mrs. Arion where it mattered the most, the heart. So to assume he would cave in to unwarranted demands for the duration of his high school days, for the duration of his life, was erroneous, for the existence of other options he held to be self-evident. The course of action he had decided upon was strategic in nature in that he had a goal in mind, a mission to accomplish. And so although it would appear on the surface that he was condoning that which he considered to be inappropriate behavior on the part of a teacher, he was looking at the complete, far-reaching picture.

When the dreaded day of standing before his classmates at last arrived, he found himself lucidly aware of the ignorance of the society in which he lived. There was a certain myth being perpetuated, the myth that it was a necessity for a student to undergo this. Opinions varied down the path of life, and it would be naive to expect total agreement on a controversial issue. But there was one thing he did know better than any other human being on the face of the earth, that being the emotions of his own inner being, his own self. That was why he could say with veritable certitude that the quality of his life had been diminished by the demands placed upon him by Mrs. Arion. Yet despite his jarred emotions, he could rise above whatever was cast his way as long as his heart was in the right place, as long as he traveled the path to sound reasoning, as long as he allowed love to be the dominant theme of his life.

As he began speaking on his chosen topic, he could feel his body tensing; yet he stood firm, realizing that emancipation would ultimately be had. Looking to the back of the room, he saw Mrs. Arion staring at him in a manner which seemed to signify some measure of satisfaction over his efforts. Yet did she understand the reasons for his improvement? It would seem not, for she had a justified look about her, as though she felt her classroom policies deserving of the credit, as though she felt she had been right all along in the demands placed upon him and every other student in days gone by.

It was not until his speech was over and he was heading back to his desk that Dwight regarded Jana for more than an instant. Without a doubt it was easy to detect the admiration she held for him over his courage to persevere in a world that did not understand his fears, in a world that all too often was unyielding in its demands. Certainly she had been of comfort to him in his hour of need, this girl who possessed an awareness of what he was up against.

Listening to other students deliver their reports, Dwight felt compassion for the ones he detected discomfort within, for he could identify with them all too well. ... Then, according to plan, when the bell rang and everyone rose from their respective seats, Mrs. Arion called out for him to stay after class.

Walking up to her desk as the room cleared of students, Dwight asked what she wanted. And he did so solemnly, for even though he was not embittered with her for demanding another oral report of him, he was not pleased with her either.

"I just wanted to say that I saw a big improvement in your speech, Dwight," she stated with a glimpse of personal pride. "It was delivered so much better than last year, even though you did have a shaky start. I'm sure you're pleased with your grade." When he said nothing in response to her assumption, she added, "You should be delighted, you know. You...."

"I don't even know what my grade is," he impulsively blurted out. "I didn't look at the grade card you handed me."

Stunned by his contention, Mrs. Arion asked him why he had behaved so.

"I was sure you'd be anxious to look at it," she deduced.

"Were you?" he merely stated. Holding her in his gaze, he subsequently made the announcement that knowing his grade didn't interest him.

"You went from a D+ to a B+ and you're not interested!" she chided him. "Is that what you're telling me!"

"Yes," he dared to admit. "That's what I'm telling you."

In a fit of exasperation the woman retaliated by saying, "I want you to know you can really be irritating at times!"

"And did it ever occur to you that you may have irritated some of your students throughout the years?" he keenly brought to her attention.

Casting his insinuation aside, Mrs. Arion boldly declared, "I should think you'd be appreciative of your grade instead of disinterested!"

"Appreciative!" Dwight incredulously reacted. While shaking his head, he wasted no time whatsoever in adding, "That's the last thing I feel right now. .... But you don't understand that, I know," he almost sadly reminded himself.

"You're right. I don't!" she was quick to confess while crossing her arms. "So why don't you try to explain it to me?"

"Alright," he obliged her. In thinking about it for awhile, he added, "I know I gave a better speech this year, but that's beside the point, because I only did it to please you. I'm not pleased with myself, because I was fulfilling your expectations of me, not my expectations of me. That's why I considered refusing to give one. That's why the next time it's asked of me I may."

"Even if it means a failing grade!" she sharply pointed out.

"Yes, even then," he freely told her. "Because my mental health is far more important to me than a grade ever will be."

"And what does your mental health have to do with this?" she confusedly inquired of him with fading patience.

"It suffers whenever I'm forced to address people before I'm ready. And Mrs. Arion, I have news for you. I haven't been ready," he made the claim with absolute conviction.

"But if you feel so strongly about that, then why did you give today's report?" she interrogated him.

"Because I thought if I didn't, you'd respond the way you are right now, with resentment." As she briefly lowered her gaze, he added, "I also figured that if you got angry with me, you'd be more determined than ever to require oral reports."

"But you spoke so much better than last year, which proves to me something positive occurred, which proves to me you're headed in the right direction!" she passionately insisted.

"Mrs. Arion, reaping something positive from something negative doesn't justify the negative thing," he sought to impress upon her. "It only means I was trying to make the best of a bad situation." Detecting her lingering doubts, he added, "There's a kinder, gentler way to get the results you're seeking."

"And what would that be?"

"Freedom of choice," he told her with utmost certainty. "If you only knew how hard it is to concentrate in a class you're on guard in, you'd realize what I mean." In noticing her prevailing skepticism, he advised her, "Ask other students how they feel about this. Find out what they have to say."

There was now a brief silence in which Mrs. Arion seriously pondered his suggestion.

"Alright, I shall," she then decided. "But tell me something. If what I'm requiring is so wrong, then why were you able to speak so much better this year?"

Regarding her, Dwight openly admitted, "Because I prayed for strength to see me through this, and it happened." While she continued to observe him, he went on to reveal, "I prayed for something else, too. I prayed that you'd have more concern for other people's feelings."

In hearing these words, Mrs. Arion looked all the more intently upon him, for even though she believed there was a higher power, she had never relied on God to see her through a difficulty in the manner this boy was claiming to have done.

"Don't you see, Mrs. Arion, overcoming one's fears happens a little at a time, not overnight," Dwight went on to introspectively say. "I'd gladly give an oral report if and when I felt ready to take that step. It's not your encouraging them that bothers me, because I think giving them can boost a person's confidence. It's your requiring them that I don't like."

Moved by his insight, Mrs. Arion at long last felt mildly receptive to that which he had to say. Yet in inching his way into her firmly-held beliefs, she became disconcerted enough to rather curtly say, "You're excused to your next class."

Sensing her pressed state of mind, Dwight departed from the room without uttering another word. In doing so he left behind a woman who was beginning to second guess what she had intended to be of benefit to her students all along. In more than one instance throughout history a person's firmly held beliefs have been called into question when those beliefs were seen from a different perspective, a different light. Therefore by all indication a boy was beginning to influence her way of thinking. He was a burdened young man who managed to portray such confidence regarding his convictions. He was a persevering individual who had given her a sense of the reality of his world and the things which frightened him. He seemed to have a purpose in mind, born of his compassion for other people's feeling, particularly the sorely constrained, the ones he could identify with so well whenever he reflected on days gone by when he, too, was so heavily immersed in the anguish of it all.

* * *

Ever since Jana's recovery from her life threatening illness, a stronger bond had been developing amongst the members of her family. It was no coincidence that such was the case, for in the course of a person's affliction changes often take place on the part of the people closest to them, compelling them to focus on what's really important in life. ..... And so because of her father's mellowed disposition, Jana was granted permission to invite Dwight over for supper one evening to get better acquainted with the family.

Though Dwight was appreciative of the opportunity to dine with the Rossis, he was apprehensive about meeting Jana's father, for he could not help but wonder how the man would treat him. Yet he fully intended to show up at the appointed time, for he knew that when it got right down to it, his only obligation was to treat others the way he himself desired to be treated, with common courtesy and respect.

Walking up to the Rossis' mansion when the day in question arrived, he felt a dichotomy within himself, as though he realized his place of belonging would never be amongst the luxury Jana was accustomed to. Yet Jana had proven that being from a wealthy family was not an impenetrable obstacle to true riches as long as one saw money for its true worth, its true limitations. She had set a good example for others to live by in that she had taken the initiative to strive for spiritual wealth in the midst of the financial wealth she had been born into through no choice of her own.

Greeted at the front door by Mrs. Rossi, Dwight was invited into her home with a smile that confirmed her ongoing receptivity to his presence.

"Jana will be downstairs shortly," she informed him as he entered the foyer. "Please come into the living room to meet my husband."

"But are you sure he wants to meet me, Mrs. Rossi?" Dwight was inclined to ask as they proceeded to make their way there.

"I can assure you he does," the woman sought to convince him. Detecting the lingering doubt on his face, she added, "I can't blame you for feeling as you do. I can hardly believe the change in him myself."

Noticeably relieved by what had been told him, Dwight entered the room with the woman to find Mr. Rossi seated in a lounge chair reading a book.

"Clayton, Dwight's here," she immediately stated to gain his attention.

Raising his head, Mr. Rossi said while standing, "So we're finally meeting." To Dwight's relief he initiated a handshake.

"How do you do?" Dwight addressed him. "Thank you for allowing me to come to your home."

"You're... ah, welcome," he said while uneasily glancing at his wife. "We... ah..would have invited you sooner, but... well, sometimes it takes a while to get around to it."

Realizing what he was admitting to, Dwight said, "I've found that to be true myself, Mr. Rossi." Indeed there was something profoundly revealing about the way in which he spoke these words.

At this stage Mrs. Rossi encouraged Dwight to sit on the sofa while awaiting Jana.

"Supper will be ready shortly," she informed him while turning about. "I'll check in with Alice to see how it's coming along."

Being alone with Mr. Rossi, Dwight could tell that the man felt awkward in his presence. So in an effort to put him at ease, he introduced dialogue by asking him how things were at his place of employment.

"Very good as a matter of fact," the man eagerly welcomed the topic. "I've been at the bank nearly twenty-five years now." Shaking his head, he added, "How time does fly."

"Do you enjoy your job?" Dwight asked.

"For the most part," he contended. "What about your interests? What would you like to do after high school?"

"I'm still thinking about that," Dwight let it be known. "I think I'd like to be involved in some sort of public service. Hopefully I'll have my mind made up by the time I graduate. I'm still in the searching stage."

"Did you ever consider pursuing a banking career?"

"No, I really don't think that type of work would appeal to me," Dwight was honest enough to admit as Jana and Cynthia entered the room.

"Dwight, it's so good to see you," Jana wasted no time in saying as he rose to greet her. "I take it you and father have gotten acquainted." As he nodded his head and smiled in a way that led her to believe all was going well, she looked to her father with appreciative eyes.

Saying hello to Cynthia, Dwight inquired how her classes were coming along.

"Actually quite well," she responded as Mrs. Rossi stepped into view to announce that supper was ready to be served.

"Dwight, I do hope you like Italian cooking," she made it a point to say as everyone headed for the dining room. "I meant to have Jana ask you beforehand."

While smiling, Dwight told her, "Mrs. Rossi, I'll have you know I've yet to find a form of cooking I don't like."

In the laughter that ensued Dwight saw evidence that the Rossis had warmed to him after all. Yet he was wise enough to realize that a person's outward bearing didn't always reflect their innermost feelings. And so when he detected a look of escaped unease in Mr. Rossi's eyes just a short time later, his suspicions were thereby aroused. Surely the only reason the man had accepted him in Jana's life to begin with was that he didn't want to run the risk of becoming estranged from his wife. And if that be the case, perhaps he was lapsing into his former ways of thinking. Only the naive and non-discerning expect perfect results in the course of positive change. No one is above reproach. We dwell upon the testing ground, forced to run the gauntlet. And surviving the gauntlet is really a matter of moral and spiritual resolve. Strength lies in the faith. All things considered, was Dwight's presence in the Rossi household in vain? Not as long as social barriers were being toppled. We have a right to present ourselves to the world free from prejudice. And if it comes to pass that we are liked by someone, a budding friendship may be in the making. .... Therefore surely two people can go from unintroduced, to uninterested, to uncomfortable, and finally to becoming friends in the course of time. Stranger things have happened. The personality sets the stage; the heart rules the outcome.

* * *

As Scott was taking a drive one evening, he happened to see Dwight nearing the road that led to the O'Maleys' farm, so he honked his horn while pulling over.

"Care to go to The Gulf," he said as Dwight opened the passenger door.

"Alright," Dwight spoke up with a smile. "It's not often I get a ride. I do like walking, though. It does me good, clears my mind." But he would not divulge the diminished quality of a summer spent wondering if Carl would show up on the scene.

"That's what my father used to say about walking," Scott informed him.

"How is your father, anyway?" Dwight inquired.

"He's doing alright I guess... but he's not too pleased with me right now. He doesn't like that my interest in football isn't what it used to be."

"And why has your interest changed?" Dwight asked of him.

"I suppose it's because I've changed the way I look at the game." With an upraised fist, he stated with emphasis, "I had to win first and foremost!" Shaking his head as he let out a sigh, he declared, "Why can't you lose and feel like a winner if you've tried your best?"

"I think you can... but yes, I know it's easier said than done." In an attempt at evaluation, he went on to say, "I guess when it comes right down to it people sometimes tire of the pressure to win, which apparently has happened to you."

"Ya, it really has, and Roberta understands that. She doesn't pressure me to play sports like my dad does."

"I get the feeling you found a friend in her," Dwight commented. "I'm happy for you." Freely he smiled, but it was only for a brief instant, for when a certain thought entered his mind, he was prompted to say, "Yet I wonder if you're breaking away from football for the right reasons, Scott."

"What do you mean by the right reasons?" Scott inquired of him with piqued interest.

"Well, it seems ironic you'd give up football now that you could enjoy it like never before." Determining that Scott had become perplexed by his remark, he sought to better explain himself by adding, "Consider this. If you played for the wrong reasons in the past and suffered for it, then it stands to reason that if you played for the right reasons in the future, you could benefit from it."

"Gee... I never thought of it that way," Scott stated in response to his perspective. "But what about the people who have attitudes I don't like? Not only would I be forced to be around them, it'd remind me of the way I used to be."

"True," Dwight acknowledged. "But if you set a good example, maybe you'd end up reaching them where it matters the most."

"And where would that be?" Scott asked.

"The conscience," Dwight so matter of factly replied that Scott felt somewhat embarrassed for even asking.

Thinking of his father, Scott pointed out in earnest, "But my dad, I doubt if I could ever get him to see things differently."

"But even if you can't, knowing what you know now, you just might find football rewarding after all," Dwight suggested to be the case.

Briefly glancing his way as he continued to drive along, Scott barely nodded his head before saying, "I guess I'll have to give that some serious thought in the months to come." Though he didn't know it, he was right on the threshold of becoming an exemplary football player because of a long-overdue attitude adjustment. His broken leg would ultimately be seen as a blessing in disguise, for it had resulted in a humbling of the athlete. What valuable lessons he was learning as a result. He had been in need of being put on the bench, taken out of the game, to refine his outlook towards life. .... And Dwight and Roberta had played a significant role in steering him in the right direction. Therefore, yes, Scott Weston would likely be considered one of the best quarterbacks ever to come out of Fulton High after all.

Arriving at the beach, the two boys advanced to the shoreline, in the event of which Scott told Dwight he'd been reading the Bible from time to time.

"That's commendable," Dwight replied. Lowering himself to the ocean, he did that which was a given each and every time he came here; he felt it. Standing up, he was inspired to add, "You know something, Scott, I found that life got much better when I started looking to God. It was so much easier to see past my unhappiness. And I want you to know that the first step is the most important one to take, because it's the one that involves the most surrender."

"Surrender to what?" Scott asked in his failure to fathom his meaning.

"To the temptation to hold a grudge," Dwight inferred. "Bitterness is such an easy feeling to give in to." Raising his eyebrows, he continued, "That's why it's so commonly felt in the world."

Readily accepting his viewpoint, Scott said, "You seem to understand more than most people our age."

Dwight knew that people in general had the ability to acquire wisdom, but he deemed it unnecessary to make mention of, comprehending that Scott was already aware of this. ... So in response to the bond that was developing between them, he instead suggested, "Let's run down the shoreline! It might do us both some good!"

"Do you think you can outrun me?" Scott challenged him on a humorous note.

"It wasn't my intention, but I do feel energetic today," Dwight warned him.

"You're on!" Scott exclaimed in anticipation of competing on a level where the outcome mattered little to either participant. Quickly departing, each of them witnessed the freedom to be themselves they wished could always be the case. ... So where were their critics now? Who amongst humanity was in their midst to weigh them down? There was no such person to be found. Therefore herein lies the nature of what they had discovered; that feeling better about life is possible after all. Was that why they were taking advantage of this moment? It would seem so. And in this shared moment, in their quest for contentment in the time and place they were in, they felt another link break away from their chains of mental bondage. Surely they recognized more than ever that the worst type of life is one in which a person is lost within themself, tormented by their own mind. So take heed, for choice is all around you, ever in your midst, to influence the condition of your existence.

* * *

It was an eventful occurrence that took place in Scott's life the following evening. Doing homework in the privacy of his room, he discovered that he was unable to concentrate on the subject matter, in large part due to his strained relationship with his father. He wondered what course of action should be taken to bring about a positive change. Sadly, a viable solution seemed beyond his reach.

Yet someone was in need of availing themself to set the stage for satisfying results. Progression needs a starting point.

In a desire to find solace in sleep, he rose from his desk to retire for the evening. ... But then suddenly, just as he was about to reach for the light switch, he was surprised to hear a knock upon his door, surprised because it had been a long time since it last occurred.

"Scott, it's dad," a voice sounded out then. "I'd like to talk to you, son."

In nervous anticipation Scott allowed a few seconds to pass before inviting the man to enter. Then, while he held him under his scrutiny, his father stated with difficulty, "I've... ah... had a lot on my mind lately, so I thought we had better talk." Truly he found it challenging to maintain eye contact with his son because of the communication gap between them.

"I'm listening, dad," Scott stated while sitting on the edge of his bed. If ever the boy had reason to be captivated, this was it.

For an instant Mr. Weston observed his son before casting his eyes downward and saying, "Scott, this really isn't easy for me." Walking past him to the window, he peered into the distant night before finding the strength to introspectively add, "I realize I haven't been an ideal father, but I didn't know what to expect of fatherhood. I guess I never learned how to be a good father... and then, when your mother died, well... I just tried to do what I thought was best for you, though now I see it hasn't been to your total bene-fit. I've... ah... always wanted good things for you, though," he then went on to say as Scott became thoroughly amazed by the sight of the man's dampening cheeks. "Pushing you in sports, in everything, was done out of something I couldn't seem to express any other way. You see, son, I..." The words were not easy to come by after years of repressed feelings; and so Scott coaxed him along by saying, "You what, dad?"

Turning to regard him, he announced, "I love you, Scott." There, he had finally said it, and eventually even smiled in welcome relief as he felt a certain calmness engulf him.

Scott could not have prevented tears from coming to his own eyes even if he had tried.

"I love you, too, dad," he said while rising from his bed. Staring at one another for a few heart-wrenching moments, they drew together and hugged. As they clung to each other in their long-overdue embrace, Scott whispered above a sob, "I can't tell you how long I've wanted to hear you say that, dad."

"I know, son," his father responded with increased tears while patting him on the back.

"Dad."

"Yes."

"I want you to know I prayed for us. I've discovered I'm in need of God."

After a period of silence the man stated, "I haven't looked to God much since your mother died. I remember a time when she encouraged me to, but I've had a difficult time accepting her death. I've been angry, and anger is a distraction."

Drawing away from him, Scott said, "Maybe we've found what's been missing in our lives all along."

"Maybe so, son, maybe so," his father contended. With a slight smile, he added, "I do find myself feeling different... better."

Looking upon him, Scott sensed that because of what had just happened, they would begin to enjoy life as never before. Wise is the person who seeks fulfillment according to the moral standards handed down a long time ago, moral standards which were lived and preached by Christ to perfection.

* * *

When Dwight learned of Scott's improved relations with his father, he was genuinely glad for the both of them. Yet in the midst of the gladness he bore for a father and his son, he so desired to discover news of his own father's whereabouts. ... But surely the right degree of wanting something was in need of being had while one bided one's time, for the ticking of the clock takes its toll in the interim. Put another way, it can be self-defeating to spend a great amount of time yearning for that which draws our attention away from today. When one craves answers, though, when one is filled with discontent, living free from distractions is easier said than done, all the more reason to rely on God while we await resolution.

* * *

Carl Barnet had never known a very satisfying home life, and as of late things were deteriorating even further, for through the progression of years his parents had gradually sunk deeper and deeper into the trap of worldly addictions. Such is the lure of that which is thought to be gratifying to our wants and needs, the temporary offerings where many have blinded vision. Vices had gotten the better of them. Allow your own imagination to complete a general overview of the troubling details, for you need not go far to see evidence of it within your own community. And yet, if asked, they, like so many other people who are enmeshed in an unhealthy lifestyle, would freely have claimed to have faith in God even though they refused to take life seriously. .... Therefore, yes, Carl certainly was a troubled youth who had been misled by his parents over the years. But there was for him, too, hope; yes, hope, the bright side of sad situations.

* * *

The movie that Dwight and Jana saw at the Perinon was a comedy they both enjoyed a lot. Afterwards, at Sam's Place, they met up with Scott and Roberta and had a bite to eat before departing in the O'Maleys' car, which the couple had allowed Dwight to use.

Pulling before the Rossis' home, Dwight casually put his hand under the front seat and withdrew a small package.

"Here, I want you to have this," he told Jana then while handing it to her.

"Oh, a gift! You shouldn't have! But I'm so glad you did!" Lightheartedly she laughed. "I just love surprises!" With a burst of enthusiasm she removed the wrapping in the dim rays of the streetlight. "Oh, it's beautiful!" she exclaimed while holding up a dainty necklace that had a small heart attached.

"I bought it with some of the money the O'Maleys paid me for watching over their farm while they were gone to Natchez," Dwight informed her. "I thought it suited you. After all, you've got heart."

"Oh, thank you," Jana stated with warmth. "I'll wear it often."

Gently she kissed him on the cheek before placing the jewelry about her neck.

Shortly thereafter, while he still had the opportunity to do so, Dwight told her that he had been thinking a lot about his father's whereabouts as of late.

"Sometimes I do wonder, though, if I'd be better off not thinking about it. I can't change the truth anyway."

"But knowing the truth helps with closure," Jana made the assertion.

"Maybe so, but there's a difference between needing to know the truth, and wanting to know the truth. Maybe I don't need to know what happened after all. Maybe I can find closure without it. ... It's really a matter of choice, isn't it, Jana?" Firmly he fixed his gaze upon her in a most intuitive of ways.

"Putting it like that, I would say so," she stated in the realization that his perspective often held credence. To reveal her willingness to assist him in his efforts, she openheartedly added, "I'll be there for you, Dwight, in whatever way I can."

"Thank you. We can all use a helping hand from time to time," he replied while looking into her eyes. "And your hand is one hand I'm comfortable accepting help from." Surely unconditional love is what he was alluding to.

Having said that, Jana softly touched his arm as they felt their trust take on a heightened dimension. Do be made aware that they were quite content to leave it at that; no further touching, no kissing, no additional physical contact to distract from the progress being made in their relationship. There was a meeting of the minds in the making, a most rewarding of occurrences when neither mind has the least bit desire to dominate, take advantage of, or control the other one.

* * *

In the weeks to follow Dwight was pleased by that which he saw within Jana's parents, for they continued to make him feel welcome in their home. Then one day Mr. Rossi asked him whether he had given any additional thought to his future schooling.

"Actually I have," Dwight told him, "but sometimes I worry about my mother being left alone if I go away to college." With somber resignation he added, "I guess I'll have to accept that I can only do so much for her. After all, I am only human."

A short time later, in leaving the house with Jana, Dwight realized as he looked at her that she was a part of his desire to take an interest in his future, for she encouraged him to be conscientious of such things. How he did love her for being such a supportive friend.

Back inside the mansion, Mrs. Rossi heedfully stated, "He's got something I find myself wishing I had. Jana told me he loves God, and from the way he speaks, it seems to be true." Staring at her husband, she thought it commendable for a boy who didn't like his mother to care about her so much.

* * *

Alice loved Jana and her family a whole lot, yet it wasn't until witnessing what Dwight and Jana had been up against, and ultimately overcome, that she felt a greater hope engulf her for people in general to improve their standing with one another. The walls of doubt and cynicism were breaking down within her, for if the family of man began to think and act as Dwight and Jana, then surely an improvement in human relations was well within the realm of possibilities.

While preparing supper for the family one evening, she thought of this only to be pleasantly surprised when the kitchen door swung open and Dwight entered the room.

"Hi, Alice," he spoke while making his way to her side. "I thought I'd come see how you're doing."

"Oh, I's jus fine," the woman stated with a broad grin. "In fact I ain't never been bett'r it seems, but I sur kin use a visit from ya jus da same. Is Miss Jana upstairs?"

"No, we were both in the library studying," Dwight informed her. "She's still there."

"Well den you and me kin have a nice lit'le chat. Would ya like a cup a coffee?"

"I've only tasted coffee once or twice, and I didn't care too much for it,"Dwight told her. "But I'll try another cup, with milk and plenty of sugar. Maybe I'll like it that way."

"Well ya sure is diff'rent den me when it comes ta dat," Alice declared as she began pouring each of them a cup. "I was raised drink'in it. My mama couldn' go th'out er daily coffee." Raising a cup to her lips, she eagerly took a sip. "I's like my mama I reckon." Quite heartily she laughed in a manner Dwight found himself following suit with.

"You're a nice lady, Alice," Dwight subsequently noted while she handed him his cup. "I can see why Jana likes being around you so much." As she warmly cast her eyes upon him, he added, "You're the only black person I ever had as a friend."

"Well, dose ole prejudices is still so strong. It ain't easy fer da white folks and da black folks ta be friends too off'n," she told him outright. "We's friends, dough, Mist'r Dwight," she made it a point to stress. "We's got dat fer sure."

"Ya, and I'm sure glad we do," Dwight responded as he stirred his coffee. "You and Jana are friends, too, it's plain to see."

"Oh, yessum, I love dat girl so much dat I was datermined we'd be friends!" Alice nearly exclaimed. "Why, I done changed her diapers when she was jus a babe, and oh, what a pretty babe she was. I watched her grow up. I couldn' help but love her. I saw ina'cence in her, dat's fer sure. And she done always had such a good heart."

"I know what you mean," Dwight recalled. "She's tried so hard to help me change my life for the better, and she never gave up trying even though I became discouraged more than once."

"She done loves ya a whole lot, Mist'r Dwight," Alice told him with a spark of emphasis. "She done tole me dat."

"How fortunate I am then," Dwight nearly whispered with an appreciation that went beyond words. In looking at her he realized that she knew what happened to her father at the hands of the Ku Klux Klan was not meant to be bitterly stored in one's heart, for so true it was that the world was changing all the time; and if it be that people learned from mankind's past mistakes and injustices, then at least it could be said that something good had been retrieved from something terrible for future generations to be wiser for, to be conscientious over.

Continuing to prepare supper while she chatted with Dwight, Alice felt even better about his involvement in Jana's life, for it was quite apparent to her that he and Jana complemented one another, which surely is what any healthy relationship should gravitate towards.

* * *

Quite often Dwight thought about the difficulties people encounter in their quest to overcome the haunting resurgence of the former self. Diligence was their ally, not complacency. Change rarely takes place without struggles concerning our previously held ways of living, thinking, acting. And why was this so? In Dwight's estimation it was a reaction, a most common of reactions, to the weakness of the human intellect. Old habits die hard, despite the fact that surrender is such a rich find, a veritable treasure. So upon consideration of this, he knew how important it was to be understanding of the time element involved in altering one's thought patterns. .... Hence, as he took a ride on Zuzueca one day, he foresaw that as long as he managed to focus on that which mattered the most in life, he would never be defeated by the scorn of others, regardless of its magnitude.

It wasn't until he was about a half-mile or so from The Gulf that he brought Zuzueca to a full gallop. Arriving at the beach, he attempted to veer along the shoreline only to find that the horse was somewhat intimidated by the action of the incoming waves. Prompted to dismount, he touched the water in the belief that it would calm the animal down, which it seemed to do, for in a matter of moments the stallion drew to the surf and put his nuzzle to it. Remounting at this time, Dwight made his way onward until his eyes beheld an upsetting sight about fifty feet or so from the water's edge. ... It was litter, and plenty of it, all of which appeared to be the remnants of a beach party, considering the large number of cans and bottles, some of which were broken, strewn about the blackened remains of a fire.

Coaxing Zuzueca to approach the unsightly spot, Dwight ran his gaze across the scattered debris.

"This tells me something, and it isn't good," he was inspired to say in his disappointment. "What's to become of us?" In his heartfelt way of looking at things, a tear came to his eye.

Just moments later, as though sensing Dwight's upset state of mind, Zuzueca walked away without any physical or verbal command to do so. In heading homeward a rush of determination soon replaced Dwight's heavy heart, and he knew what was in need of being done; something redeeming. So after allowing Zuzueca a brief rest, he proceeded back to The Gulf with a large burlap bag, in the event of which he began to pick up the debris, including every piece of broken glass he could find. He was convinced that this was the right thing to do, and not merely in that others would see and enjoy a cleaner beach whenever they came here. No, more importantly than that, he had taken the initiative to make restitution for humanity. And why? Because he felt he should put into practice his regard for the land. Feeling badly about what had taken place and doing nothing about it was not a valid option, not for someone who took an interest in the beauty of Mississippi, not for someone who knew full well the appreciation one should have for the land one dwelled upon.

* * *

In school Dwight noticed changes within students whom he had never before spoken to. To his utmost gratification they began saying hello to him, which gave him the unmistakable impression they were willing to be his friend.

Focusing on the trend of his life, he realized that he rarely got depressed any more, even though there had once been a time when he went to sleep in anguish. The reason was obvious. In learning what was expected of him he had acquired hope for a better future. In fact, it was through this awareness that he was compelled to walk to The Gulf one day after a rain had fallen and write a poem in the wake of a beautiful rainbow. It went:

ARC OF SPLENDOR

An arc of splendor across the sky,
It dazzles the attentive, naked eye.
As its many bright colors spread forth in great hues,
For all to take notice, for me and for you.
Some call it a highway to a new world beyond,
Where peace, love and justice, and beauty abound.
So this I must tell you; it could be you'll agree,
At the end of the rainbow, a pot of gold waits for thee.

In finishing this piece of poetry, a feeling of tranquility engulfed him, and he knew that he would never stop seeking the really meaningful things in life, the things of significance which gracefully bear witness to the spiritual realm, the things which were allowing him to feel so content within himself on the soil of Mississippi.

CHAPTER 21

IS THERE OPPRESSION
IN MICHIGAN?

Dwight's confidence soared to new heights through the enlightenment he constantly strove for. It was a soul-searching enlightenment which he knew full well couldn't be achieved apart from God, even though this was something many a person tried to disprove the truth of.

It was on a Sunday in late February, as he was walking home after having visited with the O'Maleys, that he saw a car pull into the driveway. Noticing a tall, slender woman step out from it, he approached with a great deal of interest as to her identity, that is until he found himself stopping in his tracks a few yards away from her as he recognized her facial features.

"Aunt Lorraine! Is it really you!" he virtually exclaimed.

Tenderly regarding him, the lady smiled and said, "You've got to be Dwight." When he nodded his head, she added while stepping forward, "If it wasn't for the fact that you resemble your father so much, I'd have never recognized you. It's really been much too long." Drawing closer, she embraced him endearingly.

It wasn't until they were again regarding one another that Dwight inquired why she hadn't let him know she was coming.

"But I did!" she reacted in dismay. "I sent two letters, in fact, the first one stating that I might come, and the next one confirming it."

"But I never saw either one," he informed her.

"Well then... you don't know what happened," she suddenly realized. Gazing arrestingly at him, she added, "Your Uncle Louis passed away a month and a half ago. He had a bad case of pneumonia and didn't pull through. I've been going through a period of adjustment ever since."

"You have my condolences, Aunt Lorraine. I hope he felt ready when his time came."

Aunt Lorraine suspected what Dwight meant by ready; and so she said, "Yes, I believe he was, and that has been of comfort to me. ..... Tell me, how is Clair doing?" she then asked in a change of topics.

"Quite well actually," Dwight was glad to divulge. "She likes living in Jackson. She says she's making more and more friends as time goes by. And then just last week we found out she's pregnant."

"So she's going to be a mother!" Aunt Lorraine declared. "Which means I'm going to be a great aunt!" As Dwight nodded his head, she went on to say on a sober note, "I do hope she's prepared for motherhood, though, because parenting is such an important responsibility."

Recalling what life with his mother had been like in recent years, Dwight was prompted to tell her, "I know parenting should be seen that way, Aunt Lorraine, but in my mother's case it no longer applies." With an earnest expression he added, "I think you had better prepare yourself to face her. You'll be seeing someone much different than the person you remember her to be."

"Then your father's disappearance has been even harder on her than I realized," she thereby determined.

"Some days are worse than others, but even if this were one of her better ones, I don't know how she'll react to seeing you. She's moody, and if she received your letters and didn't tell me, that's proof enough." Looking a bit downward in the unpleasant thought of that likelihood, he continued in sad reflection, "I can't seem to reach her no matter what I say or do. I try, but it just doesn't happen."

In an effort to offer a ray of hope, his aunt stated, "Don't fret. You may be reaching her far more than you know. The proof may unfold right before your very eyes some day." As Dwight dutifully beheld her in light of that prospect, she said with a hint of optimistic resolve, "It appears as though I've got a challenge on my hands then, doesn't it, because I intended to stay for awhile. But I have been known to take on challenges before, so I do feel ready to face her."

"You mean this is going to be a long visit!" Dwight exclaimed in the hopes that it would be.

"How long depends on whether or not I'm welcome here, of course, but I'm in no hurry to return to Michigan now that Louis is gone."

"Aunt Lorraine, I do believe you're a godsend!" he sounded out in elation. "I really want you to live with us!"

"I think we had better take it one step at a time, because I didn't intend to carry it that far," she so quickly replied that they were both inspired to smile. Removing her keys from her purse, she asked, "Could you help me with my luggage?"

"I sure will," Dwight eagerly complied. Yet as she handed him the keys, he was insightful enough to add, "Why don't you go in the house to talk to mother first, though. That might be best."

"Alright, that sounds like good advice," she assented.

Moments later, upon entering the dimly-lit living room, Lorraine laid eyes upon her sister.

"Hello, Marie," she spoke up in anxious expectation. "It's Lorraine."

Raising her head to regard this family member whom she had not seen in such a long time, Marie initially looked surprised by her presence; yet very soon after that it faded into an expression of disinterest.

"It's been a while, Lorraine," she gravely acknowledged the fact. "What brings you here?"

"I wanted to see you and the children," Lorraine told her. "I wrote you two letters. Didn't you receive them?"

"Ya, I got them, but I still didn't think you'd come." Steadfastly staring at her, she added, "You should have stayed away. I thought you'd realize that when I didn't answer those letters."

"But I grew concerned," Lorraine swiftly countered.

In a burst of annoyance Marie exclaimed, "Oh, stop pretending, Lorraine! You're thinking of yourself only! Louis is dead and you've got nowhere else to go, no one else to see! Coming here was your lonely escape!"

"That's a terrible thing to say!" Lorraine reacted in immediately hurt feelings.

"Well, I don't recall that you were any too eager to visit when Louis was still alive," Marie insinuated in her insistence to be insolent, in her insistence to be negatively focused.

"But I wrote to you a number of times telling you I wanted to come," Lorraine defended herself. "You know full well Louis didn't like to make the trip down here. He didn't like traveling. And it wasn't until his health began to fail him that I eventually learned how to drive, but by that time I couldn't very well leave him alone."

"A likely story," Marie suspiciously imparted. Lighting a cigarette, she began to smoke it without paying her any further attention.

For a few moments Lorraine seemed astonished by the extent of her sister's acrimonious disposition.

"Dwight told me you were in a bad way, but I didn't expect it to be this extreme," she consequently stated while shaking her head. "It's no wonder you never answered any of my letters. You were wallowing in your self-pity instead of helping yourself." Though Marie glared at her in response to her bold contention, she went on to say, "You're not going to succeed in getting me to feel guilty. I came here with good intentions, out of a genuine concern for the welfare of this family." In the onset of sentimentality, she was of a persuasion to softly add, "Because whether you believe it or not, Marie, I do care." Yet when there still was no mellowing to be seen within her, she ended up asserting, "It's as plain as can be you're filled with bitterness."

"Maybe I have a right to be bitter!" Marie angrily alleged. "You didn't have to endure the rumors about what happened to your husband, rumors that were sometimes ugly, so go back to Michigan where you came from! You don't belong here!"

"I'm not going to be driven away that easily," Lorraine firmly insisted. Walking forward, she continued, "And I think you'd do well to remember that despite what people say, you can rise above it. They can't control your outlook. Only you can make yourself bitter."

Still detecting no outward sign of receptiveness on her part, she was compelled to announce with a sigh, "Michigan is far away, so if it wouldn't be too much trouble, could you at least put me up for awhile? I'm very tired. I drove right through the night to get here."

Marie threw her arms up in surrender.

"Okay, you can use Clair's room!" she shouted in a fit of frustration. Yet one could not help but wonder whether she in fact wanted her sister to remain in her home. Certainly she would not admit to this, yet from the depths of her soul there was a yearning for some type of alteration in her life.

Lorraine thanked Marie for permitting her to stay. Yet before departing, in an effort to vindicate herself, she was inspired to point out from the doorway, "And you're wrong about my having nowhere else to go. I've got my children whom I'm very thankful for." And with that she headed for the kitchen where Dwight anxiously awaited her with her luggage.

* * *

The following Tuesday morning, as Dwight and Jana were walking to their first class of the day, Dwight stopped in his tracks at the sight of Carl, for he had a blackened eye which was so severely swollen it partially blocked his vision.

"Jana, what on earth happened to him?" he whispered in an immediate flood of concern.

"Cybil told me the word's going around his father did it to him. I even heard it's happened before, but that the bruises were in places he could hide them."

Looking at her, Dwight said, "If that's true, then I understand more than ever why he treats people badly." Directing his gaze at Carl, he saw him turn aside and dart into a rest room so that he couldn't be stared at.

"Jana, you go to class alone," he advised her as the hall began to clear of students. "There's still some time left before the bell rings, and I wanna talk to him."

"But are you sure that's wise?" she fearfully inquired. "He's likely to resent it."

"And yet I'll only find out by trying, won't I?" he told her before making his way down the hall.

Entering the rest room, Dwight found Carl standing before the mirror with his head held down in what he imagined to be a blend of anger and humiliation.

When Carl gazed in the mirror and saw Dwight in the room, he said nothing because of the presence of two other boys; yet after peering at one another in the time that it took for privacy to be secured, he stated with a tone of bitter defeat, "If you've come to gloat, then go ahead! I suppose you've earned the right!"

"I'm not here to gloat, and I don't have the right, either," Dwight strove to convince him. .... "Who did this to you?" he was then compelled to ask.

"What are people saying?" Carl merely responded.

"They say it was your father. ... Is that true?"

Continuing to regard him in the mirror, Carl harshly conceded, "Ya, it's true!" In remembrance of the unpleasant details, he inadvertently drifted off into a state of deep thought before adding, "I was only trying to protect my ma, and my pa resented that." Yet when he realized what he had admitted to, he grew defensive and clammed up, as though he believed that confiding in Dwight, or anyone else for that matter, would make him appear weak, as though he believed the truth was best kept a secret, a particularly troubling outlook for a boy in great need of sound counsel.

Dwight realized why Carl was reluctant to relay what had happened; and so he said, "You can trust me with the truth. I'm not going to use it against you. And I won't pretend to know how you feel."

Turning to face him, Carl sternly clamored, "You're right! You don't know! Nobody does!"

Unable to totally agree with him, Dwight rebounded by saying, "I can't believe you really mean that."

Carl was initially perplexed by his statement. ... Yet in remembering his past reference to God, he realized the point he was making.

"I don't get it!" he for that reason replied. "Out of everyone I expected you to be the gladdest for what happened to me, yet you seem the sorriest!" Nearly laughing in absolute amazement, he stated while shaking his head, "You're hard to figure out!"

"I'll admit I don't like how you've treated me, but there's a difference between disapproval and vengeance," Dwight brought to his attention. "I try not to cross over that line." Intently he then added, "You just don't understand that, do you?"

In scrutinizing him, Carl attempted to discover a sign of insincerity; but when he found himself unable to detect any, he slowly ran his gaze about the room in a threatening manner before saying, "Weren't you afraid to come in here?"

"Suddenly I'm not afraid of you any more," Dwight was relieved to tell him. "I realize I don't have to be, because I'm much more than this body, this life." With conviction, he purported, "There's a part of me you can't touch. It's beyond your grasp."

Carl was intimidated enough by his allegation to want to distance himself from him.

"I've gotta get to class!" he thereby announced in a gruff manner. "You should, too!" Abruptly departing, he left Dwight to ponder the significance of their encounter.

We have the ability to acquire a greater awareness of what's important down the path we travel. The proof that there is a right road is constantly in our midst, every passing hour of every passing day. Hark! Look into your heart and you shall see that it is so.

* * *

Aunt Lorraine remained in the Enhart household after all, but it wasn't because she had been given permission to stay. No, instead it was because she had not been ordered to leave, which she took as an invite, for the time being anyway. So in regard to this unspoken arrangement, she assigned herself to the domestic chores to assure they'd get done. Cooking and cleaning now filled her days, and it was not uncommon for Dwight to see clothes hanging on the line whenever he arrived home from school. .... Then one late evening, after having helped his aunt with the supper dishes as he usually did, Dwight sat down at the kitchen table to play a game of rummy with her only to take her by surprise when he asked if there was very much oppression in Michigan.

"My goodness, what ever would compel you to ask such a thing?" she reacted in a confused manner.

"It just interests me," he let it be known as plainly and simply as he could, this having come to be the nature of his personality. "I'd like to know what's happening in other parts of the country."

Aunt Lorraine thought about Dwight's question for awhile as she continued to play her rummy hand. Then she stated, "As a matter of fact I do know of several incidents that are believed to involve oppression."

"Tell me about them," Dwight urged her.

"Well, the first case involved a woman who was told years after inheriting some lake property that motor boats could no longer be used on even that portion of the lake her land bordered, because it had been designated a wilderness area. She maintained her rights had been violated, and I tend to agree with her." Following a brief pause, she went on to say, "In another case a man built ponds on his land only to be told he had to restore his land to its former condition even though he created a wildlife habitat. Any number of people sided with him, but the court ruling didn't go in his favor, so he and his wife fled the state to avoid arrest after refusing to comply with the court order." With forethought she further informed him, "In another case some people purchased some land and put up a gate. At first they said it was to keep out only vandals, but after awhile it went beyond that to involve the general public, including people in the community who had used the road on that property for many years."

"But why was it taken to that extreme?" Dwight asked of her.

"Partly because hard feelings developed," Aunt Lorraine informed him. "You see this land provided access to a beautiful beach, not to mention a trout stream, and even a piece of private property that was owned by some people who didn't have an ease-ment. They who were locked out came to resent it, and neither side seemed any too willing to compromise. Some people even retali-ated by trying to wreck the gate, or glue the lock, or tear down fences and no trespassing signs, but they soon found that all that served to do was strengthen the resolve of the gate backers. It was as though their methods reinforced the belief that it was right to lock the public out. In other words they made matters worse without even realizing it." Widening her eyes expressively, she added, "It was a very volatile situation."

"It sure does sound like it was," Dwight noted. Gravely he then added, "I guess people often self-defeat their cause." While looking upon her, he asked, "Are there still hard feelings?"

"Yes, there's some, but the people have mellowed a lot. The issue went to court and the judge ruled that since the gate owners owned the land the gate was on, they could lock the public out, and even the land owners beyond the gate who didn't have an easement." After a brief silence, she continued, "I must say I've learned something over these issues. I've learned that oppression comes in various forms. In the gate controversy, for example, the public was in a sense oppressed when they were deprived access, yet the gate backers were oppressed by the public when their gate, their property, was vandalized by angry citizens. In addition, the case only went to court because some of the people who were directly involved had the money to pay the legal fees. Justice should never be contingent on personal wealth. In a true democracy the poor are able to seek justice, too. .... So yes, oppression has many facets to it, I've learned." And she raised her eyebrows to lend credence to the point she was making.

"Who did bring this to the state's attention?" Dwight inquired.

"There was a man who tried to negotiate on behalf of the people. He wrote letters to various officials and tried to bring both sides together... but it never turned out the way he intended. So that means this case could set a legal precedent in Michigan."

"You mean other people around the state might do the same thing with the same result?" Dwight asked more than stated. Seeing his aunt nod her head, he felt compelled to add on an optimistic note, "The disappointments of this world are only temporary, though, and it's reassuring to know that, isn't it?"

Aunt Lorraine gazed at him with great affection. Then she concurred by saying, "Yes, that is of comfort." With that having been emphasized, she placed a hand upon his cheek to let him know how much she appreciated his perspective on things.

Later, in thinking about all the oppression there was in the world, Dwight realized that anyone who oppressed others was already in a state of deep personal bondage, for if it were not the case they would not be downcasting their fellow man. Do be made aware that where he himself was concerned he experienced no complacency whatsoever in that regard, for he knew that this could just as likely be him if he wasn't careful, wasn't vigilant, wasn't on guard to the worldly influences which lure one into such a mind set. Certainly immunity from this sort of thing was never a foregone conclusion where mankind was concerned, ethical shortcomings being what they are, moral shortcomings being what they be.

* * *

Jana liked Dwight's Aunt Lorraine right from the very start. In her she saw a woman who had Dwight's best interest at heart. Consequently, she and Dwight began to spend an ample amount of time with her on weekends, time in which they took rides to Fulton to shop, or picnicked at The Gulf, all of which was done with the additional hope that Dwight's mother would join in on these activities. ... And so through the involvement of Aunt Lorraine and the transportation that she provided, Dwight and Jana began to share even more time together, which brought them to feel increasingly attached from an emotional standpoint. Then one warm evening in March, their scruples were put to the test. It was a weekend, and Dwight's aunt had allowed them to use her car for an outing at the beach.

Initially in arriving at their destination they leisurely strolled the shoreline. ... Then lo and behold, they found themselves gazing into one another's eyes; and Dwight realized they were about to discover whether they would be true to their convictions.

With the respect for Jana he had come to know, he continued to peer into her eyes. Then he said, "I think we should talk about our feelings for one another."

"I do, too," she readily agreed. "After all, it is important."

Forcing himself to look away from her, Dwight stated, "I'm getting a feel for what people are up against when they're in the midst of temptation." Regarding her once again, he asked, "Do you know what I mean?"

"You know I do," she told him. "You feel it in me just as I feel it in you."

Determined to get to the heart of the matter, Dwight insightfully pointed out, "It's said that the thought is the father of the deed, but the thought has to be entertained for the deed to take place." Imploringly he added, "Let's not become distracted, Jana. Otherwise we'll limit all we can be."

"Don't worry, Dwight," she replied with utmost assurance. "We'll continue to grow as friends, because I've heard it said that physical attraction alone isn't nearly enough." With believable overtones, she professed, "I'm still interested in exploring the broader side of life with you."

So impressed was Dwight by her affirmation that he was inspired to convey, "That's one of the most encouraging things I've ever heard you say."

Jana tenderly smiled, realizing in doing so that by not allowing their passions to predominate, their relationship was much better off. Each of them seemed to comprehend that they could be as fulfilled as they made up their minds to be. The opportunity was theirs for the choosing. Yet in the midst of it all, what really added to their overall zone of comfort was the realization that the love of God is ever constant, and not contingent on being righteous. .... Yet God's wrath does at times arise in spite of love, for the sin can tarnish the standing, particularly great sins, great moral wrongs, against one's fellow man. Yes, some acts are so utterly immoral, so utterly reprehensible, that the spiritual implications are dire indeed. Salvation, a great gift, can in some instances be forever forfeited, even in the midst of love's triumph, when all is said and done.

* * *

When Dwight told Jana he would no longer put forth a conscious effort to be on the lookout for Carl, she expressed fearful concern for his well-being.

"But he might do you great harm!" she exclaimed.

"But don't you understand!" he emphatically told her. "I'm not willing to live that way any more! I want to be set free no matter what! I'm tired of hiding!"

Having made his claim with such an ardent yearning for deliverance, Jana eventually felt acceptance transcend her heavy heart.

"Alright, Dwight, I can't very well argue with that," she said, neither one of them realizing that a meaningful occurrence was on the horizon, one which would shed light on the phrase, "Hope springs eternal."

* * *

The very next day, as Dwight was walking down Kirkland Road towards the O'Maleys' farm, he felt so at peace within himself that he could barely believe it was true.

Why does life have its ironies? Could it be it dissuades complacency? There's something to be said about the timing of things, of lessons to be learned about where we stand in our resolutions. A testing was about to take place, one in which Dwight would discover just how determined he was to lean on his faith.

Vaguely aware that a car was approaching from behind, he did not turn to see who was coming, for he knew he was not alone. In truth he had never been alone, only now he was aware of that fact like never before. ... Then suddenly his assertion that he would rely on God was brought to a climax as he noticed some boys, including Carl, staring at him from within a stopped vehicle.

Time seemed to stand still as Dwight regarded Carl's fixed gaze. In no uncertain terms it should be emphasized that Carl was studying Dwight's reaction to discover whether his actions would support the words he had spoken in the rest room at school. The seconds continued to pass, seconds that seemed like hours in which all that could be heard was the purr of the car's engine. Then, finally, one of the boys shouted, "What are you waiting for, Carl! He's not even making a run for it!" And Dwight was able to easily hear these words, given that one of the car windows was partially open.

With an endurance he was grateful to be able to retain, Dwight stood his ground without so much as flinching a muscle, despite the fact that his human nature did allow a certain degree of unrest to penetrate the very core of his emotions in response to being threatened. The suspense mounted until it got to the point where Carl, at long last, began to grasp the authenticity of his virtues. If the truth be known, he was so impressed by his stand that it was he himself who ended up feeling intimidated.

"Let's get outta here!" he as a result told Ben, who was driving the car.

"But you've been waiting a long time for this moment!" Ben protested in near disbelief. "Go get him before he runs...."

"I said drive on!" Carl sternly insisted. "Just shut up and drive on!"

Amazed by Carl's unusual behavior, Ben reluctantly obeyed his command by turning the car around to head back into Fulton.

Reestablishing eye contact with Dwight as he was being driven away, Carl could not help but admire his ability to face an outnumbered opposition with such unyielding composure. Never did he think he would harbor respect for Dwight as a person, and yet it was happening. And never did he think he would directly witness the effect that a spiritual connection had in a person's life, and yet this, too, was happening.

Watching the vehicle disappear from sight down the dusty dirt road, Dwight stated with humility, "He's changing his direction." With that having been cited, he turned about, smiled with difficulty, and looked skyward with tear-filled eyes.

"Thank you so much!" he whispered with moving conviction.

Do we ever attain our full level of satisfaction in life? It would seem one would never know; and yet suddenly it didn't matter to Dwight, for in his way of seeing things it was enough that progress had been had. What was the perfect result anyway? And if the answer to that question was known, was it realistic to expect it for himself? ... Rather, a positive direction was what he sought. And in this stroke of time he saw a glimpse of the recompense which could be. ... So pay attention, for here is the irony in the timing. He had been feeling at peace within himself in the moments just before Carl happened along. Then, in the aftermath of having that good feeling interrupted, his contentment was supremely surpassed, proving that yes, reclamation is sometimes only a heartbeat away. We live in a world of change, so be receptive to that which the moment has to offer. Tomorrow may bring difficulties, but the day after that may offer relief. The distraught state of mind is temporary. The solaced state of mind is temporary. A blend of the two is the way of the world, but one's outlook will determine which condition predominates when all is said and done. Let the theme of your life be triumphant in the ways of love, for time wasted is time lost. The opportunity for healthy living is a terrible thing to abandon.

* * *

When Lorraine asked Marie if she could have a telephone installed so that she could communicate with her son and daughter back in Michigan, she was told in no uncertain terms that she could only do so if she agreed to incur the entire phone cost for as long as she was in the house, to which she consented.

Dwight and Jana were glad to have a phone to converse with. In fact, each of them personally thanked Aunt Lorraine for having it installed, even though they realized her reason for having done so had nothing to do with them.

Then one evening while eating supper, Dwight sought to open the lines of communication between his mother and aunt by inquiring what sort of things they did as they were growing up in Michigan, it being his intention to break down barriers by way of pleasant memories of a shared past.

"I do remember swimming a lot in Lake Superior in the summertime," his aunt informed him with a burst of enthusiasm. "It was usually chilly, but oh, so refreshing. Do you remember doing that, Marie?"

"It's rather a blur to me," she would only say. "Most of my past is."

"Well, I remember it well," Lorraine related. "You could, too, if you put your mind to it."

"I don't like being reminded of a time I enjoyed life," she sullenly stated. "It only makes me feel worse." In a rather poignant manner, she remarked, "You can't bring those days back anyway. They're gone forever." For a moment or two it even appeared as though she was about to weep.

410

"Marie, I don't think it's in anyone's best interest to yearn for the past," Lorraine told her. "I merely meant it might give you reason to smile if you thought about those days every now and then. You seem to think there's no bright side to life, yet in pleasant memories we have proof of how good life can be."

Even when someone makes so much sense one knows there is wisdom in their words, when one is engrossed in a habitually negative mode of thinking, they tend to gravitate in that direction, which is why Marie stated in response, "You're right about one thing, Lorraine. Life isn't very bright to me any more."

In a plea for help, Lorraine looked to Dwight, who spoke up by saying, "Mother, all of us have the choice to dwell on the positive or the negative. You could help yourself a lot by remembering that."

"I may dwell on the negative," she acknowledged, "but neither of you understands exactly the way I feel." With added emphasis, she bluntly concluded, "You aren't me!"

At first Dwight and his aunt were at a loss for words, for they realized there was truth in what she had said.

"Yet is it really necessary we understand everything about you?" Dwight was then driven to ask. "Isn't it enough that we care?" In the time that ensued, he further said, "Anyway, who but God understands us completely? I know I don't totally understand myself."

Unwilling to admit the truth in his statement, yet reluctant to speak out against God, his mother abruptly left the room, so self-conscious was she over what he had so aptly made reference to.

"I like what you said, Dwight," his aunt was quick to lend her support. "I think it was in need of being said."

"But still her attitude is so grim," Dwight told her with a distant stare. "It's like watching someone slowly take their own life." As he began to feel tears well up in his eyes, he said with a measure of defeat, "I love her, Aunt Lorraine, but I don't like her."

For a few moments there was silence as his aunt gazed at him with a flood of compassion. Then, eventually, she stressed with clear purpose, "You must realize, Dwight, that there was something missing in your mother's life long before you were born. You see our father showed favoritism towards me, and it hurt your mother. I think it made her feel less important." In seeing that his undivided attention had been captured, she continued, "When your father came along, he gave your mother the security she was searching for, but then, when he disappeared.... well, I'm afraid he took with him that security." In the pain that her words brought her to feel, she, too, began to cry. "I'm afraid that whenever your mother looks at me she's reminded of things she wants to forget. Maybe that's why I should leave after all."

"Oh, no, Aunt Lorraine, please don't leave us!" Dwight pleaded. "I think in her heart she wants you to stay. I know I do. You've been very good to us in our time of need. And you were kids when that favoritism took place. It won't do anyone any good to brood over it. People make mistakes. Besides that, was it really a good thing that my dad was my mother's emotional security? I mean look where it got her." In saying this it was his intention to point out that had his mother been secure in spirit, she would not have become the embittered woman she was. We sometimes look to mankind for every aspect of our fulfillment only to find ourselves starved of that which we're actually in need of. We have the means to acquire gratification through the love of God. And when one discovers that, they are well on their way to becoming a person solid in their standing.

For a few moments Lorraine pondered the words Dwight had spoken. Then, with motherly affection, she touched his arm and said, "You have a God given gift for knowing just what to say to help someone feel better." Barely nodding her head while smiling, she added, "Alright, I'll stay a while longer if you want me to, but I really would like to start going to church. I rarely missed at home."

"That sounds like a good idea. I'll go with you," Dwight stated. "We'll go where Jana and the Willards go, and I'll pray my two main prayers there."

"And what would they be?" she asked of him.

"That something good will result from my father's disappearance, and that my mother becomes enlightened," he said, for these were things he'd been praying for for months, knowing full well that even though there would always be certain things beyond his grasp, things were always very much within God's grasp; yes, God's, the true source of the solution in asking.

* * *

Quite often Dwight took Zuzueca for rides in the surrounding countryside, yet it would not be until the near future that the beauty of the land would in his eyes be truly spectacular, for it was almost springtime, his favorite season of the year, the rebirth of life, a time when the azaleas, magnolias and dogwoods were in full bloom throughout the South. This, without question, was something he looked forward to with unprecedented zeal in the calendar year of 1948.

As it turned out, the coming of spring brought with it something else, for it was during this period of time that Mrs. Arion announced she would no longer require oral reports in her classes.

"I've come to realize that most of you would prefer to be given a choice," she went on to explain herself, "and... well, to be truthful, it was one of you who convinced me that that's the way it should be." Without the least bit hesitation her eyes gravitated towards Dwight for a few seconds.

Certainly Dwight was delighted over this news, but it was mainly because he wanted students in general to be spared the emotionally-wrenching ordeal he had suffered through. .... Yet sadly, even now, he at times had nightmares concerning past strains within the classroom. Hence it could be said he had been left with a mental scar of inadequacy that hopefully time, the proper course of events, and his relationship with God would fade the haunting resurgence of. But it would be wrong to assume he desired to forget his former difficulties, for that was not conducive to reaping something positive from a life experience, however unpleasant that experience may have been.

When class was over, Dwight waited for the other students to leave before walking up to Mrs. Arion's desk and telling her how pleased he was with the change in her classroom policy.

Peering at him with a note of endorsement, Mrs. Arion said, "I thought you would be, and I saw it in your reaction... and the reaction of other students, too, I must admit."

"They're relieved, Mrs. Arion," Dwight was quick to point out. "In fact I wouldn't be a bit surprised if you notice grades improving for some of them."

"Do you really think this can do that much for them?" she inquired with a hint of skepticism.

"Ya, I really do," Dwight said in all honesty. Taking a step forward, he readily added, "Today you lifted a burden from their minds. Now that they're free from that distraction, they'll be better able to focus on what you're teaching."

"But something still troubles me, Dwight," Mrs. Arion acknowledged. "I find myself wondering how far this should be carried, because sometimes children need to follow rules without being given a choice in the matter."

Making his way to the doorway with his head held down in contemplation, Dwight turned to say, "I know what you mean." After further thought, he added, "I guess it has to be decided what's necessary and what isn't. Require the children to do the necessary, and give them a choice in the other things." With a shrug of his shoulders, he laid claim as though it were blatantly obvious, "Oral reports aren't necessary."

Moved by his insight, Mrs. Arion raised her eyebrows.

"Thanks for talking," she actually found herself saying.

"You're welcome," he responded in the solemn awareness of having come to terms with her at long last. Saying good-bye, he left the room in a thought-provoked frame of mind; whereupon, in arriving at his locker and retrieving a book for his next class of the day, he happened to overhear a girl from Mrs. Arion's class telling another girl how relieved she was, how glad she was that oral reports were no longer required, it being a statement which encouraged him to smile with much-awaited gratification. ... Thus it had come to pass that his mental strains had not been in vain.

CHAPTER 22

A MIGHTY TEST OF FORGIVENESS? ? ?

In the days to follow, Aunt Lorraine made a concerted effort to seek out the historical sites of the region, for she wanted to attain a greater insight into the things which contributed to the shaping of one's culture. Additionally, she felt as though it'd benefit Dwight to be amongst the public eye, for she knew he had led a sheltered life. ... So with Jana as their guide, they began visiting various state and local attractions such as the sternwheeler, Sprague, in Vicksburg, and the Mississippi Monument in Vicksburg's National Military Park, not to mention The Old Spanish Fort in Pascagoula, Natchez Trace along the Mississippi riverbank, and Nanih Waiya, mother mound of the Indians near Noxapater.

True as it was that the three of them enjoyed these outings, Dwight was especially appreciative to be witnessing the many features of his state's heritage while in the companionship of people who had his best interest at heart.

Then, during one of their weekend excursions, it was mutually decided upon to visit Clair and her husband in Jackson, for Aunt Lorraine had not seen them since arriving in Mississippi, given that Clair had never returned home since her marriage because of the unpleasant encounter she'd had with her mother the last time she'd seen her.

Though physically Clair was doing well and was healthy in her pregnancy, her unrest over her relationship with her mother she did make known, conceding that she still at times yearned to visit her.

"It's not too late," Dwight reminded her. Yet in detecting her prevailing reluctance, he found it a necessity to add, "Perhaps I shouldn't encourage you to go back there, considering all that's happened." With sought-after resolution, he told her, "You do what's best for you. Enough is enough."

After a brief deliberation, Clair responded, "I'll do what I can, but I've got a baby to think about now." Glancing sideways at her brother, she was motivated to ask, "Is there any improvement in her at all?"

"I believe so," Dwight stated without reservation. "It's subtle, but I do sense it." And Clair believed him, for she saw him to be both honest and perceptive.

When the time came to leave, Dwight encouraged his sister to take care of herself.

"And try to rest easy," he further advised her.

Smiling with difficulty, Clair impulsively hugged him before walking into the next room crying, this serving as a sure sign that she had grown to cherish his undying love for her.

Driving homeward, Dwight found himself thinking about the various forms of life which dwelled upon the earth, and he suddenly wondered if it had ever occurred to the people who claimed to be evolutionists that the changes which had taken place within certain species, both present day and extinct, was a part of God's choice in how he designed the course of things in the aftermath of creation.

It was after having dropped Jana off in Fulton and driven to Chism that Dwight and his aunt became quite concerned over the sight of a police car in the driveway. Anxiously parking, they rushed indoors to find an officer seated at the kitchen table with a broken down, sobbing Marie.

"What's going on here?" Dwight wasted no time in asking only to see the policeman slowly lower his head while shaking it as his mother cried all the harder.

By way of their joint reactions Dwight suspected this somehow concerned his father. As his mother raised her tear-filled eyes to regard him, she proved him right by wailing, "Your father is dead... murdered!" Indeed she was so overwhelmed, so ashamed, for having assumed the man abandoned her that she returned to sobbing.

Firmly planting his attention on the policeman as his aunt released an audible gasp of distress, Dwight asked, "Are you sure?" Observing the man nod his head, he inquired how he had come to gain knowledge of this.

At this point the officer stood up before saying, "A man came forth at the Central Mississippi Correctional Facility and confessed to the crime. He said he was a desperate man on the run at the time he killed your father, and that he dragged his body into a cave before driving away with his car, which he later abandoned."

"But are you sure this is true?" Dwight asked of him.

"Yes, I'm afraid so," he regretted to inform him. "You see he told us exactly where he hid the body, and sure enough, we found skeletal remains there. So then we took it upon ourselves to obtain your father's dental records to see if they matched the remains... and they did." Again he lowered his gaze in his displeasure to be informing them of this disturbing revelation.

Dwight instantly felt a combination of emotions engulf him, some of which were comforting, some of which were not. Certainly he experienced a sense of relief in learning some of the facts behind his father's disappearance at long last; yet there were also feelings of anguish concerning the way in which he had died. But he realized his prayers had been answered, and for that he was thankful. Now that the truth had surfaced, though, he knew he would be forced to address it; and hopefully in a manner free of scorn.

Walking to the doorway, the policeman stopped short to say, "The prisoner is going to be brought to Fulton any day now. An inquest is scheduled for a week from Tuesday. You might want to be there. .... Again let me tell you how sorry I am." Making his exit, he gently closed the door behind himself. Clearly the moment was for him deeply heartrending.

After a thought-filled silence in which there was an obvious accumulation of wrath within her, Dwight's mother ended up saying with vehemence, "The man who killed my husband deserves to die! He has no right to live after what he did to us!"

In reaction to her seemingly endless disposition of hate, Dwight swiftly turned his attention upon her.

"Will you learn nothing from this!" he forcefully stated. "You spent how many years hating a man you thought was alive, and now that you've found out he's dead, you're choosing to transfer that hate to someone else! Where will it end! It's as though.... as though you despise yourself!" So thoroughly disgusted was he by her attitude that he strode to the hallway where he turned to emphatically add, "You've hurt yourself far more than that man ever could! When will you see that!" Unwilling to risk listening to any more of her acrid words, he darted to his room.

Though she knew it would be difficult to do so, Lorraine attempted to console her sister by saying, "You've waited a long time for the truth, Marie, and now that you have it, I hope you come to terms with it."

"Just leave me alone!" she coldly replied in fast approaching despondency. "I don't even want to think about this right now."

Determined to respect her wishes, Lorraine exited the room without saying another word only to find herself inspired to seek out Dwight. Ascending the stairs, she knocked upon his door. When she heard him bid her to enter, she found him seated before his window. In making her way to his side, she gently placed a hand upon his shoulder before recommending, "Give her some time. She's feeling overwhelmed. It's going to take her a while to accept this fully."

"I know," he gravely acknowledged. "She's surprised she was wrong."

"Yet you, Dwight, I gathered you weren't surprised in the least by this terrible news of your father," she solemnly stated more than asked.

"No, I wasn't surprised," he freely admitted. "For a long time now I felt he was dead. I was just waiting for proof of it." Looking at her, he added, "Finally I have that proof. That's why I've been sitting here thanking God for answering my prayers." Having voiced that, he again peered out his window.

"But is it also that to know your father didn't abandon you allows your respect for him to stay intact?" she insightfully pointed out.

"Yes, I believe that's a part of it," Dwight had to confess. "I think a reputation is important. .... But I like to think I could have dealt with whatever the truth had been." In saying this he was in effect telling her that unconditional love should flow freely from the heart. "Oh, when will my mother see the error of her ways, Aunt Lorraine!" he dejectedly cried out. "She's poisoning her mind! ... But the world is so like that, isn't it? Sometimes I wish I could distance myself from it. I know as long as I'm alive I can't escape it, though. It's all around me. All I can do is persevere and hope I'm not consumed by it, too." He so seemed to comprehend that diligence was in great need of being an ongoing virtue.

"Yet as filled with contempt as your mother is, don't you think she should desire justice? After all, a murder was committed, and that's a serious offense."

"Justice!" Dwight somewhat startled her as he rose to his feet and strode to the center of the room in contention. "Is justice an eye for an eye! Is it really healthy to feel that!" Shaking his head, he further said, "No, my mother and so much of the world desire something far more than justice! They want revenge! Their hate is proof of that!" In the onset of tears, he proclaimed, "I want the streets to be safer, too, Aunt Lorraine! I want justice, but it doesn't interest me to hand victory to the ways of hate by caving in to that hate myself!" With a discerning look, he added from the depth of his heart, "My mother allowed a terrible thing to happen to her. She allowed herself to lose her friendliness, her hope. The killer took her husband's life, and she took her own, because the person she used to be is dead, dead by her own choosing." At the conclusion of these words it seemed as though he was about to physically collapse.

Mindful of the point he had succeeded in getting across to her, Aunt Lorraine told him with mellow acceptance, "I believe you're right, so let's hope your mother turns over a new leaf before it's too late. Let's hope and pray for her resurrection so that the person she used to be returns." Approaching him, she added with utmost regard, "I love you, Dwight, and I like you, too." Taking him into her arms, she gently pressed her cheek to the side of his face, not realizing in doing so that he was about to suffer a relapse in how he felt about his father's murder, a relapse which would very much disappoint him in more ways than one.

* * *

When the people of the area discovered what happened to Mr. Enhart, many of them found it difficult to imagine that such a terrible thing had taken place so close to the peaceful surroundings of their homes. All things considered, it seemed as though Dwight was the only one who wasn't surprised by the news of what happened to his father, so willing had he been to give him the benefit of the doubt despite the opinions of the scoffers. Why, even Clair, in spite of her life's change for the better, had been taken by surprise by what she discovered, for she, like her mother, had believed the rumors which surfaced throughout the years, rumors strictly based on assumption. ... But as for Dwight, he was a boy who believed in his father's integrity because the man had never given him any reason not to. He was a boy who realized that when you looked up to someone, you expected the best in them and gave them the benefit of the doubt until such time that they gave you just cause for thinking otherwise. ... Yet he was only human, and so now that he knew some of the details behind his father's disappearance, he at times found his mind bombarded by thoughts which were much less than wholesome, thoughts which called into question whether he would practice what he preached in the face of stark realities. ... So here is a glimpse of what recent days had been like for him:

He had not been able to sleep well ever since the police officer's visit. Intense disgust over his father's murder was the primary reason behind his insomnia. But despite his indignation, he was wise enough to realize that if he hoped to ever recapture any semblance of the peace of mind he had previously known, he would have to defeat his unhealthy thoughts, and triumph in the healthy ones.

So in standing at the cemetery with his family and friends under a gray overcast sky on the day of his father's funeral, a solemn Dwight found himself so focused on his mother's plight that he became endowed with a greater awareness of what she was up against in turning her life around. He could identify with her like never before, which influenced him profoundly.

Listening as the pastor, Preacher James, spoke t.. words of the graveside service, Dwight began to cry along w. family and friends as he reflected on days gone by when his fau. was alive and well. The time one had to share with someone could be so unexpectedly cut short, all the more reason to try one's best to establish and maintain good human relations so that regrets were kept at an absolute minimum.

When the people were in the process of dispersing, Preacher James approached Dwight and his family and said, "If any of you would like to talk to me in private, please feel free to stop by the parsonage any time."

"Thank you, we'll keep that in mind," Aunt Lorraine spoke up on behalf of all concerned as Dwight sensed the comfort he'd likely be able to feel if the day ever dawned that he chose to confide in the man.

Walking beside Dwight, Jana wished she could take upon herself a portion of his grief. At a later date she would come to see that through her loyal support she had in effect already accomplished that goal, for when the strong love one has for someone is practiced in the face of sorrowful moments, that sorrow is in essence shared to lighten the burden for all concerned.

Falling back from the crowd to gain privacy in conversation, Dwight said, "I haven't been liking my thoughts very much lately, Jana. I'm getting a feel for what my mother is up against."

"But you shouldn't expect to come to terms with this overnight," Jana was quick to emphasize.

Following a brief silence in which they continued to stroll along, Dwight stated, "Perhaps I shouldn't at that, but I assumed I was beyond this. .... I guess I underestimated my reaction to murder." As a sign of the shame he felt, he went on to say, "I'm aware that the quality of my life will diminish if I'm embittered, and yet I'm struggling with my feelings because.... because what happened involves such a mighty test of forgiveness." By way of additional insight, he felt motivated to add, "Maybe I should focus on surrendering instead, and cast aside forgiveness." Releasing a sigh, he noted, "I can't tell you how disappointed I am in myself over this."

"Oh, Dwight, there you go again being much too hard on your-self," Jana mildly reproached him as she had been known to do before. "Don't you see that in the long run this will pass? It's just too far removed from your usual self to remain constant."

"Then you have far more confidence in my character than I do," Dwight commented. As she looked at him in a strikingly discon-certed way, he brought to her attention, "You seem to think I could never hold a grudge, but I've found that I'm not immune to that possibility. ... I suppose I shouldn't really be surprised by that, though, because I saw it happen to my mother, a person I hadn't expected it in. ... I guess in some respects we're all vulnerable to it."

At this juncture Jana said nothing, for she saw in his admittance the deliverance he was so earnestly seeking. Put another way, his realizations were his strengths.

Nearing his aunt's car moments later, Dwight realized that the love Jesus preached could reverse his setback as long as he allowed that love to reside in his heart. But it wasn't easy to walk the path of righteousness, particularly in times of adversity or temptation. Surely for some of us it takes years of stumbling and falling before we finally attain a true semblance of unaltered direction. Why? In part it's because we allow the negative aspects of this world to sorely affect our ways of thinking and acting. In our desire to fill our every need we often blindly indulge ourselves in vanishing relief. Sometimes a person even becomes so perverse in their quest for fulfillment that they're a hazard to others. .... Therefore a total surrender to God is most elusive, indeed rare, so multifaceted is its complete attainment.

When the family arrived home, Clair and Stuart decided to stay for supper before heading for Jackson.

While everybody ate in the doleful silence that seemed to typify this day, they were taken by surprise when out of the clear blue sky Dwight suddenly announced that he wanted to meet the man who killed his father.

At first everyone stared at him and one another in total amaze-ment.

"Are you out of your mind!" his mother angrily lashed out at him then. "What would that accomplish!"

"That man didn't have to confess what he did," Dwight logically brought to her attention. "He must be a changed man to have done so after all these years, and I'd like to know what brought that about. Maybe we'd feel better if we understood where he was coming from. I for one want answers."

"But are you sure you're prepared to face him?" Aunt Lorraine interceded. "It could end up being very disturbing for you, and make matters even worse in the long run."

Regarding her with firm resolve, Dwight stated, "Right now I feel ready to face anything, so I'd like to see him as soon as possible if that can be arranged."

Downright disgusted over his decision, his mother irately rose from the table and left the room without uttering another word.

"Dwight, it seems odd to me that you're not concerned about our feelings," Clair tersely made comment in regard to his plans. "A person's got to draw the line somewhere."

"Don't you realize it's out of concern that I want to visit that man!" Dwight adamantly told her. While briskly scooping up a forkful of food, he strongly added, "And besides, isn't it far better to try to understand what happened instead of being lost in our grief?" With an eventual return of calm introspection, he found himself asserting, "Anyway, I think I might find it therapeutic to meet with him, and I could use a dose of that right now." With that being projected, he continued eating in what appeared to be an appeased state of mind.

Struck by the authoritative manner in which he expressed himself, nobody dared say anything more to him at this time, for it was almost as though he was speaking God's will more than his own, which would beg the all-important question: If it was God's will that he meet with his father's killer, then when should that meeting take place? Should it be sooner or later, and in the aftermath of what, for the timing of things is quite relevant to the results?

* * *

When Dwight called the Fulton police department the following evening and found out that the man who confessed to killing his father had already been brought there for his inquest, he asked his Aunt Lorraine if he could use her car to drive into Fulton to meet him. Yet before doing so, he sought his mother's permission, for he was not at all comfortable over the thought of defying her.

"Do what you must!" she rather impatiently bellowed. "I don't like it, and I don't understand it, but do what you must!"

Subtle as it may have been, there was something different about her. Had this change come about because she knew she had not been forsaken by her husband? Or did it range much deeper than that? Whatever be the case, Dwight saw a glimpse of illumination within her, which pleased him for what it was symbolic of.

"Thank you," he told her before anxiously walking away, his devotion to his mission gaining momentum through each passing moment it seemed.

Handing her car keys over to her nephew, Aunt Lorraine once again called into question the wisdom behind his intentions.

"Well, if I don't go to see him, I'll be discontent, so what's a person to do?" Dwight so matter of factly replied that she concluded nothing more was in need of being said about it.

Shortly thereafter, while driving down Kirkland Road, Dwight attempted to free himself of biases concerning a man who had wounded and scarred him through the murder of a loved one. In the shadows of his mind conflicting emotions loomed, so much so that upon arriving at the Fulton police station, he walked indoors rather tentatively only to be greeted by the very same officer who delivered the news of his father's death a few days beforehand.

"What can I do for you?" the officer asked, recognizing him immediately.

"I came here to talk to the man who was brought here for the inquest," Dwight was quick to speak up. In noticing the policeman's unmistakable surprise, and eventual uncertainty as to what course of action he should follow in regard to such an unusual request, Dwight forged onward by saying, "Please don't refuse me. I feel the need to see him... and I believe it's for the right reasons."

For a few moments the officer continued to stare at Dwight.

"Alright, if that's what you really want," he finally complied, even though he, like the world in general, found it difficult to comprehend why someone in Dwight's position would want to do such a thing. "Just follow me."

Making their way down a corridor into a plain room with a table and a few chairs, Dwight was told to wait there. In doing so, he was pleased to retain a level of composure which he felt would assist him in being tactful.

Moments later, when the door reopened and the officer entered the room with the handcuffed and shackled prisoner, Dwight stood up, in the event of which he and the man exchanged a brief eye contact, given that the man was quite apprehensive in his presumption that he had come here to tell him how much he despised him. Yet in spite of his expectations, he felt obligated to meet with him anyway, believing he owed him at least that much after what he had put him and his family through.

"When you're finished talking, just knock on the door," the officer told Dwight with a look of lingering doubt over his wisdom in being here. Following an obedient nod of Dwight's head, he left the room but kept close tabs on them through the windowed door.

At this point the prisoner forced himself to regard Dwight before saying with obvious tenseness, "I was told there'd only be an inquest when they brought me here. I didn't expect something like this."

"No, I imagine you didn't," Dwight responded, "but still, now that I'm here, can't you understand why I'd want to meet you?"

With a lowering of his shoulders, he frowned a bit before stating, "I figured ya hated me enough to wanna tell me so. Can't say I don't deserve it." In a manner as resolved as ever, he beheld Dwight as though he fully accepted this to be his status for the remainder of his life for what he had done.

Dwight studied the man's face for a few moments to get a feel for his bearing. Then he asked, "What would you say if I told you I don't hate you?"

For a while the man wondered what Dwight was leading to.

"I'd say it's not possible," he made the determination then.

With an even greater conviction, Dwight rebounded by asserting, "Then I'd say you can't know what can be accomplished in life." Sitting down at this point, he regarded him with a great deal of acuity.

Trying to gain a grasp of his meaning, the prisoner said, "You're right. I don't know about that." The spiritually-minded individuals of the world will readily take note of the sad element that his acknowledgment was indicative of.

In an effort to explain where he was coming from, Dwight began, "I try to put God first in my life. I've found that if I'm focused on doing that, I won't let hatred rule my life, even though I may have a relapse from time to time."

In looking at the man one could tell he was moved by Dwight's words; yet all too soon it changed into an expression of mistrust, for in many respects he was unenlightened about the ways of integrity, the story of his life having encouraged him to expect the worst in people. Our beliefs are a reflection of our view of the world. When we don't realize the capacity that exists for healthy living, when our cynicism overrides our better judgment, faith, hope and love do not flourish. The emotions become numbed and we stagnate in our frustrations. Discontent is ours to be had because our mind is not receptive to understanding that which can so enrich our lives.

"I don't think ya can prevent yourself from hating me," he told Dwight as a result. "It doesn't make any sense."

"Yet even though you expect that, you confessed your crime, a crime you hadn't been charged with," Dwight reminded him. "That tells me something. It tells me that in your heart you couldn't escape from what you did."

Shuffling to the table, the man sat down across from him before saying, "You're right. What I did caught up with me. I found out I had a conscience after all."

"And how did that come about?" Dwight took an interest in knowing.

With a fixed expression, he vividly recalled, "For some reason my memories began to haunt me, especially in my dreams. I couldn't take it any more. I had to do something."

"Do you think God was trying to get your attention?" Dwight was bold enough to ask, and believing enough to insinuate.

Nearly inclined to laugh over that which he considered to be a farfetched notion, the man professed, "I've never been one to give God much thought."

"But that doesn't mean what I suggested couldn't be true," Dwight argued. Detecting a look of confusion on the man's countenance, he sought to better explain himself by adding, "You see, I've been praying for news of my father's whereabouts for some time now. ... Now do you get my point?" His gaze could be described as thoroughly penetrating.

Taken by surprise, the man could not find any words to say in response; and so Dwight spoke up instead by asking, "What has your life been like?"

In a wave of exasperation he replied, "Ya ask a lot of questions!" ... Yet soon his annoyance faded into oblivion as he saw in Dwight's eyes a genuine interest in his past free of scorn. "You're making me feel even worse than before," he as a result emphasized. "If ya hated me I reckon I wouldn't feel so bad right now."

"For a while I did find myself heading in that direction," Dwight honestly admitted. "In killing my father you took him away from me and my family. Your choice forever changed our lives... and yours." At the sound of these all-inclusive words the man's attention was additionally secured; after which Dwight solemnly added, "It took me a while to come to terms with what you've done. I had to separate hating the act from hating the person, and that can be a very difficult thing to do."

"If ya don't hate me, then what is it that ya feel towards me?" he was curious enough to ask.

"Some people would expect me to say forgiveness, but it's not that at all," Dwight was inspired to confess. "You see I've recently come to believe that God doesn't expect me to forgive you. He expects something else."

"And what might that be?"

"To see beyond my pain," he informed him. "To look past the moral offense, which doesn't mean I can't be angry with you." In saying this he meant that if his anger did not consume him, if it was in the background of his emotions rather than the forefront, if it was under his control rather than in control of him, then that was quite acceptable. "I think a person who refuses to see beyond their pain is trapped in their grief."

Impressed by his insight, the man decided to confide in him

after all by stating with some measure of admission, "Most of my life hasn't been very good. .... I suppose that's what ya expected, though."

"I really don't think there's anything you could say that'd surprise me," Dwight freely contended. "I've learned to expect the unexpected. I'm beginning to believe that anyone can go down the wrong path in life if they've a mind to. Even if two people were raised identically, they could have very different outlooks, because I have news for you, it depends on the thoughts they entertain." Indeed he believed that everyone experienced some type of transgression if they lived long enough, and that any transgression was easier to address in its early stages before deep-rooted addictions set in. .... Yet when an addiction does lead to a great trespass against mankind, can love be the victor ultimately? If we truly have faith in God the answer to that question will invariably be a resounding yes. .... And so even though their physical lives have been taken away from your loved ones, their spiritual lives are beyond the grasp of he who was so conniving. He is powerless to prevent a redemptive end result. From a moral standpoint he has disgraced himself. So take heed, for all is not lost. The final result did not take place with his death or the death of the 33. The conclusion is yet to be realized, for God will compensate all concerned for their painful losses. All will receive their just recompense.

By this time the man realized Dwight had an outlook towards life he had never before been exposed to. Substantially influenced by that, he said, "I find myself liking how ya think. I don't understand it, but I like it." Rather hesitantly he then asked, "How does the rest of your family see things?"

Looking at him, Dwight made the disclosure, "My mother doesn't feel as I do. She's very bitter. In fact in some respects her guilty conscience has been no less crippling than your own."

"But why should she feel guilty?" he desired to know in his perplexity.

Quite soberly Dwight informed him, "Because she didn't give my father the benefit of the doubt. Because she thought he abandoned her."

Following a few moments of silence, the man made the

confession, "At times I'm afraid I'll go to hell for what I did. Do ya think I will?"

"Do you mean a hell where you'll suffer in eternal misery?" Dwight delved into the matter.

With a confused look, he responded, "What other kind would there be?"

"It just might be that the hell of this life is the worst you'll ever know," Dwight dared to suggest.

"Ya make it sound like ya don't even think there's a hell," he stated.

"Oh, I believe there's a hell," Dwight openly admitted. "But there's a religion that claims God would never sentence you to eternal misery for the limited amount of time you did wrong, because it runs contrary to justice. ... But I don't know if that's true. Who am I to say? I only know that salvation is possible." Indeed he felt God would not hold a flawed belief system against anyone as long as their heart was in the right place, for perfect understanding is not ours to be had. Mercy can make up for our shortcomings quite magnificently, and mercy is only a breath away.

"I'd like to know more about many things," the man said with a believable overtone.

"It's still not too late," Dwight brought to his attention.

"A preacher did give me a Bible the other day," he told him.

"Do you plan to read it?" Dwight inquired, wondering if it was Preacher James who had visited him. Yet no sooner did he ask the question than he noticed a sudden discomfort within him; and so, after some time, he was motivated to add, "Do you even know how to read?" The man would not answer him, however, which prompted him to say, "It's nothing to ashamed of if you can't. It's something we all have to learn."

Realizing Dwight made good sense, he at last admitted, "Ya guessed right. I can't read but a few words." In stating the truth he felt a rush of relief engulf him, for he had lied about his illiteracy for many years.

Pondering the situation, Dwight eventually inquired, "Are you interested in learning how to read and write?"

"It's too late for me," he was quick to assume. "I'm a lost cause."

"You sound as though you're determined to prove yourself to be just that, a lost cause," Dwight said with outright directness.

Momentarily tongue-tied, he stated, "I... have no choice. There's nobody to teach me."

With very little forethought Dwight proposed, "I could be your teacher."

Totally amazed by the offer, the man suspiciously stated, "Why would ya go through all that trouble after what I did?" Indeed it could even be said there was a hint of resentment in his voice, for he wondered if Dwight was being patronizing.

Thinking about his question for a while, Dwight announced, "I'd do it in the hopes that you wouldn't be at odds with humanity any longer. After all, hasn't there been enough hurt already?" Getting up, he walked to the door and knocked upon it before turning to add, "I'll be at the inquest Tuesday. Then afterwards I'll try to get permission to start our lessons." Before anything additional could be said, the door opened and he exited the room, leaving behind a man who was so astounded by that which had transpired that all he could seem to do was stare blankly into space, for he was not used to being shown this much concern by anyone, and he certainly didn't expect it to be coming from the son of the man whom he had killed.

* * *

"I thought he left me for another woman!" Marie lamented from where she sat at the kitchen table with her sister. "I should have given him the benefit of the doubt, but I was so convinced he didn't care about us any longer!"

"But in your heart of hearts did you really believe he'd abandon you and the children?" Lorraine inquired of her.

"At first I didn't, but after awhile I brainwashed myself into thinking it was true," she recalled with bitter regret. "And the rumors didn't help any. ... Oh, how I detest that awful man who murdered him!" she vehemently hissed while clenching her fists tightly. "He's caused us so much grief!"

"Marie, you're tormenting yourself to no useful purpose.

Thinking that way isn't going to do you or anyone else any good," Lorraine fervently advised her as Dwight was heard pulling into the driveway from his visit at the jail. "And please don't be hard on him," she swiftly added. "He's got to cope, too, and he did what he felt he had to." But in her rekindled embitterment, Marie frowned disgustedly.

When Dwight walked through the doorway, he wasted no time in saying, "I'm glad I went to see him. I learned something valuable today."

"And what was that?" his aunt questioned him with bona fide interest.

"I learned that it's important to see past what happened." Because of the manner in which he expressed himself, even his mother believed him to be speaking from the heart. ... "But I learned something else," he felt motivated to add. "I learned that that man could be released from jail today and still be a prisoner in his own mind for what he's done. What a punishment that is!" Placing his undivided attention upon his mother, he went on to relate, "So you see he's being punished, and yes, he deserves to be punished... but he's got potential in him, too. I felt it. That's why I intend to teach him how to read and write so that...."

"No, I forbid it!" his mother suddenly shrieked while standing. "He doesn't deserve it, and you're not going to embarrass this family any further! People will think we're crazy! I can hear the talk now!"

At this stage Dwight stated quite emphatically, "Don't you realize it's the people who are the most critical that understand the least?"

"You're just trying to defy me to get back at me for the past!" she sorely rebuked him. "That's why you're doing this! It's in retaliation!"

As Dwight stood there thinking about the accusation his mother had made against him, a wave of guilt promptly began to flood his emotions as he recalled in vivid detail how he had at one time urged Jana to respect her parent's wishes. And so in light of that former advice, he realized that if he didn't do the same thing, he would be a hypocrite for not practicing what he preached. Such is what happens when a person loses sight of the far-reaching aspects of a situation.

"Mother, I'm sorry I upset you," he therefore told her. "I won't

tutor him if you don't want me to, even though I still would like to."
With that being said, he slowly turned to leave in his surrendered
state of mind, yet not before stopping short to add, "I guess good
intentions aren't always enough." All things considered, he discovered that you could hurt someone even when you had absolutely no
intention of doing so, as he had done to his mother, because he
hadn't taken her feelings into proper consideration. But where was
one to draw the line concerning such things, he found himself
wondering? The answer: To be in good standing with God his
mother's feelings were to be respected, because to disregard them
would self-defeat all other courses of action. The repercussions
would travel with him. .... Thus he had learned a valuable lesson
concerning choices. And yet perhaps everything would turn out
well if his mother experienced an epiphany. Certainly this was
much more likely to occur now that he had capitulated to her
wishes, for in doing so he had shifted upon her shoulders the
responsibility for what was to further take place. From now on she
couldn't rant and rave that he was defying her. Seen from another
perspective, the quality of her life would further digress if she
continued to feed a hardened heart. He had fed it by defying her, but
she had fed it for many years. That was a foregone conclusion.
Always, though, in his estimation, there was a bright light of hope
at the end of the tunnel, and in time that light could shine forth,
given a favorable set of circumstances, a favorable chain of events.

* * *

Dwight was glad when his aunt informed him of his mother's
plans to be at the upcoming inquest, because he somehow sensed
that the inquest held the potential of helping her come to terms with
her past.

"I only hope she doesn't create a scene, though," he felt
disposed to say. "We both know she's angry enough to do it."

"Try not to concern yourself about that," Aunt Lorraine urged
him. "If she gets out of hand, they'll simply remove her from the
courtroom. ... But I'll try my best to pacify her," she added on a
reassuring note.

Conveying his appreciation by manner of a look, Dwight stated, "I wonder what sentence the judge will decide upon."

"Yes, I've been curious about that myself. Maybe we'll find that out tomorrow, too."

"But I thought that's what this was all about," Dwight confusedly reacted.

"No, I think they'll substantiate his guilt at the inquest," Aunt Lorraine apprised him. "The sentencing may be at a later date."

"Well, whatever be the case, I'm interested in the outcome," he made it a point to declare.

As it turned out, Dwight and his family weren't the only ones who took an interest in the inquest, for when they arrived at the courthouse on the morning of the summary proceedings, they discovered a courtroom nearly filled to capacity with concerned citizens, including the Willards, the O'Maleys and the Rossis, not to mention Carl Barnet, Scott and Roberta, and many others who had read in the local newspaper, or heard through the grapevine, about the break in the case concerning the disappearance of Mr. Enhart.

Sitting toward the front of the room with his mother and aunt, Dwight waited, and then listened with keen interest as Lester Madaylion, the man who had confessed to killing his father, told the prosecutor, the judge, and the courtroom the events leading up to the crime he committed.

Focusing on his testimony, Dwight had no trouble detecting the man's poor self-image as he reiterated some of the dreadful moments of his dark past. What he didn't realize, however, was that because of the impression he had had upon him during their meeting at the jail, he was having a much more difficult time speaking than he otherwise would have had, given that he liked him and didn't want to divulge harsh realities in his presence, facts which would undoubtedly be very painful for him to listen to.

"I hadn't intended to kill him," he then went on to say. "He tried to overpower me and I struck him on the head. At first I thought he was unconscious, but then I... I found out differently. I thought I had it planned so well, and it turned out so wrong." Gazing at Dwight at this time, he added with pronounced depth of feeling, "But no matter how sorry I am, I can't change the past."

And he lowered his head in abject despair.

Looking at him, Dwight got a feel for the extent of his regrets. But make no mistake about it. Had it not been for the fact that Lester had come forth by his own volition to confess his crime, he would not have been so quick to accept his claim of remorse. Indeed he had acquired a healthy skepticism, for he understood that appearances didn't always reflect what was within the mind of the individual.

Was his mother actually crying? To his utmost captivation he saw that she was, which made him wonder if it was in response to Lester's subdued bearing. Could it be that the surrender in the man was bringing about a surrender in the woman? And if that be the case, how thoroughly she must realize the futility of her bitterness over the years, and the fact that she had significantly contributed to her anguish by refusing to set her hardened heart aside. It would be so ironic if now, through a prisoner's confession, she saw the error of her ways in clear focus. Dwight so hoped this was taking place anyway.

Because Lester was currently serving a one-year sentence for a recent infraction, the decision on the part of the judge entailed how much additional time should be served based upon his admission. .... And so, when the testimony, which barely lasted an hour, was over, Judge Mackelin adjourned the proceedings, telling everyone he'd return to the bench at one o'clock that afternoon to pass sentencing.

While the people filed from the courtroom in low-pitched conversation, Dwight and Lester exchanged a prolonged eye contact. In doing so Dwight sensed a certain desperation within the man, as though this troubled individual trusted him enough to reveal honest emotion rather than false indifference. Was it a plea for help to travel down a different path in life? Dwight was inclined to believe it was so.

Going to lunch at a local restaurant with his mother and aunt, Dwight became very preoccupied in thought as he reflected on Lester's confession. ... Then suddenly, as though he were hit by a bolt of lightning, he came up with an idea, a judgment call, which he had the good sense to keep to himself this time around so as not to upset his mother any further. Was he being tactful or self-serving for taking this approach? It was actually a combination of the two. Yet in all fairness to him, his mother was largely responsible for the method he was opting to assume, for when someone is petulant and unreasonable in the demands they impose upon their children, the result is that their children are not as likely to confide in them. Avoiding a potentially unpleasant encounter was something Dwight felt justified in seeking; and so, to ward off any suspicion, he completed his meal before telling his mother and aunt that he wished to return to the courthouse to await the arrival of one o'clock.

"But why don't you stay with us instead?" Aunt Lorraine suggested. "I'm sure the time will go by much quicker for you."

"No, I'd rather go to the courthouse," Dwight told her while standing. "It won't be that long of a wait, especially after walking there." Saying good-bye, he left the two women before anything additional could be said to hold him back.

As he proceeded down the sidewalk, Dwight thought about something Lester had said in the courtroom, of the decision he had made to rob from people to get by in life, even though getting by in life doesn't compare to getting sight of life. No, it just couldn't compare.

Dwight arrived at his destination about fifteen minutes later. Heading directly to Judge Mackelin's chambers, he tentatively knocked on his door. When he was invited to enter, he found the man seated behind a paper-filled desk.

"Yes, what can I do for you?" he immediately asked Dwight.

"Judge Mackelin, I'm Mr. Enhart's son," he informed him while standing by the doorway. "I came here to talk about the sentencing you're about to rule on."

Frowning a bit, the judge said, "Dare I assume you want to influence my decision."

"Yes... I was hoping to," Dwight somewhat apprehensively conceded while stepping forward a bit.

With a look of disapproval Judge Mackelin stated, "This isn't the first time a family member has tried to get me to do that. I'm guessing you want me to give your father's killer life imprisonment, or was it something more drastic you were interested in?"

In a burst of urgency Dwight exclaimed, "Oh, no, you've got it all wrong! I didn't plan to ask you to add to his punishment! In fact I may want it lessened!"

Caught off guard by his atypical request, Judge Mackelin stated, "You may want it lessened?" When Dwight nodded his head, he added somewhat disconcertedly, "I don't know what to make of this. It's most unusual."

"Well then permit me to explain myself," Dwight eagerly volunteered while sitting on one of two chairs before the man's desk. With forethought he told him, "If Lester had committed first degree murder, I'd probably be the first one to say he should be jailed for a very long time, because people should be held accountable for their actions. Not only that, society does have a right to protect itself from that type of person. ... But Lester claims he didn't intend to kill my father, which is manslaughter, and I believe him."

"And why exactly do you believe him?" Judge Mackelin earnestly inquired.

"Because he chose to confess what he did... and because I visited him in jail and got to know something about him." Without the least bit hesitation he added, "I think he's being honest."

"I see," the judge replied. Leaning back in his chair, he placed a hand under his chin to ponder the situation before asking, "And what sentence do you feel would be appropriate under the circumstances to achieve justice?"

"One that isn't too lenient or too harsh," Dwight told him. "I guess you could say I want compromise, a healthy balance."

Clearly the judge was moved by Dwight's generosity, which compelled him to probe further into the matter by saying, "I know Lester said he was a desperate man back then, and that he panicked, but you, why are you so determined to speak up on behalf of this man? Surely you must realize society doesn't expect it of you."

"Oh, I'm well aware of society's expectations," Dwight solemnly apprised him in memory of the scars he bore. "More than once I've had a taste of it." Yet in being swept by a burst of inspiration, he added, "In answer to your question, though, I like to think of myself as fair-minded, and when a person is that way, they try to do what's in everyone's best interest. In that way they'll really be helping society, too, whether society knows this to be true or not." With a soft gaze he revealed unto him, "I told God last night as I was kneeling at my bed that I wanted closure at last, for myself, for my mother, for all concerned. So I've got to be free of scorn, because if I'm not, I'll never find the closure I'm seeking. It'll always elude me."

Fascinated, as people so often were, by the nature of his insight, Judge Mackelin scrutinized him for a while before saying, "I'll seriously consider your suggestion. I agree Lester's got to be a changed man to have confessed to something he wasn't even charged with."

"Could I ask one more thing of you?" Dwight beseeched him.

"And what would that be?"

"I'd like you to allow Lester's sentence to be served here in Fulton. You see, I want to teach him how to read and write so he'll be better prepared to face the outside world. As of now my mother has forbidden me to do this, but just in case she changes her mind, I'd like him kept here."

"I wasn't aware that he was illiterate," Judge Mackelin stated. ... "And yet I can't really be surprised by that," he then went on to say. "From my past experience on the bench I've found it to be more common than most people realize."

"Then that's all the more reason why something should be done to change that, Judge Mackelin." Raising both of his hands and drawing them inwardly toward himself, he said with clear meaning, "I'm only one person. I can only do so much, but I want to do something." His point was made with such heartfelt admittance and sought after determination that the judge's attention was thoroughly seized.

"Yes, I can see that you have an interest in making a difference," he noted. ... "Actually this plan of yours does interest me," he told him then. "God knows I've seen too many repeat offenders in the courts." Taken by surprise by his own reference to God, he paused briefly before chuckling and saying, "I do believe you're rubbing off on me." In noticing that Dwight had cast him a smile, he added, "I'm going to grant your request. I'll have to go through the state judicial system of course."

"All I ask is that you try," Dwight replied. Putting out a hand, he said while standing, "I'm hoping for the best possible outcome."

"I can't very well argue with that, now can I?" Judge Mackelin conceded while completing the handshake. "You've got a good purpose in mind."

Dwight reflected his gratitude through the warmth in his eyes. Turning to leave, he walked as far as the door before swinging about to say, "Please don't tell anyone I spoke with you about this. I don't want my mother to find out. She wouldn't like it. She's very bitter, I'm sorry to say."

"My lips are sealed," the man assured him. "I've been around long enough to know there's differing opinions within the same family. But tell me something, hasn't it been difficult for you to forgive this man for what he's done to your father?"

"But I haven't forgiven him, Judge Mackelin," Dwight straightforwardly acknowledged. "I don't have to. That's for God to decide, not me." His words seemed to flow from the depth of his soul. "When I think of all the unpleasant things that happen in the world, I'd be foolish to make matters even worse by holding a grudge. Why add to the misery?" Shrugging his shoulders, he held eye contact with the man a few seconds longer before saying good-bye and leaving the room in appreciation of the consideration afforded him.

In the aftermath of Dwight's departure, Judge Mackelin thought about his coming here, knowing full well that an official's position very often intimidated people and discouraged them from speaking out in the manner he had done about an idea which held the potential of making a worthwhile difference in someone's life. Indeed, if for no other reason than that, he found himself liking the boy.

* * *

Awaiting the arrival of one o'clock in the hall outside the courtroom, Dwight prayed that his mother would conduct herself in a dignified, ladylike manner during the sentencing, for he didn't want an already unpleasant situation made worse by way of harbored resentments.

When Judge Mackelin sentenced Lester to only three to five years of jail time followed by a probationary period, Dwight became convinced that his mother had been positively influenced by Lester's testimony, for she did not seem upset in the least. Had Clair been in attendance, would she have responded just as favorably to the ruling? Dwight could not be sure, but he did feel it was highly conceivable.

Driving homeward a short time later, Dwight sensed more than ever that his mother was a changed woman, for she was far removed from her usual self, as though she finally realized the futility of her years of hostility, as though she finally was drained empty of hate, and had come to understand that if she ever hoped to pave the way to sound mental health, she would have to come to terms with her past once and for all. A successful turnaround occurs in stages. Temporary setbacks can temper the convictions. Therefore all is not in vain as long as we grow and mature by our faults. Moral advancement is a most achievable of outcomes. We are well-advised to search for the truth about life, the road to peaceful living, the trail to heartfelt compassion. Our existence can be miserable enough to be deemed downright pathetic if we drift into a depraved condition, for whenever one reaches that dire state, death can be a merciful deliverance from that which we've become. It can be successfully argued that to continue living in moral squalor is a far worse punishment than the death that has been ordered. The ultimate retribution isn't what society imagines it to be. There are hidden truths within the sentence.

Lingering in thought, Dwight and his aunt were overcome by a clear measure of relief when his mother suddenly announced, "I can't get anywhere hating that man." Shaking her head, she somberly added, "I was expecting him to be different." With a subdued look she regarded her sister before concluding, "I think the man who killed Jarod is dead."

Dwight and his aunt instantly regarded one another in the car's rear view mirror. Then Lorraine stated, "Count your blessings, Marie, that you found that out today. You could have gone to your grave without making that discovery."

Marie did not respond to her sister's comment, yet even though she didn't, Dwight, driven by an earnest desire to aid Lester in some way, was daring enough to ask, "Mother, does this mean you'd no longer object to my visiting Lester in jail to tutor him?"

Liberation from the bondage of hatred sets the captive free from a prison within themselves. To be delivered from that burden soothes the soul and suppresses the emotions. So it came to be that his mother told him with utmost believability, "You can tutor him if you want. Suddenly the thought of your doing so doesn't matter to me any more."

Dwight knew that the moment at hand was a deeply defining one, and not meant to be marred by any display of triumph. Even the slightest hint of zeal would be inappropriate. Humble and heart-felt appreciation was instead in order. That was the respectable way to conduct oneself. In fact, in his estimation, the change that had taken place on the part of his mother was actually sacred, for she had finally been reached by a gentler side of life. Therefore even though the mood of tomorrow might be one of enthusiasm, he had the wherewithal to fathom that today he should take great strides to cloak himself with virtual gratitude, which is why he simply stated, "Thank you, mother."

Quite befittingly, nothing more was said for the remainder of the ride home as all three of them briefly and intermittently cried for their own particular reasons.

CHAPTER 23

YANKEES, GO HOME!

It was as soon as the following Friday evening that Dwight began tutoring Lester at the Fulton jail, and although this was something which initially perplexed the police officers, they soon came to accept the way things were, to one degree or another anyway.

Dwight was notified that Judge Mackelin had arranged to have six months of Lester's sentence served in Fulton before his transfer to the state penitentiary. In the opinion of the man that was more than ample time to teach Lester the basics of reading and writing in preparation for his release to the outside world.

Two lessons a week were decided upon, and although Lester did not speak very much at the outset, Dwight foresaw the moment when he would. Then sure enough, during their fourth lesson, the man began to feel enough at ease in his presence to inquire how his mother was coping with the knowledge that her husband was dead.

"I know there's a change, a positive change, taking place within her," Dwight informed him, "because ever since that day in the courtroom she's been different... less angry, less harsh."

Though Lester was genuinely glad to hear the news, he felt so responsible for the woman's suffering that his speech was somewhat labored as he said, "I hope so." Allowing some time to pass, he confided, "There's something I've been meaning to ask you, but I've been afraid to, probably because I might not like your answer."

"There's no need to fret about that," Dwight told him, "because even if you don't like what I have to say, it'll be said without malice."

Satisfied that Dwight was to be believed, Lester took in a deep breath before inquiring, "I wanna know if ya think I was let off too easily for what I did?"

Without revealing the request he had made to Judge Mackelin, Dwight noted, "No, I don't think the sentence was too lenient. I think it was just right." While Lester beheld him in a combination of surprise and relief, Dwight felt compelled to add, "I'm interested in justice, Lester, not revenge. I must tell you, though, that I wouldn't have liked the ruling if your attitude had been the same as when you killed my father."

"And what would you have wanted my sentence to be back then?" Lester's curiosity prompted him to inquire.

Thinking about it for awhile, Dwight said with gravity, "It should come as no surprise to you that there's a number of people who would have wanted you put to death for what you did, but I don't agree with them." With additional contemplation, he continued, "I would have wanted you to serve a long jail sentence, but while you were doing so, I would have also wanted you to be taught how to read and write so that you'd be better prepared to find a place in the world if you ever walked out of that prison door." Regarding him most intensely, he stated with all the fervor he could muster within himself, "But woe to you if you were ever foolish enough to commit another crime against humanity. In fact if you did do that, I might be angry and disgusted enough to ask to lock your prison cell door myself and throw away the key." As he observed the man's wide-eyed reaction to his words, he brought to his attention, "You only have so many chances to get it right, Lester. There is a limit you know."

One could see that Lester was moved by Dwight's perspective on the matter, which is why he replied in a near whisper, "I respect your answer."

Feeling as though enough had been said for the time being, Dwight turned his attention to the lesson they were currently working on, a lesson which Lester was doing quite well at, given his strong desire to learn, given his heightened self-esteem, given his interest in his future, and yes, given his liking for his tutor.

* * *

Dwight appreciated the emotional support Scott lent him at the inquest. The eye contact they exchanged spoke a thousand words, so much so that even though they had not verbally communicated with one another on that day, they nonetheless knew where they stood in their relationship. It was known by way of a look. It was the look of friendship. .... And yet each of them wondered if theirs would be a relationship that would stand the tests of time, for so true it was that only a few short months ago neither one of them possessed an inkling that friendship was on the horizon for them. But in those days they had seen themselves to be so exceedingly different, whereas in these days they had discovered themselves to be so very much the same. Shared insecurities were at the root of their emotional bond. They could relate to one another so well in that area of their lives. Yet sadly, we sometimes lose sight of what's really important in the entire scheme of things, even going as far as to throw a budding friendship away. .... And it remained to be seen whether they would take that route.

* * *

With the arrival of warmer weather, the Willards once again began to frequent The Gulf for picnics; and Dwight and Jana, having always enjoyed these outings so much, went along with them whenever possible. Occasionally during these fun filled excursions Aunt Lorraine even took it upon herself to drive the short distance to the shoreline to pay everyone a brief visit. Ironically, though, it was during this period of time in which Dwight felt himself well on his way to becoming a secure individual, that he began to experience something unsettling, something which would highly test his faith and trust in God.

It was on a Sunday evening in early May, after having taken a relatively long ride in the countryside on Zuzueca, that the manifestation of his condition first presented itself. He was in the barn at the time and had already seen to the chickens' needs when he noticed in walking up to where Hazel stood at the corral's edge that her drinking bucket was empty.

"I bet you'd like some fresh water, wouldn't you?" he spoke up. Yet just as he bent over to pick up the pail, he grew dizzy and nearly fell over. ... "Gee, what's wrong with me?" he casually commented while standing upright as though what had just occurred was not all that serious. But no sooner did he say this than the dizziness abruptly became replaced by a surge of pain that was so sharp it caused him to involuntarily throw his hand to his head.

Forced to take a few moments to regain his faculties, Dwight soon felt stable enough to carry Hazel's bucket to the faucet and begin filling it, strongly sensing in doing so that he was on the verge of being thrust into an ordeal which would involve coming to terms with certain issues he wouldn't have the luxury of putting off until later in life.

* * *

As the weeks sped by, Dwight more and more frequently experienced attacks of dizziness, pain, and the nausea that eventually followed; yet even though this was so, he was uncomfortable with the notion of telling anyone about it; and these were his reasons why:

First of all, he knew that people had a tendency to worry about things which were beyond their control, and he didn't want any of that worry channeled around him. Secondly, he didn't want to listen to unsolicited advice concerning what he should do about the state of his health. And lastly, he knew that God could heal even the worst of afflictions, therefore revealing his condition to family and friends, or even a doctor for that matter, might be wholly unnecessary. Eventually, though, his symptoms became so severe that he felt compelled to tell Jana on the last day of the school year that he had not been feeling well as of late, for in view of the trusting nature of their relationship, he felt as though she of all people deserved to be filled in on what was taking place within his body.

"I thought you seemed different," she stated from where they were seated on the school's lawn at lunchtime. "Do you have any idea what's wrong?"

"Not exactly. It's a pain that I feel in my head, and it's getting worse, and happening more and more often."

With concern for his well-being, Jana declared, "You make it sound like you've been feeling that way for a long time!"

"Well, that depends on whether or not a month is a long time to you," he told her with an ease of speech she found difficult to comprehend.

"A month!" she exclaimed. "You shouldn't be so casual about this after a month!"

"But why not?" Dwight inquired. "Don't you think my faith should sustain me?" Apprehending that her uneasiness persisted, he felt moved to express, "Oh, I can see you're worried about me, Jana, and I appreciate that, but how is worrying going to do me any good?"

"That's not the point!" she firmly retaliated. "You should see a doctor now or your condition might worsen to the point where no one will be able to help you!" With an eventual return of calm insight, she stated with undying devotion, "You'll be hurting the people who love you the most if you sit by doing nothing."

"But I haven't been sitting by doing nothing," he counteracted. "I've prayed for strength." Yet in seeing that she remained unappeased, he soon stated, "Alright, I'll see a doctor if you want me to. But I'm not going to worry. I just want to know what's wrong with me."

* * *

In the kitchen shortly after arriving home from school, Dwight told his aunt about his failing health. Then he requested that she drive him into Fulton the following day to see a doctor.

"I don't think I should drive there myself," he explained. "If I got dizzy, it could cause an accident."

"Of course I'll take you there," the woman solemnly assured him. "Would you like me to make an appointment for you?"

"No, I've already made one," Dwight informed her. "I called from school today. It's for ten o'clock in the morning." Having no trouble whatsoever detecting the worried look on her face, he felt inclined to point out, "Aunt Lorraine, I know you're concerned about me, but whatever we find out tomorrow, I'll do my best to face it. I'm aware of what life can be like."

"I know you are," she stated with difficulty before turning her attention to the supper she was preparing, this seeming to be her only recourse from crying. Surely she wondered if he'd be forced to suffer over this, or whether he'd survive it at all. Yet she also wondered how his mother would cope with another emotionally-wrenching situation, for so true it was that the guilt-ridden in society find it especially distressing to live life when the ones they've scorned become afflicted. Therefore in her way of seeing things an apology on the part of her sister towards Dwight would go a long way in restoring good family relations to the extent that was humanly possible.

* * *

That night, while kneeling at his bedside, Dwight prayed that he would be able to cope with whatever was discovered at the doctor's office the following day. But this was not all he prayed for. No, he also prayed that God would aid his family and friends in accepting whatever was told them about the nature of his health, for he realized by way of the mounting severity of his symptoms that his condition was in physical terms quite serious.

When he arose the next morning after what turned out to be a fairly good night's sleep, he and his aunt ate breakfast before readying themselves to depart for Fulton. This sparked his mother's curiosity enough to compel her to ask them where they were headed so early in the day.

"Dwight's got a doctor's appointment," Lorraine informed her. "He hasn't been feeling well lately. We thought it best to wait until morning to tell you."

To verify that her outlook had changed since that day in the courtroom, Marie said with a discernible hint of unease as to how it would be accepted, "I'm sorry to hear that." Then she quickly recoiled from her remark and walked away, so greatly was she yet struggling with the admittance that she felt love toward her son, so greatly was she grappling with surrendering her former ways.

Regarding Dwight, his aunt easily saw in his eyes the satisfaction he felt in having been correct in his belief that his mother was capable of again fostering empathy.

In the driveway shortly thereafter, while walking toward the car, Dwight experienced such an intense attack of pain that he had to momentarily delay his advancement.

"Dwight!" Aunt Lorraine exclaimed while rushing to his side and grabbing hold of his arm. "Let me help you!"

"It'll pass. ... Don't worry," he found it a challenge to tell her as he waited for the discomfort to subside. "It just takes time."

"Oh, Dwight, I just know you'll get through this," she bravely tried to assure him even though her quivering voice betrayed the essence of her emotions, emotions which converged on being distraught.

"Ya, I know I will," Dwight acknowledged. "I'm just not sure whether it'll be through my death or my life." In saying this he meant that one way or another his suffering would come to an end.

Moments later, while heading in the direction of Fulton, neither Dwight nor his aunt were inclined to be any too communicative, for the seriousness of the situation at hand weighed heavily on their minds.

Parking on the main street and making their way into the waiting room of the general practitioner whom Dwight had made an appointment with, Aunt Lorraine greeted the receptionist and told her who they were.

"Oh, yes, the doctor will be with you shortly," she said without delay. "Please sit down and make yourself comfortable."

Thanking the woman, Aunt Lorraine and Dwight heeded her suggestion. Yet when Dwight began to feel nauseous, he found it impossible to relax; and his aunt, in noticing this discomfort within him, ached for him in a way that went beyond words.

Once inside the examining room, Dwight relayed to Dr. Leyland the symptoms he was experiencing, after which Dr. Leyland asked him to remove his clothing for a complete physical, including X-rays.

During the examination Dwight felt the presence of God within him, and he knew he was not alone. In fact he seemed to comprehend that it would only be through his own fault if the day ever dawned that he came to feel alone, for he had sought and acquired spiritual sustenance in the recent months of his life. And if his focus on God had upheld him in the past, then it would continue to do so in the future as long as he allowed it to be so.

When Dr. Leyland completed the examination and Dwight was again seated in the waiting room, his aunt inquired if he had been told what was ailing him.

"No, I wasn't told a thing," he apprised her, knowing that sometimes saying nothing says a lot.

A short time later, when the receptionist called Dwight back into Dr. Leyland's office, his aunt requested to accompany him there to hear whatever the doctor had to say.

"Yes, I'd like you to be with me," Dwight stated without reservation.

Moments later, in being confronted by the somber stare of Dr. Leyland, Dwight ascertained that the time had come for his faith to brace him for some very sobering news.

"This is my Aunt Lorraine," he was quick to impart. "I'd like her to hear whatever it is you have to tell me."

Briefly regarding her, Dr. Leyland nodded his head in compliance before forcing himself to address the crux of the matter by reporting, "What I found out wasn't very encouraging."

In an immediate rush of fortitude Dwight proclaimed, "I'm ready to hear it, no matter what it is."

In Dr. Leyland's way of seeing things it was irrelevant whether Dwight was prepared to hear the truth, because the stark truth was in need of being conveyed no matter what, which is why he said in a low pitched, grave tone of voice, "You've got a brain tumor."

"Oh, no!" Aunt Lorraine gasped in response to the doctor's cutting words. .... Yet in the midst of her reaction Dwight was so unshaken by this news that one was inclined to presume he was neither surprised nor intimidated by it.

"What can be done to help him!" the woman swiftly inquired in a burst of apprehension.

As Dr. Leyland observed Dwight's stable bearing, he stated, "I've seen this type of tumor before, so I know that if there's an operation, he may die, but if there isn't an operation, he'll surely die." When Dwight still did not exhibit any of the typical emotional responses, the man was moved to emphasize, "You do realize this is extremely serious, don't you, Dwight?"

Driven to at last say something, Dwight replied, "I understand that this seems serious to you, but how do you know I'll die without an operation?"

"Because as I've already told you, I've seen this type of tumor before," Dr. Leyland succinctly reminded him in defense of his medical judgment. "Of course you're free to get a second opinion from a specialist, but...."

"But what if the tumor were to suddenly shrink or even dissolve," Dwight suggested in all earnestness.

"It'd be wonderful if that were possible," the doctor stated, "but I know of no current treatment that can bring about such a cure."

"Well, I do," Dwight told him. In noticing the man's skepticism, he freely added, "I believe God can be the treatment. It's a proven fact."

"But I hardly think you can count on that for something this serious," Dr. Leyland retorted. "I'm afraid your only chance for survival is to have an operation as soon as possible. It really is all the hope I can offer you."

Clearly disappointed by the doctor's worldly outlook, Dwight sensed that it would be difficult, if not impossible, for him to find comfort in his care. But it went beyond that, for in recent days he had been swept by an inspiration to rely on the spiritual realm; and so, with absolute certainty, he felt encouraged to say, "I'm not going to have an operation by you or anyone else. If my time to die is at hand, then I'll die, but if it isn't, then God will rescue me from my affliction. It's as simple as saying, 'Your will be done.'"

"But Dwight, aren't you making a hasty decision?" Aunt Lorraine earnestly intervened in her reluctance to disregard a doctor's advice.

"But I'm not making a hasty decision at all, Aunt Lorraine," Dwight aimed to convince her. "I've anticipated this moment and given it a lot of thought, and my decision is based on that."

"Well then you must feel God can work through Dr. Leyland to cure you," she anxiously pressed on in her dread over the thought of losing him.

"Yes, I believe that's possible," Dwight was willing to admit. "But so often people think a cure can never be had without medical treatment, and I find myself wondering what they think faith involves. Don't they believe God can directly intervene on a person's behalf?" Gazing at Dr. Leyland at this time, he matter of factly added, "I'm not against doctors, and I do know they're needed and have their place in the world, but as for me, I'll be cured directly by God this time around or not at all." Getting up, he added with surety, "I won't be in need of your services any longer."

"Start thinking realistically!" Dr. Leyland strongly objected. "You're a sixteen year old boy signing his death certificate, and that's too young to die!"

With a great deal of composure Dwight replied most pointedly, "And would my death really be so tragic if I left this world knowing a better life awaits me?" In his faith-filled frame of mind he slowly turned to leave, yet not before stopping short to draw to the man's attention, "As I was walking in a cemetery one day I saw many tombstones of people who had died young. I'll have you know it's not about my being sixteen, Dr. Leyland. My age isn't really that relevant." At the articulation of that, he left the room without waiting for his aunt to join him.

It was easy to see that Dr. Leyland remained non-receptive to the decision Dwight had made.

"Try to talk some sense into him!" he advised his aunt as she, too, rose to leave. "He's being unreasonable!" A combination of anger and disgust was at the root of his emotions.

Pondering his request, Lorraine said with an obvious change of heart, "You can call it what you may, but if you're so right, then why do I find myself admiring him so much?" Briefly holding the man under her scrutiny, she slowly exited the room in a resigned frame of mind.

Still believing Dwight and his aunt to be guilty of misplaced priorities, an incensed Dr. Leyland shook his head in the certainty that a teenage boy was about to die. And yet even though he considered this to be a foregone conclusion, why did he, too, detect something admirable about the boy's outlook? Rest assured that a part of him wanted to understand why this was so. But he, in his worldliness, was not of a persuasion to fathom that the reason had already been revealed to him just moments ago.

* * *

As the three boys were strolling down the main street of downtown Fulton, they happened to see a car with the license plate of a northern state pull over to the side of the road.

Inside the car sat a man and his wife. They were two individuals new to the area who were unable to locate the address of the people they had journeyed to see; and so, in noticing the three boys nearing their vehicle, they decided to ask them for directions. Yet before they were able to make any attempt whatsoever to do so, they heard one of the boys shout, "Yankees, go home!" And if that wasn't bad enough, as soon as he had finished doing so, the other two boys shouted the same sarcastic remark.

If there be any measure of truth to the belief that the timing of things transcends coincidence, then Dwight's departure from Dr. Leyland's office provided proof of it, for as it so happened, he and his aunt witnessed the rude behavior on the part of the boys while making their way down the sidewalk toward their own car, which happened to be parked directly in front of the out-of-state vehicle.

In the course of his short life thus far, Dwight had heard other biased, derogatory statements made against people, statements which he had for the most part kept silent about because of his lack of assertiveness to get involved. But that was then and this was now. Yet to put it in clear perspective, there was more behind his willingness to get involved than his increased self-assurance. For one thing, if he was going to die in the near future, then he wanted to say whatever he felt should be said while he still had the time and the ability; and secondly, he had read quite a bit about the Civil War, so he knew that there had been transgressions committed by both the North and the South. The South had greatly wronged a people by enslaving them, whereas the Northern army, going far beyond targeting instruments of war, had ravaged and pillaged

Southern homes in its march across it, particularly during the close of the war. Then, in the immediate aftermath of reconstruction, many greedy, selfish Northerners persecuted Southerners by unjustly confiscating their property, which was a blatant denial of their constitutional rights. This only served to add fuel to the fire of resentment, thereby widening the gap between the North and the South even further. Keenly Dwight recognized the hypocrisy of allowing the Southern people to be treated that way after having fought a war that was aimed at ending oppression. Certainly there was solid proof that what had been preached on the part of the North had not been widely put into practice. And yet even though the mistakes of the past had contributed to present-day strains, society at large was expected to put forth an honest effort to end the cycle of bigotry between the North and the South for the sake of all concerned. Hence, in a determined effort to take a step in that direction right here and now, Dwight deliberately placed himself in the path of the oncoming boys to delay their advancement. Then, as all three of them were gaping at him, he said in a voice that almost seemed to reverberate, "Why did you speak to them that way!" Never had his stare been quite so piercing.

At first the three boys merely continued to observe him. ... But then, as a rush of scorn took hold of their emotions in response to his daring intervention, one of the boys harshly told him in defense, "Because they're Yankees! We don't like Yankees!"

Initially Dwight was so repulsed by the boy's statement that all he could seem to do was shake his head and close his eyes in a fit of annoyance. Without question he felt tempted to cast aside sound advice and allow his emotions to get the better of him. Yet he somehow managed to formulate his thoughts enough to say, "It's a sad state of affairs when a war that was fought to make the country better ends up with comments like that being made! Did all of those people die in vain!" When none of boys said anything in response to his bold reprimand, he wasted no time in adding, "Don't you think it's about time for friendly relations to replace the bitter ones?"

Having recognized Dwight from school, the boys knew he was a Southerner. But they also knew from what they remembered of him that he had challenged people before with his words of advice.

Therefore even though they primarily took it upon themselves to remain defiant, they eventually became so intimidated for their lack of justification in what they had done that they abruptly brushed past him down the sidewalk. It was then, in his anger and humiliation for having been put on the spot, that the boy who had instigated the entire incident turned to call him a traitor. Of interest to note, however, was that even though Dwight's reprimand had embarrassed him, he actually respected his position so greatly that all he really wanted was to escape the situation at hand as quickly as possible without being seen as cowardly. Therefore even though Dwight had succeeded in getting him to feel ashamed regarding his poor conduct, he feared being seen as weak and noncommittal to the stand he had endorsed only moments ago.

Dwight had absolutely no desire to respond to the boy's rash comment, for he was aware of the methods resorted to whenever people felt cornered. Yes, he knew that in situations such as this they very often reduced themselves to name calling in a vain and desperate attempt to support their adverse views. And why was this so? In his way of seeing things it was because sound principles ran contrary to their claimed beliefs, wherefore all they had left as a means of defending their actions was irrational reasoning.

Making his way to the out-of-state vehicle, Dwight bent over to say to the couple within it, "I'm sorry for what happened. It should never have."

"We heard what you told them," the woman spoke up without delay. "It was reassuring." As Dwight looked at her in modest response, the man conveyed, "We were going to ask those boys for directions. We're trying to find Cypress Street. We've got friends who live there."

"Oh, I know where that is," Dwight was quick to inform him, for it was not very far from the Willards' residence. In pointing the way, the man thanked him and stated, "If you ever get to Pennsylvania, pay us a visit. I like the way you think." Having said that, he notified him of his and his wife's identity, in addition to the name of the small Pennsylvania town from which they had come.

Was the invitation indicative of something, being extended as it was following a prognosis of impending death from a doctor? In the timing of it all Dwight saw a message in the making, so much so that he gratefully replied, "I just may be at your doorstep some day. If you represent the hospitality of the people of Pennsylvania, I know I should like to go there. Besides, I've heard it said that Pennsylvania is most beautiful, and I do like to look at such land." The calm, free-flowing manner in which he said this carried the distinctive essence of his view of things.

With amicable adieus having been sufficiently exchanged, the couple warmly smiled and waved good-bye before resuming to drive onward, all of this taking place as Aunt Lorraine stood in loving admiration of a boy's incentive to be so concerned about the quality of other people's lives despite what he had just found out about his own.

* * *

When Dwight and his aunt arrived home, they found his mother seated at the kitchen table, and although she wouldn't admit she'd been awaiting their return, it was obvious she desired to be told what had been discovered at the doctor's office.

Feeling fatigued, Dwight was quick to excuse himself to the privacy of his room. Kneeling at his bed, he prayed for the strength to endure his plight, while in the meantime his aunt related to his mother all that had happened in Fulton.

In learning of Dr. Leyland's prognosis for her son, Marie experienced the same motherly concern she felt earlier in the day.

"I never considered that he might die before me," she made the confession. As the thought of that possibility sank in, she became inclined to query, "Will my feeling badly about life ever end, Lorraine?" Certainly her statement reflected an underlying admission, an awareness of the person she could and should have been, yet refused to be.

"Yes, Marie, it'll end, but your choices will determine just when." As Marie swung her gaze upon her in response to a point well made, she added with gentle urging, "Please come to terms with your past for the sake of everyone."

"But I don't think I can," Marie voiced the claim in harsh

acceptance, as though she believed herself to be hopelessly in a position of having no choice in the matter. "Too much has happened for the conclusion to be a good one for me."

Rising from the table, Lorraine stated, "Don't you know you wouldn't be alone in your efforts?"

Marie understood the message her sister was aiming to get across to her, which is why she countered with grave undertones, "I've forsaken God for so long I don't even feel justified to seek his help any more."

"I should think your admittance of having forsaken God would lead you to realize you're in need of God," Lorraine wisely emphasized. "And it's still not too late to do something about that." After a brief period of deliberation, she was of an inspiration to add, "I'm going to my room to pray for Dwight now. After all, time is of the essence." Slowly proceeding to walk away, she felt the great need to halt her departure to say, "I hope you realize that despite everything, Dwight still loves you so."

When Lorraine was out of sight, Marie began to cry over circumstances as they turned out to be. Remorse was so thoroughly hers to be had, a remorse of the beckoning heart.

"I have to change the direction of my life," she poignantly whispered above a sob. "I simply must do something." Laying her head on crossed arms, she lamented Dwight's life threatening condition. ... And if the truth be known, she found herself witnessing a considerable amount of empathy for her son. ... And the truth was known.

* * *

When Jana called Dwight that afternoon and found out about his decision not to have an operation, she began to fear for his life.

"But Dwight... I don't want you to die," she as a result stammered. "I really wish you'd reconsider this."

"But what makes you so certain I'll die without an operation?" Dwight was quick to ask. "I think you're jumping to conclusions, don't you?"

"Maybe so... but.. well, the doctor knows best and...."

"Jana!" he suddenly exclaimed in such an unusually stern

manner that she became startled. Then, after a rather long pause in which he organized his thoughts, he earnestly added, "Jana, I'm very appreciative of all you've done for me, and I know you're my friend, but if you're finding it hard to support me in my decision, then maybe it'd be for the best if we didn't see each other for a while. I've got enough to contend with right now. I'm not going to argue with you or anyone else on top of that." As she became appalled by what he had dared to suggest, he was hasty to convey, "I've got to go now. Bye." And before she could even respond, he hung up the phone on her.

Walking up the stairs, Dwight realized how little people really understood or accepted him for what he was, for even Jana found it difficult to do so at times.

Hearing the phone ring as he reached the landing, he suspected the caller was Jana, so he waited for his aunt to answer it. Then, when the woman was peering up at him to confirm his expectations, he wasted no time in stipulating, "Tell her to call back some other time. She needs to do some serious thinking, maybe even soul-searching. I do, too." Somberly walking away, he comprehended how challenging it could be to retain a supportive relationship with someone when opinions varied as to what course of action should be taken in a given situation.

Imparting Dwight's message, Lorraine sympathetically stated, "I overheard some of the things he said to you, Jana. Please try to accept his decision. I have, and I was upset over it, too, in the beginning."

"I'll try," Jana sobbed in her emotional distress, "but it won't be easy. You see I don't want to lose him. Maybe I love him too much."

"No, not too much, my dear," Lorraine compassionately told her. "It's just that you must respect his wishes. We must respect his wishes. If his time to die is at hand, then we have to accept that, or it'll only make it all the harder on all of us, including Dwight."

Moments later, in hanging up the telephone, Jana began to cry profusely, wishing as she did so that she was better prepared to accept what she didn't want to. She didn't seem to comprehend that Dwight's affliction was an opportunity for her to enhance her own standing with God by determining who was most precious to her, and hopefully concluding that the right choice really is always God.

In other words, it was extremely important that she reach the realization that she could lead a very satisfying life without Dwight's future involvement in it if that was the way it had to be. Stated another way, she could learn to do well in life without Dwight, but not without God. ... Yet surely, quite understandably, one is reluctant to think about the untimely death of a much cherished friend; the comfort, the rapport that one knows in socializing with one such as this being the valuable find that it is. Coming to terms with even that really can and does happen, though, for those of us who are of a constitution that is broad and sweeping enough to absorb the loss.

* * *

The emotions experienced during the days of Dwight's tribulation ended up being felt by Lester Madaylion, too, for when Dwight visited him in jail to tell him that they would have to discontinue their lessons because of the physical discomfort he too often felt lately, Lester grew both saddened and disappointed by the news.

"What's wrong with you anyway?" he rather tentatively inquired as though he feared the answer.

"I've got a brain tumor... and I may die. It's all up to God now," Dwight notified him with the inner strength he had come to know. "I didn't tell you this before because I wasn't sure what was wrong with me." Disregarding the worried look on the man's face, he felt disposed to say, "Your reading's become good enough for you to improve on your own, though." With previously prepared thought, he wasted no time in adding, "My father used to tell me to expand my vocabulary so that I'd be better at expressing myself. He said that it'd help me in life, and he was right. So Lester, force yourself to read, and look up the definition of words you don't know. Keep a dictionary close to you, but mostly keep God close to your heart. Learn from your mistakes so that you don't repeat them." .... Suddenly sensing that he was on the verge of being overcome by a wave of nausea, he stood up and concluded in rather labored words, "I'd like to stay longer... but I can't. .... You take care of yourself, ya hear. God willing, we'll see each other again some day." As he slowly began to depart in humble acceptance of circumstances as they stood, Lester, in the sober realization that he might never again have the opportunity to do so, rose to the occasion by exclaiming, "I love you, Dwight!"

Stopping in his tracks, Dwight closed his eyes tightly as he felt tears build up within them. Then, without turning to face Lester directly, he stated in full affirmation, "Yes, I know you do. I've known for a while now... but thanks for saying it, hey. ... I love you, too."

Seated alone, a grief-stricken man became profoundly aware of the extent of his attachment to the son of the man whom he had killed. Throwing his hands to his face then, he began to bitterly weep, hoping and praying as he did so that the God he had forsaken for such a long time would mercifully intervene on Dwight's behalf and allow him to live.

* * *

It had taken Jana a few days to come to terms with Dwight's decision not to have an operation.

Calling him up from the foyer of her home and divulging all progress made in that regard, she further stated, "I'm asking you to forgive me, Dwight. I know I didn't respect your feelings enough, and that's not being a very supportive friend."

"Forgiving you comes easy, because I know you have my best interest at heart," Dwight would only say before letting the topic come to rest. "I'd like to see you today," he told her then. "I'd like to spend the day together. I have to admit I wanted to call you more than once since we last talked, but I decided we both needed our space."

"I understand," Jana assented in memory of that conversation. "And yes, I'd like to spend the day with you, too. In fact there probably isn't anything you could have said or done to keep me away," she so dramatically added that he was inspired to take on laughter. Looking at the clock that hung in the foyer, she said, "I've got to run an errand for my mother first, though, but I'll be there in about an hour and a half."

"Alright, I'll be waiting for you," Dwight responded.

"And Dwight."

"Yes."

"I want you to know I've begun to examine my spiritual life."

"I'm glad for you," he congratulated her. "That makes me feel you'll be able to accept whatever happens. ... Tell everyone I said hello. I haven't seen them in a while."

"I shall," she assured him. "They send their love."

"And Jana, let's not be sad while we're together today," he urged her. "We can do better than that."

Jana doubted whether she'd be able to live up to that standard, which is why she merely stated, "I'll try." Suddenly noticing that Alice was gesturing to speak to him, she informed him of this before turning the phone over to the woman.

"I's ben pray'n fer ya, mist'r Dwight," Alice was quick to bring to his attention. "I jus wanted ya ta know dat."

"Thanks, Alice," he replied. "Prayer really can help. Perhaps I'll even be tasting some of your fine cooking again, or delivering that flower you once said you wanted."

Smiling to herself in recollection of that day, Alice told him, "I'll look forward ta dat."

"And Alice," Dwight now stated with a sudden tone of solemnity. "I want to thank you for making me feel welcome whenever I went over there for visits. A person remembers those things, especially when they're taking stock of their life."

Dwelling for only a moment or two on his acknowledgment, Alice professed, "It was easy, Mist'r Dwight. It's done easy when ya like someone." In the heartfelt affection she felt for him, she suspected she might break down in tears at any given moment, which is why she forced herself to cut the conversation short by saying, "Ya take care a yerself, ya hear."

"I will," Dwight sought to appease her. "Good-bye."

Moments later, in hanging up their respective phones, each of them felt the pleasant sensation that a genuine concern for another human being brings to a person's heart. ... Therefore undoubtedly it could be maintained they cared about one another as people without even the slightest regard for skin color or social standing.

* * *

When the people of the area found out about Dwight's malady, they sought to console him as best they could, none of them seeming to understand the extent to which he had accepted his plight. Yet the end of a journey can sometimes be the most difficult part of the road that's traveled, often testing one's fortitude in no uncertain terms. And so whenever anyone suggested or insinuated that he should fight for his life with modern medicine and the hope that an operation held to offer him, it only served to call into question his spiritual resolve. The people who brought this upon him did not seem to realize what they were doing to him, so much so that he wondered at times if he could ever get them to apprehend that his reason for not having an operation was based on much more than the freedom of choice they imagined it to be.

So as time marched onward, it came to be on a warm afternoon in the middle of July, as he was coming out of the barn, that Dwight happened to catch sight of Scott pulling into the driveway in his father's car.

Warmly receptive would best describe the greeting Scott received from Dwight as he stepped out of the vehicle.

"How have you been anyway?" Dwight subsequently inquired.

"I'm doing fine," Scott said while slamming the car door shut. Immediately noticing Dwight's downgraded appearance since last seeing him, he was quick to add, "I heard about you, though, and I wanted to let you know how sorry I am. I hope you get well soon."

"Thanks, Scott, that means a lot to me," Dwight reacted in a way that led Scott to believe his mental health was as vibrant as ever.

"I thought you might like to take a ride to The Gulf," Scott proposed at this time. "That is if you're up to it."

"Alright, I think I'd like that," Dwight consented. "I'm feeling good at the moment. First I had better tell my family where I'm going, though. I'll be right back."

Scott sympathized with Dwight as he watched him walk into the house, so much so that he said a prayer on his behalf right there and then.

A short time later, while the two of them strolled along the beach after having had a rather conversational ride there, Scott broke the silence that had in the meantime ensued by asking, "Dwight, do you ever find yourself afraid to die?"

Gathering his thoughts, Dwight told him, "I've heard it said that fearing death is quite common, but fear, no, it's not fear I have. It's actually something I've yet to discover, a mystery of some sorts. It's interesting because even though I'd like to be cured of what ails me to spend more time with people, sometimes I feel like I don't even belong in this world. I just don't seem to fit in too well." Stopping now, he gazed out to sea in a deep sense of awareness, as though in some respects he had just made an important discovery about himself. Poignantly he then concluded, "Odd, isn't it, to feel such opposing things. Maybe I shouldn't even be admitting it to you." And with that he grew silent.

"I won't tell anyone if you don't want me to," Scott solemnly declared.

Looking at him, Dwight saw in his eyes the empathy he felt for him, which encouraged him to say, "I'm glad we're on the road to friendship, Scott."

"So am I," he acknowledged with held-back tears, in the aftermath of which they drew together and hugged in the non-suggestive, childlike innocence God so loves to see within people. Could that be why, in walking along the shoreline once again, they owned the realization that they existed in a place in time where pretense bore no hold on them whatsoever?

* * *

When Lorraine drove into Fulton to do some grocery shopping one Saturday morning, she and Dr. Leyland found themselves standing face to face to one another in the store's parking lot.

Recognizing each other immediately, Dr. Leyland was the first one to say hello. Then, after placing within his car the two bags of groceries he was carrying, he said while standing upright, "It appears we have the same thing in mind today." In seeing Lorraine nod her head and smile, he felt free to inquire how Dwight was getting along as of late.

"He has his difficult days, and I have the feeling they're getting worse," she was honest enough to admit. "But he doesn't complain. In fact his endurance rather astounds me."

"I'm still upset over him," Dr. Leyland nonetheless stated. "For a young person to be so accepting of death when the one hope to save their life is through an operation, well...." Shaking his head disapprovingly, he boldly alleged, "I think it's downright irresponsible."

"Irresponsible?" Lorraine took issue with him. "I should think coming to terms with one's mortality is a sign of responsible thinking. It's not often one sees that in someone so young. I would even go as far as to say his outlook is quite enviable. He's not bitter, not forlorn, and not afraid to die."

"But why give up the years that could be?" the man persisted.

"Dwight is more interested in the quality of his life than the quantity of his years," she was swift to point out. "I think you should know he's had his share of difficulties, which has left him very focused on what's really important in life. Feeling at peace within himself matters far more to him than a cure for a disease."

"Even if it means a sure death?" he inquired with an incredulous overtone.

"Yes, in his case even then," she firmly insisted. "Though I don't think he'd state it quite that way, because he believes with God all things are possible."

In his refusal to surrender his position, Dr. Leyland fervidly told her, "Well, if he were my nephew I'd insist he have an operation!"

"You haven't heard a word I've said, have you?" Lorraine admonished him in fast approaching exasperation. Emphatically she then added, "There's a great deal to be said about respecting someone's personal choice to receive treatment or not. If we don't give people that much, then we aren't really respecting their lives. I for one would miss that boy very much if he died, yet I still intend to support him in his decision, because he needs that now more than ever." Still detecting prevailing disapproval on the part of the man, she felt inclined to additionally say, "I'm not going to add to his difficulties on top of everything else he's had to endure. In my way of seeing things I'd be lacking in sensitivity if I were to do that." Feeling as though enough had been said on the topic, she quickly continued before he could voice any further protest, "I really must get to my shopping now. Dwight's awaiting my return with one of his favorite foods." Nodding her head, she commenced to walk away, not realizing in doing so that a troubled boy had overheard her entire conversation with Dr. Leyland from where he sat in a car only a few feet away. Thus the timing of her encounter with the man held more significance than she could ever have imagined, for born of remorse there was an increase in moral consciousness in America on this day. And as it so happened, that moral consciousness had arisen within a boy named Carl.

CHAPTER 24

I'D BE DYING A VIRGIN

D wight felt the great need to be more intimately in touch with God as the days drifted by.

Taking long, reflective walks, he endured the bouts of pain he had come to expect. Yet even though he was able to persevere through his discomfort, by worldly standards it appeared as though he would not be recovering from what ailed him.

Leaning on the fence one day as he watched Hazel and Zuzueca grazing in the open pasture, he was thrust into such a deep state of thought that he did not even notice his Aunt Lorraine approaching from his right.

"Care to talk about it?" she spoke up when she was standing beside him.

Turning to regard her, Dwight softly smiled and said, "I didn't think it was that obvious." In recognizing the extent of her concern for him, he eventually added, "I was just wondering if I'll ever set foot on the soil of Pennsylvania."

Quite aware of what he meant by that, Aunt Lorraine told him, "Yes, I've wondered about that myself from time to time." Then, despite a rather long interlude in which she sensed his propensity to be uncommunicative, she informed him that she had seen Dr. Leyland a few days earlier at the grocery store.

"And what did he have to say this time around?" Dwight somberly asked.

"He wanted to know how you're doing," she confided.

"And what did you tell him?"

"The truth as I saw it, and he didn't like hearing it, because I stood up for you concerning the decision you've made."

Dwight's manner of looking at her confirmed his appreciation.

"You're an understanding person whose support means a lot to me." As she warmly beheld him, he went on to say, "I wish Dr. Leyland would accept things for what they are. He was so arrogant in his office that day. I can't help but feel he resents me because I chose to rely on God rather than him."

"And yet despite everything I think he means well deep down," she saw fit to lay claim. "Because to him death is synonymous to defeat when someone as young as you dies. He's probably conditioned himself to think that way over the years."

"Him and many others," Dwight staidly affirmed. "But it's really a matter of the way we choose to look at things, isn't it, because even though I have a desire to live, it's tempered by my faith in a better life beyond this one." Taking a few moments to examine his thoughts, he pensively added, "I have the feeling I've got to be willing to lose my life to acquire it, to surrender it to have it. ... Oh, I know what some people are saying, 'He doesn't value his life enough.' But they're wrong, Aunt Lorraine. I value it much more than they realize, and at times the thought of dying so young does make me feel sad."

"I wish you peace of mind," she told him in the near onset of tears. "It takes a determined heart to follow a course of action that's different from what's expected. People often take issue with that, even at times taking it personally."

"I know," he conceded. "It's as though they think the same choice should be made by everyone. And yet I've made a medical decision that applies strictly to me at this stage in my life." By saying this he meant that if he were to survive his affliction, the day could very well dawn in future years when he would choose to be treated by a doctor for whatever ailed him.

Nodding her head, his aunt stated, "That's a point well taken, for I must admit, if God cures you of this, it'll serve as a testimonial to Dr. Leyland, and others, too, of the possibilities that exist."

"And if I die, I'll have deliverance through that," Dwight noted. "But I must say I don't want to linger for weeks on end hooked up to feeding tubes, or other forms of life support. I didn't come into this world that way, and I don't think God expects me to leave it that way either." Pausing momentarily, he was prone to add, "A little while ago I was thinking about a day in school when I over-heard some boys saying something."

"And what was that?" his aunt inquired with ongoing interest.

With the memory of that day clearly etched in his mind, Dwight told her, "They were talking about sex and frowning upon being a virgin, as though it wasn't a desirable thing, as though a person should make every effort to put an end to their virginity. They spoke as though being a virgin was something to be ashamed of."

"It is a world of the flesh," she replied, "but that doesn't mean you have to think as they do, even though it is an easy trap to fall into. ..... I think you already knew that, though, didn't you?" she stated more than asked.

"Yes," he acknowledged. "It's just that in thinking of what they said, I was reminded that if I die now, I'd be dying a virgin."

"And is there really anything else God expects you to be?" she reasoned quite succinctly.

"I've asked myself that very question, and I can honestly say no, there isn't." With clear understanding he cast his eyes upon her.

Though she was impressed by his outlook, Aunt Lorraine knew that he was not immune from going astray. His knowledge of the ways of the world had served him well, however, for he was not as naive as people imagined him to be. He so seemed to have a firm grasp of what he was up against, which is a strength, not a weak-ness, in the world as we know it.

* * *

Dwight believed that whenever anyone was given a gift, they were not bound to it. In other words there was no requirement that the recipient of that gift use it or keep it. So in the spirit of that belief, when he decided to sever his hold on the past, he took it upon himself to place the conch back where Sandy had found it months ago.

Watching the ocean reclaim the former keepsake, he knew that he had done the right thing in releasing it. The return of the shell to the sea was symbolic of freedom. Sandy was free, and one way or another he, too, was going to be set free. To the best of his ability the things of this world were to have as little hold on him as possible as he prepared himself for whatever was in store for him.

* * *

Marie continued to doubt her ability to implement a healthy and lasting change in her life. Could the past really be put behind her? She asked herself that very question on more than one occasion. Certainly she was reluctant to let the love flow in as she had in bygone years. Restructuring her outlook was not going to come easy for her, even though she recognized the need for such an occurrence to take place. ... Yet she had a major dilemma in that time seemed to be running out for her where her relationship with her son was concerned. Hurdles were in need of being cleared. And clearing those hurdles would require a contrite heart.

As for Dwight, he could see that his mother was in the midst of an ongoing struggle. By her own free will she had to decide which path she was going to follow in life. .... So take heed, for comfort is possible for they who realize the supreme reward life has to offer, the solace and saving grace of a loving God.

* * *

Dwight knew that God is often forsaken when adversity comes our way. We even at times find ourselves placing qualifications and limitations on what we're willing to deal with. Our faith and trust are not always what they should be. .... And yet he at times cried passionately in the emotionally-wrenching tug-of-war he was in the midst of, hoping and praying as he did so that old resentments would be kept at bay, never again to surface as a driving force in his life.

* * *

With tensions in the Enhart household having been lifted, the atmosphere became much more conducive to relaxation. But what really pleased both Dwight and his Aunt Lorraine for the positive change, the turnaround that it signified, was when his mother decided to attend church with them the following Sunday morning.

From a physical standpoint Dwight did not feel well on this day. Yet in spite of it, he decided to attend church anyway, so determined was he to persevere for as long as he was able to do so. Sincere as his wish was, though, not to attract unwanted attention, once he arrived at church, they who had come to know him well noticed his downgraded appearance.

Seated in one of the pews with Jana, his mother, and aunt, Dwight listened as Preacher James spoke of that which pertained to wholesome living, namely Jesus Christ and the wonderful example he had set forth for the world to live by. Yet it wasn't until he was being stared at by the minister that he began to sense he was on the threshold of witnessing a profound occurrence in his life, one which would cast a firsthand knowledge on the depth of God's mercy. Interestingly, the preacher directed his sermon next to the topic of adversity.

"Some people seem to think it's the people without hardship who have it the best, but I say onto you that it's the people who face life's many hardships with faith and trust in God who are truly well off. ... Please don't fail in that regard, I beseech you. Nurture a positive outlook. Learn to be patient."

When the service was over and Dwight was outside the church, he quickly caught sight of the heavy hearts in his midst, given the manner in which glances were being cast his way. Both friends and acquaintances seemed to be speaking an unspoken farewell, as though his days amongst them were surely few in number. How little people's faith really could be, he thought, for even though God had created the world, a miracle was often dismissed from the realm of possibilities. ... And now suddenly, in response to his faith filled mind set, he once more felt that he was on the verge of experiencing an eventful occurrence in his life.

Looking at Mrs. Willard at this time, Dwight at long last saw within someone the belief that he could be healed of what ailed him.

"I'll be seeing you around, Dwight," she consequently told him with tender regard. "Our picnics await you."

Smiling effortlessly, Dwight turned and walked away with Jana following close behind.

"You look so pale today, Dwight," she made it a point to tell him when they had reached the car. "I'd like to pay you a visit later to check in on you."

"Why!" he impulsively snapped. "Are you wondering if it might be your last chance to say good-bye!"

Following a rather lengthy pause in which Dwight's mother and aunt in the meantime arrived on the scene, Jana had to admit, "Maybe that is a part of it, but is that really so bad?" The hurt in her eyes could not be concealed from him.

Eventually regretting having been so abrupt with her, Dwight ended up saying, "No, I suppose not. I'm sorry, Jana. I guess I'm tired and my patience is running thin." As an expression of grave significance overcame his features, he was prompted to tell her, "I'd like to spend the day with you, but I can't. I have the feeling I should be alone instead."

"Are you feeling that poorly?"

"Yes," he confided as his mother and aunt listened from the front seat of the vehicle. "But that's not the main reason I need to be alone."

"Well then what is?" she intently asked of him.

At first Dwight was at a loss for words, because he didn't understand why he had said what he had.

"I... I've got to spend the day in prayer," he ultimately told her in a near whisper, as though he had just received a mandate from God. Quite ardently he therefore exclaimed, "Yes, I must pray!" Yet as he bent over to get into the car, he was stricken by such an intense surge of pain that he could not prevent himself from crying out in agony.

Unable to endure Dwight's suffering, Jana looked grievously away. When he was sitting in the back seat of the car, she, in her overflowing compassion, found it difficult to convey, "I'll pray today, too, Dwight, for you." In her anguish she then darted off while beginning to bitterly weep.

Dwight was not able to dwell on Jana's departure. All he could think about at this stage, and all he really wanted, was to feel close to God in the privacy of his room. That was his burning desire.

"Dwight, maybe we should take you to the hospital?" his aunt recommended while looking upon his ashen countenance. "It's tearing me apart to see you this way."

"Ya, I know... and I'm sorry about that, but please take me home anyway," he softly requested while laying his head back. Then, as tears began to well up in his eyes, he stated in a strained voice, "I just wanna go home!"

Regarding her sister, Lorraine knew the time had come for total support of Dwight's wishes without question. No more suggestions as to what course of action he should follow, no more unsolicited advice, only support without question.

Heading home, Dwight took the opportunity to regain his faculties in the hope that it'd enable him to enter the house without difficulty. When they parked in the driveway, he initially was able to do so; but then, in another attack of pain, he leaned against the wall near the entrance to the dining room to support himself. While waiting for his discomfort to subside, he was inspired to say to the two women behind him, "I... can't be interrupted by anyone today. It's... very important." Unsteadily edging his way to the stairwell, he climbed it to his room and fell to his knees at his bedside. Once there, he did that which he felt so strongly inspired to do. He prayed, and not for only a minute or two. He did it for an hour before placing his head on his bed and losing consciousness. ... Then, upon suddenly being awoken and attempting to rise, he was subjected to the worst blast of pain he ever experienced in his entire life. It was in fact so extreme that he fell to the floor and cringed in utter and abject misery.

Driven to the point of crying uncontrollably, Dwight ultimately exclaimed in a burst of great despair, "Oh, God, let me die or cure me, but don't let me go on like this! I just can't take it any more!"

Was it because he knew God was there for him? Was it because he had passed an important test? Whatever be the case, who but God himself can know or understand the complete reasoning, the deeply profound variables, for divine intervention? Yet in seeing fit to grant Dwight's request, how would it be carried out? Would it be by manner of his death or his life, for surely either outcome represented deliverance from the ravages he was longing to be set free from? Either result would thereby be merciful.

Allow it to be emphasized at this time that there was a wonderful place awaiting Dwight, a place free of harshness where time holds no purpose. That place was not about to go away. It was there for him now as it would be there for him later. Physical death is not the defeat it's often imagined to be. Yet can victory be found in a physical cure? Certainly so, if the recipient of the cure knows who to thank and is enriched by the experience. Was Dwight a worthy prospect? Did he know the true value of that which could be gained? In other words would he be profoundly grateful of a physical cure while knowing there was something far better to be had in the life beyond this one? ..... The verdict was in. The moment was at hand. And here is the decision God made: It was to allow Dwight to spend more time upon the earth as a testimonial to others. And though it be true that a healing was not the best of what was available in terms of zones of comfort, it was the choice God made for Dwight. Yet was it also possible God desired Dwight be given the opportunity to enjoy the good things life had to offer, particularly now that he had acquired a firm grasp of how one should live, really live, to reap the most from their worldly experience? One could not help but wonder.

In a flash of time the state of our lives can take on a changed dimension, for suddenly on the wings of love and compassion Dwight felt the healing power of God descend upon him and cloak him with such virtual tranquility that he was induced to stop crying. Eventually rising to his knees, he witnessed a further decline of pain to the point where it almost completely left him; and he realized that he was well on his way to being healed. ... Then quite instantaneously, in a most deep and intimate of ways, he was compelled to lie down on his bed. Yes, even now it seemed as though God desired something of him. Hence, without delay, he did that which he felt so strongly directed to do, staying there for the remainder of the afternoon into the early evening, seven hours in total. ... And then he was completely healed of his affliction.

Inspired to get up from the bed, Dwight stepped in front of his mirror and saw that he was beaming with health, a health which was even better than before his illness had stricken him, a health which encouraged him to smile as he realized that he was hungry, really hungry, for food.

"I knew all along you could do this!" he found it befitting to say while looking upward. "I just wasn't sure you would! Thank you so much!" Rushing from the room, he made his way downstairs only to surprise his mother and aunt when he swept past them towards the kitchen.

In the course of events a timely incident had only moments earlier taken place, for as it so happened, after having spent an afternoon of anxious expectation in the living room with her sister, Dwight's mother, in looking out the living room window and seeing Zuzueca running in the open pasture, was inspired to say, "He said he wanted to come home. Despite everything that's happened, he only wanted that."

"Yes, even then," Lorraine gently responded in serious thought from where she sat on the sofa. "Yet I'm not so sure he meant here when he said that, Marie. I think he may have meant a different place."

Having become receptive to that possibility, Marie stated, "Yes, I think you're right about that." Surely something significant had taken place on the part of the woman, which seemed to indicate that she was willing to journey a different path after all. .... Then, lo and behold, Dwight had shortly thereafter rushed past them on his way to the kitchen.

Momentarily looking at one another with dumbfounded looks on their faces, the two women eventually stood up and proceeded to investigate the change which had so obviously taken place within Dwight in such a short amount of time.

Arriving at their destination, they found him searching the refrigerator, which prompted their curiosity to reach an even greater extreme, given that as of late his appetite had been lacking.

"Dwight, what on earth are you doing!" his aunt asked of him then.

"I'm hungry," he commented while continuing his search as

though it were a perfectly normal thing to be feeling. Then, when he had emerged with some leftovers from the day before, he enlightened her by saying quite emphatically, "Isn't it obvious to you that God's cured me?"

To say the two women were incredulous would be an understatement; and yet upon closer examination of the picture of health Dwight epitomized, they attached credibility to his claim.

Screaming out in jubilation while praising God, Lorraine asserted, "Oh, Dwight, we simply must tell Dr. Leyland about this!"

"But I don't need him to tell me I'm cured," Dwight was confident in deeming as he placed the food upon the table. "I already know I am."

"But Dr. Leyland doesn't know that!" she quickly reminded him. "And this could affect him greatly! He may even see the light!"

After a brief deliberation Dwight was inclined to concede, "I think you're right." Centering his attention on the food, he added with a burst of energy, "But that can wait until later, because right now I'm going to eat every morsel of this food and savor every bite of it!" Eagerly commencing to prepare himself a plate of it, his aunt readily volunteered to do so on his behalf to make known her happiness over his cure. Then, quite befittingly, they locked gazes with the warmest of glows, at which time she touched his arm with that same motherly affection he so vividly recalled experiencing in days gone by.

"What has happened today is truly a miracle," she made the determination. "And I don't need Dr. Leyland to tell me it's so."

With tears coming to her eyes over this tender scene, Marie retreated to the living room to do some soul-searching. A most solemn of expressions overtook her features as she sat on the edge of the sofa. Whether she liked it or not, her day of reckoning was at hand.

Moments later, in exiting the kitchen, Aunt Lorraine proceeded directly to the telephone to call Dr. Leyland. As it turned out, the man would not believe the miraculous news she relayed to him. In fact, he flat out told her in no uncertain terms that even though it was a Sunday evening he wanted her to drive Dwight to his office for an examination, so anxious was he to prove them wrong concerning that which he considered to be a ridiculous claim.

Lorraine said nothing to further incite the man. She merely told him she'd inform Dwight of his request. Yet in hanging up the phone, she decided not to do so until he had finished eating, for she did not want to distract from the enjoyment of his meal in any way.

Shaking his head in disappointment, Dwight later declared, "People always seem to want visible proof before they're willing to believe. I wish they'd realize that that doesn't take faith at all." With further emphasis he stated, "I'm willing to drive into Fulton to see him, Aunt Lorraine, but he'll have to be patient because I'm not rushing there. Actually it might do him some good to wait. You can call him when I leave to tell him I'm on my way."

Less than a half hour later, while Dwight was headed for Fulton, his aunt began telephoning people to inform them of his cure, so genuine was her belief that God had healed him.

Arriving at his destination, Dwight found out firsthand just how unwilling Dr. Leyland was to give him the benefit of the doubt, for he was somewhat flip with him. Yet in his confidence regarding his cure, Dwight became tight-lipped. He, like his aunt, knew that the truth would prevail anyway, therefore what purpose would a defensive bearing serve anyone?

Once inside the examining room, Dr. Leyland began to experience some degree of doubt as he noted Dwight's outward signs of good health. *Could he really be cured?* he found himself wondering for a few fleeting moments before again giving way to the pull of this world. Reverting to his prior convictions would not change the truth, however. Nor would it diminish a boy's certainty that he was not about to die from a brain tumor.

"You're not very talkative today," Dr. Leyland soon mentioned in an effort to shatter Dwight's confidence.

Recognizing the tactic he was employing, Dwight sought to set him straight by saying, "I'm only here for your sake, Dr. Leyland, not mine. I already know where I stand."

Dr. Leyland saw such confidence within Dwight that he began to witness a resurgence of doubt concerning his medical prognosis. Then, in peering into his eyes as the examination continued, he detected an alluring quality which in some respects frustrated him in that it went against and called into question the ways in which he had approached life for such a long time. Something had actually been missing all along, and it was that something he saw within Dwight. Yet he deeply fought, deeply resisted, the notion that he was lacking in something, because he wasn't willing to adopt a different outlook in order to have it. He had been indoctrinated by secular values, shaped and molded into the man he had become in the course of time, which was a stumbling block to a changed way of living.

Minutes later, as he awaited the test results, Dwight felt the sudden impulse to leave for home, so certain was he that he had been healed of what ailed him. And yet something was holding him back, as though God desired he be available to converse with Dr. Leyland once his cure was medically proven.

Though the confirmation of a miracle can be a life-altering experience, it can also be somewhat disconcerting. And so when Dr. Leyland entered the room a short time later, he shook his head unknowingly and stated in absolute amazement, "I can't understand it. The test results are negative." Gazing at Dwight in his baffled frame of mind, he added, "Maybe I should take more tests."

"No, Dr. Leyland, enough is enough. You should know by now that that's not necessary," Dwight told him. Then, after a period of time in which they scrutinized one another, Dr. Leyland acknowledged, "It really bothers me that I don't understand this. It's beyond reason."

As Dwight searched his mind for the right words to say, he happened to see a plant situated atop the man's desk.

"Dr. Leyland, do you know why a plant grows?" he asked.

Barely registering the question, he shrugged his shoulders a bit before answering, "Because it's got roots."

Smiling, Dwight said, "How true." As Dr. Leyland released a grin himself, Dwight added, "But what about its structure, all of the things which make the plant what it is?"

"No, a complete understanding of that I don't have," he admitted.

"Well that's what it's like for a person who's searching for the truth about life," Dwight intimated. "Looking at the complexity of the world, one can see evidence of a greater power, but never comprehend all that makes things what they are. That's what faith is all about, believing in what we don't fully understand." Getting up and walking to the doorway, he turned to additionally say, "I hope that what happened to me will help you in some way." Feeling free to leave, he began to do so, in the event of which Dr. Leyland suddenly surprised himself by blurting out, "Am I still your doctor?" Yes, for some reason this seemed to matter to him very much right now.

In light of all that had been said and done, Dwight saw the irony in his appeal, for which reason he dared to assume, "I guess if you can accept a stubborn, uncooperative patient in your life, then I can accept a stubborn, uncooperative doctor in mine!" The end of his statement had been stressed the hardest.

By this time Dr. Leyland had become humbled enough to accept that which had been told him without taking offense, so much so that he began to chuckle over the clever manner in which Dwight had chosen to criticize him.

"Alright, I get the point!" he stated with feigned harshness. "And yes, I deserved that!" Widening his eyes for the added emphasis, he went on to advise him, "I think it's about time you went home now, don't you! .... to live your life." His final words were spoken with a particular softness of speech, a trait long absent within him.

"I intend to do just that," Dwight responded with clear conviction. "After all, I have much to live for." Exiting the room, he felt at peace with the parting.

In prevailing astonishment over that which had transpired, Dr. Leyland took it upon himself to do something he had seldom done before. He thought about where his spiritual life was headed.

Driving homeward, Dwight felt so content within himself that he wondered if he might never know anxiousness again. How very possible it was to reap victory after all, even in the aftermath of adversities that once seemed insurmountable.

To one degree or another we are all touched by an exacting side of life. Yet in Dwight's case a miracle had ultimately been bestowed. Many people may ask why the results vary from person to person, but Dwight was not about to ask that of God. He considered it none of his business, for in a stroke of time he had been delivered from a grueling reality; and that was enough for him.

Nearing home, he saw a number of people awaiting his arrival, some of whom had greatly touched his life. When he pulled into the driveway and got out of the car, he was confronted by the many curious stares of they who were standing before him. Word of his healing was the news they anticipated, which brought him to wonder if some of them still doubted whether he had actually been cured. But he understood why this was so in that it was he himself who had directly experienced what God had done for him, no one else, therefore how could any of these people really know the extent of what had taken place in his room earlier that day.

"Dwight, what did the doctor have to say!" Jana was finally compelled to ask in total suspense.

Gazing at her in the grace of the given moment, Dwight thrilled her by saying, "He said the tumor is gone."

Rushing over to him, Jana tightly wrapped her arms around his neck. Then, as everyone voiced their amazement, she stepped back to view him before crying out, "Oh, Dwight, you're cured! You're really cured! It's too wonderful to be true!"

"And yet it is true," Dwight told her with tear-filled eyes as everybody gathered about him. "And oh, Jana, I shall never again be the same for it!"

When an event as profound as this takes place, words that convey the essence of what is felt are not easy to come by; and yet really, how could words fully define what was happening here anyway, for the presence of the Holy Spirit surely was amongst the people.

Savoring this beautiful moment as he looked into Jana's eyes, Dwight knew that his relationship with her had gone far beyond a foundation of love, for there was such a feeling of respect, and admiration, and consideration for one another as people that he knew they would always desire to keep in touch.

Focusing at this time on the fact that she would soon be returning home, Aunt Lorraine anxiously stated, "Dwight, now that you're cured, I want you and your mother to come to Michigan with me for a visit before school begins!"

"I'd like to go there with you," Dwight sought to assure her as best he could. "But not just yet." Looking intently at the faces about him, he added with utmost affection, "First I want to spend time with all my friends, and ride Zuzueca, and go on picnics to The Gulf... and just enjoy life!" In particular he looked at Mrs. Willard as he said this, for it was she who indicated earlier in the day that he could be healed. Undeniably from this day forward the appreciation they held for one another would be ever enhanced.

There are wonderful things to be reaped from a miracle, and today wise discoveries had been made. Dwight's pain had not been in vain, because the future held everlasting hope. .... Therefore in reviewing the trials and tribulations of his life, here is a summation of the person he had come to be:

He realized that actions spoke louder than words, and that it was much more of a challenge for someone to live wholesomely than to speak it.

He believed that people got so wrapped up in forgiveness that they lost sight of seeing beyond their pain. To forgive every transgression is not as expected as we may think. Forgiveness is not a cure-all for that which dwells within our troubled minds. To give up resentment is a definition of forgiveness that merits adoption in our lives, but it is not for us to pardon, excuse, remit or cancel a moral offense. Sometimes we are much better off placing forgiveness where it truly belongs, at the foot of God, for within that jurisdiction the issue will be properly handled.

He believed that if people didn't celebrate religious holidays with Jesus Christ and God the father first and foremost in their hearts and minds, then it was for the best that they not celebrate those holidays at all.

He knew that true love didn't encompass possessiveness. It was instead secure enough to be free from that bondage.

He realized that no person on the face of the earth could ever meet his every need no matter how much he was loved by them, for only God held the potential to fill in the void that remained.

He believed that the habitual offender was their own worst enemy, for the mind is a terrible thing to waste.

He understood that what God thought of him was much more important than what the world thought of him.

In his heart he foresaw that when it really came down to it, in the end result of it all, each individual had to earnestly seek God for themselves if they intimately desired to know him.

He realized that there was false guilt in the world, for he had sometimes felt it over the way in which his mother treated him, blaming himself at times for her bitterness as though he was in part responsible for it.

He felt that even though the word promise was often used in a well-meaning way by well-meaning people, they of proven integrity rarely used it in connection to their deeds.

He sensed that God wanted people to be a light to others rather than their judge, for it was an approach which set forth a good example from which to emulate.

He had come to believe that even though God expected him to love others, liking them was quite a different story. Surely Jesus Christ himself had not liked everything about everyone, yet his love for people was to the spiritually minded as obvious as the realization that the sun rises in the morning.

He knew that things weren't always as they seemed, and that a person was well-advised to keep that in mind whenever they evaluated something.

Lastly, to attain peace of mind, he saw three major components. First, one was in need of seeking God as earnestly as they possibly could. Secondly, one had to repent of their sins. And finally, one had to come to terms with the issues of their life.

It had not gone unnoticed that he was not present. ... But then suddenly there he was pulling over to the side of Kirkland Road in his father's car. Did he know what had taken place? Was that why he had come? Dwight sensed it was so, which he was right about, for only minutes earlier an informative telephone call had been received from Roberta. This compelled Scott to so abruptly leave the house that his bewildered father was left talking to a non-present son. Even the door had been left unshut in his dash to be by the side of someone whom he had heard was the recipient of a miracle.

There was no delay whatsoever on Dwight's part concerning his advancement toward Scott. In fact by the time they were facing one another they were very close to where Scott had exited the vehicle.

It was Scott who spoke up first by saying, "I had to come as soon as I heard, to find out if it's true.... that you're really healed."

"Yes, Scott, it's true," Dwight told him. "I just got back from seeing a doctor, and he confirmed what I already knew."

If ever it were possible to reveal sheer delight through the look in one's eyes, it was taking place right here and now on the part of Scott.

"So it's a miracle," he stated without reservation.

"Yes, Scott, a miracle," Dwight said with complete assurance.

Following a few moments of eye contact, Scott stated with oncoming tears, "I hope you don't mind that I've come here without notice, Dwight, but I just had to know."

"Oh, no, Scott, I'm glad you're here," Dwight endeavored to convince him. "I was hoping you'd come, because it's at times like this you want your friends by your side to share in your joy... your true friends." With that being said, he warmly smiled with heartfelt gratitude.

To be on the road to acquiring rapport with another individual is a most meaningful of life experiences. Undeniably it was happening where Scott and Dwight were concerned, which is why they took it upon themselves to hug with the conviction of pure intent. Surely, in the given moment, there was a commanding force rising to the occasion. Surely the power of unconditional love was splendidly in their midst.

"I'm so happy for you," Scott whispered above a sob as they separated to regard one another. "I..." Quite suddenly he became absorbed by the presence of her, for he had not seen this woman in many a year. In fact he was nearly catapulted into a trance-like state by the very observance of her.

It was obvious to Dwight that Scott's attention had been captivated by something or someone. As he rather tentatively cast his gaze in the direction of Scott's focus, he, too, saw her, a woman whom he had not beheld in many a year. With his emotions nearly overwhelmed by the sight of her, he gradually took on tunnel vision, as though all else faded into oblivion in the time and place he was in, as though only he and she and the spirit of God remained. The power of love drew him toward her then, this radiant lady in fine dress and swept up hair, in the event of which he stated with a quiver in his voice, "You have that look about you, of the mother I remember you to be."

Was that soft smile forming on her lips truly genuine? It had to be so, because pretense could not be detected within her in the least. Like sweet music from heaven a voice clearly stated then with absolute believability, "I'd like to again be the mother you remember me to be... if you'll have me."

Dwight was so seized by the moment at hand that for the time being he was not even able to find words to express himself. It was as though he was in witness of another miracle on the same day. To him her turnaround was that momentous, that significant. .... But was he expected to be receptive toward her? Certainly so, if he wanted to promote God's will. After all, was it not the right thing to do in the aftermath of positive change? Was it not the right thing to do in the advent of a restructured outlook? Without a doubt he should commend her, encourage her, reward her, embrace her. Therefore as far as he was concerned the slate of transgressions had been wiped clean.

In the course of our lives many tears are shed for various reasons. Dwight knew this to be true; and yet never had he shed them quite like today. He was reminded by this woman who stood so humbly before him that with God all things are possible, so much so that he thoroughly believed tonight he would go to sleep as he had as a little boy, you know, with a clear mind free of disturbances.

So with love being in his midst so magnificently, Dwight soon managed to tell her in a resonating tone of voice, "You've come home! You've been gone so long, and I've awaited your return many a day... and now finally... you've come home!" It seemed as though he might physically collapse at any given moment in his utter joy.

When a mother's love is brought to the surface, there's bound to be moving results. This became all the more evident as she drew toward her son and hugged him with long overdue affection.

Because a momentous occurrence had been witnessed, it seemed impossible that anyone could refrain from crying. Certainly there was not a dry eye to be seen. Yet the scope of it all did not end there, for to everyone's gratification, lo and behold, Marie did something truly moving. She cupped Dwight's face within her hands and told him she loved him. And at the very moment she did this she felt a barrier crumble within her as the love of God rushed in. If ever there was an incentive to continue heading in a positive direction in life, this was it. The proof was in the results.

Scott and Jana in particular were so affected by what they were observing that they cried all the harder. They knew that the moment was steep in moral content, so steep in fact that they would not likely be losing touch with its implications for the rest of their lives. Moral excellence had won a victory on this day, and it was right before their very eyes in gorgeous view.

It has been written that to whom much is given much is expected. And Dwight had been given much. Therefore he knew that it would behoove him to reflect his appreciation through his interaction with his fellow man. Do onto others as you would have them do onto you. Even though he had sought to live by that virtue in the past, from this moment forward he would seek to live it like never before, for after all, he was walking proof that miracles really do occur.

In the eyes of they who knew him well, Dwight had done something admirable by persevering through his difficulties in a troubled world. Surely he had proven it could be done. Surely he had proven he was aiming to be in good standing with God. Therefore now, with the gap between mother and child having been securely bridged, he and she began to affably mingle amongst the people with hugs of warmth, in the event of which Zuzueca whinnied from the corral's edge with unbridled enthusiasm as though he, too, possessed some level of understanding concerning the significance of all that had happened. Quite unexpectedly, the horse backed up then for a running start and jumped the fence with graceful ease only to trot over to Dwight's side.

It wasn't until the stallion had nuzzled Dwight from behind for some share of the attention that laughs of delight were ultimately heard.

Turning about, Dwight freely joined in on the laughter and

embraced the animal's broad neck, all of which reminded they who had come to see and know the very essence of him, of the profound transformation that had taken place within his personality, his character. ... And so it was that where Dwight Enhart was concerned there was a boy, a very loving boy, who had in the course of time discovered that it was a distinct possibility to experience The Fading of the Scars.

THE BEGINNING

May 14, 1992 - First draft completed
May 10, 1994 - Second draft completed
November 27, 1997 - Thanksgiving Day - Third draft completed
July 26, 2001 - Fourth draft completed
March 5, 2003 - First computer editing completed
January 17, 2004 - Second computer editing completed
April 5, 2004 - Final computer editing completed

God save humanity. Author - Orrin Michael Carpenter

The Final words from the autobiography of Joseph(John)Carey Merrick, also known as the elephant man.

'Tis true my form is something odd, but blaming me is
    blaming God.
Could I create myself anew, I would not fail in pleasing you.
If I could reach from pole to pole, or grasp the ocean with a
    span.
I would be measured by the soul, the mind's the standard of
    the man.

To order additional copies of *The Fading of he Scars*, call:
866-909-BOOK, or log on to Amazon.com to place your order

Printed in the United States
39765LVS00007B/112-117

9 781597 810296